the complete book of baking

the complete book of baking

Over 350 recipes for breads, tarts, cakes, biscuits and pastries

Edited by Deborah Gray

Colour Library Direct

A QUINTET BOOK

CLD 21337

This edition published in 1999 for
Colour Library Direct, Godalming Business Centre,
Woolsack Way, Godalming, Surrey GU7 1XW

Reprinted 1999

ISBN 1-84100-146-5

This book was designed and produced by
Quintet Publishing Limited
6 Blundell Street
London N7 9BH

Creative Director: Richard Dewing
Art Director: Clare Reynolds
Designer: James Lawrence
Senior Editor: Sally Green
Editor: Deborah Gray

Typeset in Great Britain by
Central Southern Typesetters, Eastbourne
Manufactured in Hong Kong by Regent Publishing Services Ltd.
Printed in China by Leefung-Asco Printers Ltd.

THE MATERIAL IN THIS PUBLICATION PREVIOUSLY APPEARED IN:
The Pumpkin & Squash Cookbook, *Rosemary Moon*;
The Bread Book, *Audrey Ellison*; The Bread Machine Book, *Marjie Lambert*;
Breakfast Bakes, *Elizabeth Wolf-Cohen*;
The Chocolate Book, *Valerie Barret*; Coffee, *Rosemary Moon*;
The Complete Book of Gingerbread, *Valerie Baxter*;
Desserts, *Elizabeth Wolf-Cohen*;
High-Fibre Cooking, *Rosemary Moon*; Irish Cooking, *Ethel Minogue*;
Leith's Cookery School, *Prue Leith and Caroline Waldegrave*;
Low-Fat Vegetarian Cooking, *Jenny Stacey*;
New Jewish Cooking, *Elizabeth Wolf-Cohen*;
Recipes from a Polish Kitchen, *Bridget Jones*;
Scandinavian Cooking, *Sonia Maxwell*;
Traditional Cakes and Pastries, *Barbara Maher*;
The Ultimate Bagel Cookbook, *Sarah Maxwell*;
Vegetarian Pizza Cookbook, *Maureen Keller*.

CONTENTS

INTRODUCTION

Enjoy your baking.

Few things are more welcoming than the smell of home baking and nothing more appetizing than hot muffins at breakfast time or a scrumptious snack of tea and biscuits on returning from school or work. Anyone who bakes knows the satisfaction of presenting the family with a delicious cake, or setting an indulgent pie down at the dinner table. Many of us are tired of the synthetic tastes that purchased foods offer us and value the good wholesome tastes of fresh, natural ingredients. Nothing can equal home cooking for flavour.

There is no great mystery to the art of baking. It is simply a matter of careful measuring and following the instructions. Nor need baking take a great deal of time. There are many recipes in this book that take only a few minutes to prepare, particularly with the help of electric mixers and food processors.

Let this book indeed become your Baker's Bible. In it you will find all you will ever need to know about baking techniques. There are comprehensive sections on baking basics covering all the various types of pastries, cakes, biscuits and breads, large and small, baked with and without yeast. Whether you want to make a fancy, rich pastry, learn how to bake bread, or make the perfect birthday cake, all the knowledge is here. In addition, there are hundreds of recipes from home and abroad, traditional and contemporary to inspire your baking. The information and recipes are written in a clear style so that whether you are an experienced cook or a novice you will find the instructions easy to follow.

Baking Tips

- Always measure ingredients precisely and use the exact ingredients suggested. It can make a difference if you substitute different types of flour or sugar for example.
- Use medium-sized eggs unless otherwise specified.
- Pre-heat the oven to the given temperature. Some ovens are very hot, particularly fan-assisted ovens, in which case, follow the manufacturer's recommendations for heat reduction.
- As a general rule, yeast mixtures and pastries should be placed near to the top of the oven, cakes and biscuits in the middle.
- Avoid opening the oven door while baking. This is particularly important in the first 15 minutes of baking (5 minutes for biscuits) when a sudden blast of cold air can ruin a cake by making it sink in the middle.
- Prepare can tins or sheets prior to making up the batter. This is particularly important for cakes as the rising agent begins work immediately on contact with liquid.
- Always lightly dust the work surface with flour before rolling out pastry and biscuits (if you use too much flour it will become incorporated into

the dough). If pastry or biscuit dough proves very difficult to roll out, return to the refrigerator for 30 minutes. If it is too hard after refrigeration, leave to stand at room temperature for 5 minutes.
- Test cakes using a wooden cocktail stick for sponge-type cakes and a metal skewer for fruit cakes. Insert into the centre of the cake and if it comes out clean with no batter clinging to it, then the cake is cooked. Repeat at 5-minute intervals.
- If the cake or pastry is over-browning, cover with foil or greaseproof paper.
- Leave cakes to sit in their tins for 5 minutes before turning out. They will come away from the sides more easily.
- Baked foods are more easily removed from their pans when cooked on baking parchment.
- Double up ingredients and make double the quantity; most cakes (uniced), breads and pastries can be frozen for 3 months. Most will keep in an airtight container for up to 2 weeks.

Pastry

Almost anything can be encased in pastry
to form a pie or tart. Featured in this
section are a wide range of pastry types
to suit every filling of your choice from fruit
and chocolate to vegetables and meat.
There are also wonderful recipes ranging
from classical pastries from France and
Austria to modern tarts and desserts, using
ingredients once thought of as delicacies
but now available in every market.

INTRODUCTION

Tarts and pastries feature in many culinary traditions, but play a very important part in British, American, and French cuisines. Most are easy to prepare and, with a little forethought, can be put together quickly. Remember pastry can be bought from markets and home-made pastry freezes well, so make it in batches and freeze ahead. Fillings can be assembled in no time, so use your imagination and enjoy the treat of a simple tart or pie made with delicious light pastry, warm from the oven.

Every cook I know aspires to make successful pastry. There are a few basic rules that must always be obeyed, regardless of what kind of pastry you are making:

- **Chill all the ingredients.**
- **Work as quickly as possible and, unless you are one of those natural-born pastry makers, use a pastry blender or a food processor.**
- **Chill the pastry after every stage of making and assembling: chill after patting into a disc and after rolling out and lining the tart or pie pan. Do not be tempted to cheat – your pastry will shrink unevenly.**
- **Pastry likes a hot oven; butter-rich pastries and puff pastry especially require a hot blast of heat to seal the pastry and release the steam. If longer cooking is required for a filling, the temperature can be reduced so the pastry does not burn.**

A succulent slice of the ever-popular lemon tart.

Ingredients

Most kinds of pastry are made with a combination of flour, fat and a liquid to bind. The texture, flavour and colour of the resulting pastry will vary tremendously depending on the proportions and types of ingredients used.

Flour

Plain flour is used throughout this section. Even the same brand of flour can vary from season to season, depending on humidity or how long it has been stored, so the amount of liquid necessary to bind the pastry will always vary; 1/4 teaspoon baking powder can be added to 175 g/6 oz flour to achieve a lighter result. Wholemeal or rye flour can replace some of the white flour but produces a heavier result. Use equal amounts or more white flour proportionally to wholemeal or other flours for easier handling. Please note that it is always essential to be consistent when using either metric or imperial measures, and not to mix the two.

Fat

Lard was probably the first fat used in pastry making, but has fallen out of favour for health reasons. It does make a very short and light pastry, but has a distinctive taste. Pure butter gives pastry a rich flavour and colour and a crisp texture, but it can be difficult to handle. Most bakers use a combination of butter or hard margarine (not the soft tub variety) and white vegetable fat to achieve a balance of good buttery colour and flavour with the short, flaky texture provided by white fat. Unsalted butter is preferable because it has a lower water content and the amount of salt can be more easily controlled. Experiment until you find your own preference.

The normal proportion of fat to flour is usually half fat to flour (i.e. one part fat to two parts flour), although some rich European-style pastries, such as *pâte sucrée* have a higher percentage of fat. The more fat the dough has, the more difficult it will be to handle, so be sure the dough is chilled at all stages of preparation.

Liquid

Most pastry is bound with water, although milk or other liquids can be used. Normal tart pastry uses about 1 teaspoon of water per 25 g/1 oz flour; this varies if eggs or an egg yolk is added. The water should be iced so it does not melt or soften the fat(s). Too much water will make a sticky dough, which is difficult to handle and makes the pastry tough. Be careful when using a food processor, since the mixture can form into a pastry before the correct quantity of liquid has been added. This can produce a dough that is too short and difficult to handle and results in a brittle, crumbly pastry. Many recipes call for an egg yolk mixed with water to a certain measure. This adds a golden colour and helps to bind the pastry. Sometimes a little juice is added for flavour, but be careful as certain juices, such as lemon, contain a high proportion of acid, which can shorten the pastry too much for easy handling. A little grated orange or lemon rind should add just the right kind of flavour. Flavourings such as vanilla, almond, or lemon can be used to enhance the chosen fillings, as can spices such as cinnamon, nutmeg, ginger or cardamom.

Eggs

Eggs are added to pastry for richness in texture and flavour, and because they help bind all the ingredients. Normally only the yolk is used and, for a very rich biscuit-like pastry, yolks are used without any other liquid.

Sugar

Sugar is used both to sweeten the final pastry and create a crisper texture. A teaspoon or two is often added even to savoury doughs, because the sugar helps the pastry to colour and gives a more golden look. Caster or icing sugar is usually used because these types dissolve more quickly than granulated. Granulated sugar can be used but can result in a crunchy texture, which is not always desired.

Commercial Pastry

Excellent quality shortcrust, puff and filo paste can be purchased chilled or frozen, and all give good reliable results. Shortcrust and puff pastry are available ready-rolled and give excellent results. Filo pastry is a great freezer stand-by. These paper-thin sheets of pastry need to be defrosted before being carefully unwrapped. Because the thin layers dry out so quickly, it is advisable to cover them with a damp cloth when working.

Although many good-quality, ready-made pastries are available, there is nothing quite as satisfying as making your own. The method for making Basic Pie Crust is easy to follow and, once mastered, can be adapted for both sweet and savoury tarts simply by adding a few extra ingredients.

250 G/8 OZ QUANTITY

250 g/8 oz flour

½ tsp salt

1½ tsp caster sugar, optional

120 g/4 oz cold unsalted butter, cut into small pieces

2 Tbsp cold margarine or white vegetable fat, cut into small pieces

2–4 Tbsp iced water

Basic Shortcrust (*Pâte Brisée*)

Brisée in French means broken. In this pastry the flour and fats are 'broken together', or cut in. After adding the liquid, the pastry is blended until the mixture begins to bind together. If the pastry becomes sticky at any stage, refrigerate until it is easy to handle. This recipe should produce a firm, but flaky crust which can support a filling but at the same time is still light. Sifting flour is not absolutely necessary, but it can help lighten the pastry if you are using the hand method.

Hand Method

1 Into a large bowl, sift the flour, salt and sugar if using. Sprinkle the pieces of butter and margarine or vegetable fat over the flour mixture. Using a pastry blender or two knives cut in the fat scissor-fashion, until the mixture forms coarse crumbs. Do not over-work, or the pastry will be tough.

2 Sprinkle about 2 tablespoons of the water over the flour-crumb mixture and toss lightly with a fork. Gather the parts of pastry that have bound together to one side of the bowl. Add a little more water to any dry crumbs and toss again.

3 Gather the pastry into a rough ball and turn on to a sheet of clingfilm. Lightly press the pastry into a round and flatten slightly. Wrap the pastry tightly and refrigerate for at least 1 hour or overnight.

Food Processor Method

If you have warm hands, are working in hot weather or tend to have a heavy touch, the food processor should be the answer to your prayers. Used carefully, it produces perfect pastry every time; just take care not to over-process. Although shortcrust pastry is easily made by hand, the sweeter pastries do benefit from the food processor method. The more sugar and fat added to the pastry, the more difficult it is to handle.

1 Put the flour, salt and sugar in the bowl of a food processor fitted with the metal blade. Process for 5–7 seconds just to blend. Sprinkle the pieces of butter and margarine or white vegetable fat over the surface and process for 10–15 seconds until the mixture resembles coarse crumbs.

2 Sprinkle about 2 tablespoons of the water over the flour-crumb mixture and, using the pulse button, process the mixture until the pastry just begins to hold together, 10–15 seconds. DO NOT OVER-PROCESS.

Test the pastry by pinching a piece between your fingers: if it is still too crumbly, add more water, little by little, and process again until the pastry begins to stick together in clumps.

Do not allow the pastry to form into a ball or add too much water because the baked pastry will be tough. Turn the pastry on to a sheet of clingfilm and continue with step 3 on page 12.

Rich Shortcrust Pastry (*Pâte Brisée Riche*)

Richer than basic shortcrust pastry, this is excellent for fruit tarts and special-occasion pies.

250 G/8 OZ QUANTITY

250 g/8 oz plain flour	**¹/₂ tsp salt**
120 g/4 oz cold unsalted butter, cut into small pieces	**I egg yolk beaten with 2 Tbsp iced water**

Proceed as for Basic Shortcrust Pastry (*Pâte Brisée*), using the beaten egg yolk and water to bind.

Rich Herb Pastry

This light, green-flecked pastry is ideal for vegetable pies and tarts. Vary the herbs to suit the filling and your taste.

250 G/8 OZ QUANTITY

250 g/8 oz plain flour	**2 Tbsp chopped chives**
¹/₂ tsp salt	**I Tbsp fresh parsley, chopped**
120 g/4 oz cold unsalted butter	**4–6 fresh basil leaves, torn into small pieces**
¹/₂ tsp fresh thyme or ¹/₄ tsp dried thyme	**I egg yolk beaten with 2 Tbsp iced water**
¹/₂ tsp fresh oregano or marjoram, chopped or ¹/₄ tsp dried oregano or marjoram	

Prepare as for Rich Shortcrust Pastry, adding the herbs when the flour and butter have been combined to form coarse crumbs, and before adding the water.

Light Wholemeal Pastry

This wholemeal crust remains light and flaky by substituting less than half the white flour for wholemeal. Substitute 1 tablespoon of white vegetable fat for that amount of butter if you want to produce a very flaky pastry.

250 G/8 OZ QUANTITY

175 g/6 oz flour	**25 g/I oz white vegetable fat or hard margarine**
³/₄ cup wholemeal flour	**I egg yolk beaten with 2 Tbsp iced water**
¹/₂ tsp salt	
50 g/2 oz cold unsalted butter, cut into small pieces	

Proceed as for Basic Shortcrust Pastry, combining the two flours and salt before cutting in the fats.

Basic Sweet Pastry (*Pâte Sucrée*)

Pâte sucrée, "sweetened pastry", is made in the same way as *pâte brisée*, but contains more sugar and is generally bound with egg yolks or a combination of egg yolks and water. Use icing sugar as it dissolves instantly, although caster sugar can also be used. These additions make the pastry sweeter and a little crisper than ordinary shortcrust pastry, which is ideal for dessert and fruit tarts. After the dough is formed, it is lightly kneaded by a process the French call *fresage* where the heel of the hand blends it until it is soft and pliable. The addition of sugar and egg yolk makes the dough softer and more difficult to handle, so be sure to chill all the ingredients and work quickly. However, because this is a soft pastry, it is easy to patch; just press any tears together – they will not show. This pastry can be made by hand by following the instructions for Basic Shortcrust Pastry, but it is easier to use a food processor.

175 G/6 OZ QUANTITY

175 g/6 oz plain flour	120 g/4 oz cold unsalted butter, cut into small pieces
½ tsp salt	
3–4 Tbsp icing sugar	2 egg yolks beaten with 2 Tbsp iced water and ½ tsp vanilla essence (optional)

- ● Put the flour, salt and sugar in the bowl of a food processor, fitted with the metal blade. Process for 5–7 seconds. Sprinkle the butter over the flour mixture and process for 10–15 seconds until the mixture resembles coarse crumbs. Pulse 2–3 times more if the crumbs are not evenly distributed.
- ● With the machine running, pour the yolk-water mixture through the feed tube and process just until the pastry begins to hold together. **DO NOT OVER-PROCESS.**

  Test the dough by pinching a piece between your fingers; if it is still crumbly add a little more water and pulse once or twice. Do not allow the dough to form into a ball at this stage because the baked pastry will become tough. Turn out the dough on to a sheet of clingfilm.
- ● Using the clingfilm as a guide, hold each side with one hand and push the dough away from you, turning it and holding the opposite sides of the clingfilm to contain it, until it is smooth and just blended. Flatten into a round and wrap with the clingfilm. Refrigerate for 1 hour or overnight.

Extra Sweet Pastry (*Pâte Sucrée Riche*)

With a little more sugar and egg yolk, pastry becomes a melting, rich biscuit, or shortbread pastry, that is ideal for encasing fruit tarts and tartlets. This pastry is very tricky to handle; although chilling is important, do not chill for too long or it will be too firm to roll out. If you cannot roll it out, simply press it in the tart tin using flour-dipped fingers.

175 G/6 OZ QUANTITY

175 g/6 oz plain flour	3 egg yolks beaten with 1 Tbsp iced water and ½ tsp vanilla essence (optional)
½ tsp salt	
4–5 Tbsp confectioners' sugar	
120 g/4 oz cold unsalted butter, cut into small pieces	

Proceed as for Basic Sweet Pastry.

Easy Nut Pastry

This is a delicious crust, which makes an ideal base for custards and cooked fillings. It does not need rolling out and can be pressed straight into a pie dish with lightly floured hands, chilled and then baked without being weighted with beans.

250 G/8 OZ QUANTITY

250 g/8 oz unsalted butter at room temperature	250 g/8 oz plain flour
	½ tsp sugar
1 egg, lightly beaten	
1 tsp vanilla or almond essence (optional)	120 g/4 oz walnuts, peanuts, almonds, hazelnuts or macadamia nuts, finely chopped

- ● Lightly spray or brush the pie dish with a vegetable cooking spray or a little melted butter or oil.
- ● Using an electric mixer, cream the butter in a large bowl. Add the egg and vanilla or almond essence and beat until blended. Sprinkle over the flour, sugar and nuts and beat on low speed until well blended.
- ● Scrape the mixture into the prepared dish and press evenly on to the bottom and up the side of the pie dish. Using a fork, prick the bottom of the pastry. Chill for at least 30 minutes in the refrigerator.
- ● Preheat the oven to 350°F/180°C/Gas 4. Bake for 6–8 minutes until set. Remove to a wire rack to cool. It must be completely cool before filling.

Cream Cheese Pastry

Cream cheese pastry is a moist, flaky pastry often used with sweet or nut-flavoured fillings. It is ideal for rich tartlets and tiny petit fours.

FOR A 22-CM/9-IN FLAN TIN OR
TWELVE 5–7-CM/2–3 IN TARTLET TINS

175 g/6 oz plain flour	125 g/4 oz unsalted butter, at room temperature
1/2 tsp salt	
1 tsp sugar	125 g/4 oz full-fat soft cheese, at room temperature

● In a large bowl, sift together the flour and salt. Add the butter, sugar and soft cheese and, with an electric mixer, beat the ingredients together until well blended and a soft pastry forms. Shape into a ball, flatten to a disc and wrap tightly. Refrigerate about 1 hour before rolling and shaping.

Crumb Crust

This easy crumb crust, popular for cheesecakes, is ideal for chilled tarts since it remains crisp and crunchy, and is particularly good for ice-cream tarts and chilled chiffon mixtures. For alternative flavourings to suit different fillings, use vanilla, ginger, chocolate or Amaretti biscuits (about 24) instead of digestive biscuits, or replace 50 g/2 oz of the crumbs with 50 g/2 oz chopped nuts for a Nut Crumb Crust.

FOR A 22 CM/9-IN FLAN TIN OR PIE PLATE

175 g/6 oz digestive biscuit crumbs or other biscuit crumbs	90 g/3 oz butter or margarine, melted
	1–2 Tbsp sugar, or to taste

● Put the biscuits in the bowl of a food processor fitted with the metal blade and process for 20–30 seconds until fine crumbs form. Alternatively, put them in a heavy-duty freezer bag and press into fine crumbs with a rolling pin. Pour them into a bowl and stir in the melted butter or margarine and sugar. Pour into a flan tin and press crumbs on to the bottom and up the side of the flan tin or pie plate. Chill, uncovered, for at least 20 minutes in the refrigerator.

● Preheat the oven to 375°F/190°C/Gas 5. Bake the crust 6–8 minutes until set. Remove to a wire rack to cool. It must be completely cool before filling.

Rich Cheese Pastry

This pastry is based on a Rich Shortcrust Pastry. Use a grated hard cheese, such as Cheddar.

250 G/8 OZ QUANTITY

250 g/8 oz plain flour	3 Tbsp cold white vegetable fat, cut into small pieces
1/4 tsp salt	
1/8–1/4 tsp cayenne pepper	3/4 cup grated mature Cheddar cheese
1/2 tsp dry mustard	
120 g/4 oz cold unsalted butter, cut into small pieces	1 egg yolk beaten with 3 Tbsp iced water

Proceed as for Rich Shortcrust Pastry, adding the cheese after the butter and white vegetable fat are cut in, and mix well to combine.

Chocolate Pastry

This makes a stunning base for fruit tarts and tartlets, as well as chocolate fillings.

250 G/8 OZ QUANTITY

150 g/5 oz butter, softened	3 tsp vanilla essence
120 g/4 oz caster sugar	120 g/4 oz cocoa powder
1/2 tsp salt	250 g/8 oz plain flour

● Put the butter, sugar, salt and vanilla into the bowl of a food processor fitted with the metal blade and process for 25–30 seconds until creamy. Add the cocoa and process about 1 minute, until well blended. Add the flour all at once and, using the pulse button, process for 10–15 seconds until the flour is well blended. Scrape the pastry out on to a sheet of clingfilm and shape into a flat circle. Wrap and refrigerate.

● Soften the pastry for 10–15 minutes at room temperature. Unwrap and sandwich between two large pieces of clingfilm. Roll out to about 1/2 cm/1/4 inch thick. Peel off the top sheet and invert into a greased flan tin. Ease on to the bottom and sides of the tin, then remove the bottom layer of clingfilm. Press the pastry around the pan, then roll the rolling pin over the top of the tin to cut off any excess pastry. Prick the base of the pastry with a fork and refrigerate 1 hour.

● Preheat the oven to 400°F/200°C/Gas 6. Bake blind for 10 minutes. Remove the paper or foil and beans and continue baking for 5 more minutes until just set. Transfer to a wire rack to cool.

Rolling and Shaping the Pastry

If the pastry has been refrigerated for more than an hour, allow it to soften slightly at room temperature for about 10 minutes.

To Form a Pastry Circle

1 Unwrap the pastry and place on a lightly floured surface. Using a lightly floured rolling pin, press parallel grooves into the pastry. Turn the pastry 45˚, flouring the surface underneath, and press more parallel grooves. Continue rotating and pressing the pastry, being careful the pastry does not stick, until it is about 1 cm/½ in thick. This method avoids overworking the pastry before actually rolling it.

To Form a Square or Rectangle

Proceed as for rolling out a circle but rotate the pastry 90˚ rather than 45˚ when making the grooves. This will elongate the pastry to fill a square or rectangular tin.

2 Beginning from the centre, lightly roll out the pastry to the far edge, but do not actually roll over the edge. Return to the centre and roll to the near edge, but do not roll over the edge. Turn the pastry 45˚ and continue rolling until it is about 3 mm/ ⅛ in thick and forms a 30–35-cm/12–14-in round. Do not allow the pastry to stick to the work surface; lightly flour the surface and rolling pin as necessary, using a small pastry brush to remove any excess flour from the pastry.

3 If the pastry is tender or tears, patch it with a small piece of moistened pastry. As the pastry circle enlarges, fold it in half or into quarters to rotate and dust with flour to avoid stretching it.

Lining a Pie Dish

The traditional pie dish is shallow with no rim. It usually has a fluted side and removable base that gives the characteristic edge and allows the side of the pan to be removed for presentation without disturbing the base of the tart. Tart rings are generally smooth-sided rings which are set on a heavy baking sheet to form its base; these are generally used by professionals. The best pans are dull metal or non-stick since shiny metal reflects the heat and prevents the pastry from browning properly. Butter-rich pastry does not generally stick, but lightly spray the pie dish with a vegetable cooking spray. Alternatively, brush the bottom and side of the pie dish with a little oil.

Lining Tartlet Tins

For very small tartlet pans (less than 5 cm/2 in), arrange the pans on the work surface close together and unroll the rolled-out pastry over them, loosely draping the pastry into them. Roll the rolling pin over them to cut off the excess pastry, then, using a floured thumb, press the pastry on to the bottom and up the side of the tins. Prick the bottoms with a fork. For larger tartlets, follow the steps for lining a round pie dish, since this gives adequate pastry and a firm high edge to support any filling.

1 To transfer rolled-out pastry to a pie dish, set the rolling pin on the near edge of the pastry round, square, or rectangle. Fold the edge of the pastry over the rolling pin, then continue to roll pastry loosely around the pin.

2 Hold the far edge of pastry and rolling pin over far edge of the pie dish and gently unroll the pastry, allow it to settle into the dish without stretching or pulling.

3 Using floured fingertips, lift the outside edge of the pastry and ease into the bottom and side of the dish, allowing excess pastry to overhang the edge. Smooth the pastry on to the bottom of the dish and press the overhang down slightly toward the centre of the pan, making the top edge thicker.

4 Roll the rolling pin over the edge, cutting off any excess pastry and flattening the top edge. Press the thickened top edge against the side of the dish to form a stand-up edge. This makes the edge slightly thicker and higher, reinforcing the side of the pastry. Prick the bottom of the pastry with a fork and, if you like, crimp or decorate the edge. Refrigerate 1 hour or freeze for 20 minutes.

Tips for Filling Tarts

- For easier handling, and to avoid any overflows, always set flan tin on a heavy baking sheet.
- Beat the eggs and milk or cream mixture in a large measuring cup or jug, rather than a bowl, since it will be easier to pour.
- To fill the tart case with a liquid filling, set the tart on a baking sheet. Pull out the middle oven rack halfway and set the tart on its baking sheet on the rack. Pour in as much filling as possible and gently slide the rack back in place. Bake 5 minutes as this allows a thin crust to form over the top. If any mixture remains, pull the oven rack out and carefully pour the remaining mixture into the centre of the tart. Slide the rack back in place.
- To remove the side of the flan tin, set the bottom on a sturdy can and allow the side to drop down gently on to the surface, leaving the tart on the bottom of the pan. Slide on to a serving plate.
- For a vegetable or meat tart, sprinkle cheese over the partially baked tart case to keep the pastry from getting soggy. When the cheese melts it forms a barrier between the pastry and the filling.
- Rubbing an unbaked tart case with 1 tablespoon of softened butter and chilling before filling helps prevent a soggy crust.
- Brushing a warm, blind-baked tart case with a little beaten egg or egg white and returning it to the oven for 2 minutes, creates a seal between pastry and filling, preventing a soggy crust. Brushing a baked tart case with melted jam helps prevent a fruit tart becoming soggy.
- There are many flan tins on the market. Use a dull metal or non-stick one as they produce the best-cooked, crisp pastry. Shiny metal reflects heat, and glass and china absorb it, preventing the pastry from browning well. To present or transport a tart, bake the tart in a metal, loose-bottomed tin. Remove the side of the tin from the baked tart, leaving it on the metal bottom, then slide into a quiche dish of the same size.
- To test if the filling is set, insert a sharp knife into the centre. It should come out clean and should feel hot to the touch.
- If the pastry edge begins to brown before the filling is set, cover with foil.

Baking Blind

Baking blind is a method of pre-baking a pastry case, either partially or completely, to prevent the pastry from becoming soggy and to ensure the base cooks evenly.

1 Cut out a circle of greaseproof paper or foil about 7 cm/3 in larger than the flan tin. Fold the paper or foil in half and lay it across the centre of the pastry-lined tin. Unfold it and press on to the bottom, into the edge and up the side of the pastry.

2 Fill the paper- or foil-lined pastry base with dried beans, rice or pastry weights, spreading them evenly over the bottom and up the sides. The dried beans, rice or pastry weights can be cooled and used again.

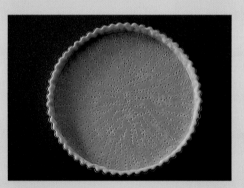

3 To partially bake blind: bake in a 400˚F/200˚C/Gas 6 oven for 15–20 minutes until the pastry is set and the rim looks dry and golden. Remove to a heatproof surface and remove the paper or foil and beans. The base can now be filled and the baking completed.

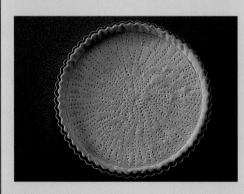

4 To completely bake blind: bake in a 400˚F/200˚C/Gas 6 oven for 10 minutes. Remove to a heatproof surface and carefully remove the paper or foil and beans. Prick the pastry bottom again with a fork and bake for 5–10 minutes until golden. The bottom should look dry and set. Cool on a wire rack before filling.

Hot Water Pastry

This is made by heating water and fat together and mixing them into the flour. Because of the high proportion of water, this pastry is inclined to be hard. Its strength and firmness allows it to encase heavy mixtures, as in the traditional pork pie, without collapsing. As the fat used is generally lard, the pastry can lack flavour, so add a good spoonful of salt. Many old recipes recommend throwing the pastry away uneaten once it has done its duty as a cooking container. The recipe for veal and ham pie is a better-tasting modification of hot water crust, containing butter and egg.

Do not allow the water to boil before the fat has melted. If the water reduces by boiling, the proportion of water to flour will not be correct.

Quickly mix the water and melted fat into the flour in a warm bowl, then keep it covered with a hot damp cloth. This prevents the fat from becoming set and the pastry flaking and drying out.

MAKES 500 G/1 LB HOT WATER PASTRY

500 g/1 lb plain flour	175 ml/6 fl oz water
1 tsp salt	60 g/2 oz butter
2 eggs, beaten	60 g/2 oz lard

- Sift the flour and salt into a bowl. Make a well in the centre, break the eggs into it and toss a liberal covering of flour over the egg.
- Put the water, butter, and lard into a saucepan and bring to the boil. Once the liquid is boiling, pour it on to the flour, mixing with a knife as you do. Knead until the pastry is smooth. Wrap in a piece of plastic wrap and refrigerate for 15 minutes.

Choux Pastry

This pastry contains water and eggs and depends on the rising of the steam within it to produce a puffy, hollow pastry case. It is easy to make if the recipe is followed closely. The following points are particularly important:

- Measure ingredients exactly. Proportions are important with choux pastry.
- Do not allow the water to boil until the butter has melted, but when it has, bring it immediately to a full rolling boil. Boiling the water too soon will cause too much evaporation.
- Have the sifted flour ready in a bowl so that the minute the rolling boil is achieved, you can tip in the flour all in one go.
- Beat fast and vigorously to get rid of lumps before they cook hard.
- Do not overbeat. Stop once the mixture leaves the sides of the pan.
- Cool slightly before adding the egg – otherwise you'll scramble them.
- Do not beat in more egg than is necessary to achieve a dropping consistency. If the mixture is too stiff, the pastry will be stodgy. If it is too thin, it will rise unevenly into shapeless lumps.
- Bake until it is a good even brown, otherwise the inside of the pastry will be uncooked.
- If the pastry is to be served cold, split the buns/rings, or make a slit in each of them with a skewer or sharp knife to allow the steam to escape. If steam remains trapped inside, the pastry will be soggy and a little heavy.

- Opened-up pastry or small buns with holes in them can be returned to the oven, hole uppermost, to dry out further.
- Serve the pastry on the day it is made (or store frozen), as it stales rapidly.

Choux Pastry

MAKES 1 QUANTITY CHOUX USING 120 G/4 OZ FLOUR

125 g/4 oz unsalted butter	⅛ tsp salt
250 ml/8 fl oz water	4 eggs, lightly beaten
125 g/4 oz plain flour	

- Put the water and the butter, cut into 3–4 pieces, into a heavy saucepan and place over gentle heat.
- Bring to the boil slowly so that by the time the liquid boils all the butter has melted.
- As soon as the liquid is boiling fast, tip in all the flour and remove the pan from the heat.
- Beat vigorously until a smooth paste is formed. The trick is to beat out the lumps before they are cooked solid by the heat. Once the mixture curls away from the sides of the pan, stop.
- Allow the choux pastry to cool slightly then beat in the liquid egg, a little at a time. It may not be necessary to add all the egg.
- Continue adding egg until you achieve a soft dropping consistency. The mixture will be shiny and smooth and will fall reluctantly from a spoon if it is given a sharp jerk.

Suet Pastry

This is made like shortcrust pastry except that the fat (suet) is generally chopped or shredded before use. Because self-rising flour (or plain flour and baking powder) is used in order to produce a less heavy, doughy pastry, it is important to cook the pastry soon after making while the raising agent is at its most active. During cooking the raising agent causes the dough to puff up and rise slightly and as the pastry hardens during cooking, air will be trapped. This makes the suet crust lighter and more bread-like.

Butter for greasing

375 g/12 oz self-raising flour

Salt

175 g/6 oz shredded beef or vegetable suet

Water to mix

- ● Grease a pudding basin.
- ● Sift the flour with a good pinch of salt into a bowl. Blend in the shredded suet and add enough water to mix, first with a knife, and then with one hand, to a soft dough.
- ● Roll out the pastry and line the oven-proof bowl or pudding basin.
- ● Fill with the desired mixture.

Lining a Pudding Basin

- ● Cut a third from the prepared suet pastry and reserve it. Roll the rest out on a lightly floured board to a round about 1 cm/½ in thick. Flour the round well on top then fold it lightly in half, bringing the far edge towards you when you fold.
- ● Gently roll it to a round again, pushing the flat folded edge into a curved shape. Use floured hands to separate the two layers of pastry to give a bag-shape. Carefully lift the "bag" and ease gently into the greased pudding basin or bowl.
- ● Trim off the excess pastry leaving 2.5 cm/1 in above the edge. Fill. Roll out the remaining third of the pastry to make a round lid. Put in place, wet the edges and press them together securely.

Flaky and Puff Pastry

These are made rather like the first stage for preparing shortcrust pastry, though the consistency of these pastries is initially softer and less "short", containing a high proportion of water. Then more fat is incorporated into the pastry, which is rolled, folded and rolled again several times. This process creates layers of pastry which, in the heat of the oven, will rise into light, thin layers. For instance, puff pastry, which is folded in three and rolled out six times, will have 729 layers.

As the aim is to create the layers without allowing the incorporated fat to melt, everything should be cool, including the bowl, the ingredients and even the worktop if possible. Short, quick strokes (rather than long steady ones) allow the bubbles of air so carefully incorporated in the pastry to move about while the fat is gradually and evenly distributed in the pastry. Work lightly and do not stretch the pastry – or the layers you have built up will tear and allow the air and fat to escape. Chill the pastry between rollings or at any point if there is a danger of the fat breaking through the pastry, or if the pastry becomes sticky and warm. Although it sounds complicated, it is easy to do.

Pastry rises evenly to a crisp crust in a steamy atmosphere. For this reason flaky and puff pastries (which are expected to rise in the oven) are generally baked with a roasting tin full of water at the bottom of the oven, or on a wet baking sheet. The oven temperature is set high (about 425°F/220°C/Gas 7) to cause rapid expansion of the trapped layers of air and quick cooking of the dough before the fat has time to melt and run out.

Flaky Pastry

250 g/8 oz plain flour

Pinch of salt

90 g/3 oz unsalted butter

120 ml/4 fl oz cold water

¾ cup white vegetable fat or lard

- ● Sift the flour with a pinch of salt. Blend in half the butter. Add enough cold water to mix with a knife to a doughy consistency. Turn out on to a floured board and knead until smooth.
- ● Roll into an oblong about 13 x 25 cm/5 x 10 in. Cut half the shortening or lard into tiny pieces and dot them evenly all over the top two thirds of the pastry, leaving a good margin.
- ● Fold the pastry in three. Fold the third with no fat up, then the top third with fat down. Press well to seal the edges.

- Repeat the rolling and folding process (without adding any fat) once more so that the folded, closed edge is on your left.
- Roll out again, dot with butter as before, fold and seal as before to prevent the fat escaping during rolling.
- Roll out again, dot with the rest of the lard, fold, seal and roll once more.
- Fold, wrap the pastry and "relax" (or chill) for 10–15 minutes.
- Roll and fold once again (without adding any fat) and then use as required.

Puff Pastry

500 g/1 lb plain flour	300 ml/10 fl oz iced water
2 tsp salt	1 tsp lemon juice
500 g/1 lb unsalted butter	

- Sift the flour and salt into a bowl and blend in 120 g/4 oz butter with the fingertips or pastry cutter. Add sufficient water and lemon juice to bind into a pliable dough. Turn on to a lightly floured surface and lightly knead until smooth.
- Shape the pastry into a round and cut a cross in the top to about half its depth. Open out the resulting four flaps and roll them out until the centre is about four times as thick as the flaps. Shape the remaining butter to fit the centre of the dough and fold over the flaps envelope-style. Seal the edges with the fingertips.
- On a floured surface, roll out the dough into a rectangle 20 x 40 cm/8 x 16 in using quick, short strokes. Fold the dough in three. Wrap the pastry in clingfilm and leave for 20 minutes in the refrigerator.
- Fold the pastry in three and roll into a rectangle as before. Fold into three again. Repeat the rolling and folding for a total of six times. Leave the dough to chill for at least 30 minutes before using it. Puff pastry should rise to about six times its height and should be cooked at 450°F/230°C/Gas 8.

NOTE

If the pastry becomes too warm or sticky and difficult to handle, wrap it up and chill it for 15 minutes before proceeding.

Strudel Pastry

This differs from most other pastries in that it actually benefits from heavy handling. It is beaten and stretched, thumped and kneaded. This treatment allows the gluten to expand and promotes elasticity in the dough. The pastry is rolled and stretched on a cloth (the bigger the better) until it is so thin that you should be able to read fine print through it. Keep the pastry covered and moist when not in use. When the pastry is pulled out, brush it with butter or oil to prevent it cracking and drying, or keep it covered with a damp cloth. Strudel pastry can be bought in ready-rolled sheets from specialist food shops, especially Greek-owned ones. Called 'filo' or 'phyllo' pastry, it is used to make the Middle Eastern baklava.

TIP

Bought filo pastry is obtainable frozen from good supermarkets and from specialist food shops. It comes ready-rolled and in convenient sheets.

---

300 g/10 oz plain flour	60 ml/2 fl oz water
Pinch of salt	1 tsp oil
1 egg	

- Sift the flour and salt into a bowl.
- Beat the egg and add the water and oil. Using first a knife and then one hand mix the water and egg into the flour, adding more water if necessary to make a soft dough.
- Beat until smooth and elastic, as follows: lift the dough up in one hand and with a flick of the wrist throw it on to a lightly floured marble slab or board without letting go of it. Gather it up again and repeat the process. Keep doing this for a few minutes. The pastry will gradually become more elastic and also less sticky.
- Keep folding and flicking until the pastry is smooth, shiny and elastic. Cover and leave in a warm place for 15 minutes.
- Put the pastry into a clean floured bowl. Cover and leave in a warm place for 15 minutes.
- The pastry is now ready for rolling and pulling, as described.

Vegetarian Tarts

Sun-dried Tomato and
Mozzarella Tart

Spinach and Walnut
Wholemeal Quiche

Ratatouille and Goat's
Cheese Quiche

Sweet Garlic, Thyme and
Olive Tart

Spinach, Camembert and Pine Nut
Square

Courgette and Provolone Tart

Aubergine and Pepper Pie

Asparagus Tranche

Cheese Soufflé Tart

Sun-dried Tomato and Mozzarella Tart

Transform the idea of the classic tomato and cheese pizza by updating the ingredients and arranging them on a pastry base.

MAKES 6–8 SLICES

1 quantity Rich Shortcrust Pastry (*Pâte Brisée Riche*, see page 13)

175 ml/6 fl oz home-made thick tomato sauce or ready-made pizza topping

300 g/10 oz grated mozzarella cheese

4–5 large plum tomatoes, sliced

6 sun-dried tomatoes, packed in oil, drained and sliced

250 g/8 oz smoked mozzarella cheese, sliced

6–8 fresh basil leaves, torn into small pieces plus extra for garnish

Virgin olive oil for drizzling

Freshly ground black pepper

Preheat the oven to 400°F/200°C/Gas 6. Roll out the pastry into a 22-cm/11-in round and use to line a 20-cm/10-in lightly greased pizza plate or shallow flan tin. Prick the bottom and blind bake for 10 minutes.

Remove from the oven and prick the bottom again. Immediately spread the base evenly with the tomato sauce or pizza topping and sprinkle with the grated cheese. Return to the oven until the cheese just begins to melt, 3–5 minutes. Remove from the oven and cool slightly.

Arrange the sliced tomatoes, sun-dried tomatoes and smoked mozzarella overlapping on the surface of the pastry base in a decorative pattern. Sprinkle with the torn basil. Drizzle with about 1 tablespoon of olive oil and season with the pepper.

Return to the oven until the pastry is golden and the cheese melted, and just beginning to color, about 8 minutes. Serve hot, drizzled with additional olive oil, and garnished with fresh basil leaves.

Spinach and Walnut Wholemeal Quiche

The fillings in vegetable quiches can easily become one dull mass of indistinguishable textures. In this quiche, walnuts are mixed with the spinach, giving a good crunch to the filling.

SERVES 4–6

PASTRY	FILLING
120 g/4 oz butter	500 g/1 lb frozen chopped leaf spinach
175 g/6 oz wholemeal flour	Salt and freshly ground black pepper
Pinch of salt	Freshly grated nutmeg
	60 g/3 oz walnut pieces, roughly chopped
	120 g/4 oz blue cheese, crumbled (Stilton or Danish)
	300 ml/10 fl oz milk
	2 large eggs

Preheat the oven to 400°F/200°C/Gas 6. Blend the butter with the flour and salt in a bowl until the mixture resembles fine crumbs. Mix to a manageable dough with warm water, then roll out and use the pastry to line a 22-cm/9-inch loose-bottomed pie dish. Line with kitchen paper then fill with baking beans. Bake blind for about 20 minutes.

Cook the spinach gently in a covered pan until piping hot; shake from time to time to prevent it from burning. Squeeze the spinach dry then season to taste with salt, pepper and nutmeg.

Remove the paper and beans from the shell and fill with a layer of the spinach, then a layer of walnuts. Crumble the blue cheese over the top of the filling.

Beat the milk and eggs and season with salt and pepper. Pour the custard over the spinach filling then grate a little nutmeg over the top. Reduce the oven temperature to 375°F/190°C/Gas 5 and bake the quiche for 25–30 minutes, until the custard has set. Serve warm or cold.

Ratatouille and Goat's Cheese Quiche

Fillings for quiches are almost infinitely variable and this one is great for using up leftover ratatouille. Alternatively you can use a tin of vegetables and add chopped nuts – about 50 g/2 oz to add interest to the texture.

SERVES 4

PASTRY	
90 g/3 oz butter	1 Tbsp basil leaves, roughly torn
150 g/5 oz flour	120 g/4 oz soft goat's cheese
Pinch of salt	Salt and freshly ground black pepper
400 g/15 oz tinned or fresh ratatouille	300 ml/10 fl oz milk or milk and single cream, mixed
	2 large eggs, beaten

Preheat oven to 400°F/200°C/Gas 6. Prepare the pastry by blending the butter into the flour and salt until the mixture resembles fine breadcrumbs. Mix to a firm, manageable dough with warm water, then knead lightly on a floured surface and roll out to line a deep 18-cm/7-in pie dish. Chill the pastry lightly for 10–15 minutes, then line the pastry base with kitchen paper and fill with baking beans. Bake for 15 minutes.

Remove the paper and the beans and spread the ratatouille over the partly cooked pastry. Sprinkle the basil leaves and goat's cheese over and season with pepper. Beat together the milk, the eggs and some seasoning, then pour the mixture over the vegetables and cheese. Return the quiche to the oven, reduce the heat to 375°F/190°C/Gas 5 and cook for a further 35 minutes or until set. This quiche is best served warm.

Ratatouille and Goat's Cheese Quiche ▶

Sweet Garlic, Thyme and Olive Tart

This strong-flavoured tart is served with goat's cheese and basil on top – it makes a great talking point. Substitute rocket or watercress for basil if you like.

SERVES 6

20–22-cm/8–9-in flan tin lined with Rich Shortcrust Pastry (*Pâte Brisée Riche*, see page 13) partially baked blind

25 g/1 oz butter

4–6 large young garlic cloves, unpeeled

2 tsp fresh thyme leaves, chopped, or 1 tsp dried thyme

2 Tbsp extra-virgin olive oil

1 large sweet onion, thinly sliced

250 ml/8 fl oz whipping cream

2 eggs

175 g/6 oz good-quality black and green olives, rinsed, pitted and halved

120 g/4 oz diced feta cheese

$^1/_2$ tsp dried pepper flakes

Handful fresh basil leaves, watercress or rocket

In a small saucepan over low heat, melt the butter. Add the garlic and thyme and cook, covered, for 15–20 minutes, stirring occasionally, until the garlic is soft. Remove from the heat to cool slightly. Squeeze the garlic from its skin and discard skins. Mash the pulp to combine with the butter and thyme.

Preheat the oven to 375°F/190°C/Gas 5. In a medium frying pan, heat 1 tablespoon of the olive oil. Add the onion and cook, stirring frequently, until soft and translucent, about 10 minutes. Spread evenly over the bottom of the flan tin.

Beat the cream and eggs and stir in the garlic purée. Pour into the onion-filled tart case and sprinkle the olives over the top. Bake until just set and lightly coloured, about 30 minutes. Remove to a wire rack to cool slightly.

In a small bowl, toss the diced feta cheese in the remaining olive oil with the pepper flakes. Arrange on the warm tart with the basil leaves, watercress or rocket. Serve.

Spinach, Camembert and Pine Nut Square

The Camembert and soured cream combine to create a rich creamy filling in this tart.

SERVES 4

25-cm/10-in square flan tin lined with Rich Shortcrust Pastry (*Pâte Brisée Riche*, see page 13) baked blind

25 g/1 oz butter

2 shallots, finely chopped

250 g/8 oz baby spinach, washed and dried

175 g/6 oz Camembert, Brie or other semi-soft cheese, rind removed and cut into small pieces

60 ml/2 fl oz soured cream

2 eggs

salt

Freshly grated nutmeg

2 Tbsp pine nuts

Preheat oven to 350°F/175°C/Gas 4. Place shell on a baking sheet for easier handling. In a frying pan over medium heat, melt 1 tablespoon butter. Add the shallots and cook, stirring often, until just softened, 3–5 minutes. Spread evenly over bottom of shell.

Melt the remaining butter in the same pan and add the spinach, stirring gently, until it wilts, about 1 minute. Spread over the bottom of the shell and sprinkle the cut-up cheese over the spinach.

Beat the soured cream and eggs until well blended. Season with salt and nutmeg and pour into the shell. Sprinkle over the pine nuts. Bake until set and golden, 20–25 minutes. Transfer to a wire rack to cool slightly; serve immediately.

2828 VEGETARIAN TARTS

Courgette and Provolone Tart

If yellow squash is hard to find or out of season, simply use young zucchini.

SERVES 4

22-cm/9-in flan tin lined with Rich Shortcrust Pastry (*Pâte Brisée Riche*, see page 13), baked blind

1 Tbsp olive oil

1 Tbsp butter

300 g/10 oz courgettes, diced

1 small red pepper, diced

½ tsp salt

Freshly ground black pepper

2 Tbsp bottled pesto sauce

250 ml/8 fl oz single cream

2 eggs

120 g/4 oz grated Provolone cheese

Preheat the oven to 375°F/190°C/Gas 5. Set the shell on a baking sheet for easier handling.

In a large frying pan over medium-high heat, heat the oil and butter. Add the courgettes and red pepper and cook, stirring frequently, until just beginning to soften, about 5 minutes. Season with salt and pepper and spread over the bottom of the shell. Drizzle the surface with the pesto sauce.

Beat the cream and eggs until blended., Stir in the grated cheese and pour over the filled shell. Bake until set and golden, about 35 minutes. Transfer to a wire rack to cool slightly. Serve hot or warm.

Aubergine and Pepper Pie

Grilling the vegetables before baking them in the tart really intensifies the flavours and brings out their sweetness.

SERVES 6

22-cm/9-in flan tin lined with Rich Shortcrust Pastry (*Pâte Brisée Riche*, see page 13), partially baked blind

1 medium aubergine, thinly sliced crossways

2 courgettes, sliced diagonally crosswise

60 ml/2 fl oz olive oil

1 red pepper, quartered and seeded

1 yellow pepper, quartered and seeded

1 large red onion, thickly sliced

120 g/4 oz soft goat's cheese, crumbled

120 ml/4 fl oz whipping cream

1 egg

1 egg yolk

1 oz Parmesan cheese, freshly grated

½ tsp dried oregano

1 Tbsp tomato purée

¼ tsp dried pepper flakes

Preheat the grill. Line the grill pan with foil and arrange the aubergine and courgette slices in a single layer on the foil. Brush the surfaces generously with some of the olive oil. Grill the vegetables until just beginning to char, about 5 minutes. Turn and grill 5 more minutes. Arrange on the bottom of the shell. Set on a baking sheet for easier handling.

Arrange the red and yellow pepper quarters, skin-side up, together with the onion rings, on the foil and brush with the remaining oil. Grill until just beginning to char, about 6–7 minutes. Remove any loosened skin and arrange them over the other vegetables in the shell, distributing them evenly. Sprinkle the crumbled goat's cheese over the vegetables.

Preheat the oven to 400°F/200°C/Gas 6. Beat the cream with the egg and egg yolk. Stir in the Parmesan cheese, oregano, tomato purée and pepper flakes until well blended. Pour over the vegetables in the tart case. Bake until the filling is set and top is well coloured, about 25 minutes. Transfer to a wire rack to cool slightly. Serve warm.

◀ *Aubergine and Pepper Pie*

Asparagus Tranche

Atranche is a "slice" in French. This rectangular tart makes an elegant presentation, as well as being easy to slice.

SERVES 4

14 x 10-cm/4-in flan tin lined with Rich Cheese Pastry or Rich Shortcrust Pastry, see page 13, partially baked blind

15 g/½ oz butter

500 g/1 lb thin asparagus tips, well washed

120 ml/4 fl oz double cream

2 eggs

1 egg yolk

½ tsp salt

¼ tsp cayenne pepper

3 Tbsp freshly chopped dill or chives

2 tsp Dijon mustard

Preheat the oven to 350°F/175°C/Gas 4. Set the shell on a baking sheet for easier handling. In a large frying pan over medium-high heat, melt the butter. Add the asparagus tips and cook, tossing gently until tender-crisp and brightly coloured, 1–2 minutes. Remove from the heat and cool slightly. Arrange the asparagus spears crosswise and top to tail in the shell.

Beat the cream, eggs and egg yolk until well blended. Season with salt and cayenne pepper, then stir in the dill or chives and mustard. Pour into the shell. Bake until set and golden, about 25 minutes. Transfer to a wire rack to cool slightly. Serve hot or warm.

Cheese Soufflé Tart

This cheese soufflé in a pastry shell makes a great supper dish. For a special presentation, make individual tartlets but bake 10 minutes less.

SERVES 6

22-cm/9-in flan tin lined with Rich Pie Crust (*Pâte Brisée Riche*, see page 13), partially baked blind

30 g/1 oz Parmesan cheese, freshly grated

25 g/1 oz butter

1 small onion, finely chopped

25 g/1 oz plain flour

300 ml/10 fl oz milk

2 eggs, separated

1 Tbsp Dijon mustard

175 g/6 oz grated Cheddar cheese

Salt

Cayenne pepper

1 egg white

Preheat the oven to 425°F/220°C/Gas 7. Sprinkle the shell with Parmesan cheese. Set on a baking sheet for easier handling.

Melt the butter in a medium saucepan over medium heat. Stir in the onion and cook for 1–2 minutes. Stir in the flour all at once and cook, stirring constantly, for 2 minutes. Gradually whisk in the milk, stirring until thick and smooth. Bring to the boil and cook for 1 minute. Remove from the heat. Beat in the egg yolks, one at a time, then beat in the mustard and cheese. Season with a little salt and cayenne pepper. Set aside.

In a medium bowl, with an electric mixer, beat all the egg whites with a pinch of salt until soft peaks form. Stir a spoonful of the whites into the cheese sauce to lighten it, then gently fold in the remaining whites and spoon the mixture into the shell.

Bake until the soufflé is puffed and golden, about 25 minutes. Serve immediately in the same way as you would a traditional soufflé.

Asparagus Tranche ▶

Meat and Fish Pies, Quiches and Tarts

Broccoli, Ham and Cheese Pie

Spanish Tortilla Tart

Quiche Lorraine

Smoked Salmon, Leek and Orange Tart

Crab and Red Pepper Tartlets

Beef Wellington

Steak and Kidney Pudding with
Smoked Oysters

Scandinavian Meat Loaf en Croûte

Game Pie

Veal and Ham Raised Pie

Chicken and Mushroom Pie

Broccoli, Ham and Cheese Pie

The classic flavours of ham and cheese marry well with broccoli.

SERVES 8

20 x 30-cm/8 x 12-in rectangular flan tin lined with 250 g/8 oz Cheese Pastry, partially baked blind

2 cups broccoli florets, blanched

250 g/8 oz diced cooked ham

120 ml/4 fl oz whipping cream

120 ml/4 fl oz milk

3 eggs

2 egg yolks

Salt

Freshly ground black pepper

150 g/5 oz grated Gruyère or Cheddar cheese

Preheat the oven to 375°F/190°C/Gas 5. Arrange the blanched broccoli evenly over the bottom of the flan tin, then sprinkle over the ham pieces or slices.

Mix the cream, milk, eggs and egg yolks until well blended. Season with salt and pepper and stir in the cheese. Pour over the filling. Bake until set and golden, 30–35 minutes. Transfer to a wire rack to cool slightly. Serve hot or warm.

Spanish Tortilla Tart

The pastry provides a light, flaky base for an omelette-like filling with typically Spanish flavours.

SERVES 6

22-cm/9-in flan tin lined with 175 g/6 oz Rich Shortcrust Pastry (*Pâte Brisée Riche*, see page 13), partially baked blind

1 Tbsp olive oil

1 small onion, thinly sliced

1 red or green pepper, seeded and thinly sliced

2 garlic cloves, chopped

2–3 sun-dried tomatoes packed in oil, chopped

8–10 black olives, stoned and chopped

1 large potato (about 250 g /8 oz), cooked and sliced

50 g/2 oz chorizo, cut into thin strips

2 tsp chopped tinned jalapeño chillies

4 eggs

150 ml/2 fl oz milk

60 ml/2 fl oz whipping cream

½ tsp salt

Freshly ground black pepper

½ tsp paprika

90 g/3 oz grated Cheddar cheese

Preheat the oven to 375°F/190°C/Gas 5. In a medium frying pan over medium heat, heat the oil. Add the onion, pepper and garlic and cook, stirring occasionally, until softened, about 8 minutes. Reserve one quarter of the mixture and spread the remainder evenly over the pastry base. Set on a baking sheet for easier handling.

Sprinkle the onion mixture with three-quarters of the sun-dried tomatoes and olives, and arrange the potato slices over the top. Sprinkle over the remaining onion-pepper mixture, sun-dried tomatoes and olives.

Beat the eggs, milk and cream. Season with salt, pepper and the paprika, then stir in the cheese. Pour over the vegetable layers. Bake until set and golden, about 30 minutes. Transfer to a wire rack to cool slightly. Serve hot, warm or at room temperature.

Quiche Lorraine

The authentic 'quiche', which originates in the Lorraine region of France, is a custard-based tart containing bacon, cream and eggs, and is served as an appetizer. Purists say that only this tart can truly be called a quiche. If you like, add 1 cup grated Gruyère or Cheddar to the custard mixture.

SERVES 6

22-cm/9-in flan tin lined with 175 g/6 oz Rich Shortcrust Pastry (*Pâte Brisée Riche*, see page 13) partially baked blind

250 g/8 oz bacon, cut into 1-cm/½-in strips

375 ml/12 fl oz whipping cream

3 eggs

1 egg yolk

½ tsp salt

Freshly ground black pepper

Freshly grated nutmeg

Preheat the oven to 375°F/190°C/Gas 5. Set the flan tin on a baking sheet for easier handling.

Put the bacon in a frying pan over low heat. When the fat begins to melt, increase the heat to medium and fry, stirring occasionally, until crisp. Drain on kitchen paper, then sprinkle over the pastry base.

Beat the cream and eggs until well blended. Season with salt and pepper and a little grated nutmeg. (Stir in the cheese, if using.) Pour into the pastry base. Bake until the filling is set and golden, about 35 minutes. Transfer to a wire rack to cool slightly. Serve at room temperature.

Smoked Salmon,
Leek and Orange Tart

A hint of orange brings out the flavour of the leeks and smoked salmon.

SERVES 6

22-cm/9-in flan tin lined with 175 g/6 oz Rich Shortcrust Pastry (*Pâte Brisée Riche*, see page 13), partially baked blind

3 leeks, trimmed, washed and cut into ½-cm/¼-in slices

250 ml/8 fl oz whipping cream

Grated rind of ½ orange

2 Tbsp chopped fresh chives or dill

Freshly ground black pepper

250 g/8 oz smoked salmon, cut into thin strips

3 Tbsp soured cream

1 egg

1 egg yolk

Preheat the oven to 375°F/190°C/Gas 5. Put the leeks, whipping cream and orange rind into a medium saucepan. Set over medium-high heat and bring to the boil. Simmer until the leeks are tender and cream reduced to a thick purée consistency. Remove from the heat and stir in the chives or dill and season with pepper. Spread evenly over the pastry base.

Arrange the smoked salmon strips evenly over the leek mixture. Set on a baking sheet for easier handling.

Beat the soured cream, egg and egg yolk and pour over the leeks and smoked salmon strips. Bake until the filling is set and golden, about 25 minutes. Transfer to a wire rack to cool slightly. Serve warm.

Crab and Red Pepper Tartlets

Buy good-quality fresh white crabmeat for these delicate tartlets. Use a mini-muffin pan to make small tartlets.

MAKES 8

4 sheets filo pastry, defrosted if frozen	1 Tbsp chopped dill
60–90 g/2–3 oz butter, melted	60 g/2 oz Parmesan cheese, freshly grated
3 red peppers, seeded and cut lengthwise into thin strips	250 g/8 oz fresh white crabmeat
	2 Tbsp mayonnaise
	1 Tbsp lemon or lime juice

Melt 2 tablespoons of the butter in a large frying pan over medium heat. Add the red pepper strips and cook until softened. Remove from the heat and stir in the dill.

Preheat the oven to 350°F/190°C/Gas 5. Grease eight 5 x 3-cm/2½ x 1¼ in deep tartlet tins. Stack pastry sheets on a work surface. Cut into 10–13-cm/4–5 inch squares.

Place one square on the work surface and brush lightly with a little butter; do not brush right up to the edge. Sprinkle with a little Parmesan cheese. Place a second square on top of the first at a right angle, to create a star shape. Brush lightly with butter and sprinkle with a little Parmesan. Top with a third square, at an angle to the first two, but do not brush with butter. Ease into one of the tartlet tins, keeping the edges pointing up to form a flat-bottomed tulip shape. (Keep the filo pastry sheets you aren't working with covered with a damp tea-towel to prevent them from drying out.) Line the remaining tins.

Bake until crisp and golden, about 10 minutes. Transfer to a wire rack to cool slightly. Carefully remove each filo case and set on a rack to cool. Divide the pepper mixture evenly among the filo cases and top each with a little crabmeat. Mix the mayonnaise with the lemon or lime juice and drizzle a little sauce over the crabmeat. Garnish with dill sprigs.

Beef Wellington

Served hot or cold, this pastry-wrapped beef makes an impressive pastry dish.

SERVES 6

500 g/1 lb flaky or puff pastry	300 g/10 oz mushrooms
1-kg/2-lb beef fillet, in one piece	1 medium onion
	2 garlic cloves
Salt and pepper	Mixed fresh herbs
175 g/6 oz butter	1 egg, beaten, to glaze

Preheat the oven to 425°F/220°C/Gas 7. Make the pastry dough and chill in the refrigerator.

Trim the beef and season with salt and pepper. Rub with butter and roast in a hot oven for about 10 minutes.

Finely chop the mushrooms, onion, garlic and herbs and cook in the rest of the butter. Drain well and arrange in a layer over the beef.

Roll out the dough large enough to fit around the beef and meet at the top. Brush beaten egg on the edges of the dough and squeeze together with your fingers. If you are worried about the dough opening during cooking, put the seam under the beef and decorate the top with dough leaves made from the trimmings. Brush all over with beaten egg and roast for about 20 minutes or until the pastry is golden. Serve hot or cold.

Steak and Kidney Pudding with Smoked Oysters

This is a classic English pudding. The smoked oysters (and indeed the kidney) can be omitted if preferred. Mushrooms could be substituted for the oysters.

SERVES 4

12 oz flour-quantity Suet Pastry	1 small tin smoked oysters, drained
700 g/1½ lb chuck steak	Salt and pepper
250 g/8 oz lamb's kidneys	2 tsp chopped onions
Flour	2 tsp chopped fresh parsley

NOTE

Traditionally, steak and kidney pudding served from the bowl is presented wrapped in a white linen napkin. Alternatively, it can be unmoulded on to a large deep-lipped dish and cut like a cake.

As the filling of the pudding may, with long cooking, dry out somewhat, it is worth having a gravy boat of hot beef gravy or stock handy to moisten the meat when serving.

Cut the steak into 20 mm/¾-in cubes. Chop the kidneys, discarding any sinew. Place both the steak and the kidneys in a large sieve. Pour over the flour and shake until the meat is lightly coated.

Line the pudding basin with the prepared suet pastry. Fill the lined basin with the meat and add the smoked oysters. Sprinkle plenty of seasoning, chopped onion and parsley between the layers. Add water to come three quarters of the way up the filling.

Roll the remaining third of suet pastry ½ cm/¼ in thick and cover the pudding filling.

Cover the pudding with a piece of greaseproof paper, pleated down the centre (this is to allow room for the pastry to expand), and a similarly pleated piece of foil. Tie down with string.

Place in a saucepan of boiling water with a tightly closed lid, or in a steamer, for 5 hours, taking care to top up with boiling water occasionally. (If using the saucepan method, the water should come two thirds up the side of the pudding basin. If too full the water bubbles over the top. If too empty it risks boiling dry.)

Remove the paper and foil and serve.

▲ *Beef Wellington*

Scandinavian Meat Loaf en Croûte

The chicken liver filling adds a gourmet touch to this meat loaf. An attractive dish which tastes as good as it looks.

SERVES 4–6

PASTRY

500 g/1 lb Basic Shortcrust Pastry

MEAT LOAF

90 g/3 oz dried breadcrumbs

120 ml/8 fl oz single cream

120 ml/4 fl oz water

½ onion, chopped

Butter for frying

120 g/4 oz frozen chicken livers, thawed

400 g/14 oz minced beef, veal or pork

1½ tsp white pepper

½ tsp salt

Prepare the pastry and leave to rest in the refrigerator for 1 hour.

Mix the breadcrumbs with the cream and water. Fry the onion in a little butter. Slice the chicken livers, fry and season. Mix the minced meat with salt, pepper, breadcrumb mixture and fried onion. Pat the mixture into a meat-loaf shape on moistened greaseproof paper. Cut a line along the top and fill with the livers, season then smooth over to cover.

Preheat the oven to 425°F/220°C/Gas 7. Roll out the pastry between sheets of clingfilm. Remove the clingfilm now and then to sprinkle with flour. Roll out one rectangle large enough to wrap around the meat loaf. Trim away uneven edges and save for decoration.

Ease the meat loaf on to the pastry. First fold up the short ends, trimming away the pastry at the corners so that it is not too thick. Fold up the long sides but not too tightly. Seal the join. Ease the parcel on to a greased baking sheet. Decorate with pastry trimmings. Bake for 30–35 minutes.

If liked, serve with chopped iceberg lettuce and peppers dressed in a mixture of 3 tablespoons mayonnaise, 2 tablespoons tomato paste, 3 tablespoons water, salt and pepper.

Game Pie

It is not really worth making a game pie for fewer than eight people.

SERVES 8–10

500–700 g/1–1½ lb Basic
  Shortcrust Pastry

1 kg/2 lb stewing venison, or
  a mixture of rabbit and
  venison

250–375 g/8–12 oz pheasant,
  partridge or pigeon

1 onion

2 leeks

2 carrots

1 turnip

Fresh parsley, thyme and bay
  leaf tied together

120 g/4 oz butter

30 g/2 oz chopped shallots

375 g/12 oz chopped
  mushrooms

250 g/8 oz bacon rashers

250 g/8 oz veal, ham or pork

120 g/4 oz chicken livers

2 Tbsp chopped fresh thyme

Chopped fresh savory,
  tarragon, and parsley

Grated rind of 1 orange

Salt and freshly ground black
  pepper

Pinch of ground cloves

Pinch of grated nutmeg

2 cups fresh breadcrumbs

1 egg, beaten

1 glass Madeira or port

5 hard-boiled eggs, chopped

1 egg, beaten, to glaze

Put any bones you have, together with the venison trimmings, in a pot. Add the onion, leeks, carrots and turnip with enough water to cover. Add the herbs and simmer while you prepare the rest of the pie.

In 50 g/2 oz of the butter, fry the jointed birds until cooked 'pink'. Remove. Fry the shallots and mushrooms in a little more butter.

Preheat the oven to 375°F/190°C/Gas 5. Line a 25–30-cm/10–12 in deep baking dish with half the bacon rashers. Grind the rest of the bacon with the veal, ham or pork. Add the chicken livers and the reserved livers from the birds used in the pie. Put the minced meat into a bowl and mix with the fried shallots and mushrooms, herbs, orange rind, salt, pepper and spices. Add the breadcrumbs, the whole egg and the Madeira. Mix well.

Put a layer of game joints over the bacon rashers. Season and sprinkle with parsley. Add a layer of hard-boiled eggs, then the cooked liver mixture rolled into balls. Continue until full, cover with foil and bake for up to 1 hour.

Take out of the oven and cool. Put a pie funnel in the middle, cover with the pastry dough and let some of the funnel protrude. Glaze with egg and cook in a hot oven until the pastry is golden. Serve with a fruit jelly.

Veal and Ham Raised Pie

This traditional pie makes an impressive centre-piece for a buffet party and is excellent served with beetroot or potato salad.

SERVES 4

500 g/1 lb Hot Water Pastry (see page 19)	1 onion, finely chopped
700 g/1½ lb boned veal shoulder	2 Tbsp chopped parsley
120 g/4 oz ham	1 hard-boiled egg
Salt and pepper	1 egg, beaten
	600 ml/1 pt meat aspic

Preheat oven to 325°F/160°C/Gas 3. Cut the veal and ham into very small cubes. Season with a little salt, plenty of pepper, onion and parsley. Reserve.

Wrap a large piece of greaseproof paper around the outside of a tall, wide jar. Smooth it down as well as possible and try to cover the jar tightly. Leave upside down while you make the pastry.

Reserve about a quarter of the pastry for the lid, keeping it covered. Roll out the remaining pastry to a round and shape to cover the upturned jar. Leave to chill until really firm, about 20 minutes. When hard turn the jar over and remove it carefully, leaving the greaseproof paper inside the pastry case. Trim and carefully remove the greaseproof paper from the pastry. Stand the pastry case on a baking sheet.

Fill the pie, pushing the filling well into the corners, with half the seasoned meat. Press in the hard-boiled egg and cover with the remaining meat. Shape the filling so that there is a central dome.

Cover the pie with the pastry reserved for the lid. Using a little water secure the lid to the sides of the pie. Press firmly together. Cut off any excess pastry and "crimp" the top edge. Secure a double piece of greaseproof paper around the whole pie with paper clips at top and bottom to prevent the sides from bulging.

Make a few pastry leaves from any pastry trimmings. Brush the top of the pie with egg white. Make a neat hole (for the steam to escape) in the middle of the lid and decorate the top with the pastry leaves.

Bake for 2 hours. After 1½ hours remove the paper and brush the sides evenly with the egg glaze. Remove from the oven and allow to get completely cold on a wire rack, but do not refrigerate yet.

Warm the meat aspic until just runny. Using a funnel, fill the pie with aspic. The aspic will take some time to filter through the meat so keep repeating the topping-up process until you are sure that it is absolutely full. Leave to cool and set before serving.

TIP

For curly pastry leaves cut diamonds from a wide pastry strip. Use the blade of a knife held at a non-cutting angle to mark the leaf 'veins', while pulling the leaf into a curved shape.

Thicker, more robust leaves can be curved in situ. The leaves can be glazed with egg to stick them in place and to give them a shine when baked.

Chicken and Mushroom Pie

A timeless favourite with a light rich pastry.

SERVES 6–8

500 g/1 lb Flaky Pastry	500 g/1 lb button mushrooms, or wild mushrooms, if available
1 good-sized chicken	
1 Spanish onion	Knob of butter, softened and worked with 1 Tbsp flour
Fresh parsley, thyme and bay leaf tied together	1 Tbsp chopped fresh herbs, including tarragon
Carrots, celery and leeks	1 egg, beaten, to glaze
Dry white white (optional)	

Place the chicken in a pot with the onion, bouquet garni and vegetables. Cover with water and some dry white wine, if you have any.

When the chicken is cooked, remove it from the pot and reserve the stock. Take off all the skin and remove the bones and any tough sinews. Cut the chicken into bite-sized pieces.

Sauté the mushrooms in a little butter. Remove from the butter and place in a deep baking dish together with the prepared chicken.

Into the pan juices from the mushrooms, gradually add 600 ml/1 pt or more of the reserved chicken broth. Cook for a few minutes over high heat. Thicken with a knob of butter worked together with 1 tablespoon of flour. Add the fresh herbs and seasoning and pour over the chicken and mushrooms. Cool.

Roll out the flaky pastry dough. Cover the contents to the edges of the baking dish, and brush an egg glaze on the pie. Cook in the oven, preheated to 425°F/220°C/ Gas 7, until golden brown.

Fruit and Nut Tarts and Pies

Summer Berry Tart

The hazelnut pastry goes beautifully with the sweetness of summer berries or substitute other favourite fruits cut into bite-sized pieces.

SERVES 6

22-cm/9-in flan tin lined with Easy Nut Pastry made with hazelnuts (see page 14), baked blind

700 g/1½ lb mixed summer berries, such as strawberries, raspberries, red or blackcurrants

⅓ cup redcurrant jelly or raspberry jam

2 Tbsp raspberry-flavored liqueur

Mint leaves for garnish (optional)

Cut any large strawberries in half or quarters and put in a large bowl. Add the remaining fruit and then toss lightly to combine.

In a small saucepan over medium heat, heat the jelly or jam with the liqueur until melted and smooth, stirring frequently. Drizzle over the fruit and shake the bowl to lightly coat the fruit.

Pour the fruit mixture into the shell, gently distributing the fruit evenly over the surface and into the edge. If you like, garnish with fresh mint leaves.

Blueberry Pie

Asimple classic. If fresh blueberries are unavailable, frozen blueberries work equally well.

SERVES 4

PASTRY BASE

25 g/1 oz butter

90 g/3 oz sugar (optional)

1 egg

90 ml/3 fl oz whipping cream

150 g/5 oz plain flour

FILLING

500–700 g/1–1½ lb blueberries

Sugar to taste (optional)

1 tsp breadcrumbs or potato flour

Soften the butter and add the sugar, if using. Mix in the egg thoroughly, then add the cream and flour. Mix well, but do not beat the dough. Leave the dough to stand in a cool place for 15 minutes.

Preheat the oven to 400°F/200°C/Gas 6. Roll out the dough into a thin sheet and transfer to a greased baking sheet, shaping a raised edge all the way around. Mix the blueberries with the sugar, if using, and the breadcrumbs or potato flour. Spread the filling over the base. Bake until the pastry is golden brown.

Cottage Cheese Strudel

Cottage cheese and soured cream make a light filling for this unusual Strudel.

SERVES 6–8

FILLING

60 g/2oz Sultanas

1 Tbsp rum

120 g/4 oz butter, softened

200 g/7 oz caster sugar

4 egg yolks

375 g/12 oz cottage cheese, sieved

60 ml/2 fl oz soured cream

1 tsp lemon rind

1 quantity Strudel Pastry or 12 sheets of filo pastry

Icing sugar to dust

Soak the sultanas in the rum for 30 minutes to plump. Beat the butter and sugar until light and fluffy. Beat in the egg yolks one at a time. Mix in the cheese, sour cream and lemon rind.

Pre-heat the oven to 400°F/200°C/Gas 6. Roll out the pastry on to a teatowel and brush with melted butter. Spread the filling over two-thirds of the pastry and sprinkle with sultanas and rum. Using a teatowel to help, roll the pastry loosely over the filling; tuck in the ends carefully, so that the filling cannot leak out, and transfer to a large, greased baking sheet, seam side down. Brush with more melted butter and bake for 30 minutes until crisp and well-browned. Serve warm or cold, dusted with icing sugar.

If using filo pastry, use six sheets at a time. Brush one sheet with melted unsalted butter and cover with a second sheet of pastry; brush with more melted butter and continue layering and brushing with butter with the remaining layers. Place half the cheese filling in the middle and roll up in the same way as for Strudel. Finish with the rest of the filo sheets in the same way.

Summer Berry Strudel

This is a delicious summer recipe – the almond cream adds a distinctive richness and flavour.

SERVES 6–8

ALMOND CREAM

120 g/4 oz blanched almonds

50 g/2 oz sugar

2 Tbsp plain flour

90 g/3 oz unsalted butter, softened and cut into pieces

1 egg

1 egg yolk

½ tsp almond essence

STRUDEL

175 g/4 oz butter, melted

120 g/4 oz fresh breadcrumbs

1 kg/2 lb mixed summer berries, such as raspberries, blueberries, strawberries (hulled and chopped), extra for serving

120 g/4 oz sugar plus extra for sprinkling

Grated rind of 1 lemon

8 large sheets filo pastry

Icing sugar for dusting, sifted

Whipped cream or crème fraîche for serving

For the cream: Grind almonds, sugar and flour in a food processor. Blend in the butter a little at a time, then add the egg, egg yolk and almond essence.

For the Strudel: Heat 5 tablespoons of the melted butter in a large frying pan, then add the breadcrumbs and stir-fry for 5 minutes.

Pre-heat the oven to 375°F/190°C/Gas 5. Grease a large baking sheet. Toss the berries in a large bowl with 120 g/4 oz sugar and lemon rind.

Place a filo pastry sheet on the work surface. Brush with a little melted butter and sprinkle with about 20 g/1 oz of the breadcrumbs. Lay a second sheet of pastry over the top, and repeat. Continue layering the remaining filo sheets with butter and crumbs.

Spread the almond cream over the stack of pastry. Spoon the berry mixture over the centre and roll up like a Swiss roll. Slide the Strudel, seam-side down; on to the baking sheet. Brush with any remaining butter and sprinkle with a little sugar.

Bake for about 45 minutes until crisp; cover with foil if it browns too quickly. Cool on a wire rack. Dust with icing sugar and serve with whipped cream or crème fraîche and extra berries.

Lemon and Almond Strudel

This Strudel, with a rich but light tangy filling, goes well with coffee.

SERVES 6–8

60 g/2 oz butter

2 egg yolks

I whole egg

300 g/10 oz caster sugar

Grated rind of 2 lemons

1½ Tbsp lemon juice, strained

2 egg whites

I portion Strudel Dough or 12 sheets of filo pastry

180 g/6 oz ground almonds

Icing sugar, to dust

Beat the butter until pale and creamy. Whisk in the egg yolks one at a time then the whole egg. Beat in 250 g/8 oz sugar and mix in the lemon rind. Set aside. Beat together the lemon juice and remaining sugar. Whisk the egg whites until they stand in stiff peaks and beat the lemon juice and sugar mixture into them until they are thick and glossy.

Brush the dough with melted butter and cover two-thirds with the butter and egg yolk filling. Scatter the ground almonds all over and cover with the lemon and egg white mixture. Roll up the Strudel lightly. Brush with melted butter.

Preheat oven to 400°F/200°C/Gas 6. Bake for 30 minutes until crisp and well-browned. Serve dusted with icing sugar.

Fruit Tarts

These classic tarts are easy to make and always look impressive filled with fresh fruits. Soft fruits do not need to be cooked so make a quick and easy dessert. Simply bake a 20–25-cm/8–10 in pastry case blind using Rich Shortcrust Pastry as described on page 13, and fill shortly before serving to prevent the pastry from going soggy.

For the simplest fruit tart, fill the pastry case with the prepared fruits arranging them attractively in concentric rings or in colourful segments as desired. The fruit can then be glazed with 3 tablespoons redcurrant jelly or raspberry jam warmed with 2 tablespoons kirsch or lemon juice.

Many fruit tarts include a custard filling known as crème pâtissière (pastry cream). Fill the case with the custard filling before topping with the fruit.

Crème Pâtissière (Pastry Cream)

4 eggs	1 litre/1¾ pt milk
150 g/5 oz caster sugar	60 g/2 oz butter
120 g/4 oz flour	Few drops vanilla essence

Beat together the eggs and sugar until the mixture becomes pale in colour. Add the sifted flour. Bring the milk to the boil and pour over the custard, beating continuously.

Transfer the custard to the pan and cook over low heat, stirring with a wooden spoon until the mixture thickens as it begins to boil. Remove from the heat.

Cut the butter into small cubes and stir into the custard along with the vanilla essence.

Place a sheet of dampened baking parchment or sprinkle caster sugar over the custard until it is cold to prevent a skin from forming.

Tarte Tatin

This classic French tart was originally made famous by two sisters in the small town of Sologne in France; now it is served all over the world. It is equally delicious made with pears.

SERVES 6–8

375 g/12 oz ready-made puff pastry or 1 quantity Basic Sweet Pastry (*Pâte Sucrée*, see page 14)	120 g/4 oz unsalted butter
	300 g/10 oz sugar
	¼ tsp ground cinnamon
10 large Golden Delicious apples	Soured cream for serving
Juice of 1 lemon	

On a lightly floured surface, roll out the pastry into a 30-cm/12-in round, about ½ cm/¼-in thick. Slide on to a lightly floured baking sheet and refrigerate until needed.

Using a swivel-bladed vegetable peeler, peel the apples, then halve and core them. Sprinkle the apples with a little lemon juice as you work, to prevent them from discolouring.

In a 25-cm/10-in heavy-based, ovenproof deep frying pan over a medium-high heat, melt the butter. Add the sugar and cinnamon, stirring occasionally, until the sugar dissolves. Cook, stirring occasionally, until the sugar is a rich golden caramel colour. Remove from the heat.

Carefully arrange the apple halves, rounded side down, around the outside edge of the pan, pressing them together tightly. Press the remaining apple halves into the centre, squeezing them into a circle (remember the apples will shrink as they cook). Be very careful not to touch the caramel as it is dangerously hot.

Return the apple-filled pan to the heat and bring to the boil. Simmer until the apples begin to soften and the caramel darkens, about 20 minutes. Remove from the heat to cool slightly.

Preheat the oven to 425°F/220°C/Gas 7. Remove the pastry round from the refrigerator and allow to soften slightly, about 5 minutes. Carefully slide the rolled-out pastry round over the apple-filled pan, centring the pastry over the apples. Using a knife, carefully tuck the overhanging dough inside the edge of the pan. Pierce the pastry in 2 or 3 places. Bake until golden, 25–30 minutes. Transfer to a wire rack to cool, about 5 minutes.

Run a knife round the edge of the pan to release any pastry that might be stuck. Place a heatproof serving plate over the pan and, using oven gloves, carefully invert them together (unmould this tart over the sink in case the caramel oozes out). Gently remove the pan, loosening any apple that may have stuck. Serve warm or at room temperature with soured cream or crème fraîche.

Lavender-scented Apple Tart

The heady scent of lavender in this tart evokes the hills of Provence in France. Fresh lavender gives the best flavour but rosemary or thyme are equally intriguing. For a pretty effect, do not peel the apples, but core and thinly slice them. The peel on the edge gives the cooked tart a colourful finish.

SERVES 6

25-cm/10-in flan tin lined with Basic Sweet Pastry (*Pâte Sucrée*, see page 14)

4 large Gala or Golden Delicious apples

120 ml/4 fl oz Pineaux de Charente or other sweet dessert wine

3 Tbsp granulated sugar

GLAZE

60 ml/2 fl oz honey

1 tsp dried or fresh lavender or to taste

Pre-heat the oven to 400°F/200°C/Gas 6. Using a swivel-bladed vegetable peeler, peel the apples, if desired, then halve and core them. Place cut-side down on a work surface and cut crossways into thin slices. Toss with 3–4 tablespoons of the wine and 2 tablespoons of the sugar.

Starting at the outside edge, arrange the apple slices in overlapping concentric circles in the pastry case. Sprinkle with the remaining sugar. Bake until the apples are tender and the pastry crisp and golden, about 40 minutes. Transfer to a wire rack to cool slightly.

In a small saucepan over medium-high heat, simmer the remaining wine, honey and lavender until reduced by half, about 5 minutes. Carefully brush the hot glaze over the tart. Serve warm.

Plum Crumble Tarts

Almost any firm fruit can be substituted for the plums. The sharpness of the fruit contrasts perfectly with the sweet crumble topping.

MAKES 6

six 8-cm/3¹/₂-in tartlet pans, lined with Basic Sweet Pastry (Pâte Sucrée, see page 14), partially baked blind	**¹/₂ tsp ground cinnamon**
	FILLING
CRUMBLE TOPPING	**700 g/1¹/₂ lb plums**
120 g/4 oz plain flour	**15 g/¹/₂ oz butter**
120 g/4 oz cold butter, cut into small pieces	**2 Tbsp sugar**
50 g/2 oz sugar	**¹/₂ tsp ground cinnamon**
3 Tbsp light or dark brown sugar	**Lemon juice**
50 g/2 oz walnuts or pecans, chopped	

Prepare the crumble topping. Put the flour in a large bowl and sprinkle the pieces of butter over the top. Using a pastry blender, cut in the butter until the mixture resembles coarse crumbs. Do not over-blend or the topping will be too dense. Stir in the sugars, nuts and cinnamon until well blended. Refrigerate until ready to use.

Preheat the oven to 400°F/200°C/Gas 6. Halve the plums and, using a small spoon, remove the stones; chop coarsely. In a large frying pan over medium-high heat, melt the butter. Add the plums and toss to coat. Sprinkle with the sugar and cinnamon, and cook for about 1 minute. Cool slightly.

Divide the plum mixture equally among the tartlet shells and set them on a baking sheet for easier handling. Spoon the crumble mixture over the plums, mounding it generously. Bake for 15–20 minutes until the topping is crisp and golden. Transfer the tartlets to a wire rack to cool. Serve warm with soured cream, if liked.

Apple and Sultana Crumble

The quantity of cinnamon can be adjusted according to taste.

SERVES 4–6

CRUMBLE TOPPING	**FILLING**
175 g/6 oz plain flour	**1 kg/2 lb apples**
Pinch of salt	**Butter**
120 g/4 oz butter	**2 Tbsp sultanas**
120 g/4 oz sugar	**3 Tbsp brown sugar**
	Squeeze of lemon juice
	Pinch of cinnamon

Pre-heat the oven to 400°F/200°C/Gas 6. Prepare the crumble by sifting the flour into a bowl with the salt. Rub in the butter using a pastry blender until the mixture resembles coarse crumbs. Stir in the sugar.

Peel, quarter, core and slice the apples thinly into a deep, buttered pie plate. Mix in the sultanas, sugar, lemon juice and cinnamon. Press down firmly to flatten.

Sprinkle the crumble mixture evenly over the apple so that it is well sealed. Bake for 30 minutes until golden brown.

> **TIP**
> *For the crumble, use a deep dish that takes apple and topping easily. The apple swells slightly as it cooks and can push bits of crumble off the top if the dish is overfilled, and the juices can overflow.*

Plum Crumble Tarts ▶

Strawberry Heart Tart

A heart-shaped tin can be used to make this tart, carefully unmoulding the pastry before filling. Alternatively, cut out your own heart shape on a baking sheet.

SERVES 6

300 g/10 oz ready-made puff pastry

700 g/1½ lb strawberries

120 g/4 oz redcurrant jelly

2 Tbsp Kirsch or water (optional)

Preheat the oven to 425°F/220°C/Gas 7. Lightly spray a 22-cm/9-in heart-shaped cake tin with vegetable oil. On a lightly floured surface, roll out the pastry to a circle about 3 mm/⅛ in thick. Line the cake tin with the pastry, pressing into the base. Trim and crimp the edges.

Line the heart-shaped dough with foil and fill with beans. Bake blind for 10–15 minutes. Reduce the oven temperature to 400°F/200°C/Gas 6, remove foil and beans and continue baking until crisp and golden brown, about 15 more minutes. Transfer to a wire rack to cool completely. Carefully remove the pastry heart from the tin.

Cut off the stem end of the strawberries and slice each lengthwise. If they have a rounded not pointed tip, cut them through the narrowest part to make them appear more pointed. Arrange them, tightly together, pointed ends up, in the pastry case.

In a small saucepan over medium heat, heat the jelly with the liqueur or water until melted and bubbling. Cool slightly, then brush the berries with a thick layer of glaze, allowing it to dribble between the berries. Serve at room temperature.

Strawberry Rhubarb Pie

The classic strawberry-rhubarb combination is an ideal filling for an easy-to-make pie. It is also excellent made with apples and blackberries.

SERVES 6–8

1 quantity Basic Sweet Pastry (*Pâte Sucrée*) or Extra Sweet Pastry (*Pâte Sucrée Riche*, see page 14)

15 g/½ oz butter

500 g/1 lb rhubarb, cut into 2.5-cm/1-in pieces

Sugar

2 Tbsp plain flour

500 g/1 lb strawberries, hulled and halved if large

2 Tbsp fresh breadcrumbs, toasted, or 4 Tbsp home-made dried breadcrumbs

Lightly spray or oil a large baking sheet. On a lightly floured surface, roll out the pastry to a 32–35-cm/13–14-in round; it doesn't matter if the shape is not perfect or if the edges tear, as this is a rustic pie. Slide on to baking sheet and refrigerate 30 minutes.

Melt the butter in a large pan over high heat. Add the rhubarb and stir-fry until the juices begin to run and it just begins to lose its colour. Sprinkle in 3–4 tablespoons sugar and the flour and toss to coat. Remove from the heat and add the strawberries, tossing lightly to combine. Cool for about 5 minutes.

Preheat the oven to 400°F/200°C/Gas 6. Remove the pastry round from the refrigerator to soften for about 5 minutes. Sprinkle the surface of the pastry with the toasted or dried breadcrumbs and spoon the fruit on to the pastry to within 7–10 cm/3–4 in of the border.

Using your fingertips, fold and crimp the wide border of the pastry over the fruit toward the centre. Sprinkle with a little sugar. It doesn't matter if the pastry cracks or is uneven, just pinch it together. Bake until the pastry is crisp and golden and fruit is bubbling, 35–40 minutes. Transfer the pie on its baking sheet to a wire rack to cool slightly. Serve hot or warm.

Summer Fruit Tart

This free-form tart resembles a pizza – top with any soft fruit you like. It is delicious served with ice cream.

SERVES 10–12

1 quantity Basic Sweet Pastry (*Pâte Sucrée*, see page 14) or Walnut- or Almond-Enriched Basic Shortcrust Pastry (see page 12)	120 g/4 oz halved or quartered strawberries
	50 g/2 oz raspberries
	50 g/2 oz blackberries
2 Tbsp honey	50 g/2 oz blueberries
1 small peach, thinly sliced	15 g/½ oz butter, melted
1 small nectarine, thinly sliced	2–3 Tbsp sugar

Lightly spray or brush a large baking sheet with vegetable oil. On a lightly floured surface, roll out the pastry to a 27–30-cm/11–12-in round, about 15 mm/ ⅝ in thick. Transfer to a baking sheet. Crimp the edge and prick the bottom all over. Refrigerate for 30 minutes.

Preheat the oven to 400°F/200°C/Gas 6. Line the pastry round with foil and weight with the bottom of a pie dish or ovenproof dinner plate. Bake for 10 minutes until the pastry edge begins to colour. Remove the weight and foil.

Gently brush the surface with the honey and arrange the fruit in triangles or circles over the surface of the pastry. Brush the fruit with the melted butter and sprinkle with the sugar.

Bake until the fruit is tender and pastry is golden, 5–7 minutes. If you like, turn on the grill and grill the tart until the fruit begins to caramelize, 1–2 minutes. Cover the edge of the pastry with foil if it browns too quickly. Cool slightly and serve warm.

Pecan Pie

This classic American pie is delicious served warm with whipped cream, soured cream or vanilla ice cream.

SERVES 8–10

1 22-cm/9-in flan tin, lined with Basic Sweet Pastry	60 ml/2 fl oz golden syrup
	Grated rind and juice of ½ lemon
300 g/10 oz pecan halves	
3 eggs	50 g/2 oz butter, melted
250 g/8 oz dark brown sugar	½ tsp vanilla essence

Pre-heat the oven to 350°F/175°C/Gas 4. Pick out about 120 g/4 oz of perfect pecan halves and set aside. Coarsely chop the remaining nuts.

Beat the eggs and sugar together in a large bowl. Then beat in the golden syrup, grated lemon rind and juice, melted butter, vanilla essence and the chopped pecans. Pour this mixture into the pastry case and carefully set on to a baking sheet.

Arrange the perfect pecans in concentric circles on top of the egg-sugar mixture and bake until the filling is set and slightly puffed and pecans are well coloured, about 40 minutes. Transfer to a wire rack to cool. Serve warm or at room temperature.

◀ *Summer Fruit Tart*

Prune Linzer Tart

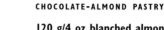

This tart is popular in Eastern Europe. Dried apricots or fresh cherries can be substituted for the prunes.

SERVES 6–8

375 g/12 oz ready-to-eat stoned prunes

Grated rind and juice of 1 orange

175 ml/6 fl oz water

2 Tbsp sugar

½ tsp ground cinnamon

½ tsp almond essence

CHOCOLATE-ALMOND PASTRY

120 g/4 oz blanched almonds

150 g/5 oz caster sugar

175 g/6 oz plain flour, sifted

2 Tbsp unsweetened cocoa powder, sifted

1 tsp ground cinnamon

½ tsp salt

Grated rind of 1 orange

250 g/8 oz unsalted butter, cut into pieces

2–3 Tbsp iced water

Icing sugar to dust, sifted

Bring the prunes to the boil with the orange rind and juice and water. Simmer until the liquid is absorbed and the prunes are soft and plump, 15 minutes. Stir in the sugar and the cinnamon and almond essence. Process in a food processor, 20–30 seconds. Cover and chill.

Spray or butter a 27-cm/11-in flan tin. Process the almonds and half the sugar to fine crumbs. Add the remaining sugar, flour, cocoa powder, cinnamon, salt and orange rind and process to blend. Add the butter and process until coarse crumbs form, about 20 seconds. Add the water a tablespoon at a time and process until the dough just begins to form.

Turn the dough on to a large piece of clingfilm and knead lightly. Press half the dough on to the bottom and sides of the tin. Prick the bottom and refrigerate for 30 minutes. Roll out the remaining dough and cut into 1-cm/½-in strips.

Pre-heat the oven to 375°F/190°C/Gas 5. Spread the prune filling on to the pastry-lined flan tin. Arrange the dough strips on the top in a lattice pattern. Bake for about 35 minutes. Cool then dust with icing sugar.

Coffee and Apple Parcels

These unusual little parcels make a decorative dessert.

SERVES 4

400 g/14 oz flour	Rind of 1 orange
Pinch of salt	4 apples
90 g/3 oz sugar	
175 g/6 oz butter	**SAUCE**
2 eggs, beaten	25 g/1 oz butter
	25 g/1 oz plain flour
FILLING	150 ml/5 fl oz milk
1 banana, mashed	60 ml/2 fl oz cooled, extra-strong coffee
2 rings pineapple, chopped finely	150 ml/5 fl oz single cream

Sift the flour, salt, and 25 g/1 oz sugar into a bowl. Blend in the butter until the mixture resembles fine crumbs. Mix to a stiff paste with the eggs.

Mix together the banana, pineapple, remaining sugar and orange rind. Peel and core the apples.

Put all the sauce ingredients into a pan, except the cream, and heat, whisking all the time. When thick, remove from the heat and use a little of the sauce to moisten the fruit filling.

Roll out the pastry to a square. Cut out four circles. Place an apple in the centre of each square and fill with the banana and pineapple mixture.

Brush the edges with water and completely enclose the apple, pressing the joins neatly together.

Place the apple parcels, join-side down, on a baking sheet and make a small hole in the centres. Decorate with pastry trimmings.

Preheat the oven to 425°F/220°C/Gas 7 and bake for 30 to 35 minutes on the middle shelf until golden.

Gently heat the coffee sauce and add the cream. Do not boil. Serve with the apples.

Traditional Fruit Pies

These classic fruit pies are guaranteed to please family and friends. Follow the instructions for the apple, pear and plum pies. For the peach pie the fruit needs no pre-cooking and the fruit can be placed directly on the pastry base.

Old-fashioned Apple Pie

300 g-/10 oz-flour quantity Basic Shortcrust Pastry (see page 12)	120 g/4 oz caster sugar
	2 tsp cornflour
1 kg/2 lb tart apples, pared	1 egg
50 g/2 oz sultanas	1 Tbsp milk
1 tsp cinnamon	1 Tbsp granulated sugar

Prepare the pastry and place it in the refrigerator.

Wash, peel (if necessary) and slice the fruit and put into a saucepan with the sultanas, cinnamon and caster sugar. Bring to the boil, simmer for 5 minutes then remove from the heat and cool.

In the meantime, remove half the pastry from the refrigerator and roll out on a well-floured surface with a floured rolling pin to a circle just larger than the pie dish. Place the pastry on the greased pie dish and cut around the edges with a sharp knife. Sprinkle the cornflour on to the base of the pie to absorb any excess juices.

Pre-heat the oven to 400°F/200°C/Gas 6. Beat the egg into a small bowl with a little milk. Remove the other half of the pastry from the refrigerator and roll out in the same way. Brush a little of the egg around the edge of the pastry base and cover with the pastry top pushing down on to the edges. Cut around the pie and crimp the edges together using either your fingers or a fork. Brush the top of the pie with the egg mixture. Decorate the pie with fruits and leaves made from pastry scraps. Make two slits in the centre of the pie with a sharp knife and sprinkle the granulated sugar over the top.

Bake in your pre-heated oven for 25–30 minutes or until the pie is golden brown. Remove from the oven and leave to cool a little before serving with whipped cream or vanilla ice cream.

VARIATIONS

Pear and Ginger Pie	Peach Pie	Plum and Mint Pie
300 g-/10 oz-flour quantity Basic Shortcrust Pastry	300 g-/10 oz-flour quantity Basic Shortcrust Pastry	300 g-/10 oz-flour quantity Basic Shortcrust Pastry
1 kg/2 lb pears	1 kg/2 lb peaches, peeled and sliced	500 g/1 lb plums
50 g/2 oz chopped crystallized ginger	1 tsp lemon juice	50 g/2 oz chopped mint
120 g/4 oz caster sugar	120 g/4 oz caster sugar	175 g/6 oz caster sugar
2 tsp cornflour	¼ tsp cinnamon	2 tsp cornflour
1 egg	2 tsp cornflour	1 egg
1 Tbsp milk	1 egg	1 Tbsp milk
1 Tbsp granulated sugar	1 Tbsp milk	1 Tbsp granulated sugar
	1 Tbsp granulated sugar	

Custard and Cream Tarts

Orange Cardamom Tart	Raspberry Tart
Pear and Chocolate Cream Tart	Prune and Walnut Tart
Cherry Almond Tart	Pumpkin Pie with Pecan Praline Topping
Lemon Tart	Gingered Crème Brûlée Tartlets
Key Lime Pie	Chocolate Ganache and Berry Tart
Strawberry Shortcake	Butterscotch Pie
Chocolate Banoffee Pie	Coconut Custard Pie
Paris–Brest	Millefeuille with Raspberries or Strawberries
Coffee Pear Tart	

Orange Cardamom Tart

This delicious orange tart is flavoured with cardamom seeds, which give it a slightly exotic touch. Topped with orange slices, it looks stunning.

SERVES 6–8

- 22-cm/9-in flan tin lined with Extra Sweet Pastry (*Pâte Sucrée Riche*, see page 14), partially baked blind
- 5 Tbsp fine-cut orange marmalade
- 600 g/1¼ lb sugar
- 300 ml/10 fl oz freshly squeezed orange juice, strained
- 2 large navel oranges, thinly sliced
- 120 g/4 oz unsalted butter, softened
- 2 eggs
- 2 egg yolks
- 150 ml/5 fl oz whipping cream
- Seeds from 4–5 cardamom pods, lightly crushed
- Grated rind of 3 oranges
- 50 g/2 oz sultanas, plumped

In a small saucepan over low heat, heat 3 tablespoons of the marmalade until melted. Use to brush evenly over the bottom of the tart case. Set on a baking sheet for easier handling.

In a medium saucepan, combine 300 g/10 oz sugar and 250 ml/8 fl oz of the orange juice. Bring to the boil and cook until thick and syrupy, which should take about 10 minutes. Add the orange slices to the syrup and simmer gently until they are completely glazed, about 10 minutes. Carefully transfer to a wire rack set over a baking sheet to catch any drips. Reserve the syrup.

Pre-heat the oven to 375°F/190°C/Gas 5. With an electric mixer, beat the butter, eggs, egg yolks and 300 g/10 oz sugar until lightened, about 2 minutes. Gradually beat in the cream, cardamom seeds and the remaining marmalade. Finally stir in the orange rind, remaining juice and the sultanas. (The mixture may look curdled at this stage, but don't worry, it will be fine.)

Pour the mixture into the pastry case. Bake until the filling is just set, about 35 minutes. Transfer to a wire rack to cool slightly. Arrange the orange slices in overlapping concentric circles on top of the tart. Bring the reserved syrup to the boil and brush over the orange slices to glaze. Serve at room temperature.

Pear and Chocolate Cream Tart

Sweet ripe pears baked into a rich, creamy chocolate custard are a heavenly combination.

SERVES 6

22-cm/9-in flan tin lined with Extra Sweet Pastry (*Pâte Sucrée Riche*, see page 14), or Chocolate Pastry	120 g/4 oz caster sugar
	1 egg
	1 egg yolk
120 g/4 oz plain chocolate, melted	1 tsp vanilla or almond essence
250 ml/8 fl oz whipping cream	3 medium ripe pears

In a medium saucepan over low heat, melt the chocolate, cream and 2 tablespoons of the sugar, stirring frequently, until smooth. Remove from the heat and cool slightly. Beat in the egg, egg yolk and vanilla or almond essence and spread evenly in the pastry case.

Pre-heat the oven to 375°F/190°C/Gas 5. Using a swivel-bladed vegetable peeler, carefully peel the pears, then halve and core them. Put them on a work surface cut-side down and cut crossways into thin slices.

Arrange the pears spoke-fashion in the crust and gently with the heel of your hand fan out the pear slices towards the centre. Tap the tart gently on the work surface to eliminate any air bubbles.

Bake for 10 minutes. Reduce the oven temperature to 350°F/175°C/Gas 4. Sprinkle the surface of the tart with the remaining sugar and bake until the custard is set and the pears are tender and glazed, about 20 more minutes. Transfer to a wire rack to cool slightly. Serve warm.

Cherry Almond Tart

In this tart, dried cherries are combined with fresh cherries for maximum flavour.

SERVES 6–8

22-cm/9-in flan tin lined with Basic Sweet Pastry (*Pâte Sucrée*, see page 14)	2–3 Tbsp sugar
	½ tsp almond essence
150 g/5 oz dried cherries	1 egg
120 ml/4 fl oz water	1 egg yolk
90 g/3 oz blanched almonds	300 g/10 oz fresh sweet cherries, stoned
2 Tbsp plain flour	Icing sugar to dust
90 g/3 oz unsalted butter, softened	

In a small saucepan, combine the dried cherries and water. Bring to the boil over medium-high heat. Reduce the heat and simmer over low heat until the water is absorbed and cherries are soft and plump, about 15 minutes. Cool completely.

Pre-heat the oven to 400°F/200°C/Gas 6. Put the almonds in a food processor fitted with a metal blade. Process until fine crumbs form. Add the flour and pulse to blend. Add the butter, 250 g/8 oz sugar, the almond essence, the egg and egg yolk and process for 10–15 seconds until smooth and creamy, scraping down the sides of the bowl once. Spread the mixture evenly over the pastry case.

In a bowl, combine the fresh cherries and plumped dried cherries and sprinkle with 2–3 tablespoons of sugar (or to taste). Toss well and spoon over the almond mixture, distributing the cherries evenly.

Bake for 15 minutes. Reduce the oven temperature to 350°F/175°C/Gas 4, sprinkle the surface with another teaspoon of sugar and continue baking until the filling is puffed and golden, about 25 more minutes. Transfer to a wire rack to cool slightly. Serve warm or at room temperature.

Pear and Chocolate Cream Tart ▶

Lemon Tart

A perennial favourite, with a creamy sweet-sharp lemon filling encased in crisp tender pastry – simple but delicious.

SERVES 6–8

22-cm/9-in flan tin lined with Extra Sweet Pastry (*Pâte Brisée Riche*, see page 14), partially baked blind	200 g/7 oz sugar
	120 ml/4 fl oz whipping cream
Grated rind of 2–3 lemons	3 eggs
150 ml/5 fl oz freshly squeezed lemon juice	3 egg yolks
	Icing sugar to dust

Pre-heat the oven to 375°F/190°C/Gas 5. With an electric mixer on low speed, beat together the lemon rind, juice and sugar. Slowly beat in the cream until blended, then beat in the eggs and yolks, one at a time.

Set the pastry case on a baking sheet for easier handling and carefully pour in the filling. (If you prefer a completely smooth filling, strain into the crust, removing the rind.)

Bake until the filling is just set, but not coloured, about 20 minutes. If the tart begins to colour, cover with foil. Transfer to a wire rack to cool completely. Dust with icing sugar before serving.

Key Lime Pie

Originally made with the small, yellowish limes that come from the Florida Keys, this tart can be made with any limes.

SERVES 6–8

22-cm/9-in pie dish or pie plate lined with Ginger Crumb Crust (see page 15)	120 ml/4 fl oz freshly squeezed lime juice (about 3 limes)
3 egg yolks	1 Tbsp grated lime rind
400-ml/15 fl oz tin sweetened condensed milk	250 ml/8 fl oz whipping cream

With an electric mixer, beat the egg yolks until thick and creamy, about 3 minutes. Gradually beat in the condensed milk, lime juice and rind. Pour into the pastry shell and refrigerate until completely set, for at least 4 hours or overnight.

Beat the cream until stiff peaks form. Spoon the cream into a piping bag fitted with a medium star nozzle and pipe a decorative border between the outer edge and the centre. Alternatively, you could serve cold with a bowl of whipped cream.

> **WARNING**
>
> *People with weak immune systems, children and pregnant women may wish to avoid this dish because it contains uncooked eggs.*

◄ *Lemon Tart*

Strawberry Shortcake

This mouth-watering dessert should be eaten while it is still warm. The shortcake dough may be prepared 1 to 2 hours ahead of time and kept in a cool place. Have the butter, fruit and cream ready too, so that the warm cake can be assembled in just a few minutes.

SERVES 8

PASTRY BASE

300 g/10 oz plain flour

2 tsp baking powder

½ tsp salt

Pinch of nutmeg

120 g/4 oz caster sugar

90 g/3 oz unsalted butter, chilled and cubed

1 egg

150 ml/5 fl oz cream

120 g/4 oz unsalted butter, softened, for spreading on cooked layers

FILLING AND TOPPING

175 g/6 oz strawberries, redcurrants or raspberries

3 Tbsp sugar

2 Tbsp kirsch or Grand Marnier

250 ml/8 fl oz double or whipping cream

Reserve a few berries for decoration. Slice one-third of the strawberries but leave the remaining fruit whole. Crush the rest of the fruit and stir in 2 tablespoons of sugar and 1 tablespoon of the liqueur. Fold in the sliced fruit and set aside.

Sift together the flour, baking powder, salt, nutmeg and sugar into a bowl. Drop in the butter pieces and quickly rub to a crumb texture. Lightly whisk the egg into the cream and pour on to the dry mixture. Combine quickly into a smooth dough. Butter and flour a 20-cm/8-in spring-release tin and press in the dough. Preheat the oven to 425°F/220°C/Gas 7 and bake for about 20 minutes on a wire rack.

Split the shortcake in two and spread half the butter on the bottom layer and the rest on the underside of the top layer. Spread the fruit filling over the bottom cake and sandwich with the top layer. It does not matter if the fruit oozes out.

Whisk the cream until softly peaked and beat in the rest of the sugar and liqueur. Spoon the cream on to the shortcake and decorate with the reserved fruit.

Chocolate Banoffee Pie

Banoffee pie is an all-time favourite. Covering it with white-chocolate whipped cream sends it right over the top. The toffee layer can be made ahead, but don't add the bananas and cream more than a few hours before serving.

SERVES 8

22-cm/9-in deep pie dish lined with Chocolate Pastry or Ginger Crumb Crust (see page 15), baked blind	**WHITE-CHOCOLATE WHIPPED CREAM**
2 400-ml/15-fl oz tins sweetened condensed milk	400 ml/14 fl oz whipping cream
6 oz good-quality plain chocolate, chopped	175 g/6 oz good-quality white chocolate, grated
150 ml/5 fl oz double cream	½ tsp vanilla essence
1 Tbsp golden syrup	Cocoa powder to dust
25 g/1 oz butter	
3 ripe bananas	

Puncture each of the cans of milk (this prevents any possible explosion while cooking). Put them in a medium saucepan and add enough water to cover. Bring to the boil then reduce the heat and simmer, covered, for about 2 hours. Be sure to top up with water. (Some milk may leak but this does not matter.) Carefully remove the tins from the water and cool.

In a medium saucepan over medium-low heat, combine the chocolate, double cream, golden syrup and butter (cut into pieces). Cook until smooth and melted, stirring constantly. Pour into the prepared crust and refrigerate until set, which should take about 1 hour.

Prepare the white-chocolate whipped cream. In a small saucepan over medium heat, bring 120 ml/4 fl oz of the cream to the boil. Remove from the heat and stir in the grated white chocolate all at once, stirring until completely smooth. Stir in the vanilla essence. Strain into a medium bowl and cool to room temperature.

Scrape the condensed milk into a bowl. Whisk the thickened "toffee" until smooth. Immediately spread evenly over the chocolate layer in the pie shell.

Slice the bananas thinly and arrange them in overlapping concentric circles over the toffee layer in the pastry case. In a medium bowl, whisk the remaining cream until stiff peaks form. Fold a spoonful into the white-chocolate cream to lighten it, then fold in the remaining cream. Spoon over the banana layer and spread to the edge. Dust the top with cocoa powder. Refrigerate until ready to serve.

Paris–Brest

This dessert, originally made with chestnut purée, was created to celebrate a famous bicycle race from Paris to Brest. This is a delicious variation on the classic recipe.

SERVES 6–8

CHOUX PASTRY	FILLING
150 ml/5 fl oz water	500 g/1 lb cherries, stoned and marinated overnight in kirsch
50 g/2 oz unsalted butter	
90 g/3 oz flour	300 ml/10 fl oz cream
Pinch of salt	3 Tbsp icing sugar
2 eggs, beaten	2 Tbsp instant coffee dissolved in 1 Tbsp hot water
50 g/2 oz flaked almonds	

Heat the water and butter in a saucepan until the butter melts and the water boils. Remove from the heat and quickly beat in the flour and salt. Continue beating over low heat until the mixture is smooth and comes away from the sides of the pan.

Remove from the heat and add the eggs a little at a time, beating well between each addition until the mixture is smooth and shiny.

Pre-heat oven to 400°F/200°C/Gas 6. Spoon the mixture into a piping bag fitted with a plain 2.5-cm/1-in nozzle. Pipe a circle about 4 cm/1½ in wide and 20 cm/8 in in diameter on a greased baking sheet. Sprinkle the almonds evenly over the dough and bake for 30 minutes. Remove from the oven and slice through the middle with a sharp knife. Cool both halves separately.

Place the pastry base on a serving plate, then spoon the drained cherries into the bottom half of the ring. Whip together the cream, sugar and coffee, and spoon this mixture over the cherries.

Cover with the pastry top and dust with icing sugar.

Coffee Pear Tart

T he flavour of coffee and pears works
surprisingly well in this tart.

SERVES 10

PASTRY BASE

175 g/6 oz butter

400 g/4 oz plain flour

1 Tbsp sugar

2 Tbsp powdered instant
coffee dissolved in 1 Tbsp
warm water

1 egg

FILLING

1 kg/2 lb firm ripe pears

2 eggs, beaten

90 ml/3 fl oz cream

2 Tbsp powdered instant
coffee dissolved in 1 Tbsp
warm water

1 liqueur glass of coffee
liqueur

Pre-heat the oven to 400°F/200°C/Gas 6. Blend the
butter into the flour and stir in the sugar. Mix together the
coffee and egg and use to bind the mixture together. If
more liquid is required use water. Roll out the pastry and
line a 30-cm/12 in loose-bottomed pie dish. Bake for
about 15 minutes.

Peel, halve and core the pears and arrange in a circle
in the pastry case.

Mix together the eggs, cream, coffee and liqueur. Pour
over the pears and bake for 30 minutes. Serve warm.

Raspberry Tart

A delicious tart consisting of a thin, rich pastry case filled with lemon cream and raspberries, topped with fresh lemon jelly. This makes an impressive dessert.

SERVES 6

CRUST

250 g/8 oz plain flour

Pinch of salt

120 g/4 oz soft butter

2 Tbsp sugar

I egg yolk

LEMON CREAM

2 egg yolks

2 Tbsp sugar

¾ Tbsp cornflour

250 ml/8 fl oz single cream

25 g/I oz softened butter

Grated rind of ½ lemon

JELLY

½ Tbsp gelatine

250 ml/8 fl oz water

2 Tbsp sugar

juice of ½ lemon

250 g/8 oz fresh or frozen raspberries

Pre-heat the oven to 200°F/100°C/Gas 3. Place the flour and salt in a bowl, then blend in the butter until the mixture resembles crumbs. Stir in the sugar. Add the egg yolk and stir until it forms a dough. Add water as necessary. Knead lightly. Use to line a shallow, straight-sided 22-cm/9-in flan tin. Bake blind for about 10 minutes, until golden. Cool slightly, then release carefully from the tin.

For the lemon cream, whisk together the egg yolks, cream, cornflour and sugar in a saucepan. Simmer the mixture, whisking, until the cream is thick and fluffy. Remove from the heat, add the butter, and whisk occasionally while it cools. When cold, flavour the cream with the lemon rind.

Dissolve the gelatine in the water for the jelly. Add the sugar and lemon juice.

Fill the pastry case with the lemon cream and cover with raspberries. Pour the jelly over the top when it starts to set. Leave the tart in a cold place until serving.

Prune and Walnut Tart

Baked in a crisp pastry and made with cream for a special occasion. One mouthful of this tart conjures up images of prune country in southwestern France.

SERVES 6

PASTRY

90 g/3 oz butter

150 g/5 oz fine wholemeal flour

1 Tbsp light brown sugar

1 large egg, beaten

FILLING

2 Tbsp plum jam or apple jelly

120 g/4 oz prunes, stoned, roughly chopped

120 g/4 oz walnut pieces, roughly chopped

300 ml/10 fl oz milk or single cream

2 large eggs, beaten

1 tsp caster sugar (optional)

Freshly grated nutmeg

Prepare the pastry by blending the butter into the flour and sugar. Bind with the beaten egg then knead gently on a lightly floured surface. Cover the pastry with clingfilm and chill in the refrigerator for 30 minutes.

Pre-heat the oven to 400°F/200°C/Gas 6. Roll out the pastry to line a deep, 20-cm/8-in flan or cake tin, preferably loose-bottomed. Fill the pastry case with baking parchment and baking beans, then bake for 15 minutes. Remove the baking beans and parchment and continue cooking for a further 5 minutes, until the base is dry.

Reduce the oven heat to 350°F/175°C/Gas 4. Spread the jam over the base of the pastry case then top with the prunes and walnuts. Beat the milk or cream with the eggs and sugar, if used, then pour the custard into the pastry case and grate some nutmeg over the top. Bake for 40 minutes, or until the custard is lightly set. Leave to cool, then serve warm or cold.

Pumpkin Pie with Pecan Praline Topping

This is a variation on the traditional American Thanksgiving pumpkin pie. The pecan topping is easy to make and adds a crunchy contrast to the creamy filling.

SERVES 6–8

22-cm/9-in flan tin lined with Basic Shortcrust (*Pâte Sucrée*, see page 14), partially baked blind

300 g/10 oz fresh or tinned pumpkin

250 g/8 oz sugar

120 g/4 oz light brown sugar

175 ml/6 fl oz whipping cream

5 Tbsp milk

2 eggs

1–2 Tbsp bourbon or whisky (optional)

¾ tsp ground cinnamon

½ tsp ground allspice

½ tsp ground ginger

¼ tsp ground cloves

¼ tsp grated nutmeg

TOPPING

50 g/2 oz pecans, chopped

250 g/8 oz light brown sugar

25 g/1 oz unsalted butter, melted

Whipped cream or vanilla ice cream to serve

Pre-heat the oven to 350°F/175°C/Gas 4. With an electric mixer, beat the pumpkin with the remaining ingredients (except the topping and whipped cream) until smooth and well blended. Set the flan tin on a baking sheet for easier handling and carefully pour the mixture into the crust.

Bake until the filling is just set (the pie will continue to bake once removed) and pastry is golden, about 45 minutes. Cover the pastry edge with foil if it browns too quickly. Remove to a wire rack to cool completely, then refrigerate.

Pre-heat the grill. Combine the pecans, sugar and butter, and sprinkle evenly over the pie. Cover the edge of the pastry with a strip of foil if necessary. Grill about 10 cm/4 in from the heat until the topping bubbles and caramelizes, watching carefully, about 1 minute. Leave to cool, then serve at room temperature or chilled with whipped cream or ice cream.

Gingered Crème Brûlée Tartlets

These delicately flavoured tartlets will soon become one of your firm favourites. The deliciously thick custard can be flavoured still further by infusing the cream with a split vanilla pod if you prefer, but it is the ginger that adds a subtle, exotic hint.

MAKES 4

Four 10-cm/4-in tartlet tins lined with Basic Sweet Pastry (*Pâte Sucrée*, see page 14), or Ginger Crumb Crust (See page 15), baked blind	2 egg yolks
	1 Tbsp sugar
	1 Tbsp ginger syrup (from the bottle)
300 ml/10 fl oz whipping cream	1 piece bottled stem ginger, finely chopped
1 egg	4–6 Tbsp light brown granulated sugar

Pre-heat the oven to 325°F/160°C/Gas 3. Set the tartlet crusts on a baking sheet or easier handling.

In a saucepan over medium heat, bring cream to the boil. Whisk egg and egg yolks with sugar and ginger syrup until lightened, 1 minute. Whisk in hot cream. Strain into a measuring jug. Stir in chopped ginger.

Divide mixture evenly among tartlet crusts. Bake until custard is lightly set, 15 minutes. Transfer to a wire rack to cool. Refrigerate for at least 4 hours.

Just before serving, pre-heat the grill. Sprinkle a thin layer of sugar evenly over the custard right to the pastry edge. If the pastry is already very brown, protect with a thin strip of foil. Grill close to heat until sugar melts and begins to bubble, 1 minute; do not over-grill or custard will curdle. Refrigerate immediately to allow the caramel to harden, 5 minutes. Serve.

Chocolate Ganache and Berry Tart

Summer berries make a perfect match for a rich chocolate crust filled with a dark chocolate and raspberry truffle mixture.

SERVES 6–8

22-cm/9-in pie dish lined with Chocolate Pastry, baked blind

750 ml/1¼ pt whipping cream

250 g/8 oz seedless raspberry jam

250 g/8 oz good quality plain chocolate, chopped

4 Tbsp Framboise or other raspberry-flavoured liqueur

750 g/1½ lb mixed fresh summer berries, such as raspberries, blackberries, strawberries (quartered if large) or blueberries

1–2 Tbsp caster sugar

In a medium saucepan over medium heat, bring 300 ml/10 fl oz of the cream and three-quarters of the raspberry jam to the boil, whisking to dissolve the jam. Remove from the heat and add the chocolate all at once, stirring until melted and smooth. Strain the mixture directly into the pastry case, lifting and turning the tart to distribute the filling evenly. Cool completely or refrigerate until set, at least 1 hour.

In a small saucepan over medium heat, heat the remaining raspberry jam and 2 tablespoons of the Framboise or other raspberry-flavoured liqueur until melted and bubbling. Drizzle over the berries and toss to coat well. Arrange the berries over the top of the tart. Refrigerate until ready to serve.

Bring the tart to room temperature at least 30 minutes before serving. Whip the remaining cream with the sugar and remaining liqueur until soft peaks form. Spoon into a serving bowl and serve with the tart.

Butterscotch Pie

A wickedly rich dessert for those with a decidedly sweet tooth! The cream adds the final luxurious touch.

SERVES 6–8

22-cm/9-in flan tin lined with Basic Shortcrust Pastry (*Pâte Brisée*), baked blind

500 ml/1 pt scalded milk

1 vanilla pod, split

250 g/8 oz brown sugar

25 g/1 oz plain flour

45 g/1½ oz unsalted butter

¼ tsp salt

4 egg yolks

90 g/3 oz chopped pecans

120 ml/4 fl oz whipping cream

Pecan halves to decorate

Bring the milk and vanilla pod to the boil Draw off the heat and leave to infuse for 15 minutes. Remove the pod. Place a double boiler over hot water and combine sugar, flour, butter and salt. Stir and cook until blended. Slowly add the infused milk. Beat the egg yolks until light, add a little of the milk mixture to lighten then stir into the mixture in the double boiler. Stir and cook until the mixture thickens. Remove from the heat and stir in the chopped pecans.

Pour the cooled butterscotch into the pastry case. Beat the cream until soft peaks form and spoon into a piping bag fitted with a medium star nozzle. Pipe a border of cream around the edge. Decorate with pecan halves.

Chocolate Ganache and Berry Tart ▶

Coconut Custard Pie

This is a classic pie – a sweet creamy coconut filling in a flaky pastry crust.

SERVES 4

22-cm/9-in pie plate lined with Basic Sweet Pastry (*Pâte Sucrée*) (see page 14) baked blind	175 ml/6 fl oz double cream
150 g/5 oz sugar	3 egg yolks
4 Tbsp cornflour	25 g/1 oz unsalted butter, diced
Pinch of salt	2 tsp vanilla essence
500 ml/1 pt milk	250 g/8 oz desiccated coconut
	250 ml/8 fl oz cream

In a medium saucepan, combine the sugar, cornflour and salt. Slowly whisk in the milk and half the cream and bring to the boil over medium heat.

Beat the egg yolks with the remaining cream and slowly pour into the thickened milk mixture, whisking constantly and rapidly to avoid lumps. Boil for 1 minute, whisking constantly. Remove from the heat and beat in the butter, vanilla essence and 175 g/6 oz of the coconut. Pour into the pastry case and smooth the top evenly. Cool, then refrigerate.

Preheat the oven to 425°F/220°C/Gas 7. Spread the remaining coconut on a baking sheet and toast until golden, stirring occasionally, about 5 minutes. Cool the coconut completely.

Beat the cream until soft peaks form. Spoon into a piping bag filled with a medium star nozzle and pipe a border of cream around the edge. Alternatively spoon cream on to the tart and swirl with the back of a spoon. Sprinkle with the toasted coconut and serve cold.

Millefeuille with Raspberries or Strawberries

One thousand leaves is the literal translation of 'Millefeuille', and it is almost true! By the time the puff pastry has been rolled, folded and turned half a dozen times, there are more than 700 layers of trapped air and butter dough. This feather-like dessert needs only the simplest embellishment.

SERVES 4

500 g/1 lb puff pastry, chilled (see page 21), or use ready-made puff pastry	**500 g/1 lb raspberries or strawberries, wiped but not washed**
500 ml/1 pt whipping cream	**Icing sugar to dust**
4 Tbsp vanilla sugar	
2 Tbsp kirsch or Grand Marnier	

Roll out the pastry on a chilled, floured surface to 3 mm/⅛ in thick, and use a sharp knife to cut it into three equal rectangles, 18 x 30 cm/7 x 12 in. Leave to chill for at least 1 hour, or overnight if possible.

Pre-heat the oven to 425°F/220°C/Gas 7. Chill a baking sheet under running cold water and then shake off the excess moisture. Transfer one of the pastry rectangles to the wet sheet, prick all over with a fork and bake until it is well puffed and golden. Cool on a wire rack. Prepare and bake the other pastry rectangles in exactly the same way.

Whisk the cream into soft peaks; lightly beat in the sugar and liqueur.

Smooth half the whipped cream on to a puff pastry rectangle. Cover with a second layer of pastry and spread over the rest of the cream. Reserve one perfect fruit for decoration, and stir the rest into the cream. Lay the last pastry rectangle on top. Dredge the top generously with sifted icing sugar. Heat a long metal skewer and quickly burn a trellis pattern into the sugar, reheating the skewer as necessary. Place the reserved fruit in the centre as decoration and serve on an elegant platter. Use the remaining whipped cream to pipe rosettes on the top of the dessert.

Small Pastries

Profiteroles

Chocolate-dipped Palmiers

Walnut-raisin Rugelach

Poppy Seed Parcels

Apple Pastries

Mango Galettes

Irish Cream Barquettes

Raspberry Chocolate Eclairs

Cheddar Pennies

**Parma Ham, Fig
and Fontina Barquettes**

Cheese Straws

Profiteroles

This classic dessert is a guaranteed dinner party hit.

SERVES 6

50 g/2 oz unsalted butter

150 ml/5 fl oz water

90 g/3 oz plain flour

2 eggs, beaten

FILLING

300 ml/10 fl oz double cream

50 g/2 oz icing sugar, sieved

a little Grand Marnier

2 tsp finely grated orange rind

CHOCOLATE SAUCE

150 g/5 oz plain chocolate chips

2 Tbsp orange juice

120 g/4 oz icing sugar

25 g/1 oz butter

Melt the butter in a pan with the water. Bring to the boil and immediately tip in the flour. Beat well until the mixture forms a ball that comes away from the pan. Leave to cool. Beat or whisk in the eggs, a little at a time. Continue beating until the mixture is smooth and glossy.

Put the mixture into a piping bag fitted with a 1-cm/½-in plain nozzle. Pipe about 24 small balls on to a greased and floured baking sheet.

Pre-heat the oven to 400°F/200°C/Gas 6. Bake for 15–20 minutes until well risen and golden brown. A few minutes before removing them from the oven, pierce the profiteroles with a sharp knife to release the steam. Cool on a wire rack.

To make the filling, whisk the cream until stiff. Stir in the icing sugar, Grand Marnier and orange rind. Put the cream in a piping bag fitted with a small nozzle and pipe the cream into the profiteroles through the slits.

To make the sauce, put all the ingredients into a bowl over a pan of hot water and heat until melted. Stir well.

Pile the profiteroles on a serving dish and, just before serving pour over the warm sauce.

Chocolate-dipped Palmiers

These classic French pastries are deceptively quick and easy to make as they can be made from bought puff pastry.

MAKES ABOUT 40

50 g/2 oz finely chopped hazelnuts	Sugar for rolling
2 Tbsp sugar	1 egg, lightly beaten
½ tsp ground cinnamon	250 g/8 oz plain chocolate
250 g/8 oz fresh or frozen puff pastry, defrosted if frozen	

Lightly grease 2 large baking sheets. In a small bowl, combine hazelnuts, sugar and cinnamon. Set aside.

Cut pastry into quarters. Generously sprinkle the work surface with sugar and roll out one quarter of pastry to a thin rectangle. Lightly brush the pastry with beaten egg, and sprinkle evenly with the nut mixture.

Fold the long edges of the pastry inwards to meet, edge to edge, in the centre. Brush with beaten egg, and sprinkle with more nut mixture. Fold outside edges inwards to meet, edge to edge, in the centre to make 4 even layers.

Pre-heat oven to 425°F/220°C/Gas 7. Using a sharp knife, cut the pastry crosswise into 2.5-cm/1-in strips, and place 1 cm/½ in apart on baking sheets. Open from the centre fold to form a "V" shape. Refrigerate for 15 minutes.

Bake until golden, about 10 minutes, turning half-way through. Transfer the baking sheets to wire racks to cool slightly then remove palmiers to wire racks to cool completely.

In a small heatproof bowl set over a saucepan of just simmering water, melt the chocolate until smooth, stirring frequently. Line baking sheets with greaseproof paper or foil. Dip each palmier halfway into chocolate and place on lined baking sheets. Leave to set.

Walnut-raisin Rugelach

Rugelach are popular Jewish pastries. Often made with a simple cream cheese pastry, these little filled crescents melt in the mouth. The fillings can vary from poppy seed to cinnamon and walnuts, to cheese or chocolate or, typically, raspberry or apricot jam.

MAKES ABOUT 60

CREAM CHEESE PASTRY	FILLING
250 g/8 oz unsalted butter, softened	90 g/3 oz sultanas
250 g/8 oz cream cheese, softened	120 g/4 oz walnuts, finely chopped
1 Tbsp sugar	2 tsp ground cinnamon
2 to 3 Tbsp soured cream	90 g/3 oz sugar
250 g/8 oz plain flour	Milk to glaze
¼ tsp salt	2 Tbsp sugar mixed with ½ tsp cinnamon for sprinkling

Cream butter and cream cheese in a large bowl with electric mixer (or by hand) until well blended. Add the sugar and beat until smooth, then beat in the soured cream and mix in flour and salt until a soft dough is formed. Shape into a ball and flatten to a circle. Wrap the dough well and refrigerate until firm, at least 2 hours.

Pre-heat the oven to 350°F/175°C/Gas 4. Lightly grease 2 large baking sheets. In a small bowl, toss the sultanas and walnuts with the cinnamon and sugar to mix. Set aside.

Place the dough on lightly floured surface and cut into quarters; work with one-quarter at a time, keeping the remaining dough refrigerated. Roll out one-quarter of the dough 3 mm/⅛ in thick. Using a 25-cm/10-in plate to cut the dough into a 25-cm/10-in circle. Sprinkle the dough with about one-fifth of the filling to within 2.5 cm/1 in of the edge.

Cut the dough circle into 10 to 12 equal wedges. Starting at the curved edge, roll up each wedge Swiss-roll fashion. Place each on baking sheet, point side down (so the filling will not ooze out) about 2.5 cm/1 in apart, curving ends down to form a crescent.

Brush each crescent with a little milk and sprinkle with a little sugar-cinnamon mixture.

Bake until golden brown, 20–25 minutes. Transfer to a wire rack to cool. Repeat with the remaining dough. Store in an airtight container.

VARIATION

Poppy Seed Rugelach

Use 175 g/6 oz poppy seeds, spreading a little on each dough circle before cutting. Shape and bake.

Poppy Seed Parcels

These unusual pastries come from Poland. The poppy seeds are mixed with butter, raisins, honey and nutmeg and go well with coffee.

MAKES 16

250 g/8 oz plain flour

90 g/3 oz unsalted butter

2 Tbsp caster sugar

1 egg, separated

3 Tbsp soured cream

90 g/3 oz poppy seeds, ground

25 g/1 oz butter

4 Tbsp raisins, chopped

2 Tbsp clear honey

½ tsp grated nutmeg

Caster sugar to sprinkle

Sift the flour into a bowl. Rub in the butter then stir in the sugar. Mix in the egg yolk with the soured cream to make a fairly stiff dough. Knead the dough then wrap in clingfilm. Chill for 30 minutes.

Mix the ground poppy seeds with the butter in a small pan. Cook for a few minutes, stirring constantly. Add the raisins, honey and nutmeg and set aside to cool. Pre-heat the oven to 375°F/190°C/Gas 5.

On a lightly floured surface, roll out the dough into a 35-cm/14-in square. Cut this into sixteen 8-cm/3½-in squares. Divide the poppy seed mixture between the squares, piling it in the middle of each with a teaspoon. Lightly whisk the egg white and brush it on the edges of the pastry. Fold the corners of each pastry square up to meet over the middle of the poppy filling. Pinch all the pastry edges together to seal them thoroughly. Use the blunt edge of a knife to knock the pastry edges down, holding them with two fingers, to ensure they are sealed and neat.

Place the parcels on greased baking sheets and brush them with a little egg white. Bake for 20 to 25 minutes, until golden. Sprinkle with caster sugar as soon as they are cooked. Cool on a wire rack.

Apple Pastries

These are slightly fiddly to make but are well worth the effort.

MAKES ABOUT 30

175 g/8 oz plain flour	3 apples, peeled, cored and quartered
90 g/3 oz unsalted butter	
3 Tbsp caster sugar	I egg, beaten
120 g/4 oz cottage cheese	Icing sugar to dust
2 Tbsp soured cream	

Sift the flour into a bowl. Rub in the butter and stir in the sugar. Drain any liquid from the cheese, then push it through a sieve. Mix the cheese and soured cream into the flour mixture to form a soft dough. Knead gently into a ball and cut in half.

Pre-heat the oven to 400°F/200°C/Gas 6. Roll out one piece of dough quite thinly and cut out 6-cm/2½-in rounds, using a pastry cutter. Cut each apple quarter into two or three pieces. Place a piece of apple on a round of pastry. Brush the edge of the pastry with egg, then fold it in half to enclose the apple in a miniature case. Pinch the edges together to seal them well. Place on a greased baking sheet. Fill and seal all the pastry rounds, using the trimmings to make more rounds. Repeat with the second piece of pastry. Brush the pastries with beaten egg.

Bake for about 20 minutes, until golden and cooked. Cool on a wire rack and dust with icing sugar while warm. Serve warm or cold.

Mango Galettes

This idea can be used with any soft fruit which cooks quickly, such as nectarines, or papayas. Puff pastry also makes an easy-to-make base.

MAKES 6

1 quantity Extra Sweet Pastry (*Pâte Sucrée Riche*, see page 14)	15 g/½ oz unsalted butter
	2 Tbsp caster sugar
2 medium ripe mangoes	2 Tbsp apricot jam or clear honey

On a lightly floured surface, roll out the pastry ½ cm/¼ in thick. Using a large fluted cutter or saucer as a guide, cut out six 10-cm/4-in rounds, re-rolling pastry trimmings if necessary. Transfer to a large baking sheet, scallop the edges if you like and prick the bases to within 2 cm/¾ in of the edge. Refrigerate for 30 minutes.

Pre-heat the oven to 400°F/200°C/Gas 6. Peel the mangoes. Cut off each half and lay cut-sides down. Slice thinly crosswise.

Arrange the mango slices over the pastry circles to within 2 cm/¾ in of the edge. Brush with a little melted butter and sprinkle each with a quarter of the sugar. Bake until the mango begins to caramelize and the pastry is set and golden, which should be about 15 minutes. Transfer to a wire rack to cool slightly.

In a small saucepan over medium heat, melt the apricot jam or honey. Brush over the galettes and serve warm.

Irish Cream Barquettes

These little tartlets make an ideal
accompaniment to an after-dinner coffee.
Other shapes may also be used to form the tartlets,
such as hearts, squares or circles.

MAKES 12

12 small barquette moulds or other small tartlet tins lined with Extra Sweet Pastry (*Pâte Sucrée Riche*, see page 14), baked blind	3 egg yolks
	2 Tbsp sugar
	3 Tbsp plain flour
	4 Tbsp Irish cream liqueur
150 g/5 oz plain chocolate, melted	4 Tbsp whipping cream, whipped
120 ml/4 fl oz milk	Chocolate shavings or cocoa powder to dust

Brush the base of each tartlet with a little melted chocolate. Set the tartlets on a baking sheet to make for easier handling.

In a heavy-based saucepan over medium heat, bring the milk just to the boil. Beat the egg yolks and sugar until light, about 1 minute, then stir in the flour. Add the hot milk, whisking constantly.

Return the custard to the heat and cook, until it thickens, about 2 minutes, whisking constantly. Remove from the heat and whisk in the Irish cream liqueur. Allow to cool. Gently fold in the cream and refrigerate until thickened, about 30 minutes.

Spoon the custard-cream into a piping bag fitted with a medium star nozzle. Pipe into the tartlet cases and refrigerate. Garnish with chocolate shavings or dust with cocoa just before serving.

Raspberry Chocolate Eclairs

Eclairs are irresistible and the addition of raspberries adds a juicy, sharp contrast to the sweetness of the chocolate.

MAKES ABOUT 10

50 g/2 oz butter, cut in pieces

150 ml/5 fl oz water

90 g/3 oz flour

2 eggs, beaten

FILLING

150 ml/5 fl oz double cream

120 g/4 oz raspberries

A little sugar

TOPPING

175 g/6 oz plain chocolate

25 g/1 oz butter

Put the butter and water into a pan and bring to the boil. Remove from the heat and tip all the flour into the pan at once. Beat with a wooden spoon until the paste forms a ball. Cool. Whisk the eggs into the mixture, a little at a time. Continue beating until mixture is glossy.

Pre-heat the oven to 400°F/200°C/Gas 6. Put the pastry into a piping bag fitted with a large plain nozzle. Pipe 7-cm/3-in lengths on to greased baking sheets.

Bake for about 25 minutes, until golden brown. Remove from the oven and make a couple of slits in the sides of each one to allow steam to escape. Return to the oven for a few minutes to dry. Cool on a wire rack.

To make the filling, whisk the cream until stiff. Fold in the raspberries and sugar to taste. Make a slit down the side of each eclair and fill with the cream mixture. Melt together the chocolate and butter. Dip the tops of the eclairs into the chocolate and then leave to set.

Cheddar Pennies

These spicy cheese biscuits are really popular. They are usually served with drinks and make a change from peanuts and crisps.

MAKES ABOUT 48

120 g/4 oz unsalted butter, softened

120 g/4 oz mature Cheddar cheese, grated

120 g/4 oz plain flour

3 Tbsp chopped chives

Pinch of salt

¼ tsp cayenne pepper or chilli powder

TIP

This is a good way to use up small pieces of left-over hard cheese, such as Cheddar, but the cheese should be well flavoured and not bland or the pennies will have a bland taste.

In a bowl with an electric mixer, beat the butter until creamy, 30 seconds. Stir in the grated cheese, flour, chives, salt and cayenne pepper or chilli powder to form a dough.

Scrape on to a piece of clingfilm or greaseproof paper and using the clingfilm or paper as a guide, form into a long log about 4 cm/1½ in in diameter (for smaller pennies, form dough into a 2.5-cm/1 in log). Wrap tightly, and refrigerate for several hours or overnight until firm. (The dough can be made up to five days ahead or frozen.)

Preheat oven to 350°F/175°C/Gas 4. Lightly grease 2 large baking sheets. Using a sharp knife, cut dough log (or logs) into 15-mm/⅜-in slices and place on the prepared baking sheets. Bake until slightly puffed and golden, 10 to 12 minutes. Using a metal spatula or palette knife, transfer the biscuits to a wire rack to cool. Store in airtight containers.

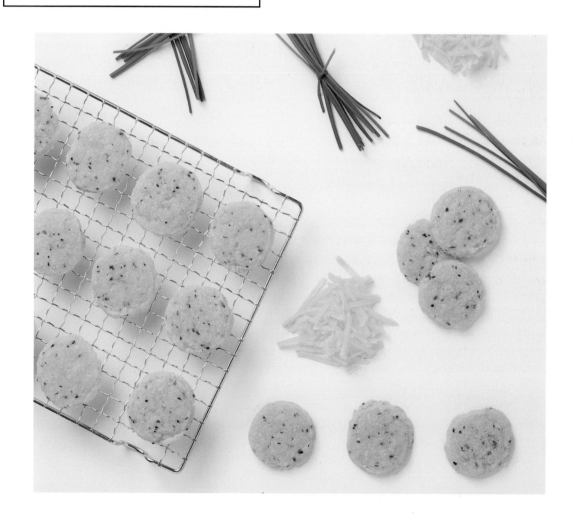

Parma Ham, Fig and Fontina Barquettes

The saltiness of the Parma ham and sweetness of the figs are balanced by the fontina cheese to create a delicious pastry appetizer.

MAKES 12

12 barquette moulds lined with Rich Shortcrust Pastry (*Pâte Sucrée Riche*), baked blind

12 slices Parma ham, trimmed and cut in half lengthwise

4 figs, halved and thinly sliced

120 g/4 oz diced fontina cheese

Freshly ground black pepper

Parsley or basil leaves for garnish

Pre-heat the oven to 375°F/190°C/Gas 5. Roll the Parma ham and fill the barquettes with fig slices and diced cheese and Parma ham rolls. Grind a little black pepper over each barquette. Then set on a baking sheet for easier handling.

Bake until the cheese is just melted and pastry is heated through, 3–5 minutes. Serve hot or warm.

Cheese Straws

This pastry uses self-raising flour. This lightens the pastry, which might otherwise be slightly heavy because of the cheese.

MAKES 30

175 g/6 oz self-raising flour

Pinch of salt

90 g/3 oz butter

50 g/2 oz grated Parmesan and Cheddar cheese

1 egg yolk

Salt and pepper

Pinch of cayenne pepper

Pinch of dry mustard

Beaten egg

Pre-heat the oven to 375°F/190°C/Gas 5.

Sift the flour into a bowl with a pinch of salt. Blend the butter into the flour until the mixture resembles coarse crumbs. Add the grated cheese, egg yolk, salt, pepper, cayenne and mustard. Mix to a stiff dough with the beaten egg. Chill for 15 minutes.

Line a baking sheet with baking parchment. Roll the pastry into a large rectangle and cut into strips about 1 cm/½ in wide. Twist each strip two or three times and press the ends down firmly on the paper to prevent unravelling.

Bake for 10–15 minutes. The cheese straws should be golden brown. Leave to cool on a wire rack.

> **TIP**
> *Bake any mixture with a high cheese content – and therefore likely to burn – on baking parchment. If twisting the cheese straws, press the ends down firmly to prevent unravelling.*

Cakes

There is no mystery to making cakes, but this section gives plenty of background information on baking techniques as well as a wide selection of recipes. There are impressive large cakes suitable for the most special occasions right down to simple little cakes suitable for more everyday eating. A selection of icings is also included and instructions on how to decorate and make the most of the finished cake.

INTRODUCTION
AND BASIC RECIPES

A deliciously tempting slice of carrot cake, a great favourite.

Successful cake baking is a most satisfying activity for the cook, but the most demanding on account of the accuracy needed in measuring the ingredients and the skill necessary in preparing certain cakes. Confidence is best built by beginning with the easier types, such as gingerbread or fruit cakes. The first attempt at making a more difficult cake such as a Genoise sponge can be disappointing. Happily, practice – with good ingredients, proper utensils, careful weighing and measuring, precise oven temperatures and exact timing (in short, careful attention to detail) – makes perfect.

Most cakes are made by mixing fat, sugar, flour, eggs, and liquid. Air or another gas is incorporated to make the mixture rise while baking. As the cake bakes, strands of gluten in the flour are stretched by the gas until the heat finally hardens the cake. It is even rising that gives a cake its light, sponge-like texture.

Ingredients

Fats

Butter makes the best-flavoured cakes. Margarine, particularly the soft or "tub" variety, has its place in baking both for speed and (if the margarine is high in polyunsaturated fats) for health reasons, though it has less flavour than butter. White vegetable fat is flavourless but produces light cakes. Lard cakes are often delicious but heavy and for this reason lard is little used in cake making. Oils are not used much as they do not easily hold air when they are creamed or beaten, and the resulting cakes can be heavy.

Sugars

The fine creaming possible with caster sugar makes it most suitable for cake making. Very coarse granulated sugar can give a speckled appearance to a finished cake unless the sugar is ground down first in a blender or food processor. Soft brown sugars give colour and flavour to dark cakes like gingerbread, but they give sponge cakes a drab look and a strong caramel flavour.

Golden syrup, honey, treacle or molasses are used in cakes made by the melting method. Such cakes are cooked relatively slowly as these thick liquid sugars tend to caramelize and burn at higher temperatures.

Eggs

Unless specified, most recipes assume a medium-sized egg weighing about 50 g/2 oz. The eggs should be used at room temperature – cold eggs tend to curdle the mixture and this results in a cake with a tough, coarse, too open texture. When using whisked egg whites in a cake, be sure that not even a speck of yolk gets into the whites. Any yolk, or fat on the whisk, will prevent proper whisking (and therefore the air-holding ability) of the whites, which will reduce the lightness of the finished cake.

Flours

Plain white flour is used in cake making unless otherwise specified. Self-raising flour has a raising agent (baking powder) added to it and should only be used if specified in the recipe. All flours should be sifted before use to eliminate any lumps and to incorporate air.

Raising Agents

Air

Air is incorporated into cake mixtures by agitating the ingredients. Methods include sifting the flour, beating the butter and beating or creaming it again with the sugar to a fluffy, mousse-like consistency, and whisking the eggs. The heat of the oven causes the air trapped in the mixture to rise and lighten the cake, either by itself or in conjunction with other rising agents.

Steam

Steam rises some mixtures even when air has not been beaten into them. Flour mixtures with a high proportion of liquid in them will rise in a hot oven since, as the water vaporizes and the steam rises, the uncooked flour mixture rises with it. While in this puffed-up state, the mixture hardens in the oven heat with the steam trapped inside. The pockets of air created by steam are uneven and very open as in choux pastry so steam is not used on its own for making cakes. But steam is a contributing factor in rising wet cake mixtures such as gingerbread.

Bicarbonate of Soda

Bicarbonate of soda is a powder which, when mixed into cake mixtures, quickly gives off half its substance as carbon dioxide gas. In a cake the trapped gas causes the mixture to puff up. Heat sets the mixture once it has risen. By the time the cake cools, the gas will have escaped and will have been replaced by air. Unfortunately, the unused portion of bicarbonate remaining can give a cake a slightly unpleasant smell and taste, and a yellowish colour. For this reason, bicarbonate is most often used in strong-flavoured cakes such as those made with chocolate or molasses. The carbon dioxide reaction is speeded up by acidic substances, so bicarbonate is usually used in cake mixtures with ingredients such as sour milk, vinegar, buttermilk, soured cream, cream of tartar and yogurt. This makes is especially suitable for quickly mixed items like fruit cakes. It also gives them a soft texture and spongy crust with a deep colour. Unfortunately the process destroys some of the vitamins present in the flour.

Baking Powder

Baking powder in commercial forms consists of bicarbonate of soda and an acid powder which varies according to the brand, plus a starch filler, usually cornflour, arrowroot, or ground rice. The starch keeps the mixture dry by absorbing any dampness in the air which might cause the soda and acid in the powder to react. The presence of the filler explains why more baking powder than mixed bicarbonate and cream of tartar would be needed to raise the same cake. A "double action" baking powder is sold which needs heat as well as moisture to produce carbon dioxide gas. The advantage of it is that it can be added to mixtures in advance of baking – it only works once in the oven.

Preparing a Cake Tin

All tins should be greased before use to prevent the cake mixture from sticking or burning at the edges or bottom. Melted white vegetable fat or oil are the most suitable fats. Turn the tin upside down after greasing to allow any excess fat to drain away. Use a pastry brush to get a thin layer.

Bread tins and non-stick spring-release tins need no preparation other than greasing. Tins for cakes made by the melting or creaming methods should be greased, then the base lined with waxed paper or baking parchment, cut exactly to size and the paper brushed with more melted white vegetable fat or oil. (To cut the

1 Cut a length of non-stick paper long enough to go round the cake tin and overlap slightly.

2 Fold the paper along one side to give a 2.5-cm/1-in margin. Make small cuts along its length up to the margin line, as shown. Cut 2 circles of non-stick paper to fit the bottom of the tin.

4 Fit the strip of paper around the edge of the tin, allowing the cut flanges to lie flat on the bottom.

5 Fit the second paper circle in the bottom to keep the cut flanges flat. Brush the side and base of the lined tin with butter or oil.

paper accurately draw round the tin, then cut just inside the line.) For cakes made by the whisking method, the tin should be dusted with caster sugar and flour after it has been lined and greased.

For fruit cakes, grease the tin, then line the sides and base with waxed paper or baking parchment following the steps as shown below:

3 Brush the tin with melted butter or oil and fit one of the paper circles in the bottom. Brush with butter or oil.

6 Finally, dust the inside of the tin lightly with flour, shaking out any excess.

A Rubbed-in Method Cake

The rubbed-in method gives a fairly substantial cake with a crumbly, moist texture. The raising agent is always bicarbonate of soda. In this example the agent is in the self-raising flour. The cake is delicious served sliced and spread with butter.

Marmalade Loaf

250 g/8 oz self-raising flour	2 eggs, lightly beaten
½ tsp salt	3 Tbsp orange marmalade
120 g/4 oz butter	3 Tbsp milk
50 g/2 oz caster sugar	

- Pre-heat the oven to 350°F/175°C/Gas 4. Grease a medium-sized (700 g/1½ lb) loaf tin or 15-cm/ 6-in cake tin or charlotte mould.
- Sift the flour and salt into a bowl and blend in the butter: to do this first cut the butter with a knife into tiny dice, and stir these into the flour with a knife, so that each piece is floured and separate. Then using the tips only of well floured fingers, or a pastry cutter, gently rub in a few dice at a time to break them up, dropping them back into the flour as soon as they are squashed or crumbled. Keep dipping your fingers into the flour and dropping the butter pieces from a height into the bowl – this both cools them and aerates the mixture.
- When the mixture resembles coarse crumbs stir in the sugar, eggs, marmalade and milk. Mix well.
- Turn into the prepared tin and bake for about 55 minutes, or until a skewer inserted into the middle of the cake comes out clean.
- Leave to cool in the tin for 10 minutes, then turn out and cool, right side up, on a wire rack. Serve cut in slices, spread with butter.

Creamed Method Cakes

All-in-one Creaming Method

The all-in-one method is any easy version of the creaming method, because all the ingredients are beaten together at the same time, but a powerful electric mixer is necessary to make these cakes really successful. Soft "tub" margarine gives a lighter result than butter.

Chocolate All-in-one Cake

This cake is made with an electric mixer.

120 g/4 oz soft butter or
  margarine

120 g/4 oz caster sugar

2 eggs

50 g/2 oz unsweetened
  cocoa powder, sifted

90 g/3 oz self-raising flour

Milk, if necessary

FILLING

120 g/4 oz plain chocolate

50 g/2 oz unsalted butter

50 g/2 oz icing sugar, sifted
  to dust

I egg yolk

NOTE

If the chocolate is hot when added it will melt the butter, which will then lose the beaten-in air that makes the frosting fluffy. This also happens if the butter or frosting is beaten for too long (and so over-heated) in the processor. In this case leave till cool and solid, then beat again.

- Pre-heat the oven to 375°F/190°C/Gas 5. Lightly oil two 18-cm/7-in cake tins and line the bottom with baking parchment. Brush with oil.
- Put all the ingredients except the milk into the bowl of a strong electric mixer or food processor and beat until smooth. Start beating slowly – otherwise the flour will shoot out of the bowl. Gradually build up speed. The mixture should have a dropping consistency, that is, it should drop slowly off a spoon. If it sticks obstinately it is too thick. Add enough milk to achieve the correct consistency.
- Divide the mixture between the tins and bake for 20 minutes or until the cakes are well risen and feel spongy to the fingertips. Allow to cool for a few minutes in the tins, then turn

out on to a wire rack, remove the baking parchment and leave to cool completely.
- For the icing, break the chocolate into small, even-sized pieces. Place on a plate and set over a saucepan of simmering water until completely melted. Beat the butter. When soft add the sugar. Beat until light and fluffy. Beat in the egg yolk followed by the melted and cooled chocolate.
- Sandwich the cakes with the icing. Dust the top with a little confectioners' sugar.

Creamed Method Fruit Cake

Fruit cakes use another version of the creamed method. Softened butter and sugar are creamed in a mixing bowl to incorporate air. The eggs and any other liquid are gradually beaten into the creamed mixture, with the flour added with the last few additions of egg to reduce the risk of curdling. After the mixture is well combined, the dry fruit is folded in well to distribute it evenly throughout the cake. The mixture should have a soft dropping consistency and be spread out evenly in the prepared tin, with a slight dip in the centre of the mixture to counteract the cake "peaking". Because these cakes are generally large and dense and contain a high proportion of fruit (which burns easily), they are cooked extremely slowly. To prevent burning they can be placed on a folded newspaper in the oven and can be covered in several layers of brown paper – but not foil, which traps the steam and produces too doughy a result.

Rich Fruit Cake

250 g/8 oz butter	300 g/10 oz seedless raisins
250 g/8 oz soft brown sugar	300 g/10 oz sultanas
300 g/10 oz self-raising flour	300 g/10 oz currants
1 tsp salt	1 tsp mixed spice
4 large eggs, lightly beaten	300 ml/10 fl oz dark beer or Guinness (for an even richer flavour replace half the beer with rum or brandy)
175 g/6 oz ground almonds	
2 Tbsp chopped mixed candied peel	
2 Tbsp chopped glacé cherries	

- Pre-heat the oven to 350°F/175°C/Gas 4. Line a cake tin as described on page 106.
- Beat the butter and sugar together until light, fluffy and pale in colour. This is easily achieved in a machine. If doing it by hand start with the butter, soft but not melted, and beat hard for a few minutes, then add the sugar and continue for at least 10 minutes more.
- Sift the flour with the salt and stir it into the butter mixture with the eggs, adding first a spoonful of flour, then a spoonful of egg and so on. Add all the rest of the ingredients, alternating spoonfuls of fruit or dry ingredients with the beer. Once all is in, beat the mixture briefly to ensure even mixing.
- Turn into the prepared cake tin and bake for 1 hour. Turn the oven down to 300°F/150°C/Gas 2. Cover the cake with a sheet or two of brown paper and bake for a further 3 hours or until a skewer comes out clean when pushed into the middle. Allow the cake to cool in the tin. Once cold store in an airtight container.

Classic Creaming Method

The creaming method, ie the creaming of fat and sugar to a mousse-like consistency (and thereby incorporating air) is the secret of lightness in this type of cake, although a little chemical rising agent is usually added. First the butter or margarine is beaten until it is smooth and very light in colour, but the fat is never allowed to melt (if it did the carefully incorporated air beaten into it would escape). The sugar is then beaten in by degrees until the mixture is pale and fluffy.

The eggs are lightly beaten and added, also by degrees, to the creamed mixture. The mix is beaten after each addition to thoroughly incorporate them. At this point the batter can curdle – usually if the eggs are too cold – but beating in a tablespoon of sifted flour taken from the recipe after each addition of egg should prevent this. Cakes made from curdled mixtures are acceptable, but they have a less delicate, more open and coarse texture than those made from uncurdled mixture.

Plain flour, if used, should be sifted with the baking powder and salt. Self-raising flour should be sifted with salt. The flour mixture is then folded carefully into the creamed mixture with a metal spoon and with as little mixing as possible to ensure a minimum loss of air in the batter.

Victoria Sponge

120 g/4 oz butter	Milk, if necessary
120 g/4 oz caster sugar	FILLING
2 eggs, at room temperature	Raspberry jam
120 g/4 oz self-raising flour	Icing sugar to dust

- Pre-heat the oven to 375°F/190°C/Gas 5. Lightly oil two 18-cm/7-in cake tins and line the bottom with baking parchment. Brush again with oil.
- Beat the butter until soft. Add the sugar and beat again until light and creamy. It should look fluffy and pale. Beat the eggs in a separate bowl until smooth. Gradually add the beaten egg to the butter mixture, beating well at the time. If the mixture begins to curdle add a little of the flour.
- Sift the remaining flour and fold it into the cake mixture using a large metal spoon. The mixture should have a dropping consistency. Add enough milk to achieve the correct consistency.
- Divide the mixture between the tins and bake for 20 minutes or until the cakes are well risen, golden and feel spongy to the touch. Allow the cakes to cool for a few minutes in the tins, then turn out on to a wire rack. Remove the baking parchment and leave to cool.
- Sandwich the cakes with the jam. Sift a little icing sugar over the top.

A Melting Method Cake

The melting method is used for very moist cakes like gingerbread. The fat, sugar, syrup and any other liquid ingredients are heated together to melt, then they are cooled slightly. The flour and other dry ingredients are sifted together and the warm sugar mixture is stirred, not beaten, into the dry mixture along with the eggs. The rising agent is always baking soda. These cakes are the perfect cake for the beginner – easy, reliable and delicious.

Gingerbread

120 g/4 oz crystallized ginger	½ tsp salt
90 g/3 oz butter	150 ml/5 fl oz milk
175 ml/6 fl oz golden syrup	I egg, beaten
120 g/4 oz brown sugar	½ tsp bicarbonate of soda
250 g/8 oz plain flour	½ tsp cream of tartar
I tsp ground ginger	

- Prepare a shallow rectangular cake tin; grease the bottom and sides and then line the bottom with baking parchment and grease again. Pre-heat the oven to 325°F/160°C/Gas 3.
- Chop the preserved ginger finely. Melt the butter, golden syrup and sugar together without boiling. When the sugar has dissolved add the ginger and allow to cool.
- Sift the flour into a bowl with the ground ginger and salt. Make a well in the centre. Warm the milk and pour it into the egg. Add it to the syrup mixture. Slowly beat the syrup mixture into the flour, pouring a little at a time into the well, and drawing the flour in from the sides as you mix. When all the flour is incorporated in the mixture, stir in the bicarbonate of soda and cream of tartar.
- Turn the mixture into the prepared tin and bake for about I hour. The gingerbread should feel moist but firm. Leave it to cool before turning it out. This will keep for about 2 weeks in an airtight tin, and freezes perfectly.

Whisked Method Cakes

In the whisking method, the only raising agent is air that has been trapped in the cake mixture during mixing. As the air extinds in the heat of the oven, the cake rises.

The simplest whisked sponge contains no fat. Sugar and eggs are whisked together until they are thick and light, then flour is folded in gently to keep in as much air as possible. In a lighter but more complicated whisked sponge, the eggs are separated and the yolks are whisked with the sugar and the flour added. The whites are whisked in another bowl, then folded into the batter. Sometimes half the sugar is whisked with the yolks, and half with the whites to give a meringue.

To make these sponges, the sugar and eggs (or egg yolks only) are whisked in a bowl set over a tin of barely simmering water. Make sure that the bowl does not touch the water or the heat will scramble the eggs.

The gentle heat from the steam speeds up the dissolving of the sugar and slightly cooks and thickens the eggs, encouraging the mixture to hold the maximum number of air bubbles. The mixture should change from yellow to almost white in colour and increase to four times its original volume. The mixture is ready when a lifted whisk leaves a ribbon-like trail. Whisking is traditionally done with a balloon whisk but a hand-held electric one works excellently. If an electric mixer is used, the heat can be dispensed with, though this process is considerably speeded up if the mixture is put into a warmed bowl.

When the flour is folded in, great care should be taken to fold rather than stir or beat, as the aim is to incorporate the flour without losing any of the beaten-in air which alone will make the cake rise. The correct movement is more of lifting the mixture and cutting into it, rather than stirring it.

A mixture is whisked "to the ribbon" when a lifted whisk leaves a thick ribbon-like trail on the surface.

Although they are light and springy, a drawback to these cakes is that they stale quickly. Always plan to make a fatless sponge on the day of serving, or freeze the cake once it is cool.

Whisked Fatless Sponge

3 eggs	FILLING
6 Tbsp caster sugar	Strawberry jam
90 g/3 oz plain flour	Double cream, lightly whipped
Pinch of salt	Icing sugar to dust

- Pre-heat the oven to 350°F/175°C/Gas 4. Prepare a deep 20-cm/8-in cake tin or Swiss roll tin. Grease the tin with oil, then line the base with baking parchment, cut exactly to size. Brush again with oil. Dust with caster sugar and then flour. Shake out any excess sugar or flour.
- Place the eggs and sugar in a bowl and fit it over (not in) a saucepan of simmering water. With a balloon whisk (or hand-held electric one) whisk the mixture until it has doubled in bulk and will leave a thick "ribbon" trail on the surface when the whisk is lifted. Start whisking slowly and gradually build up speed. It is essential that the eggs and sugar are not allowed to get too hot – do not let the water get above simmering point and take care that it does not touch the bowl. Remove the bowl from the heat and whisk occasionally until it becomes cool.
- Sift the flour and salt. With a large metal spoon sprinkle it evenly over the surface of the mixture, then fold it in gently but thoroughly.
- Turn into the prepared tin and bake in the middle of the oven for about 25 to 30 minutes. When the cake is cooked it will be risen and brown with the edges slightly shrunk from the edge of the tin and crinkled. When pressed gently with a finger, it will spring back, and will feel spongy. Another point to note is that the cake will sound "creaky" if held close to the ear.
- Leave to cool for a few minutes in the tin then turn out on to a wire rack. Remove the baking parchment and leave to cool.
- Split in half with a large serrated knife. Spread the bottom half with jam and spoon over the cream. Sandwich together again. Dust the top of the cake with a little icing sugar.

Chocolate Feather Cake with Chestnuts

This whisked cake can be made by hand, but this is time- and labour-intensive. With the help of an electric mixer and food processor or blender, it is simplicity itself. It can be served plainly dusted with icing sugar for tea, or as a dessert with a chestnut cream filling and hot chocolate sauce. It is an interesting recipe because a variety of raising methods are used: a meringue is made with the egg whites (the acid cream of tartar being added to improve volume); a mousse-like emulsion is made with the oil and yolks; the powder ingredients are sifted to aerate them; and a tiny quantity of baking powder is added to guarantee lightness.

3 eggs, separated	FILLING
Pinch of cream of tartar	300 ml/10 fl oz double cream
250 g/8 oz caster sugar	8 candied chestnuts or chestnuts in syrup
60 ml/2 fl oz vegetable oil	1 Tbsp icing sugar
1 tsp vanilla essence	HOT CHOCOLATE SAUCE
6 Tbsp water	3 Tbsp unsweetened cocoa powder
120 g/4 oz plain flour	300 ml/10 fl oz water
50 g/2 oz unsweetened cocoa powder	2 tsp cornflour
¼ tsp baking powder	3 Tbsp golden syrup
½ tsp salt	

- Pre-heat the oven to 375°F/190°C/Gas 5. Separate the eggs. Put the egg whites and pinch of cream of tartar into a bowl and whisk until they hold their shape, then add about half the sugar and whisk until stiff and glossy. (This is only possible with an electric whisk. In the absence of one, whisk the whites to stiff peaks and fold in the sugar carefully without further beating.)
- Put the egg yolks with the oil, vanilla essence and water into the processor or blender and beat until creamy, pale and smooth. If doing this by hand, use a balloon whisk. Beat well.
- Sift the flour, cocoa, baking powder and salt together and stir in the rest of the sugar. Add to the liquid mixture and whisk until smooth. Fold into the meringue mixture.
- Turn carefully into an ungreased 20-cm/8-in angel cake tin or ring tin, or into a 22-cm/9-in spring-release cake tin, prepared as for whisked cakes (page 110). Bake for 50 minutes or until the cake has slightly shrunk from the

sides of the tin and feels springy to the touch. Leave to cool and shrink in the tin, then turn out and transfer to a wire rack. Do not attempt to turn it out before it is cool – it will stick and then break.

- Whip the cream stiffly. Chop three of the chestnuts roughly. Mix into the cream. Split the cake horizontally with a serrated knife and carefully remove the top layer. Use half the whipped cream to sandwich the two layers together, and fill the central hole with the rest. (If the cake has been made in an ordinary, rather than ring-shaped, tin use all the cream to sandwich it.)
- Sift the icing sugar over the top of the cake, and decorate with the remaining five whole candied chestnuts.
- Serve the sauce separately if the cake is to be eaten as a pudding. Mix the cocoa powder with 2 tablespoons water in a saucepan until smooth. In a cup mix the cornflour with 1 tablespoon water until smooth. Add the syrup and water and slaked cornflour to the pan and stir until boiling.

> **TIP**
>
> *The cake may be split and filled as Whisked Fatless Sponge, filled and iced with a butter cream icing or eaten plain.*

The Génoise

This is a whisked sponge that has just-runny butter folded into it with the flour. Butter gives it flavour and richness and makes it keep a day or two longer than fatless sponges. A richer génoise cake (génoise fine) has a greater proportion of butter to flour, and the egg whites are whisked separately and folded in after the butter. The butter for both types of génoise sponges should be poured in a stream around the edge of the bowl and then folded in. If the butter is poured heavily on top of the whisked mixture, it forces out some of the air, and needs excessive mixing, with the danger of loss of more air.

Whisked cakes are cooked when the surface springs back when pressed with a finger. The cakes should be cooled for a few minutes in the tin and then turned out on to a wire rack. The baking parchment should be carefully peeled off to allow the steam to escape.

Rich Génoise Cake

4 eggs	Pinch of salt
120 g/4 oz caster sugar	50 g/2 oz very soft but not melted butter
120 g/4 oz plain flour	

- Pre-heat the oven to 375°F/190°C/Gas 5. Prepare a deep 20-cm/8-in cake tin as shown opposite.
- Place the eggs and sugar in a bowl and fit it over (not in) a saucepan of simmering water. With a balloon whisk (or hand-held electric one) whisk until the mixture has doubled in bulk, and leaves a thick "ribbon" trail. Start whisking slowly, and gradually build up speed. Remove the bowl from the heat and whisk occasionally until cool.
- Sift the flour with the salt and dust it evenly and lightly over the egg mixture. Fold it in gently with a large metal spoon.
- Beat the butter until it is soft enough to be just liquid without being clear or melted. It should still be opaque and have the consistency of half-whipped cream. Pour it as thinly as possible round the edge of the bowl. (Dumping it in a lump on the surface requires too much mixing and consequent loss of air.) Fold in gently.

1 Cut a circle of baking parchment to fit the base of the tin. Brush the tin with oil.

2 Put the paper in the tin and brush with oil.

3 Dust evenly all over with caster sugar. Shake off any excess. Then dust with plain flour and again shake out the excess.

4 Place eggs and sugar in a bowl over simmering water. Whisk the eggs and sugar together, slowly at first, then gradually build up speed.

5 Whisk until doubled in bulk, leaving a thick ribbon behind when the whisk is lifted. Remove from the heat and whisk occasionally until cool.

6 Sift the flour and salt over the egg and sugar mixture, keeping the sieve as close to the mixture as possible.

7 Blend in the flour with a large metal spoon. Turn the bowl with one hand and use a three-dimensional figure-of-eight movement to ensure an even fold.

8 Pour in the softened butter around the edge of the bowl. Blend in gently. Pour into the prepared tin and bake for 30 to 35 minutes.

9 Leave to cool on a wire rack. Remove the paper and cut the cake in half with a serrated knife.

● Pour the mixture into the prepared tin. Bake for 30 to 35 minutes. The cake is cooked when risen and golden brown, with the edges slightly shrunk from the edge of the tin and crinkled. The surface will feel spongy and will spring back when pressed with a finger and the cake will sound "creaky" if held close to the ear.
● Cool for a few minutes in the tin then turn out on to a wire rack. Remove the paper and leave to cool.

Icing

Not all cakes need icing, but adding one is a sure way to liven up a simple cake. Icing and garnishes should be chosen to add contrast in texture and colour. The flavour should either blend with that of the cake, such as a chocolate fudge icing on a chocolate cake, or add a contrasting taste, such as the hint of lemon in the cream cheese icing used with a carrot cake.

Frostings are nearly always used when the cake is for a gift or a special occasion. Then you have the opportunity to add various garnishes and decorations to suit the occasion. Although using a piping bag takes a little practice to perfect, it is not necessary to be highly skilled to make simple star and leaf shapes which make excellent borders and decorations. Royal Glaze and Butter Cream Icing both pipe well.

Garnish the cake with crystallized orange and lemon slices, frosted grapes, nuts, coconut or chocolate flakes and curls. There are wonderful purchased flowers that are made specially for cake decoration that add a professional touch to the cake. Some of them, such as crystallized mimosa and violets, are made from real flowers, others are made with sugar and come in a range of varieties and colours. For children, use sweets such as jelly beans and liquorice allsorts, which always go down well.

Seven-minute Frosting

2 egg whites

300 g/10 oz sugar

5 Tbsp cold water

¼ tsp lemon juice or cream of tartar

I tsp vanilla essence

● **Place all the ingredients, except the vanilla, in a heatproof bowl and place in a double boiler over a tin of rapidly boiling water. Beat continuously with a wire beater or electric mixer for seven minutes by which time the frosting should be thick and fluffy. Stir in the vanilla essence and use immediately.**

Seven-minute frosting should be used immediately.

Lemon or Orange Frosting

Use only 3 tablespoons water and omit the vanilla essence. Add 2 tablespoons lemon or orange juice and half a teaspoon grated lemon or orange zest to the finished frosting.

Marshmallow Frosting

Add 120 g/4 oz mini marshmallows to the egg white mixture. The heat and beating action will melt the marshmallow and make the frosting smooth.

Chocolate Frosting

Add 2 squares plain chocolate to the ingredients in the bowl. For chocolate marshmallow frosting, add both marshmallows and chocolate.

Cream Cheese Icing

90 g/3 oz cream cheese, at room temperature	1 tsp grated lemon rind
	1 tsp lemon juice
1½ Tbsp milk	1 tsp vanilla essence
250 g/8 oz icing sugar, sifted	

- Beat the cream cheese, milk and icing sugar until smooth. Stir in the lemon rind, juice and vanilla essence.

Fudge Icing

90 g/3 oz butter	½ tsp vanilla essence
250 g/8 oz brown sugar	500 g/1 lb icing sugar, sifted
1 Tbsp milk	

- Place the butter, brown sugar and milk in a pan and heat gently until the sugar has dissolved. Remove from the heat and add the vanilla essence and icing sugar. Beat until the icing is smooth and of spreading consistency.
- Fudge Icing can be flavoured with one of the following:

Chocolate:	add 2 squares of plain chocolate to the pan.
Coconut:	stir 120 g/4 oz shredded coconut into the finished icing.
Coffee:	omit vanilla and add 1 Tbsp instant coffee to the tin.
Nuts:	stir 50 g/2 oz chopped pecans, hazelnuts or mixed nuts into the finished icing.
Liqueur:	Add 2 Tbsp rum, Irish Cream or other suitable liqueur into the finished icing. As this makes the icing slightly runnier, add 2 to 4 Tbsp additional icing sugar.

Butterscotch Icing

50 g/2 oz butter	90 ml/3 fl oz evaporated milk
120 g/4 oz brown sugar	500 g/1 lb icing sugar
Pinch of salt	½ tsp vanilla essence

- Place the butter, brown sugar, salt and evaporated milk in the top of a double boiler over rapidly boiling water. Beat until the sugar has melted and the icing is smooth. Beat in sufficient icing sugar to make the icing of spreading consistency, then stir in the vanilla essence.

Butter Cream Icing

90 g/3 oz unsalted butter   1–2 tsp warm water or milk

300 g/10 oz icing sugar

- Beat the butter until light and fluffy, then gradually beat in the icing sugar, adding a little water if necessary to make the icing of spreading consistency. Flavour with one of the following:

Vanilla:	¼ to ½ tsp vanilla essence.
Orange/ Lemon	stir in the grated rind of 1 small orange or ½ lemon, use orange or lemon juice in place of water.
Chocolate:	add 1 square melted plain chocolate to the softened butter.
Mocha:	as for chocolate but dissolve 1 tsp instant coffee in the water or milk.
Pineapple:	omit milk or water and add 90 g/ 3 oz drained crushed pineapple to the finished icing.
Maple Syrup:	omit milk or water and add 60 ml/ 2 fl oz maple syrup or maple-flavoured syrup.

Fondant Icing

This is not as complicated to prepare as it might seem, and it does keep fresh for several months. If you make a large quantity it will always be on hand when you need it. Half this quantity will be enough to cover a 20–22-cm/8- to 9-in cake.

- Pour the water into a heavy-based pan, or unlined copper sugar boiler; add the sugar and lemon juice. Heat gently until the sugar has all dissolved, then bring to the boil and cook briskly until the syrup reaches the soft ball stage (240°F); 2 to 3 minutes of boiling. Pour the syrup straight on to a cold wet marble slab or wet work surface and leave to cool for 1 minute.
- Using a wooden spatula or metal scraper, work all round the syrup, lifting it from the edges and slapping and folding it over into the middle. It will change from a clear transparent syrup to a dense creamy mass.
- The syrup will now be cool enough to handle. Continue working – it will set hard otherwise – kneading and punching by hand, and folding in the same way as one handles dough. After about 10 minutes it should look matt white and feel smooth and firm.
- Wrap in clingfilm and leave to rest for 1 hour or store in the refrigerator. Divide the mixture in two. Store one half for later use.
- The fondant must be softened before use. Place in a heatproof bowl and set it over a tin half-filled with simmering water; in this instance the water may come up the sides of the bowl. Warm very gently and add just a little tepid water (about 2 tablespoonfuls is enough for 250 g/8 oz of fondant), for an unperfumed flavour. When the fondant mixture has the texture of thick cream it is ready for instant use.
- To colour the fondant, add a drop of orange vegetable colouring. For a liqueur flavour, use Grand Marnier instead of the water.
- Spread the fondant over the cake as you would glacé icing. Decorate with candied orange rind while still soft. Leave to set for several hours or overnight.

How Much Icing?	
Top and sides of two-layer 20-cm/ 8-in round cake	300 g/10 oz
Top and sides of two-layer 22-cm/ 9-in round cake	375 g/12 oz
Top and sides of three-layer cake	550 g/1 lb 2 oz
Top and sides of 20 x 20 cm/ 8 x 8 in square cake	375 g/12 oz
Top and sides of 22 x 13 x 7 cm/ 9 x 5 x 3 in loaf cake	300 g/10 oz
Filling 25 x 37 cm/10 x 15 in Swiss roll	500 g/1 lb
24 cup cakes	300 g/10 oz

Marzipan

250 g/8 oz icing sugar

250 g/8 oz sugar

600 g/1¼ lb ground almonds

1 tsp lemon juice

3 drops almond essence

1 egg, beaten

● Sift the icing sugar into a bowl, then stir in the caster sugar and the almonds. Add the lemon juice and almond essence, then using a wooden spoon, stir in sufficient egg to form a stiff paste. Knead lightly on a board dusted with icing sugar.

Glacé Icing

250 g/8 oz icing sugar

Water

Few drops vanilla essence or lemon juice

Food colouring, optional

● Sift the icing sugar into a bowl and stir in sufficient water to achieve spreading consistency. Stir in the vanilla essence or lemon juice. Stir in a few drops of food colouring to tint the glaze, if desired. Use immediately as the glaze sets quickly.

Royal Icing

2 large egg whites

500 g/1 lb icing sugar, sifted

½ tsp lemon juice

1 tsp glycerine

● In a bowl, break up the egg whites with a fork. Stir in the icing sugar a little a time, beating well with a wooden spoon. When about half of the sugar has been added, stir in the lemon juice. Continue adding the sugar until the icing forms soft peaks, stir in the glycerine to prevent the icing from setting rock hard. At this stage it can be used for soft icing. For piping, add a little more sugar until the icing holds its shape when formed into peaks. Do not add more sugar if the icing appears soft after adding all the sugar, continue to beat until it thickens or it will set too hard. To allow air bubbles to settle, cover with a damp cloth and leave for 5 minutes before using.

Glazed glacé fruit and nuts add a finishing touch to an iced cake.

Plain Cakes

Eivor's Orange Teabread

Acacia Honey Cake

Boiled Orange and Almond Cake
with Cottage Cheese Icing

Light Pound Cake

Passion Fruit-glazed Pound Cake

Sunshine Cake

Sandcake

Seed Cake

Finnish Lemon Cake

Soured Cream Cake

Angel Cake

Lekach

Eivor's Orange Teabread

This Scandinavian orange cake is light and airy, with a fresh flavour. Try it served with coffee or tea, or as a dessert accomtinied by fruit salad.

MAKES ONE LOAF CAKE

150 g/5 oz butter	Butter for greasing
120 g/4 oz sugar	Breadcrumbs to coat tin
3 eggs	GLAZE
Grated rind of 2 lemons	120 g/4 oz icing sugar
60 ml/2 fl oz fresh orange juice	2 Tbsp fresh orange juice
250 g/8 oz plain flour, sifted with 2 tsp baking powder	A few drops of oil and yellow food colouring

Whisk the butter and sugar until smooth and pale. Add the eggs, one at a time, stirring vigorously. Mix in the lemon rind and orange juice, together with the flour. Grease a 22-cm/9-in loaf tin with the butter, and sprinkle in the breadcrumbs. Pour the mixture into the tin. Place in a cold oven. Heat the oven to 325°–350°F/160°–175°C/ Gas 3–4 and bake for 1 hour. Turn out and leave to cool under the upturned tin.

Mix the icing sugar and orange juice to a smooth glaze. Add a couple of drops of oil, and colour the glaze light yellow with food colouring. Spread over the cake.

Acacia Honey Cake

Honey cakes are among the oldest cakes in history and were usually served for festive occasions. This is best made a week in advance.

MAKES 12 TO 16 SLICES

175 ml/6 fl oz acacia honey	120 g/4 oz coarse, ground almonds or hazelnuts
3 whole eggs, lightly beaten	2 Tbsp dark rum
300 g/10 oz rye flour, unsifted	½ tsp bicarbonate of soda
1 tsp ground cinnamon	1 Tbsp milk
Large pinch of ground cloves	Almond halves to decorate

Pre-heat the oven to 350°F/175°C/Gas 4. Grease and flour a deep rectangular tin 30 x 20-cm/12 x 8-in.

Warm the honey in the jar set in a tin of hot water, then pour it into a large mixing bowl and whisk until it is frothy, thick and white. Beat in the eggs and add the flour a spoonful at a time. Mix together the spices and nuts and stir in the rum. Combine with the honey and egg mixture. Dissolve the bicarbonate with the milk and beat it into the batter. Leave to mature in a covered bowl overnight as this helps to lighten the batter.

Press into the prepared tin. Stud with almond halves and bake for 30 to 35 minutes. Avoid letting it brown too much as this gives a bitter taste. When the cake has cooled in the tin, cut it into rectangular pieces and store for at least a week in an airtight container before serving.

Boiled Orange and Almond Cake with Cottage Cheese Icing

A simple cake with a moist texture and a sharp, tangy flavour.

MAKES ONE 22-CM/9-IN CAKE

2 oranges

6 eggs

120 g/4 oz sugar

250 g/8 oz blanched almonds, ground

1 tsp baking powder

Flour to dredge the tin

FROSTING

120 g/4 oz cottage cheese

120 g/4 oz icing sugar

2 Tbsp double cream

1 Tbsp Grand Marnier, or Cointreau

Pre-heat the oven to 375°F/190°C/Gas 5. Boil the oranges in their skins in water on top of the hob until they are very soft – this takes about 1 hour. Drain thoroughly.

Beat the eggs and add the sugar, almonds and baking powder. Purée the chopped oranges in a food processor and add to the mixture. Oil and flour a 22-cm/9-in cake tin and pour in the mixture. Bake for about 1 hour. This is a very moist cake and may be served as a dessert, plain with cream or with the cottage cheese icing.

To make the icing, put all the ingredients into a mixer or food processor. Blend. When they are well creamed, spread on top of the cake.

Light Pound Cake

Pound cake is an equal-weight cake, in which each of the main dry ingredients weighs the same as the eggs. It originated centuries ago and was highly spiced, flavoured and perfumed, and filled with seeds or dried fruit. Using potato flour gives the cake a finer flavour and the whipped egg white makes it much lighter.

MAKES ONE LOAF OR EQUIVALENT

250 g/8 oz butter	120 g/4 oz potato flour
250 g/8 oz caster sugar	1 tsp baking powder
5-cm/2-in vanilla pod, split	1 tsp orange-flower water
1 tsp lemon rind	1 Tbsp dark rum
4 large eggs	Icing sugar to dust
120 g/4 oz plain flour, unsifted	

Beat the butter and half the sugar until light and fluffy. Beat in the seeds of vanilla pod and the lemon rind. Beat in, one at a time, one whole egg and the three yolks.

Sift together the flours and baking powder two or three times then lightly beat 3 tablespoons at a time into the butter and sugar mixture, together with the orange-flower water and the rum, taking care not to over-beat. Whisk the egg whites in a separate bowl until they are firm, and beat in the rest of the sugar until the mixture looks silky and smooth. Lighten the main mixture by beating in 2 to 3 spoonfuls of the egg whites, then tip in the rest and gently fold in using a large metal spoon.

Pre-heat the oven to 350°F/175°C/Gas 4. Use a deep 20-cm/8-in cake tin or a 22 × 13-cm/9 × 5-in loaf tin or 22–25-cm/9 to 10-in ring tin. Butter well and dust with flour. Pour in the cake mixture and smooth level. Make a slight hollow in the middle. Bake in the warmed oven until well risen and golden brown, about 1¼ hours. Leave to cool in the tin for 10 minutes before turning out on to a wire rack. Dredge with icing sugar before serving. Pound cake keeps fresh for at least one week.

VARIATIONS

This basic pound cake is quite simple, but it may be enriched in a variety of exciting ways.

Dried Fruit

Try a mixture of dried fruits — apricots (soaked in water for 2 to 3 hours, then dried and chopped), 150 g/5 oz each of sultanas and raisins; you need two loaf tins for this.

Citrus Peel

Mixed candied citrus peel also tastes good.

Chocolate and Ginger

Chocolate and ginger make the cake rich and spicy. Pour half the cake mixture into an 18-cm/7-in ring tin and to the remaining mixture add 2 tablespoonfuls cocoa powder, 1 teaspoon powdered ginger and 50 g/ 2 oz finely chopped crystallized ginger. Blend the mixture well and spoon it over the mixture in the tin; gently drag a fork through it to give a marbled effect.

Fresh Fruit

Fresh fruit can also be added to the basic mixture. Choose any seasonal firm fruit, but avoid soft or citrus ones: plums, grapes, apples, cherries, rhubarb, apricots and pears are all good. You will need about 700 g/ 1½ lb stone fruits, 500 g/1 lb others.

Wash, dry, peel and core or remove the stones. Pour half of the cake mixture into the tin and cover with a layer of fruit; spoon over the rest of the cake mixture and cover with the remaining fruit. The baking time will be a little longer, and the cake will not keep for more than about 5 days.

Streusel

Combine 120 g/4 oz brown sugar, 50 g/2 oz toasted slivered almonds, ½ tablespoonful ground cinnamon and 25 g/1 oz melted butter. Spoon half the mixture into a ring tin and cover with the Streusel mixture. Cover with the rest of the mixture.

Passion Fruit-glazed Pound Cake

The flavour of this cake comes from the intensity of the passion fruit glaze. Be sure to use the blackest, most wrinkled fruits, as they are usually the ripest.

MAKES 8 TO 10 SLICES

175 g/6 oz plain flour

¼ tsp baking powder

175 g/6 oz unsalted butter, softened

250 g/8 oz sugar

Grated rind of 1 small orange

1 tsp vanilla essence

3 eggs, lightly beaten

PASSION FRUIT GLAZE

8 to 10 ripe passion fruit

50 g/2 oz sugar

4 seedless oranges, peeled and segmented

Icing sugar to dust (optional)

Pre-heat the oven to 350°F/175°C/Gas 4. Grease a 22 x 13-cm/9 x 5-in loaf tin. Line the bottom with non-stick baking parchment. Grease the paper and dust the tin with flour. Sift the flour and baking powder into a bowl.

Beat the butter until light and creamy, for 1 to 2 minutes, in a large bowl with an electric mixer. Gradually beat in the sugar until light and fluffy, then beat in the grated orange rind and vanilla essence. Beat in the eggs on low speed until well blended. Fold the flour mixture into the egg mixture, until just blended. Scrape into the tin, smoothing the top evenly.

Bake until risen and golden, and a skewer inserted into the centre comes out clean, about 1 hour. (Cover the top with foil if the cake browns too quickly.) Remove to a wire rack to cool, about 20 minutes.

To prepare the glaze, cut six of the passion fruit crosswise in half, and scoop the pulp into a nylon sieve or strainer placed over a medium bowl and press through with a wooden spoon. Stir in about 90 g/3 oz sugar; the amount required will depend on the sweetness of the passion fruit. Stir until the sugar is dissolved.

Using a long metal skewer, pierce holes from the top to bottom all over the cake. Slowly spoon over the glaze and allow to stand for about 20 minutes. Carefully unmould on to the rack, top-side up. If you like, dust with icing sugar before serving.

Meanwhile, cut the remaining passion fruit crosswise in half, and then scoop the pulp into a bowl; sweeten to taste with 2 to 3 tablespoons of sugar. Serve slices of the cake with a few orange segments drizzled with the passion fruit glaze.

Sunshine Cake

This light, simple sponge cake is easy to make.

MAKES ONE 22-CM/9-IN ANGEL CAKE

175 g/6 oz plain flour, sifted	5-cm/2-in vanilla pod
Pinch of salt	1 tsp cream of tartar
6 eggs, separated	1 tsp lemon juice, strained
250 g/8 oz caster sugar	Icing sugar to dust

Carefully wash and dry a 22-cm/9-in angel cake tin and dust with flour. Pre-heat the oven to 350°F/175°F/Gas 4.

Sift the flour and salt several times to aerate well. Whisk the egg yolks and half the sugar until thick and frothy, then mix in the seeds of the vanilla pod. Set aside. Lightly whip the egg whites in a clean bowl until they are foamy, add the cream of tartar and continue whisking until they have extinded into firm white peaks. Pour the remaining sugar in until glossy and smooth.

Carefully fold in the beaten egg yolks and lemon juice on a low speed, or by hand. Sift over one-third of the flour and gently fold it in; repeat in two more stages.

Pour the sponge mixture into the floured tin. Drag a knife through it to break any pockets of air. Bake for 50 minutes or until well risen and springy to the touch. Turn over on a wire rack to cool, leaving the cake tin in place.

Dust with icing sugar to serve.

Sandcake

Sandcake is related to pound cake, but the method of preparation is quite different. The mixture has to be beaten for a considerable time so the cooked cake has a fine, sand-like texture. Potato flour gives added refinement with a powdery dense texture and a sweet, nutty flavour.

MAKES ONE LOAF CAKE

175 g/6 oz butter	175 g/6 oz potato flour, sifted
175 g/6 oz caster sugar	¼ tsp baking powder
1 large egg	2 large egg whites
3 large egg yolks	Icing sugar to dust
1 Tbsp rum	
½ tsp grated lemon rind	

Gently melt the butter in a small pan, taking care not to let it brown. As it starts to bubble, draw the pan off the heat and carefully pour the clear liquid into a small mixing bowl, leaving the thick sediment in the bottom of the pan. Leave to cool. As it starts to solidify, set the bowl on a bed of ice cubes and beat the clarified butter for 10 minutes with a food mixer (20 minutes by hand) until it is very thick and almost white.

Pre-heat the oven to 325°F/160°C/Gas 3. Grease and flour a 22 x 13-cm/9 x 5-in loaf tin.

Transfer the butter to a large bowl. Add the sugar, egg and egg yolks a little at a time, making sure that the mixture never becomes runny, and beat for a further 15 minutes.

Slowly add the rum, beating all the time, then the rind. Sift the flour and baking powder and fold in half but do not over-blend. Whisk the egg whites until they are stiff and fold them into the main mixture in three stages, alternating with siftings of flour. Pour into the prepared tin and smooth out. Bake for 1 hour. Turn out of the tin to cool on a wire rack. Dredge with icing sugar to serve. Keeps fresh for up to a week.

Seed Cake

Seed cake, or "seedy cake" as it was known in Dublin, was very popular with the ladies. It was traditionally washed down with a glass of port.

MAKES ONE 20-CM/8-IN CAKE

250 g/8 oz butter	1 heaped Tbsp caraway seeds
250 g/8 oz sugar	2 Tbsp milk
4 eggs	2 Tbsp kirsch
175 g/6 oz self-raising flour	Icing sugar to dust

Cream the butter and sugar. Beat in the eggs, 1 at a time, adding a little flour each time to prevent the mixture curdling.

Fold in the rest of the flour and the caraway seeds. Stir in the milk and kirsch.

Bake in a round 20-cm/8-in tin, lined and greased, for about 1½ hours. Leave in the tin for a few minutes, then cool on a wire rack. Dredge the top of the cake with icing sugar, if wished. This cake keeps for a long time in an airtight container.

Finnish Lemon Cake

The sharp lemon flavour and smooth, creamy texture of this cake makes a perfect contrast to the accompanying jam or fruit.

MAKES ONE 22-CM/9-IN CAKE

4 eggs, separated

3 Tbsp sugar

5 Tbsp plain flour

Grated rind of 1 lemon

300 ml/10 fl oz double cream or soured cream, or 250 ml/8 fl oz plain yoghurt

Butter for greasing

Breadcrumbs to coat tin

Pre-heat the oven to 350°F/175°F/Gas 4.

Whisk the egg yolks with the sugar and flour. Add the lemon rind. Whip the cream, and stir it into the egg mixture. If using yoghurt, just mix it in. Whisk the egg whites into peaks, and fold into the mixture. Mix well, but do not stir or the mixture might sink.

Pour the mixture into a greased and breadcrumbed 22-cm/9-in cake tin. Bake for 35 to 40 minutes. Do not open oven door during the first 25 minutes. Serve the cake freshly baked with jam, or as a dessert with berries and soft fruit.

Soured Cream Cake

A feather-light sponge made with soured cream and delicately spiced with cinnamon, cardamom or ginger.

MAKES ONE 22-CM/9-IN CAKE

150 g/5 oz softened butter	1 tsp ground cardamom or ginger
250 g/8 oz sugar	250 ml/8 fl oz soured cream
3 eggs	1 tsp vanilla sugar
500 g/1 lb plain flour	Butter for greasing
1 tsp bicarbonate of soda	Breadcrumbs to coat tin
1 tsp ground cinnamon	

Pre-heat the the oven to 325°F/160°C/Gas 3.

Mix the butter and sugar until light and creamy. Add one egg at a time, stirring constantly. Mix all the dry ingredients together, except the vanilla sugar (sugar that has been stored with a vanilla pod to absorb the flavour) and breadcrumbs. Beat half of the flour mixture into the creamed mixture. Whisk in the soured cream, the rest of the flour mixture and the vanilla sugar.

Grease a 22-cm/9-in round cake tin with the butter, and sprinkle with the breadcrumbs. Spoon in the mixture. Bake for 50 minutes. When ready, turn out on to a wire rack and leave to cool.

Angel Cake

Although it sounds complicated, this low-fat recipe is very easy to make. Be sure to treat the mixture gently, to retain as much air as possible.

MAKES ABOUT 12 SLICES

	FILLING
3 eggs	
6 Tbsp caster sugar	200 g/7 oz low-fat soft cheese, such as curd or cream cheese
90 g/3 oz self-raising flour	
Few drops of pink food colouring	2 Tbsp icing sugar to dust
Few drops of yellow food colouring	

Pre-heat the oven to 400°F/200°C/Gas 6. Line three 22 x 13-cm/9 x 5-in loaf tins with baking parchment paper. Whisk the eggs and sugar in a large bowl until thick and pale and the whisk leaves a trail in the mixture when lifted. Sift the flour into the mixture and fold in gently.

Divide the mixture into three equal quantities and place in separate bowls. Add a few drops of pink colouring to one bowl and stir in gently. Add a few drops of yellow food colouring to another bowl and stir in gently.

Spoon the pink mixture into one prepared tin, the yellow into another and the plain mixture into the third. Bake for 10 minutes until the mixture springs back when gently pressed. Turn out and leave to cool completely on a wire rack.

Trim the sides from each cake. Mix together the filling ingredients. Place the yellow cake on a chopping board and spread half of the filling on top. Place the pink cake on top and spread with the remaining filling. Top with the white cake.

Dust with icing sugar and slice to serve.

Lekach

This honey cake is the traditional Jewish New Year cake. Strongly flavoured with ginger and other spices, it resembles German-style gingerbread.

MAKES 12 SLICES

300 g/10 oz plain flour

120 g/4 oz wholemeal flour

120 g/4 oz dark brown sugar

1 Tbsp baking powder

1 tsp bicarbonate of soda

2 tsp ground ginger

1 tsp ground cinnamon

½ tsp ground allspice

50 g/2 oz chopped walnuts or almonds, toasted (optional)

50 g/2 oz sultanas (optional)

400 g/14 oz good-quality natural honey

250 ml/8 fl oz strong black coffee

3 Tbsp whisky, brandy or water

4 eggs

60 ml/2 fl oz vegetable oil

90 g/3 oz ginger preserve or chopped stem ginger in syrup

Icing sugar to dust or honey to glaze

Pre-heat the oven to 350°F/175°C/Gas 4. Grease a 22 x 32-cm/9 x 13-in cake tin; line with baking parchment, then grease and flour paper.

In a large bowl, combine flours, brown sugar, baking powder, bicarbonate, ginger, cinnamon and allspice. Stir in the walnuts or almonds and sultanas if using. Set aside.

In a small saucepan, over medium-low heat, heat the honey with the coffee until warm. Remove from the heat. Stir in the whisky, brandy or water.

In a large bowl, beat the eggs with vegetable oil until well blended. Beat in the ginger preserve or stem ginger. Alternately, in 3 or 4 batches, stir in the warm honey mixture and the flour mixture into the beaten egg mixture until well blended.

Pour the mixture into the prepared tin. Bake until a skewer inserted in the centre comes out with just a few crumbs attached and the top springs back when gently pressed with a finger, 1 hour. Transfer the tin to a wire rack and cool completely.

Turn out the cake on to a rack and then back on to a serving plate, so the cake is the right way up. Dust with icing sugar or, if you do not mind a sticky cake, brush with slightly heated honey, and cut into squares to serve.

Family Cakes

Courgette Passion Cake

Cranberry and Coffee Cake

Coffee Almond Slice

Pear Upside-down Cake

Cranberry-orange Upside-down Cake

Apple Bran Cake

Walnut Torte

Coffee Sponge

Coffee Swiss Roll

Carrot Cake

Polish Honey Cake

Lime Coconut Layer Cake

Courgette Passion Cake

This passion cake is made with both carrots and grated courgettes.

MAKES ONE 22-CM/9-IN CAKE

250 g/8 oz plain flour	**FROSTING**
2 tsp baking powder	150 g/5 oz cream cheese
I tsp bicarbonate of soda	120 g/4 oz butter, softened
I tsp salt	½ tsp vanilla essence
250 g/8 oz caster sugar	250 g/8 oz sieved icing sugar
25 g/I oz pine nuts	Finely grated mixed carrot
25 g/I oz sultanas	and courgette for
175 g/6 oz mashed ripe bananas (about 2 bananas)	decoration (optional)
3 large eggs, beaten	
250 g/8 oz grated mixed carrots and courgettes	
150 ml/5 fl oz sunflower oil	

Pre-heat the oven to 350°F/175°C/Gas 4, and line a 22-cm/9-in deep cake tin with baking parchment – a loose-bottomed, spring-release tin is best.

Sift the flour, baking powder, bicarbonate and salt into a large mixing bowl, then add the sugar, pine nuts and sultanas. Mix well, then add the mashed bananas and beaten eggs. Stir in the grated vegetables and finally the oil, then beat the cake thoroughly for a minute, to a thick, slightly lumpy mixture.

Scrape into the prepared tin and bake for I hour, until a skewer inserted into the centre of the cake comes out clean. Leave for a few minutes, then carefully remove the cake from the tin and leave it to cool completely on a wire rack.

To make the icing, beat the cream cheese and butter together with the vanilla essence until smooth, then gradually beat in the sugar. Leave the icing to stand in a cool place for about 30 minutes, to harden it slightly, then spread over the cake. A little finely shredded mixed carrot and courgettes makes a perfect decoration, either in tiny mounds around the edge of the cake, or in the centre.

Cranberry and Coffee Cake

This is a very light sponge cake made with oil, flavoured with coffee, with dried cranberries folded into the mixture. It may be served as a plain sponge cake or decorated with whipped cream and fresh fruit, such as apricots, blueberries or cherries.

MAKES ONE 22-CM/9-IN CAKE

3 large eggs	1 tsp coffee essence
120 g/4 oz light brown sugar	50 g/2 oz dried cranberries, chopped roughly
90 g/3 oz fine wholemeal flour	
1 Tbsp sunflower oil	Whipped cream and fresh fruit (optional)

Pre-heat the oven to 375°F/190°C/Gas 5 then lightly grease a 22-cm/9-in cake tin and line the base with baking parchment.

Whisk the eggs and sugar together until pale and fluffy – this is best done in an electric mixer and may take up to 10 minutes. Fold in the flour a few spoonfuls at a time, then add the oil and essence, drizzling them down the side of the bowl. Finally, add the cranberries, folding in lightly. Transfer the mixture immediately to the prepared cake tin and bake for 20 to 25 minutes, until the mixture springs back when pressed lightly and shrinks away from the sides of the tin.

Turn the cake out on to a wire rack to cool completely. Decorate with fruit and whipped cream, if wished, then serve sliced.

Coffee Almond Slice

This sophisticated-looking cake is surprisingly easy to make and well worth the effort. A rich tea-time treat.

MAKES 10 SLICES

120 g/4 oz butter	FILLING AND TOPPING
120 g/4 oz sugar	25 g/1 oz plain chocolate
2 eggs	300 ml/10 fl oz double cream
120 g/4 oz self-raising flour	4 tsp instant coffee dissolved in 1 Tbsp hot water
1 Tbsp baking powder	
90 g/3 oz ground almonds	3 Tbsp icing sugar
2 drops almond essence	90 g/3 oz chocolate vermicelli
1 Tbsp water	

Pre-heat the oven to 350°F/175°C/Gas 4. Grease and line an 18 x 27-cm/7 x 11-in tin with baking parchment.

Put all the cake ingredients in a bowl. Mix together and beat until smooth. Pour the batter into the prepared tin. Bake for 25 to 30 minutes until firm to the touch. Turn out, remove the paper and cool.

Melt the chocolate until runny and keep warm. Whisk the cream with the dissolved coffee and icing sugar until it forms soft peaks.

Trim the edges of the cake and cut into three even-sized pieces. Spread a layer of cream on one piece, top with a second layer and spread with more cream. Top with the final layer of cake.

Spread the sides with cream and coat with the chocolate vermicelli. Spread the remaining cream on the top. Spoon the chocolate into a piping bag with a fine tip. Pipe straight lines along the length of the cake and with the point of a knife draw lines backwards and forwards across the chocolate lines creating a chevron effect. Chill for at least 1 hour and serve.

Pear Upside-down Cake

In this low-fat recipe, sliced pears are set on a caramel base and topped with a spicy sponge mixture. Once cooked, turn out and serve immediately with plain yoghurt.

MAKES ONE 20-CM/8-IN CAKE

2 Tbsp honey	60 g/2 oz caster sugar
2 Tbsp granulated brown sugar	3 egg whites
	120 g/4 oz self-raising flour
2 large pears, peeled, cored and sliced	2 tsp ground allspice
50 g/2 oz polyunsaturated margarine	Walnuts to decorate (optional)

Pre-heat the oven to 350°F/175°C/Gas 4. Heat the honey and sugar in a tin until melted. Pour into a 20-cm/8-in round cake tin lined with baking parchment. Arrange the pears around the base of the tin.

Beat together the margarine and sugar until light and fluffy. Whisk the egg whites until peaks form. Fold into mixture with the flour and allspice. Spoon over the pears.

Bake for 50 minutes or until risen and golden. Cool in the tin for 5 minutes, then turn out on to a serving plate. Remove the lining paper. Decorate with walnuts if desired, but remember that nuts are high in fat and are best saved for special occasions.

Cranberry-orange Upside-down Cake

"Upside-down" cakes became very popular in the 1940s, the most famous being made with tinned pineapple rings.

MAKES ONE 22-CM/9-IN CAKE

CRANBERRY TOPPING	CAKE
50 g/2 oz unsalted butter, melted	90 g/3 oz plain flour
250 g/8 oz fresh cranberries	1 tsp baking powder
150 g/5 oz sugar	¼ tsp salt
Grated rind of 1 orange	3 eggs
¼ tsp ground cinnamon	120 g/4 oz sugar
	½ tsp vanilla essence
	Grated rind of 1 orange
	40 g/1½ oz unsalted butter, melted

Pre-heat the oven to 350°F/175°C/Gas 4. Pour the melted butter into a 22-cm/9-in cake tin. Mix the cranberries, sugar, orange rind and cinnamon in a bowl. Spread the mixture over the bottom of the tin, pressing gently into the butter.

Sift the flour, baking powder and salt twice. Put the eggs in a heatproof bowl and set over a tin of simmering water. With an electric mixer, beat until frothy. Gradually beat in the sugar until thick and pale. Beat in the vanilla essence and orange rind.

Remove from the heat and fold in the flour mixture in three batches; drizzle in the melted butter and fold into the mixture. Spoon mixture over the cranberry layer. Bake 35 minutes. Remove to a wire rack to cool, about 7 minutes.

Run a knife around the edge of the tin to loosen the cake. Place a plate over the tin, bottom-side up, and quickly unmould the cake.

Pear Upside-down Cake ▶

Apple Bran Cake

Chunks of apple add moisture to this filling, low-fat cake. Decorate with apple slices just before serving or brush with a little lemon juice if you want to store the cake.

MAKES ONE 20-CM/8-IN CAKE

120 g/4 oz apple sauce

120 g/4 oz brown sugar

3 Tbsp skimmed milk

175 g/6 oz plain flour

60 g/2 oz all-bran breakfast cereal

2 tsp baking powder

1 tsp ground cinnamon

2 Tbsp honey

250 g/8 oz peeled and chopped apples

2 egg whites

Apple slices and 1 Tbsp honey to decorate

Pre-heat the oven to 300°F/150°C/Gas 2. Grease a deep 20-cm/8-in round cake tin and line with baking parchment.

Place the apple sauce in a mixing bowl with the sugar and milk. Sift the flour into the bowl and add the bran, baking powder, cinnamon, honey and apples. Whisk the egg whites until peaks form and fold into the mixture. Spoon the mixture into the prepared tin and level the surface.

Bake for 1¼ to 1½ hours or until cooked through. Cool in the tin for 10 minutes, then turn on to a wire rack and cool completely. Arrange the apple slices on top and drizzle with honey.

Walnut Torte

A classic cake made with ground nuts instead of flour. Keeps well for up to two weeks.

MAKES ONE 22-IN/9-IN CAKE

250 g/8 oz ground walnuts	I Tbsp toasted breadcrumbs
120 g/4 oz caster sugar	I Tbsp cocoa powder
120 g/4 oz ground almonds	I tsp instant coffee powder
4 eggs, separated	Icing sugar to dust

Pre-heat the oven to 350°F/175°C/Gas 4.

Beat the egg yolks and sugar until light and creamy. Mix the walnuts with the almonds, breadcrumbs, cocoa and coffee powders and blend well with the egg yolk mixture. Whisk the egg whites until they are firm and beat 4 tablespoonfuls into the nut mixture to lighten it. Carefully fold in the rest of the egg whites.

Pour the mixture into a buttered and breadcrumbed 22-cm/9-in spring-release cake tin and bake immediately. Leave to cool in the tin for 10 minutes before turning out on to a wire rack.

Dust with icing sugar to serve. For more elaborate occasions, brush with warm, sieved apricot jam and cover with a chocolate, vanilla or caramel icing and decorate with walnut halves.

Coffee Sponge

An airy, light coffee sponge with a rich flavour.

MAKES ONE 20-CM/8-IN CAKE

5 tsp instant coffee	**FILLING**
1½ tsp boiling water	150 ml/5 fl oz double or whipping cream
4 eggs, separated	2 Tbsp single cream
60 g/2 oz caster sugar	2 Tbsp caster sugar
5-cm/2-in vanilla pod, split	2 to 3 Tbsp Tia Maria or dark rum
120 g/4 oz ground almonds	Chocolate-coated coffee beans
2 Tbsp plain flour, sifted	Grated chocolate

Pre-heat the oven to 350°F/175°C/Gas 4. Butter, flour and sugar a 20-cm/8-in spring-release cake tin.

Dissolve the instant coffee in the boiling water and leave to cool. Beat the egg yolks and sugar until thick, pale and creamy. Beat in the seeds of vanilla pod, ground almonds and about two-thirds of the coffee liquid. Whisk the egg whites until they stand in firm, snowy peaks and fold them into the main mixture in two stages, alternating with siftings of flour.

Pour the batter into the tin and bake until well risen and brown. Leave to settle in the tin for 10 minutes before turning out to cool on a wire rack.

Whip the cream to hold soft peaks and beat in the sugar, remaining coffee liquid and liqueur.

Split the cooled cake in half and spread half the cream on the base. Cover with the top layer and smooth over the rest of the cream. Decorate with chocolate coffee beans and grated chocolate. Chill before serving.

Coffee Swiss Roll

This recipe combines the flavours coffee, chocolate and liqueur. Delicious served with a good strong cup of coffee.

25 g/1 oz butter	**FILLING**
3 large eggs	6 Tbsp warmed Morello cherry jam
90 g/3 oz caster sugar	
1 Tbsp coffee essence	150 ml/5 fl oz double cream
90 g/3 oz plain flour	1 Tbsp coffee liqueur
Pinch of salt	25 g/1 oz coarsely grated plain chocolate
1 Tbsp hot, strong coffee	

Pre-heat the oven to 425°F/220°C/Gas 7. Butter a 30 x 20-cm/12 x 8-in Swiss roll tin and line with baking parchment.

Put the eggs, sugar and coffee essence in a large bowl over a tin of hot water and whisk until the mixture is pale and leaves a thick trail. Remove from the heat and sift half the flour and salt over the egg mixture and fold in carefully, using a large metal spoon. Repeat with the remaining flour and add the hot coffee.

Turn the mixture quickly into the prepared tin, tilting it until evenly covered. Bake immediately just above the middle of the oven for about 10 minutes or until well risen and springy.

Have ready a sheet of baking parchment drenched with sugar. Turn the sponge cake out onto the paper and roll up the sponge cake at once from the short side, making the first turn firm, then rolling lightly. Cool on a wire rack covered with a clean cloth and with the join of the sponge cake underneath.

When cold, carefully unroll the cake, remove the lining paper and brush with cherry jam. Whip the cream and liqueur together, spread over the jam and carefully re-roll the cake. Sprinkle chocolate over the top.

Carrot Cake

A wonderful cake to serve both for everyday eating and for special occasions.

250 g/8 oz wholemeal flour	**ICING**
2 tsp baking powder	175 g/6 oz softened butter
1 tsp bicarbonate of soda	175 g/6 oz cream cheese
1 tsp salt	1 tsp vanilla essence
90 g/3 oz walnut pieces, finely chopped	250 g/8 oz icing sugar, sifted
3 large eggs, beaten	
150 g/5 oz mashed banana (2 medium-sized bananas)	
250 g/8 oz grated carrot	
175 ml/6 fl oz sunflower oil	

Pre-heat the oven to 350°F/175°C/Gas 4 then lightly grease a 22-cm/9-in, deep round cake tin and line it with baking parchment.

Mix all the dry ingredients together in a large bowl then add the eggs, mashed bananas and carrots. Pour the oil into the bowl and beat thoroughly to a thick, well-blended batter. Spoon into the prepared cake tin and bake in the centre of the oven for about 1 hour, until a skewer inserted into the cake comes out clean. Remove the cake carefully from the tin and leave to cool completely.

Prepare the icing by beating together the softened butter and cream cheese until blended, then add the vanilla essence and beat again. Sift the icing sugar and beat it gradually into the cream cheese mixture. Spread the icing over the cake and decorate, if wished, with finely chopped walnuts or a little extra grated carrot.

Polish Honey Cake

More of a honey spice cake, Polish Honey Cake or *Piernik* recipes do not always contain ginger, but a mixture of spices.

MAKES ONE 22-CM/9-IN CAKE

500 g/1 lb plain flour	25 g/1 oz chopped dried figs
2 tsp baking powder	25 g/1 oz chopped angelica
½ tsp ground ginger	300 g/10 oz honey
½ tsp ground cinnamon	90 g/3 oz caster sugar
½ tsp ground cloves	90 g/3 oz butter
½ tsp ground allspice	4 egg yolks
Grated rind of ½ orange	2 tsp instant coffee, dissolved in a little water
25 g/1 oz chopped hazelnuts or walnuts	4 egg whites
25 g/1 oz seedless raisins	

Pre-heat the oven to 350°F/175°C/Gas 4. Grease a 22-cm/9-in cake tin and line with baking parchment.

Sift the flour, baking powder and spices into a bowl. Stir in the orange rind, nuts, raisins, figs and angelica. Put the honey, sugar and butter into a tin and heat until completely melted. Cool slightly.

Add the melted mixture, egg yolks and coffee to the flour and mix well. In a bowl, whisk the egg whites until very stiff and then fold into the mixture.

Pour the mixture into the cake tin and bake for 1 to 1¼ hours.

If liked, you can slice the cake and sandwich the halves together with thick jam. You can also decorate the top with thick chocolate icing.

Lime Coconut Layer Cake

Delicious layers of lime-scented sponge with a tangy lime custard topped with classic seven-minute frosting and coconut – a desert island dream.

MAKES ONE DEEP 20-CM/8-IN CAKE

120 g/4 oz plain flour	**ICING**
Pinch of salt	2 egg whites
6 eggs	375 g/12 oz sugar
200 g/7 oz sugar	3 Tbsp cold water
Grated rind of 2 limes	¼ tsp cream of tartar
1 tsp lime juice	1½ tsp golden syrup
200 g/7 oz desiccated coconut	1½ Tbsp lime juice
	250 g/8 oz desiccated coconut

LIME CUSTARD

2 Tbsp cornflour

250 ml/8 fl oz cold water

2 eggs

Grated rind and juice of 1 large lime

250 g/8 oz sugar

90 g/3 oz butter

Pre-heat the oven to 350°F/175°C/Gas 4. Lightly grease three 20-cm/8-in cake tins. Line the bottom of each with baking parchment; grease and flour again. Sift the flour and salt.

Put the eggs in a large heatproof bowl and set over a saucepan of just simmering water. With an electric mixer, beat until frothy. Gradually beat in the sugar until well-blended. Continue beating until the mixture is doubled in volume and very thick. Remove the bowl from the tin of water and fold in the grated lime rind and desiccated coconut. Sift the flour mixture in three batches, folding in after each addition.

Divide the mixture evenly among the tins. Bake about 30 minutes. Cool for 5 minutes. Unmould on to a wire rack to cool completely.

Prepare the lime custard: Blend the cornflour with about a tablespoon of the cold water to dissolve. Whisk in the remaining eggs. Put the remaining water, grated rind and lime juice, sugar and butter in a saucepan and, over medium heat, bring to a boil. Whisk a little of the mixture into the beaten egg mixture, then whisk the egg mixture into the saucepan and return to the heat. Whisk until the mixture boils, about 5 minutes. Pour into a bowl and cool.

Prepare the icing: Put all the ingredients except the coconut in a heatproof mixing bowl and set over a saucepan of just simmering water. With an electric mixer, beat for 7 minutes until thick. Remove from the hot water and beat until mixture is at room temperature. Cover with clingfilm.

Remove the paper from the cake layers. Place a layer on a plate and spread with half the lime custard. Cover with a second layer and the remaining lime custard. Spread the top and side of the cake with the icing and press some of the shredded coconut on to the side of the cake; sprinkle the remaining coconut over the top.

Chocolate Cakes

Surprise Chocolate Ring

Chocolate and Soured Cream Marble
Cake

Chocolate and Raspberry Cake

Devil's Food Dream Cake

Chocolate Roulade

Chocolate-almond Zuccotto

Raisin Chocolate Fudge Cake

Chocolate and Almond Sandwich

Family Chocolate Cake

White Chocolate Mousse and
Strawberry Layer Cake

Cooking with Chocolate

Cooking with chocolate as the main ingredient can be quite spectacular, especially when other good quality ingredients are used. To prevent disappointment in your efforts, you must remember to treat chocolate with TLC: tender loving care.

Melting Chocolate

There are several different ways to melt chocolate, but to avoid ending up with a solid mass there are a few rules which must be observed. Any equipment used must be perfectly dry because any stray drops of water will cause the chocolate to thicken and stiffen. For the same reason, never cover chocolate during, or after, melting. If you do end up with a solid mass, try stirring in a little vegetable oil and mix very well. Butter or margarine will not do as they contain some water. The second thing to remember is NEVER to rush the melting process. A watched pot never boils and it can be tempting to increase the heat and speed up the process. Unfortunately this will ruin the flavour and texture of the chocolate. It is best to grate or chop the chocolate before melting for a smooth result.

Direct Heat Method

This method is only used when the chocolate is combined with butter, sugar, milk or similar ingredients, as when making some sweets and sauces. The mixture should always be stirred over very gentle heat. As soon as the mixture has melted, it should be removed, to prevent the chocolate overcooking and becoming "grainy".

Double Boiler Method

This is probably one of the best and easiest methods of melting chocolate. If you do not possess a double boiler, you can easily improvise one by placing a heatproof bowl over a saucepan. The bowl should fit securely on the pan so that neither steam nor water can escape. Water in the saucepan should never touch the bottom of the bowl. Place the chocolate in the bowl. Allow the water in the saucepan to come to the boil and place the bowl on top. Turn off the heat under the saucepan and leave to stand for a while until the chocolate is melted.

Oven Method

Chocolate can be melted in an ovenproof bowl in a very low oven (225°F/110°C/Gas ¼). If the oven has been in use for another purpose and has been turned off, it makes sense to use the lingering heat to melt the chocolate. When the chocolate has almost melted it should be removed and stirred until smooth.

Microwave Oven Method

Microwave ovens are very handy for melting chocolate, especially small quantities, quickly and safely. The chocolate should be broken into small pieces and put into a glass bowl. Microwave, uncovered, until almost melted. The manufacturer's instructions should be followed as the timing and power setting will vary according to the appliance.

On average 90 g/3 oz chocolate will melt in 1 to 1½ minutes. It is important to stir the chocolate just before the end of the cooking time to see if the chocolate has melted and thus prevent overcooking.

Chocolate for Dipping

Delicious sweetmeats such as marzipan, caramel, fudge, crystallized or fresh fruit can all be dipped in chocolate. Use either tempered couverture, or plain chocolate. Heat in a double boiler, taking care not to have the heat too high. The chocolate should be in a bowl deep enough for the confection to be totally covered. Using a special dipping fork, fondue fork or thin skewer, lower the confection into the chocolate. Turn it over and then lift out the chocolate, tapping the fork on the edge of the bowl to shake off the excess chocolate. Place the chocolate on a tray lined with non-stick or greaseproof paper. The dipping fork can be used to decorate the top of the chocolates before they set. Lay the fork on the surface of the chocolate and lift it gently to create ridges.

Storing Chocolate

Chocolate should be kept in a cool, dry place. Contrary to popular belief the refrigerator is not the best place to store chocolate other than for short periods during hot weather. When refrigerated, chocolate will absorb odours very easily and also may collect a film of moisture on the surface. Wrap the chocolate in foil, then in a plastic bag if you wish to refrigerate it. Let the chocolate stand at room temperature before unwrapping and using as this should prevent moisture condensing on the surface.

If chocolate is stored in very warm conditions, the cocoa butter or sugar crystals in it may rise to the surface giving a grayish white "bloom". This is completely harmless and although it detracts from the appearance, does not affect the flavour of the chocolate. The "bloom" will also disappear on melting so the chocolate is quite suitable for cooking.

If you wish to keep chocolate for a longer time in hot conditions, then it is best to freeze it. Make sure it is tightly wrapped. Remove it from the freezer the night before you need it, and allow it to thaw completely before unwrapping it. The freezer is an especially good place to store chocolate decorations such as squares, leaves, etc. These can then be used any time to garnish cakes and desserts and only need a few hours to thaw.

If kept in the correct conditions, plain chocolate should keep for one year and milk chocolate for about six months.

Making Chocolate Decorations

Chopped Chocolate

Use chocolate at room temperature. Break into small pieces and place on a chopping board. Using a sharp chopping knife, chop into the size required. Chocolate may also be chopped quite successfully in a food processor.

Chocolate Squares, Triangles

Melt plain chocolate and spread evenly on to greaseproof paper. Leave to set. Using a ruler, mark into squares or rectangles. Cut with a sharp knife. Cut squares diagonally to form triangles and rectangles diagonally to form wedges.

Chocolate Cups

Use two thicknesses of paper cases. If you can obtain foil cases a single layer only is necessary. Melt the chocolate and brush on the bottom and up the sides of the cases. Repeat this process until a thick layer is obtained. Carefully turn upside down on to greaseproof paper. Chill until hard. Peel paper case away from the chocolate and fill as desired.

Chocolate Curls

Melt some plain chocolate and spread out on a cool work surface to a thickness of about 3 mm/ ⅛ inch. Cool until set but not hard. Using a long knife, hold it at an angle of of 45° under the chocolate and push away from you, scraping off long curls.

Surprise Chocolate Ring

The surprise element of this luxurious cake lies in its rich treasure-trove of hidden contents – cream, fruit and cherry brandy. It's the cook's secret.

MAKES ONE 20-CM/8-IN RING CAKE

150 g/5 oz self-raising flour

50 g/2 oz unsweetened cocoa powder

175 g/6 oz soft margarine

175 g/6 oz caster sugar

3 eggs

4 Tbsp cherry brandy

250 g/8 oz fruit, such as strawberries, raspberries, stoned cherries

150 ml/5 fl oz double cream

ICING

60 ml/2 fl oz double cream

375 g/12 oz plain chocolate, grated

DECORATION

Chocolate butterflies (or other chocolate decorations) or chocolate-dipped fruit

Pre-heat the oven to 350°F/175°C/Gas 4. Grease and flour a ring tin.

Sift the flour and cocoa into a mixing bowl. Add the margarine, sugar and eggs. Beat well together. Spoon the mixture into the prepared tin. Bake for about 35 to 40 minutes. Turn out and cool.

Turn the cake upside down and cut a slice about 2 cm/¾ in deep off the flat base of the ring. Lift off the slice carefully and reserve.

With a teaspoon, scoop out the cake in a channel about 2 cm/¾ in deep and 2.5 cm/1 in wide. Sprinkle 3 tablespoonfuls of the cherry brandy over the sponge. Chop the fruit and spread in the hollow. Whisk the cream until stiff. Stir in the remaining brandy. Spread the cream over the fruit. Place the reserved slice back on the cake. Invert the cake so it is the right way up.

To make the icing, put the cream into a saucepan and bring just to the boil. Add the chocolate. Stir until the chocolate melts. Cool until the mixture is thick and smooth. Pour over the cake. Put in a cool place until set and decorate with piped chocolate butterflies or chocolate dipped fruit.

Chocolate and Soured Cream Marble Cake

A wholesome classic cake that is always popular, here made in an attractive circular shape.

MAKES ONE LARGE RING CAKE

175 g/6 oz plain chocolate	½ tsp almond essence
250 g/8 oz butter	400 g/14 oz self-raising flour
250 g/ 8 oz caster sugar	150 ml/5 fl oz soured cream
4 eggs	Icing sugar to dust
2 tsp vanilla essence	

Pre-heat the oven to 350°F/175°C/Gas 4. Butter and thickly sugar a 22–25-cm/9–10-in ring tin.

Melt the chocolate and leave to cool slightly.

Cream together the butter and sugar until light and fluffy. Beat in the eggs one at a time. Add the vanilla and almond essence. Fold in the flour.

Divide the mixture in two. Add the soured cream to one half and the melted chocolate to the other half. Put alternate spoonfuls of the mixtures into the prepared tin. Using a teaspoon, cut down into the mixture and swirl together.

Bake for about 1 hour or until a skewer inserted into the centre comes out clean. Leave for 5 minutes. Unmould on to a wire rack and cool.

Dust with icing sugar to serve.

Chocolate and Raspberry Cake

A very indulgent chocolate treat. The raspberry flavour offsets the chocolate perfectly.

MAKES ONE 22-CM/9-IN CAKE

300 g/10 oz good-quality plain chocolate, chopped

120 g/4 oz unsalted butter

8 eggs, separated

60 ml/2 fl oz Framboise or other raspberry-flavoured liqueur

¼ tsp cream of tartar

CHOCOLATE RASPBERRY GANACHE FILLING

375 g/12 oz good-quality plain chocolate, chopped

175 g/6 oz unsalted butter, cut into pieces

120 g/4 oz seedless raspberry jam

60 ml/2 fl oz Framboise or other raspberry-flavoured liqueur

CHOCOLATE-RASPBERRY GLAZE

250 ml/8 fl oz double cream

250 g/8 oz good-quality plain chocolate, chopped

2 Tbsp Framboise or other raspberry-flavoured liqueur

90 g/3 oz fresh raspberries for decoration

Icing sugar to dust

Pre-heat the oven to 350°F/175°C/Gas 4. Lightly butter two 22-cm/9-in spring-release tins. Line the bottoms with baking parchment and butter again.

Heat the chocolate and butter. Beat the egg yolks then gradually whisk into the melted chocolate. Whisk in the raspberry-flavoured liqueur. Beat the egg whites until frothy. Add the cream of tartar and continue beating until soft peaks form. Fold whites into the chocolate-egg mixture.

Divide the mixture evenly between the two tins. Bake for 35 minutes. Remove cakes to a wire rack to cool for 15 minutes. Remove sides of the tins and cool cakes. Invert on to a rack, remove tin bottoms then peel off the paper.

Heat the chocolate, butter and half the raspberry jam for the filling. Remove from the heat and stir in half the raspberry-flavoured liqueur. Heat the remaining jam and liqueur. Spread a thin layer of the jam mixture over each cake layer.

Place one cake layer in cleaned tin, jam-side up. Spread with filling. Top with second cake layer, jam-side down against filling. Refrigerate overnight.

Prepare the glaze. Bring the cream to the boil. Remove from heat and add in the chocolate all at once stirring until melted and smooth. Stir in the raspberry-flavoured liqueur and set aside to cool. Remove the side of the spring-release tin. Transfer the cake to a wire rack set over a baking sheet. Pour the glaze over the cake, smooth the top and sides and allow to set. Scrape remaining glaze off the baking sheet back into the bowl and whisk until smooth. Pipe a scroll border around the edge of cake. Decorate with raspberries and dust with sifted icing sugar.

Devil's Food Dream Cake

These rich, dark chocolate layers are filled and iced with a dark chocolate ganache, a chocolate truffle filling. Truly a wicked dream.

MAKES ONE 22-CM/9-IN CAKE

50 g/2 oz unsweetened cocoa powder	3 eggs
300 g/10 oz plain flour	175 ml/6 fl oz soured cream or buttermilk
2 tsp bicarbonate of soda	1 tsp vinegar
½ tsp salt	1 cup boiling water
50 g/2 oz plain chocolate, chopped	CHOCOLATE GANACHE ICING
120 g/4 oz unsalted butter, softened	750 ml/1½ pt double cream
300 g/10 oz light brown sugar	750 g/1½ lb good-quality plain chocolate, chopped
2 tsp vanilla essence	25 g/1 oz butter
	1 Tbsp vanilla essence

Pre-heat the oven to 375°F/190°C/Gas 5. Grease two 22-cm/9-in cake tins. Line bottoms with baking parchment; grease and flour again. Sift together the cocoa powder, flour, bicarbonate and salt; set aside.

In the top of a double-boiler over low heat, melt the chocolate, stirring frequently until smooth. Cool.

With an electric mixer, beat the butter, brown sugar and vanilla essence until light and creamy. Add the eggs, one at a time, beating well after each addition. Add the flour mixture alternately with the soured cream or buttermilk in three batches. Stir in the vinegar and slowly beat in the boiling water. Pour into the tins and bake 20 to 25 minutes. Cool cakes in their tins 5 minutes. Carefully unmould on to a wire rack to cool completely.

Preparing the icing: Bring the cream to the boil. Remove from the heat and add the chocolate all at once, stirring until melted. Beat in the butter and vanilla essence. Pour into a bowl and refrigerate until the ganache reaches a spreading consistency.

To assemble: Remove paper from cake bottoms. Slice each cake into two layers. Place one layer, cut-side up on a plate and spread with one sixth of ganache. Place second layer on top and frost with another sixth of ganache. Continue layering. Ice the top and sides of cake with remaining ganache.

Chocolate Roulade

The roulade may be made a day in advance but should be filled close to the time of serving.

MAKES 8 TO 10 SLICES

175 g/6 oz plain chocolate

5 eggs, separated

175 g/6 oz caster sugar

3 Tbsp hot water

Icing sugar, sifted

FILLING

500 ml/1 pt double cream

120 g/4 oz icing sugar, sifted

50 g/2 oz unsweetened cocoa powder

2 tsp instant coffee powder

½ tsp vanilla essence

DECORATION

Icing sugar

Whipped cream

Crystallized violets

Angelica leaves

Pre-heat the oven to 350°F/175°C/Gas 4. Grease a 22 x 37-cm/9 x 15-in Swiss roll tin and line with baking parchment. Grease again.

Melt the chocolate in a bowl over a pan of hot water.

Put egg yolks into a large bowl. Add the sugar and beat well until pale and fluffy, this is best done with an electric mixer and takes about 10 minutes. Add hot water to the chocolate and stir until smooth. Whisk into the egg mixture. Whisk the egg whites until stiff. Lightly fold into the chocolate mixture. Pour into the prepared Swiss roll tin. Cook in the oven for 15 to 20 minutes, until firm.

Remove from the oven. Cover with a sheet of baking parchment sprinkled with icing sugar. Roll up gently leaving the paper in place. Leave until completely cold.

To make the filling put all the ingredients into a bowl. Whisk until thick. Chill. Unroll the roulade and spread the filling over the cake to within 2.5 cm/1 in from the edge. Roll up again, using the paper to help.

Place seam-side down on a serving plate and chill for one hour. Dredge the roulade with icing sugar. Pipe whipped cream down the centre and decorate with crystallized violets and angelica leaves.

Chocolate-Almond Zuccotto

An extravagant variation of the cake from the preceding recipe. This Italian speciality could be served as a special cake or dessert.

MAKES 8 TO 10 SLICES

Chocolate Roulade Cake

2 Tbsp almond-flavoured liqueur

CHOCOLATE-ALMOND FILLING

500 ml/1 pt double cream

500 g/1 lb ricotta cheese

120 g/4 oz sugar

4 Tbsp almond-flavoured liqueur

175 g/6 oz plain chocolate, melted

90 g/3 oz plain chocolate, grated

50 g/2 oz chopped almonds, lightly toasted

CHOCOLATE WHIPPED CREAM

300 g/10 oz good-quality plain chocolate, chopped

500 ml/1 pt double cream mixed with 2 Tbsp almond-flavoured liqueur

50 g/2 oz chopped almonds, lightly toasted

Cool the roulade. Cut out a 20-cm/8-in circle from the cake. Cut the remaining long strip of cake into long narrow triangles, 5 cm/2 in at base end, and cut any remaining cake into pieces. Sprinkle with liqueur.

Line a bowl with clingfilm, then, with the point of each triangle in the centre, line with the triangles.

Beat the cream into stiff peaks. Beat the ricotta with sugar, and liqueur. Stir a spoonful of cream into the ricotta and fold in remaining cream. Remove half mixture to "cream" bowl.

Fold the melted chocolate into one half of the ricotta-cream mixture. Fold grated chocolate and almonds into other half. Spoon this half into the cake-lined bowl and spread on the base and up sides. Spoon the melted chocolate mixture into the centre.

Top with the remaining circle of cake, edging it in to surround the cream. Decorate with chocolate, cream, liqueur and almonds. Chill. Carefully unmould to serve.

Chocolate Roulade ▶

Raisin Chocolate Fudge Cake

A rich chocolate cake full of spicy flavours, nuts and raisins.

MAKES ONE 20-CM/8-IN CAKE

60 g/2½ oz butter	25 g/1 oz flaked almonds
400 g/14 oz brown sugar	50 g/2 oz raisins
1 whole egg	**FILLING**
2 Tbsp orange juice	120 g/4 oz unsalted butter
2 tsp grated orange rind	300 g/10 oz icing sugar
50 g/2 oz plain chocolate, melted and cooled	4 Tbsp milk
	1½ tsp vanilla essence
90 ml/3 fl oz milk	50 g/2 oz pecan nuts, chopped
90 ml/3 fl oz water	
Pinch of bicarbonate of soda	50 g/2 oz desiccated coconut
250 g/8 oz plain flour, sifted	50 g/2 oz raisins, cut in half
½ tsp baking powder	Pecan halves and flaked almonds to decorate
½ tsp ground cinnamon	
¼ tsp ground cloves	

Pre-heat the oven to 350°F/175°C/Gas 4. Grease a 20–22-cm/8–9-in spring-release tin and line with baking parchment.

Cream the butter and half the sugar. Beat in the egg and blend well. Add the orange juice and rind. Beat in the rest of the sugar and the chocolate. Combine well. Mix the milk with the water and blend in the bicarbonate.

Sift together the flour and baking powder with the cinnamon and cloves. Dust the almonds and raisins with some of the flour and set aside.

Beat one-third of the liquid into the mixture followed by one-third of the dry ingredients. Repeat in two further stages. Mix in the raisins and almonds. Turn into the prepared tin. Level the surface. Bake for 1 hour until risen and shrinking away slightly from the edges of the tin. Cool on a wire rack.

Make the filling by beating the butter until light and creamy; sift in the icing sugar, then beat in the milk and vanilla. Mix the pecan nuts, coconut and raisins and stir into the mixture.

To assemble, split the cake into three layers. Reserve just over one-third of the filling for the outside and use the remainder to sandwich the three chocolate layers together. Smooth the rest over the top and sides of the cake. Decorate with pecans and almond flakes.

The cake should settle for at least a day before it is cut. It will stay fresh for up to a week.

Chocolate and Almond Sandwich

A simple family cake, which is quick and easy to make, but quite delicious.

SERVES 4

120 g/4 oz butter

5 Tbsp sugar

1 egg, beaten

6 Tbsp plain flour

6 Tbsp blanched almonds, ground

1 Tbsp cocoa powder

1 tsp baking powder

¼ tsp salt

3 Tbsp milk

Icing sugar

CHOCOLATE FILLING

120 g/4 oz plain chocolate, grated

1½ Tbsp milk

250 g/8 oz icing sugar

90 g/3 oz unsalted butter

Dash of almond essence

Pre-heat the oven to 400°F/200°C/Gas 6. Grease two 18-cm/7-in tins and bottom-line with baking parchment.

Cream the butter and sugar together. Add the well-beaten egg. In another bowl, sift together the flour, ground almonds, cocoa, baking powder and salt. Add alternately with the milk to the creamed butter and sugar. Combine thoroughly.

Divide the mixture between the two baking tins and bake for 20 minutes. When cool, sandwich together with the chocolate filling and dredge the top of the cake with icing sugar.

To make the filling, mix the chocolate with the milk and warm over low heat until the chocolate has melted. Remove from the heat, beat in the icing sugar, then leave until cool. Cream the butter then add the chocolate mixture and the almond extract; beat until light and creamy. Use to fill the cake.

Family Chocolate Cake

A delicious basic chocolate cake, which will be requested time and time again.

MAKES ONE 19-CM/7½-IN CAKE

90 g/3 oz plain chocolate	1½ tsp baking powder
Approx 60 ml/2 fl oz clear honey	¼ tsp vanilla essence
	150 ml/5 fl oz milk
120 g/4 oz butter or margarine	
90 g/3 oz caster sugar	ICING
2 eggs	50 g/2 oz plain chocolate
150 g/5 oz self-raising flour	3 Tbsp water
	2 Tbsp butter
50 g/2 oz unsweetened cocoa powder	250 g/8 oz icing sugar, sifted

Pre-heat the oven to 350°F/175°C/Gas 4. Grease and line one 18–19-cm/7–7½-in cake tin.

Put the chocolate and honey into a small bowl over a pan of hot water. Stir until the chocolate has melted. Cool.

Cream together the butter or margarine and sugar until light and fluffy. Beat in the chocolate mixture, then the eggs. Sift together the flour, cocoa powder and baking powder. Stir in the flour mixture a little at a time, alternately with the vanilla essence and milk.

Pour the mixture into the cake tin. Bake for about 45 minutes. Turn on to a wire rack, leaving the lining paper on the cake to form a collar.

When the cake is cool, make the icing. Put the chocolate and water into a small saucepan and melt over gentle heat. Remove from the heat and stir in the butter. When the butter has melted, beat in the sugar.

Spread the icing over the top of the cake and swirl with a metal palette knife. When the icing is firm, remove the lining paper from the cake.

White Chocolate Mousse and Strawberry Layer Cake

Other fresh berries in season can be used in this cake, but ever-popular strawberries look particularly elegant.

MAKES ONE 22-CM/9-IN CAKE

120 g/4 oz good-quality white chocolate, grated or chopped

120 ml/4 fl oz double cream

120 ml/4 fl oz milk

1 Tbsp rum or vanilla essence

250 g/8 oz plain flour

1 tsp baking powder

Pinch of salt

120 g/4 oz unsalted butter, softened

200 g/7 oz sugar

3 eggs

750 g/1½ lb fresh strawberries, sliced, plus extra for decoration

750 ml/1½ pt double cream

2 Tbsp rum or strawberry-flavoured liqueur

1 Tbsp icing sugar, sifted

WHITE CHOCOLATE MOUSSE FILLING

300 g/10 oz good-quality white chocolate, chopped

375 ml/12 fl oz double cream

2 Tbsp rum or strawberry-flavoured liqueur

Pre-heat the oven to 350°F/175°C/Gas 4. Lightly butter two deep 22-cm/9-in cake tins. Line bottoms with baking parchment; grease and flour again. Put the white chocolate and cream in a saucepan and stir over low heat until melted and smooth. Stir in the milk and rum or vanilla essence. Cool.

Sift together the flour, baking powder and salt. Set aside. With an electric mixer, beat the butter and sugar until light and creamy. Add the eggs, one at a time, beating well after each addition.

Add the flour mixture alternately with the melted chocolate mixture in three batches until just blended. Scrape into the prepared tins and bake 20 to 25 minutes or until cooked through. Cool in tins 10 minutes. Unmould on to a wire rack to cool completely.

Prepare the mousse. Process the chopped white chocolate in a food processor 15 to 30 seconds. Bring the cream to the boil. Pour the hot cream through the processor feed tube and process until smooth. Pour into a bowl, stir in the rum or strawberry-flavoured liqueur and refrigerate until just set. Whisk until light and mousse-like.

To assemble: Remove the paper from cake bottoms. Slice each cake into two layers. Place on layer, cut-side up, on a cake plate and spread with one-third of the mousse mixture. Arrange one-third of the sliced strawberries over the mousse. Place a second layer on top and continue layering in this way. Cover with the last cake layer.

Whip the cream with the rum or liqueur and icing sugar until firm peaks form. Spread half over top and sides of cake. Pipe scrolls or rosettes with remaining cream around top edge of cake and in the centre. Decorate with the remaining strawberries.

Fruit Cakes

Sultana Cake

Fresh Cherry Cake

Babka

Wholemeal Courgette
and Raisin Cake

Pumpkin, Sunflower Seed
and Raisin Cake

Gypsy Cake

Pineapple Fruit Cake

Barm Brack

Irish Tea Brack

Guinness Cake

Sultana Cake

The method of preparation and baking is quite unusual and gives a not too sweet, light and airy cake that is ideal with tea or coffee.

MAKES ONE 20-CM/8-IN RING CAKE

90 g/3 oz butter	4 eggs, separated
90 g/3 oz plain flour, sifted	90 g/3 oz caster sugar
120 g/4 oz sultanas	Icing sugar to dust
1 tsp lemon rind	

Pre-heat the oven to 475°F/240°C/Gas 9. Grease and flour an 20–22-cm/8–9-in ring tin.

Cut the butter into the flour and blend to a fine crumb texture. Toss in the sultanas and lemon rind, making sure that they are well coated with flour. Set aside.

Whisk the egg whites in a large clean bowl until they stand in firm, snowy peaks and beat in half the sugar until the mixture is firm and glossy. Using a large metal spoon or the mixer on very slow, fold in the rest of the sugar and the lightly beaten egg yolks. Very carefully and lightly, fold in the flour and butter mixture in three portions.

Pour the mixture into the prepared tin. Level out and bake immediately for 5 minutes; then reduce the oven temperature to 425°F/220°C/Gas 7 for 10 minutes; finally reduce the temperature to 350°F/175°C/Gas 4 for 30 minutes. The cake puffs up high and turns a rich brown. Remove from the oven and turn out on to a wire rack after 10 minutes to cool. Dust with icing sugar to serve.

Fresh Cherry Cake

Fresh cherry cakes are traditional in central Europe, but are a popular family treat everywhere. This particular version comes from Switzerland.

MAKES ONE 22-CM/9-IN CAKE

2 Tbsp toasted breadcrumbs	250 g/8 oz ground almonds
3 small stale bread rolls	½ tsp ground cinnamon
150 ml/5 fl oz milk	1 kg/2 lb fresh cherries, washed and dried
150 ml/5 fl oz water	
120 g/4 oz butter, melted and cooled	Pinch of salt
200 g/7 oz caster sugar	Icing sugar to dust
4 eggs, separated	Whipped cream to serve (optional)

Pre-heat the oven to 350°F/175°C/Gas 4. Grease a 22-cm/9-in spring-release tin.

Butter well and coat with 2 tablespoonfuls toasted breadcrumbs.

Break the bread rolls into pieces and place them in a bowl. Heat the milk with the water and pour the liquid over the rolls. Leave to soak for about 15 minutes.

Pour the melted butter into a mixing bowl, leaving the sediment behind, mix in the sugar and egg yolks and beat until the mixture is pale and creamy. Beat in the almonds and cinnamon.

Drain the bread rolls, squeezing out any excess moisture by hand. Break them up small with a fork or blend in a food processor bowl for a few seconds. Beat the paste into the main mixture. Stir in the cherries.

Whip the egg whites with the salt in a clean bowl until they hold firm, snowy peaks. Using a large metal spoon, lightly fold the egg snow into the cherry mixture. Pour the mixture into the prepared cake tin. Bake until golden, 1 to 1¼ hours.

The cake may be eaten warm or cold. Dust with icing sugar and serve with whipped cream. It also freezes very well for up to 2 months.

Babka

This is a sponge cake with dried fruit and candied peel.

MAKES 8 TO 10 SLICES

60 g/2 oz butter	175 g/6 oz plain flour
175 g/6 oz icing sugar, sifted	I tsp baking powder
I tsp vanilla essence	60 g/2 oz seedless raisins
3 eggs, separated	3 Tbsp candied peel
60 ml/2 fl oz milk	Icing sugar to dust

Grease a 20 × 13-cm/8 × 5-in loaf tin and line with baking parchment. Set the oven at 350°F/175°C/Gas 4.

Beat the butter in a bowl until very soft, then gradually beat in the icing sugar. Stir in the vanilla and egg yolks, one by one. Slowly add the milk, mixing in the occasional small spoonful of flour to prevent the mixture from curdling. Sift the remaining flour with the baking powder and stir it into the mixture. Stir in the raisins and candied peel.

Whisk the egg whites until stiff and use a metal spoon fold them in, taking care not to knock out the air. Turn the mixture into the tin and spread it with the back of a metal spoon, hollowing out the middle slightly.

Bake for 40 to 45 minutes, until risen and golden. Turn the babka to cool on a wire rack. Dust with icing sugar while still warm.

Wholemeal Courgette and Raisin Cake

This cake was inspired by a conventional passion cake made with carrots, but is much more moist. It is excellent eaten plain, but may be spread with butter cream icing or cream cheese frosting.

MAKES ONE 22-CM/9-IN CAKE

200 g/7 oz wholemeal flour	250 g/8 oz grated courgettes
I tsp bicarbonate of soda	200 g/7 oz crushed pineapple, drained
2 tsp baking powder	
I tsp salt	50 g/2 oz grated carrot
I tsp ground ginger	150 ml/5 fl oz plain yoghurt
250 g/8 oz soft brown sugar	3 large eggs, beaten
120 g/4 oz raisins or sultanas	150 ml/2 fl oz corn oil

Pre-heat the oven to 350°F/175C/Gas 4, and line a 22-cm/9-in round cake tin with baking parchment.

Place the flour, bicarbonate, baking powder, ginger, sugar and raisins in a bowl then mix in the courgettes, pineapple and carrot. Add the yoghurt with the eggs, then finally add the oil. Mix to a thick batter then beat vigorously for I minute.

Pour the mixture into the prepared tin, then bake for I hour, until a skewer inserted into the centre comes out clean. Cool slightly, then turn out on to a wire rack and leave until completely cold.

Pumpkin, Sunflower Seed and Raisin Cake

A moist autumn fruit cake using the seasonal orange pumpkin and nutritious sunflower seeds.

MAKES ONE 20-CM/8-IN CAKE

250 g/8 oz wholemeal flour	2 eggs
Pinch of salt	2 Tbsp honey
2 tsp baking powder	2 Tbsp molasses
1 tsp bicarbonate of soda	1 Tbsp warm water
25 g/1 oz sunflower seeds, chopped	250 g/8 oz cooked pumpkin, finely chopped
25 g/1 oz raisins	

Pre-heat the oven to 375°F/190°C/Gas 5. Grease and flour a 20-cm/8-in spring-release cake tin and base-line with baking parchment.

Combine flour, salt, baking powder, sunflower seeds and raisins in a bowl and mix well.

In another bowl, beat the eggs and stir in the honey and molasses. Add 1 tablespoon of warm water with the pumpkin and beat well.

Mix all the ingredients together thoroughly and pour into the tin. Bake for 50 to 60 minutes until cooked through. Leave to stand for 10 minutes in the tin, then cool.

Gypsy Cake

This cake is based on a traditional Polish recipe. It is good just as it is but it is also very tempting when sandwiched with plum jam.

MAKES ABOUT 10 SLICES

6 eggs, separated	25 g/1 oz chopped dried figs
120 g/4 oz caster sugar	25 g/1 oz cooking dates, chopped if necessary
1 tsp vanilla essence	3 Tbsp chopped mixed peel
120 g/4 oz plain flour	Icing sugar to dust
1 tsp baking powder	
25 g/1 oz raisins	

Line and grease a 27 x 18-cm/11 x 7-in tin (a shallow tin is fine, in which case the baking parchment should stand well above the rim). Pre-heat the oven to 400°F/200°C/Gas 6.

Beat the egg yolks and sugar in a bowl until pale and thick. Lightly stir in the vanilla essence, then fold in the flour and baking powder. Stir in all the fruit. Whisk the egg whites until stiff and stir a couple of spoonfuls into the mixture to lighten it, then fold in the remainder. This is not easy as the mixture is fairly stiff but try not to over-stir while mixing in the whites. Turn the mixture into the tin and spread out.

Bake for about 20 minutes, or until risen, golden and firm to the touch. Cool on a wire rack. Dust with icing sugar before serving, cut into oblong pieces.

Pineapple Fruit Cake

This everyday fruit cake, made with an interesting selection of dried fruit, would make an excellent Christmas cake for those who are not fond of rich, dark fruit cakes.

MAKES ONE 18-CM/7-IN CAKE

150 g/5 oz mixed dried fruit (pineapple, seedless raisins, cranberries, etc.)

120 ml/4 fl oz pineapple juice

200 g/7 oz margarine or butter

250 g/8 oz wholemeal flour

2 tsp baking powder

Pinch of salt

1 tsp ground ginger

120 g/4 oz light brown sugar

2 large eggs, beaten

Soak the dried fruit in the pineapple juice for 10 minutes. Pre-heat the oven to 350°F/175°C/Gas 4 and lightly grease an 18-cm/7-in deep, round cake tin.

Blend the butter into the flour, baking powder, salt and ginger in a bowl until the mixture resembles fine crumbs. Stir in the sugar, then add the fruit and juice and the beaten eggs. Mix to a soft dropping consistency, adding a little extra pineapple juice or milk as required, then spoon the mixture into the prepared tin and smooth the top.

Bake for 35 to 40 minutes or until a skewer inserted into the centre comes out clean.

Cool briefly in the tin then turn out on to a wire rack to cool completely.

Barm Brack

Barm brack means speckled bread, referring to the fruit in the mixture. This is a traditional Irish cake.

MAKES ONE 20-CM/8-IN CAKE

375 g/12 oz plain flour

Grated nutmeg

Pinch of salt

50 g/2 oz butter

20 g/¾ oz yeast

2 Tbsp sugar

300 ml/10 fl oz milk

2 eggs, beaten

200 g/7 oz sultanas

200 g/7 oz currants

150 g/5 oz candied peel

Pre-heat the oven to 400°F/200°C/Gas 6. Sift the flour, nutmeg and salt together. Cut the butter into the flour.

Cream the yeast in a cup with 1 tsp of the sugar. Add the rest of the sugar to the flour mixture and combine well. Scald the milk; add to the liquid yeast together with all but a little of the well-beaten eggs. Stir into the dry ingredients to produce a stiff but elastic mixture. Then carefully fold in the fruit.

Butter a 20-cm/8-in round cake tin and pour in the dough. It should come halfway up the tin. Cover with a clean cloth and leave in a warm place to rise – it should double in size in about 1 hour.

Brush the top of the brack with beaten egg to glaze. Bake until a skewer inserted into the centre comes out clean, about 1 hour.

Irish Tea Brack

Two Irish fruit cakes in which the fruit is first soaked in alcohol overnight. This gives the cake a succulent moistness and a richness of flavour.

MAKES ONE LOAF CAKE

500 g/1 lb sultanas	375 g/12 oz plain flour, sifted
500 g/1 lb raisins	3 eggs, beaten
500 g/1 lb brown sugar	1 Tbsp baking powder
500 ml/1 pt black tea	2 tsp ground mixed spice
500 ml/1 pt Irish whiskey	

Soak the fruit with the sugar in the tea and whiskey overnight.

Pre-heat the oven to 375°F/190°C/Gas 5. Grease a 22 x 13-cm/9 x 5-in loaf tin or a 20-cm/8-in cake tin and base-line with baking parchment.

Add the flour, eggs, baking powder and mixed spice to the fruit mixture.

Mix all the ingredients together well and put into the prepared tin.

Bake for 1 hour. Leave to cool in the tin slightly before turning out to cool fully on a rack.

Guinness Cake

The dark Irish brew gives this delicious cake its richness of flavour.

MAKES ONE 20-CM/8-IN CAKE

120 g/4 oz raisins, soaked in Guinness overnight	3 eggs, beaten
50 g/2 oz candied peel, soaked	250 g/8 oz self-raising flour
	Pinch of salt
200 g/7 oz sultanas	½ tsp ground mixed spice
120 g/4 oz butter	50 g/2 oz glacé cherries
250 g/8 oz brown sugar	150 ml/5 fl oz Guinness

Soak the raisins and peel in Guinness overnight.

Pre-heat the oven to 350°F/175°C/Gas 4. Grease a deep 20-cm/8-in cake tin and base-line with baking parchment. Soak the sultanas in water until plump. Drain.

Cream the butter and sugar. Beat in the eggs. Add the flour, salt, mixed spice, glacé cherries and the raisins and peel. Mix in the Guinness.

Pour the mixture into the tin. Bake for about 2 hours until firm in the centre.

Irish Tea Brack ▶

CAKES 171

Special Occasion Cakes

Chocolate and Whiskey Cake

Irish Coffee Cake

Mocha Gâteau

Black Forest Gâteau

Drum Cake

Orange Mousseline Gâteau

Torta Sorentina (Easter Cake)

Sachertorte

Bouquet Cake

Star Cake

Chocolate and Whiskey Cake

This no-cook recipe is from Marlfield House Restaurant in Co. Wexford, Ireland.

MAKES ONE 22-CM/9-IN CAKE

250 g/8 oz digestive biscuits	6 Tbsp sugar
250 g/8 oz plain cooking chocolate	50 g/2 oz glacé cherries
	50 g/2 oz walnuts
250 g/8 oz butter	150 ml/5 fl oz Irish whiskey
2 eggs	90 ml/3 fl oz double cream, whipped

Crush the biscuits coarsely and set aside.

Melt the chocolate with the butter in a double boiler or saucepan. Cream the eggs and sugar in a bowl until they are pale and thickened, then fold in the chocolate.

To this mixture add three-quarters of the cherries and the walnuts; save the rest for decoration. Fold in all but 1 tablespoon of whiskey.

Oil a 22-cm/9-in baking tin, line with the crushed biscuits, then scrape all of the mixture into it. Decorate the top with the remaining cherries and walnuts and place in the refrigerator for several hours or overnight. Take it out of the refrigerator about 30 minutes before serving.

Add the whiskey to the cream. Pipe around the top of the cake and serve.

Irish Coffee Cake

A sophisticated adult cake. Great for a whiskey lover's birthday treat.

MAKES ONE 20-CM/8-IN CAKE

120 g/4 oz butter	**FOR THE SYRUP**
120 g/4 oz caster sugar	150 ml/5 fl oz black coffee
2 eggs	50 g/2 oz caster sugar
120 g/4 oz self-raising flour	1 Tbsp Irish whiskey
2 Tbsp black coffee	
	DECORATION
	300 ml/10 fl oz double cream
	1 Tbsp black coffee or black coffee and whiskey
	175 g/6 oz icing sugar

Pre-heat the oven to 325°F/160°C/Gas 3. Grease two 20-cm/8-in spring-release cake tins.

Cream the butter and sugar until light and fluffy. Add the eggs, one at a time, adding a little of the flour after each egg. Beat in the coffee then fold in the rest of the flour.

Divide the mixture in half and place in the two cake tins and bake for about 40 minutes.

To make the syrup, heat the coffee with the sugar until it melts, then add the whiskey. When the cake is almost cool, prick the underside with a fork and drizzle the syrup all over the cake. Fill the middle with whipped cream and whiskey.

Make a glacé icing by adding a few drops of coffee to the sifted icing sugar, then beating with a wooden spoon until it becomes glossy and can spread easily with a palette knife. Spread the icing over the top of the cake.

Mocha Gâteau

This gâteau is prepared a day in advance to allow the flavours to mature.

MAKES ONE 20-CM/8-IN CAKE

1 portion génoese sponge mixture (see page 112)

1 Tbsp instant coffee powder dissolved in ½ tsp boiling water

FILLING AND TOPPING

300 g/10 oz icing sugar, sifted

3 Tbsp unsweetened cocoa powder, sifted

200 g/7 oz butter

1 Tbsp strong black coffee

1 cup toasted slivered almonds

Chocolate coffee beans

Pre-heat the oven to 350°F/175°C/Gas 4. Grease and base-line a 20-cm/8-in spring-release tin.

Prepare the génoese sponge, but mix the coffee liquid into the egg yolk and sugar mixture. Pour into the prepared tin and bake until risen and golden. Cool on a wire rack.

Make the mocha butter cream icing. Combine the sifted icing sugar with the cocoa powder. Beat the butter with an electric mixer until light and fluffy. Beat in the sugar, cocoa powder and coffee.

Split the cake into three layers. Reserve about half the icing and sandwich the three cake layers together with the remainder. Fit a piping bag with a small star nozzle and fill with icing. Smooth the remainder of the icing over the top and sides of the cake and press the slivered almonds into the sides. Pipe small mocha butter cream icing stars close together in symmetrical lines. Decorate with chocolate coffee beans. Chill for a day before serving.

Black Forest Gâteau

There is still no traditional recipe for Black Forest Gâteau. It may be made with layers of plain chocolate sponge with or without butter and including nuts, but common to all are cherries, chocolate, cream and kirsch, and this tempting combination entices so many people that it is probably one of the youngest and most popular traditional cakes in the world.

MAKES ONE DEEP 20-CM/8-IN CAKE

150 g/5 oz unblanched almonds, coarsely ground

120 g/4 oz toasted breadcrumbs

1 tsp ground cinnamon

1 tsp ground cloves

2 Tbsp kirsch

120 g/4 oz caster sugar

9 egg yolks

2 tsp grated orange rind

120 g/4 oz plain chocolate, melted and cooled

6 egg whites

FILLING

1 kg/2 lb morello cherries, washed and stoned or 500 g/1 lb tinned, stoned morello cherries

250 ml/8 fl oz red wine

250 ml/8 fl oz water

250 g/8 oz granulated sugar

Cinnamon stick

2 tsp grated orange rind

150 ml/5 fl oz kirsch

500 ml/1 pt double or whipping cream

3 Tbsp caster sugar

50 g/2 oz grated chocolate and chocolate curls for decoration

Pre-heat the oven to 350°F/175°C/Gas 4. Prepare two 20–22-cm/8–9-in spring-release tins: butter, line the base with baking parchment, butter again, dredge with sugar and flour.

Mix together the almonds, breadcrumbs, cinnamon and cloves and moisten with kirsch.

In a separate bowl beat the sugar and egg yolks until thick, pale and creamy. Mix in the orange rind and chocolate. Lightly combine with the first mixture. Whisk the egg whites separately until they hold firm peaks. Lightly and quickly fold them into the main mixture until just combined.

Divide the mixture equally between the two tins. Smooth the top and tap each tin once to disperse any air pockets. Bake for 30 minutes until well risen and slightly shrinking away from the sides of the tin. Cool on wire racks.

To cook the fresh cherries for the filling, combine the wine, water and sugar in a tin and heat gently until the sugar has dissolved. Add the cinnamon stick and orange rind, and simmer for about 20 minutes. Drop in the cleaned fruit and poach lightly for 10 minutes. Lift the fruit carefully out of the syrup and drain. Boil the syrup over high heat for two minutes to reduce and thicken it slightly. Cool.

Mix 90 ml/3 fl oz of cherry syrup with 120 ml/4 fl oz kirsch. Dry the cherries with kitchen paper. Whisk the cream until softly peaked and beat in the sugar until firm; fold in the remaining kirsch. Cut both chocolate sponges across the middle. Reserve 3 to 4 tablespoonfuls cream and a few cherries for decoration.

Place a sponge base on a serving plate and sprinkle over about one-third of the kirsch syrup. Smooth over a quarter of the cream and press in half the cherries. Cover with a second sponge, sprinkle with more syrup, a layer of cream and the rest of the fruit. Place the third sponge on top, sprinkle with the remaining syrup and a layer of whipped cream. Cover with the last sponge layer and coat the top and sides of the whole cake with the rest of the cream. Dust the cake sides with chocolate.

Pipe the reserved cream in large rosettes on the cake surface and dot with cherries. Place a few chocolate curls in the middle to finish. Chill for 3 to 4 hours. Just before serving dredge a little icing sugar over the chocolate curls.

Drum Cake

The caramel can be poured on to greaseproof paper and cut into triangles. They are then embedded in the chocolate filling, slightly at an angle to create a fan effect.

MAKES ONE 22-CM/9-IN CAKE

SPONGE	CHOCOLATE FILLING
6 egg yolks	50 g/2 oz cornflour
250 g/8 oz caster sugar	375 ml/12 fl oz milk
1 tsp grated orange rind	50 g/2 oz sugar
50 g/2 oz plain flour	1 egg yolk, beaten
50 g/2 oz potato flour	250 g/8 oz butter
6 egg whites	120 g/4 oz mini marshmallows
	50 g/2 oz plain chocolate
	CARAMEL GLAZE
	175 g/6 oz granulated sugar

Pre-heat the oven to 350°F/175°C/Gas 4. Grease and flour a 22-cm/9-in spring-release tin.

Beat the egg yolks and sugar until pale and creamy. Mix in the orange rind. Sift together both the flours to aerate well and add to the egg yolks. Whisk the egg whites in a separate bowl until they are firm and well-peaked. Fold the egg whites into the yolk mixture as lightly and quickly as you can.

This quantity makes six layers. Spread a thin coating of mixture in the bottom of the tin and smooth carefully. Bake immediately for 5 to 8 minutes. (Bake two layers at a time if you have the tins.) When it is coloured light gold, remove the cake from the oven and turn out of the tin straight onto a wire rack to cool. Make the remaining layers in the same way.

Assemble the cake as soon as the layers have cooled so that they do not dry out and become crisp.

Make the chocolate filling by mixing a little cornflour with milk. Heat the rest of the milk with the sugar, add the cornflour mixture and bring to the boil stirring until thickened. Quickly stir in the egg yolk. Cool. Beat the butter until soft then beat into the cooled custard. Melt the marshmallows and chocolate over a double boiler and beat into the custard. Place in the refrigerator until firm enough to spread.

Set aside the best-looking cake layer and sandwich the rest together with chocolate filling, spreading it over the top and the sides.

Prepare the top layer. Brush any loose crumbs off the cake and lay it on a large sheet of greaseproof paper. Then take two long knives and lightly grease the blade of one with oil or butter.

Make the caramel glaze by gently heating half of the granulated sugar until golden, then add the rest of the sugar and cook until it has thickened. Quickly pour the caramel straight over the cake layer and smooth it out using the clean knife. Using the greased knife, immediately mark the cake out into 10 sections and cut through the sugar glaze. Leave to cool. Lay the caramel top on top of the filled cake layers.

Do not store in the refrigerator as this spoils the caramel surface.

Torta Sorentina (Easter Cake)

The sparkling lemon flavour balances the richness in this Italian cake.

MAKES ONE RING CAKE

250 g/8 oz unsalted butter	90 g/3 oz unsalted butter
4 large eggs	Grated rind of ½ lemon
250 g/8 oz sugar	
300 g/10 oz self-raising flour	**ICING**
Grated rind of ½ lemon	6 squares plain chocolate
	2 Tbsp cream
LEMON FILLING	2 Tbsp butter
1 egg white	Crystallized lemon slices
120 g/4 oz icing sugar	

Pre-heat the oven to 350°F/175°C/Gas 4. Grease and flour a ring tin.

Melt the butter and leave to cool. Put eggs and sugar into a bowl over a pan of hot water and whisk until they are pale and thick and leave a trail. Gently fold in the flour, rind and butter. Do not over-mix.

Pour the mixture into the prepared tin. Bake for 30 to 40 minutes. Cool slightly, then turn out on to a wire rack.

To make the filling, put the egg white and icing sugar into a bowl over a pan of hot water and whisk until a meringue is formed. Remove from the heat and whisk until cool.

Beat the butter until light and fluffy. Beat in the meringue a little at a time. Add the lemon rind.

Split the cake into three layers. Spread the lemon filling between the layers. Chill.

Put the chocolate and cream in a bowl over a pan of hot water. When melted, stir in the butter. Remove from the heat and mix until smooth.

Coat the cake with the icing. Decorate with crystallized lemon slices. Allow the icing to set.

Sachertorte

This classic cake is usually undecorated, but here chocolate leaves and flakes add interest. To make chocolate leaves, gently melt the chocolate, then brush clean, freshly picked leaves through it. Peel off the leaf when the chocolate has cooled and set.

MAKES ONE 22-CM/9-IN CAKE

120 g/4 oz butter	2 drops almond essence
120 g/4 oz caster sugar	120 g/4 oz plain flour, sifted
4 egg yolks	3 egg whites
175 g/6 oz plain chocolate, melted and cooled	Apricot jam
1 Tbsp vanilla sugar	250 g/8 oz plain chocolate

Pre-heat the oven to 325°F/160°C/Gas 3. Grease a 22-cm/9-in spring-release tin.

Beat the butter with the sugar until pale and fluffy. Beat in the egg yolks, one at a time, and the cooled chocolate. Beat in the vanilla sugar and almond essence and continue beating for 15 minutes by electric mixer (25 minutes by hand).

Sift the flour over the mixture and quickly but lightly blend it in without over-beating. Whisk the egg whites until they stand in stiff peaks and then carefully fold them into the mixture.

Pour the batter into the prepared tin – the mixture should be no more than 3 cm/1¼ in deep. Bake for about 1 hour until slightly shrinking from the sides of the tin. Cool on a wire rack.

Brush the cake with sieved apricot jam. Melt the chocolate over a double boiler and spread over the cake. Alternatively, a rich chocolate icing may be used.

CELEBRATION CAKES

There are times when a special cake is called for, such as weddings, anniversaries, special birthdays and Christmas. On these occasions it is traditional to serve a rich fruit cake commonly decorated with marzipan and royal icing. However, some people prefer a sponge cake base which is more simply decorated with butter cream icing. For these cakes, it doesn't matter how good the cake is underneath the icing, it is the decoration that is on show.

If you are not artistic, then it is best to keep the decoration simple. Mastering a couple of basic shapes with a piping bag is not very difficult although it does require a bit of practice before you get started. Visit a specialist cake shop which will stock a good range of cutters, ribbons, sugar flowers and pre-tinted icing. You will get a lot of ideas to help you cheat and might even become inspired.

The instructions here are for a simple celebration cake suitable for a birthday, anniversary, or even wedding, but the basic idea can be adapted for other occasions. We have used pansies in pink, lilac and purple, but choose your colour scheme according to the sugar flowers you have available.

For a Christmas cake, replace the bouquet with a cut-out angel made from white icing and placed in the middle of the cake. Then, make a small star from yellow icing and a tiny halo. Replace the angel with other shapes such as a Santa, animals or flowers or even a halloween witch. These figures may look even more effective if simply painted with food colouring and placed on appropriate tinted backgrounds. If the cake is for a man, how about placing a few special chocolates on top or carefully modelling the shape of a beer bottle from brown icing and laying this on the cake top. Cake shops will also have model figures that are useful for christenings and weddings and other ornaments suitable for Christmas and birthday cakes – once you get started you will be spoilt for choice.

Using a Piping Nozzle

Royal icing needs to be a little thicker than smooth icing so beat it for a little longer to thicken. If piping butter cream icing, add a little more icing sugar. Before working on the cake itself, practice with a variety of tips. Try drawing straight and wavy lines with the writing tip, stars, flower petals and chains with the star tip and shells and scroll borders with the shell tip. While piping, keep the unused icing covered with a damp cloth to prevent it from drying out.

Try drawing straight and wavy lines with the writing tip, stars, flower petals and chains with the star nozzle and shells and scroll borders with the shell nozzle.

Rough Icing

This method is particularly attractive on a Christmas cake. Simply smooth the icing over the cake and work it roughly with a knife.

Smooth the icing over the cake.

Work icing roughly with a knife.

Bouquet Cake

The perfect way to celebrate something special. This cake says "congratulations," but you can vary the words to suit the occasion.

MAKES ONE 20-CM/8-IN CAKE

One 20-cm/8-in rich fruit cake (see page 109)

900 g/1¾ lb marzipan

5-egg quantity royal icing

Lemon dusting powder

Lilac food colouring

Coloured ribbon 3 mm/⅛ in thick in three toning colours

Sugar flowers to decorate

APRICOT GLAZE

250 ml/8 fl oz apricot jam

2 Tbsp water

To marzipan the cake, cut the top off if domed, then turn upside-down to create a flat surface to work with. If the sides do not sit flat on the board, fill any hollows with marzipan to create a smooth finish on all sides.

Make the glaze by melting jam and water in a tin. Rub through a sieve. Brush over the cake.

Measure cake with thread, up one side, across the top and down the other, then roll marzipan about ½ cm/¼ in thick. Drape marzipan over a rolling pin and lay over cake. Smooth out marzipan from centre of cake with hands dusted with icing sugar. Trim around the base. Allow to dry for at least 24 hours and up to 2 weeks before icing.

Make royal icing to soft peak consistency. Spoon over the cake and spread to an even depth of ½ cm/¼ in. Remove excess icing from top edges. The top can be smoothed by dragging a ruler across the surface in one movement. Trim excess from top edges to neaten. To smooth the sides, hold a palette knife vertically against the icing and rotate the cake keeping knife on board to keep sides straight. Repeat until you are happy with the appearance. Allow to dry for 24 hours before decorating.

Make 1-egg white quantity of royal icing to hard peak stage. Tint to a pale lilac colour with food colouring. Fit a small paper cone or a piping bag with a shell-shaped nozzle. Practice on the work surface, then pipe shells all round base of cake. Pipe rows of stars around top of cake. Link with draped lines piped in white. Wrap three bands of lemon- and/or lilac-coloured ribbon around the cake. Write "congratulations" on a piece of card. Lay a sheet of greaseproof paper over the top and pipe letters over the top using a broad writing nozzle. Leave to dry.

Carefully peel off the paper and fix message to cake with a little icing If writing proves too tricky, then purchase message from a cake decorating shop. Purchase yellow and lilac pansies or similar flowers wired on to stalks and tie together in a bouquet with a little ribbon. Lay these on top of the cake.

CHILDREN'S BIRTHDAY CAKES

*A*s *with celebration cakes, children's birthday cakes are as much about the decoration as the cake. Children often challenge parents to make cakes that reflect their latest craze. If they are very fond of a pet, for instance, then it is appropriate to make a cat or rabbit shape out of a 32 x 22 x 5-cm/13 x 9 x 2-in sponge cake and ice with chocolate icing or a paler butter cream icing to match the animal's colouring. Simply draw the shape of the pet on paper, cut out and place on the cake as a template. Cover with icing and use sweets for the eyes and nose and strings of liquorice for the whiskers. Butterflies work well too. Cut out the shape of the butterfly, cover with coloured icing and decorate with sweets.*

Football, soccer and baseball pitches provide another easy option. Use green-tinted icing and coconut to form the pitches and pipe on the line markings with white or coloured icing. Cake decorating shops often carry small figures and balls for decoration, or use characters from children's toys. Similarly, a swimming pool can be made by colouring bought ready-to-roll icing pale blue and draping it over the cake. Miniature dolls and accessories to finish the cake can be found in toy shops. Specialist stores carry a large selection of ribbons, some of which reflect the latest children's crazes.

Using a shaped cake tin is a great way to create excellent birthday cakes. Number cake tins can be purchased or hired and a star or heart shape is always effective. Draped with icing or iced with the child's favourite icing, they can easily be decorated using sweets, or miniature toys. If all else fails, a simple round cake with a tasty icing, generously decorated with sweets will be sure to please.

Star Cake

No child could fail to be thrilled with this fun-shaped, colourful cake.

MAKES ONE 22-CM/9-IN CAKE

One 22-cm/9-in chocolate or sponge star cake	**I-egg quantity royal icing or ½ quantity butter cream icing**
4 Tbsp apricot glaze	
900 g/1¾ lb bought ready-to-roll white icing	**Moon- and star-shaped biscuit cutters**
Orange food colouring	**Egg white**
30-cm/12-in cake board	**Candles**
Icing sugar	**Candle holders**

Brush the cake with warmed apricot glaze. Knead icing until soft, then shape into a flattened ball. Leave white or drop several small drops of food colouring on to it and knead until the colouring is streaked throughout the icing. Do not over-knead.

Place the cake on the board. Dust a work surface with sugar. Roll out the icinge until it is about 7 cm/3 in larger than the cake and, using a rolling pin to support its weight, transfer to the cake. Smooth the icing over cake, then flare out the corners of the star and mould into shape. It is easiest to use the soft part of the palm to gently work the surplus icing into place. Trim around base of cake with a knife.

Colour some of the butter cream icing bright orange. Pipe stars around base and top edge of cake. Colour some surplus icing in solid orange. Cut out star and moon shapes and attach to the sides of cake with egg white. Cut a large star shape and, using white icing, pipe the child's name across the centre using a writing nozzle. Decorate the outer rim of the star shape with dots of icing, using writing nozzle. Attach to the top of the cake with egg white. Insert candles.

Small Cakes

Butterfly Cakes

Iced Mazurek

Mazurek

Almond Cakes

Rocky Mountain Buns

Chocolate Orange Cakes

Eliza Leslie's Ginger Cup Cakes

Chocolate Meringues

Butterfly Cakes

These little cakes are particularly popular with children.

MAKES 14 TO 16

120 g/4 oz butter or margarine

120 g/4 oz sugar

2 eggs

1 tsp grated orange rind

120 g/4 oz plain chocolate, finely grated

150 g/5 oz self-raising flour

FROSTING

120 g/4 oz butter or margarine

200 g/7 oz icing sugar, sifted

90 g/3 oz plain chocolate, melted

DECORATION

Icing sugar

Seedless raspberry jam or glacé cherries

Pre-heat the oven to 350°F/175°C/Gas 4.

Put the butter and sugar into a bowl and cream until light and fluffy. Beat in the eggs a little at a time. Stir in the orange rind and chocolate. Then fold in the flour.

Arrange cake papers in bun tins. Divide the mixture between the cases. Bake for about 15 to 20 minutes. Cool.

To make the icing, beat together the butter and icing sugar. Then gradually beat in the cooled, melted chocolate.

Starting ½ cm/¼ in in from the edge, remove the top of each cake by cutting in and slightly down to form a cavity. Pipe a little icing in the cavity of each cake.

Sprinkle the reserved cake tops with icing sugar and cut each one in half. Place each half, cut-side outwards, on to the icing to form wings. Pipe small rosettes of icing in the centre of each cake. Top with a small blob of raspberry jam or half a glacé cherry.

Iced Mazurek

Plain mazurek is a type of shortcake, which may be frosted according to taste. It is usually cut into fingers and is traditionally served at Easter.

MAKES 16

250 g/8 oz plain flour

2 tsp baking powder

120 g/4 oz butter

200 g/4 oz icing sugar, sifted

2 egg yolks

DECORATION

Seven-minute frosting (see page 114)

Crystallized orange peel, cut into strips

50 g/2 oz glacé cherries, quartered

About 2 Tbsp slivered almonds, toasted

Sift the flour and baking powder into a bowl. Blend in the butter and mix in the icing sugar. Mix in the egg yolks to make a soft dough. Wrap in clingfilm and chill for 5 minutes. Meanwhile, base-line and grease a 20-cm/8-in square cake tin. Pre-heat the oven to 350°F/175°C/Gas 4.

On a floured surface, roll out the dough into a square. Put it into the tin and press out with your fingers to cover the base of the tin. Make sure the top is smooth and the dough evenly thick.

Bake for about 35 to 40 minutes, until golden and firm. Turn out to cool on a wire rack. Coat with icing and decorate when cool. Cut into fingers to serve.

Mazurek

This improves with keeping for a couple of days before topping with chocolate and eating. The redcurrant jelly together with chocolate make a divinely complementary combination.

MAKES ABOUT 22

8 eggs, separated

120 g/4 oz caster sugar

60 g/2 oz plain flour

250 g/8 oz plain chocolate chips

250 g/8 oz ground almonds

DECORATION

175 g/6 oz redcurrant jelly

90 g/3 oz plain chocolate chips

60 g/2 oz unsalted butter

Line and grease a 27 x 18-cm/11 x 7-in tin (a shallow tin is fine, in which case the baking parchment should stand well above the rim). Preheat the oven to 400°F/200°C/Gas 6.

Beat the egg yolks and sugar in a bowl until pale and thick. Lightly fold in the flour. Whisk the egg whites until stiff and fold them into the mixture. Lightly stir in the chocolate and almonds. Turn the mixture into the tin and spread it out evenly.

Bake for 20 to 25 minutes, until firm and lightly browned. Cool the mazurek in the pan for 5 minutes, then turn out on to a wire rack to cool completely.

For the decoration, warm the redcurrant jelly in a bowl over hot water and spread it all over the mazurek. Leave to set completely, then chill for 30 minutes. Melt the chocolate and butter in a bowl over hot water. Leave to cool but do not allow the mixture to thicken. Pour the chocolate all over the mazurek and spread it evenly. Leave to set before cutting into fingers.

Iced Mazurek ▶

Almond Cakes

Easy to make, these little cakes, with their delicate almond flavour, are a mouthwatering treat. For a special occasion, soak the cakes in sherry or freshly squeezed orange juice with a little rum added, then top with whipped cream.

MAKES 16 TO 20

150 g/5 oz flaked almonds

Butter for greasing

2 eggs

3 cups sugar

150 g/5 oz plain flour

120 g/4 oz butter, melted

Pre-heat the oven to 400°F/200°C/Gas 6. Toast the flaked almonds lightly, then crumble or chop finely. Leave to cool. Carefully grease 16 to 20 small cake moulds or patty tin with soft butter, and scatter them with the chopped almonds.

Whisk the eggs until frothy, add the sugar and whisk to a fluffy mixture. Mix in the flour and the cooled butter. Stir gently to prevent the mixture collapsing. Divide the mixture between the moulds and place on a baking sheet. Bake for 15 minutes. Turn out and leave to cool under the upturned moulds.

Rocky Mountain Buns

There is a hint of coffee in these fun-to-eat small buns. The marshmallows and raisins give them a "rocky", uneven appearance.

MAKES 12

300 g/10 oz self-raising flour

½ tsp salt

60 g/2 oz polyunsaturated margarine

2 Tbsp caster sugar

3 Tbsp sultanas

60 g/ 2 oz mini marshmallows

150 ml/5 fl oz skimmed milk

1 Tbsp coffee essence

Icing sugar to dust

Pre-heat the oven to 425°F/220°C/Gas 7.

Sift the flour and salt into a bowl. Blend in the margarine until the mixture resembles breadcrumbs. Stir in the sugar, sultanas and marshmallows.

Mix together the milk and coffee essence and stir into the mixture to form a soft dough. Place 12 equal-sized spoonfuls of mixture on a non-stick baking sheet, spacing slightly apart.

Bake for 20 minutes until risen and golden. Cool on a wire rack, dust with icing sugar and serve.

Chocolate Orange Cakes

A delicious combination of chocolate and marmalade.

MAKES 18

2 eggs

60 g/2 oz sugar

150 g/5 oz self-raising flour, sifted

Approx 4 Tbsp marmalade, sieved

120 g/4 oz plain chocolate

Grated rind of ¼ orange

2 tsp corn oil

1 Tbsp water

Pre-heat the oven to 400°F/200°C/Gas 6. Thoroughly grease about 1½ bun tins.

Put the eggs and sugar into a bowl. Whisk until thick and creamy so that when the whisk is lifted the mixture leaves a trail. If using a hand whisk put the bowl over a pan of hot water. With a metal spoon, fold in the flour.

Spoon the mixture into the bun tins. Bake for about 10 minutes until golden brown.

Remove and cool on a wire rack.

Spread a little marmalade over each cake.

Put the chocolate, orange rind, oil and water into a bowl over a pan of hot water. Stir well until melted. Cool until the chocolate starts to thicken and then spoon over the marmalade. Leave to set.

Eliza Leslie's Ginger Cup Cakes

This is a modern interpretation of an old American recipe in Eliza Leslie's *Seventy-Five Receipts for Pastry, cakes and sweetmeats. By a lady of Philadelphia*, published in 1828.

MAKES 28

120 g/4 oz butter	1 tsp ground cloves
120 g/4 oz light muscovado or brown sugar	2 tsp ground ginger
175 ml/6 fl oz molasses	1 egg
250 g/8 oz plain flour	1 egg yolk
1 tsp bicarbonate of soda	4 Tbsp milk
½ tsp ground allspice	

Pre-heat the oven to 325°F/160°C/Gas 3. Gently heat the butter, sugar and molasses in a pan until the butter has melted and the sugar dissolved. (Do not boil or the cakes will be hard.) Remove from the heat to cool. Sift together two or three times the flour, bicarbonate, allspice, cloves and ginger, and finally into a large bowl. Make a well in the centre.

Whisk the egg and egg yolk with about half the milk and pour the mixture into the flour with the cooled syrup. Beat to a smooth batter, adding more milk if necessary.

Use paper cases and fill each no more than half full with the mixture, which rises a lot during baking. Bake for about 30 minutes until well risen. The cakes should feel slightly soft to the touch. Leave to cool on wire racks.

Chocolate Meringues

A delicious treat for chocoholics.

MAKES 6 TO 8

	FILLING
3 egg whites	
90 g/3 oz caster sugar	150 ml/5 fl oz double cream
175 g/6 oz icing sugar, sifted	1 Tbsp brown sugar
60 g/2 oz unsweetened cocoa powder, sifted	2 tsp unsweetened cocoa powder

Pre-heat the oven to 225°F/110°C/Gas ¼. Beat the egg whites until they form stiff peaks. Gradually whisk in the caster sugar, a little at a time. Whisk in the icing sugar. Fold in the cocoa powder.

Put the mixture into a piping bag fitted with a large star nozzle. Line baking trays with baking parchment. Pipe the mixture into spirals.

Bake for 2 to 3 hours or until the meringues are dry. Cool on a wire rack.

Whip the cream until stiff. Stir in the sugar and cocoa. Sandwich the meringues together, two at a time, with the chocolate cream.

> **TIP**
> *Make a batch of plain meringues and a batch of chocolate meringues and alternate them in a pyramid for a spectacular party dessert.*

Cheesecakes

New York-style Cheesecake

Coffee Cheesecake

Raspberry Cheesecake

Low-fat Blueberry Cheesecake

Cheese Placek

Chilled Sultana and Orange
Cheesecake

New York-style Cheesecake

Baked cheese recipes can be traced back to the discovery of curd cheese in the Middle East centuries ago. Western cheesecake as we know it is probably a descendant of the Russian Easter pashka, a tall moulded dessert of homemade cottage cheese, eggs, sugar, soured cream, butter and chopped nuts. This smooth, lemon-flavoured cheesecake makes a perfect dessert.

SERVES 8 TO 10

375 g/12 oz crushed digestive biscuits (20 to 22 biscuits)

½ tsp ground cinnamon

3 Tbsp butter or margarine, melted

750 g/1½ lb cream cheese

175 g/6 oz sugar

Grated rind of 1 lemon

1 tsp vanilla essence

3 eggs

SOURED CREAM TOPPING

250 ml/8 fl oz soured cream

2 Tbsp sugar

1 tsp vanilla essence

VARIATION

Strawberry Cheesecake

Prepare the cheesecake as above, but before serving, decorate the edge of cake with strawberries, hulled and cut in half lengthwise. In a food processor fitted with a metal blade, process 500 g/1 lb fresh strawberries, hulled, and 3 tablespoonfuls of sugar to taste. Strain and add a little lemon juice or water to thin if necessary. Serve separately with the cheesecake.

Pre-heat the oven to 350°F/175°C/Gas 4. Lightly butter a 22-cm/9-in spring-release tin. In a medium bowl, combine biscuit crumbs, cinnamon and butter or margarine. Press the crumbs over the base and sides of the tin. Bake for 5 minutes until just set. Remove to a wire rack to cool.

In a large bowl, with an electric mixer on medium-low speed, beat the cream cheese with sugar until smooth. Add lemon rind and vanilla essence, then beat in eggs, one at a time, until batter is well blended and smooth.

Carefully pour the filling into the cooled crust. Bake until firm at the edges but still slightly soft in the centre, 45 to 50 minutes. Do not allow the cake to brown; it should be puffed and slightly golden. Turn off the oven and leave the cheesecake in the oven with the door closed for 1 hour. (This helps prevent the surface from cracking.) Remove to a wire rack and leave to cool.

Pre-heat the oven to 425°F/220°C/Gas 7. Make the topping. In a small bowl, combine soured cream, sugar and vanilla essence. Carefully pour over the top of the cake and return to the oven. Bake for 5 minutes. Remove the cake to a wire rack to cool completely. Refrigerate overnight.

To serve, run a sharp knife around the edge of the pan to loosen the edges. Carefully remove the side of the spring-release tin and place the cheesecake on a serving dish.

Coffee Cheesecake

This no-cook cheesecake is set with gelatine.

SERVES 10 TO 12

120 g/4 oz butter

120 g/4 oz brown sugar

375 g/12 oz crushed coffee biscuits

4 x 25-g/1-oz sachets gelatine

6 Tbsp warm water

500 g/1 lb cream cheese

4 eggs, separated

250 g/8 oz brown sugar

2 Tbsp instant coffee dissolved in 1 Tbsp hot water

300 ml/10 fl oz double cream

Crystallized rose petals

Grease a 25–30-cm/10–12-in loose-bottomed cake tin. Melt the butter in a saucepan. Stir in the sugar and biscuits. Spoon into the tin and press down firmly with the back of a spoon. Chill.

Dissolve the gelatine in a bowl of warm water over a pan of simmering water. Beat the cream cheese in a bowl until soft and beat in the egg yolks, half the sugar, coffee and cream. Stir well. Add the gelatine to the coffee mixture and leave until it is on the point of setting.

Whisk the egg whites until stiff and whisk in the remaining sugar. Gently fold into the coffee mixture. Pour on to the chilled biscuit base. Gently tilt and tip the tin to level the surface. Chill for 3 to 4 hours.

Run a heated palette knife around the edge of the cheesecake and remove from the tin. Transfer to a plate and decorate the top with the crystallized rose petals.

Raspberry Cheesecake

Raspberry is a flavour that goes well with cheesecake.

SERVES 10 TO 12

250 g/8 oz flour quantity Rich Shortcrust Pastry (Pâté Brisée Riche) (see page 13)

2 eggs, separated

500 g/1 lb cottage cheese, pressed through a sieve

4 Tbsp sugar

4 Tbsp unsalted butter

Juice and grated rind of 1 lemon

Melted raspberry jam to serve

Pre-heat the oven to 350°F/175°C/Gas 4. Make the pastry dough and chill.

Beat the egg yolks and mix with the cottage cheese, sugar, softened butter, lemon juice and rind. Combine well. Then, whisk the egg whites until stiff. Fold them into the cottage cheese mixture.

Roll out the dough and line a 20-cm/8-in loose-bottomed cake tin. Bake blind until the edge of the pastry begins to colour, then fill the pastry shell with the cheese mixture and bake for 30 to 35 minutes.

Serve warm with melted raspberry jam brushed over the surface.

Raspberry Cheesecake ▶

Low-fat Blueberry Cheesecake

Cheesecake with a delicious muesli and dried fig base, in place of the usual crushed biscuits and butter, which gives a rich and crunchy base to the soft filling.

SERVES 6

250 g/8 oz plain muesli

150 g/5 oz dried figs

1 tsp vegetarian gelatine

4 Tbsp cold water

120 ml/4 fl oz skimmed evaporated milk

1 egg

6 Tbsp caster sugar

500 g/1 lb low-fat cottage cheese

120 g/4 oz blueberries

TOPPING

50 g/2 oz blueberries

2 nectarines, stoned and sliced

2 Tbsp honey

Place the muesli and dried figs in a food processor and blend together for 30 seconds. Press into the base of a base-lined 20-cm/8-in spring-release tin and chill while preparing the filling.

Sprinkle the gelatine on to 4 tablespoonfuls of cold water. Stir until dissolved and heat to boiling point. Boil for 2 minutes. Cool. Place the milk, egg, sugar and cheese in a food processor and blend until smooth. Stir in the blueberries. Place in a mixing bowl and gradually stir in the dissolved gelatine. Pour the mixture on to the base and chill for 2 hours until set.

Remove the cheesecake from the tin and arrange the fruit for the topping on top. Drizzle the honey over the fruit and serve.

Cheese Placek

This lattice-topped cheesecake is delicate in flavour with a crisp pastry base.

SERVES 8

BASE	FILLING
250 g/8 oz plain flour	650 g/1¼ lb cottage cheese
3 tsp baking powder	120 g/4 oz sugar
90 g/3 oz unsalted butter	2 Tbsp plain flour
60 g/2 oz caster sugar	½ tsp vanilla essence
I egg	Grated rind of I lemon
3 Tbsp soured cream	3 eggs, separated
	Icing sugar to dust

Grease a 27 x 20-cm/11 x 8-in loose-bottomed oblong pie tin or dish.

For the pastry, sift the flour and baking powder into a bowl. Blend in the butter, then stir in the sugar. Mix in the egg and soured cream to make a soft dough. Set aside one-third of the dough, then use the rest to line the base and sides of the tin. Prick the base all over, then chill the dough for 30 minutes.

Pre-heat the oven to 375°F/190°C/Gas 5. Line the pastry case with baking parchment and sprinkle with baking beans. Bake blind for 15 minutes. Remove the paper and cool.

For the filling, place the cheese in a double-thick piece of muslin and squeeze as much liquid as possible from it. Press the drained cheese through a sieve, then beat in the sugar, flour, vanilla essence, lemon rind and egg yolks. Whisk the whites until stiff and fold them into the mixture. Turn the mixture into the prepared base.

Roll out the reserved pastry into an oblong about the same size as the tin, then cut it lengthways into 1-cm/½-in wide strips. Arrange these in a lattice over the filling, trimming and re-rolling as necessary. Bake for about 35 to 40 minutes, until browned on top and firm. Leave to cool, then dust with a little icing sugar. Cut into squares to serve.

Chilled Sultana and Orange Cheesecake

Although the traditional baked cheesecakes, introduced from Europe, were favoured for many years, in recent times America has made the unbaked variation its own, and it has gained worldwide popularity.

SERVES 10 TO 12

120 g/4 oz candied peel, chopped	175 ml/6 fl oz sweetened whipped cream
120 g/4 oz sultanas	2 Tbsp Grand Marnier or Cointreau
2 Tbsp Grand Marnier or Cointreau	Candied peel to decorate
4 x 25-g/1-oz sachets gelatine	Pistachios to decorate
90 ml/3 fl oz hot water	SYRUP
375 g/12 oz cream cheese	175 g/6 oz granulated sugar
90 g/3 oz caster sugar	60 ml/2 fl oz water
175 g/6 oz lemon marmalade	3 Tbsp Grand Marnier or Cointreau
2 Tbsp grated orange rind	1 cooked Whisked Fatless Sponge 22 cm/9 in diameter (see page 111)
375 ml/12 fl oz whipping cream, softly whipped	
5 Tbsp chopped pistachios	

Soak the peel and the sultanas in Grand Marnier or Cointreau for at least 30 minutes. Make a syrup with the sugar and water boiled to thread stage (230°F/110°C). Mix in the liqueur. Cool.

Slice the sponge cake horizontally into two layers, of one-third and two-thirds thicknesses. Lightly oil a 22-cm/9-in spring-release tin and line the base with greaseproof paper. Drop the thicker cake layer into the tin and brush all over with the flavoured syrup.

Sprinkle the gelatine on to very hot, but not boiling, water in a cup and stir to dissolve. Leave to cool. The mixture should be transparent and lump-free, if it is not, place the cup in a pan of warm water and heat gently. Cool to room temperature before using. Meanwhile, beat the cream cheese with the sugar, lemon marmalade and orange rind until well blended. Gently trickle over the gelatine liquid, beating all the time. Set aside until the mixture is on the point of setting. Using a large metal spoon, lightly fold in the soaked peel and sultanas, the liqueur, whipped cream and the pistachios.

Pour the cheese filling on to the sponge cake in the prepared tin and smooth it out. Carefully cut half of the remaining sponge layer into six triangular pieces and evenly space them on top of the filling to create a fan effect.

Flavor 175 ml/6 fl oz sweetened whipped cream with 2 tablespoons of orange liqueur and pipe rosettes of cream on the cake. Decorate with candied peel and pistachios. Chill for 5 to 6 hours. The cake may be prepared 2 to 3 days ahead of time and kept in the refrigerator.

Dessert Cakes and Puddings

Pumpkin and Lemon Roulade

Cappuccino Sponges

Steamed Coffee Pudding

Banana Choc-chip Pudding

Magic Chocolate Dessert

Date and Ginger Pudding

Danish Apple Dessert Cake

Chocolate Upside-down Pudding

Individual
Sticky Toffee "Pudding" Cakes

Lemon-scented Passover Cake

Pumpkin and Lemon Roulade

Surprisingly light and tangy, this roulade or Swiss roll makes an unusual dessert. An excellent cake for the early autumn when a little culinary comfort is required.

MAKES 8 SLICES

3 large eggs	3 Tbsp icing sugar, sifted
90 g/3 oz caster sugar	175 g/6 oz thick pumpkin purée
60 g/2 oz plain flour, sifted twice	50 g/2 oz seedless raisins
Grated rind and juice of 1 large lemon	Icing sugar to dust
150 ml/5 fl oz whipping cream	

Pre-heat the oven to 425°F/220°C/Gas 7. Line a Swiss roll tin 32 x 22 cm/13 x 9 in with baking parchment.

Whisk the eggs and sugar together until very thick and pale – you should be able to leave a figure of 8 trail clearly visible in the mixture. Fold the flour and lemon rind quickly into the mixture, then scrape it into the prepared tin and gently level the surface.

Bake for 8 to 10 minutes, until spongy in texture and golden. Turn the cake on to a wire rack covered with baking parchment and sprinkled with icing sugar. Trim away the crusts of the cake and make a shallow cut a little way in from one of the short sides, then place another piece of paper over the sponge. Roll it up and leave it, entwined with the paper, until cold.

For the filling, whip the cream until almost stiff, then add the icing sugar and pumpkin purée. Beat well, then fold in the raisins. Unwrap the roulade and remove the inner paper. Spread the cream over the roulade, then re-roll it using the sugared paper to help. Transfer to a plate.

Pierce the roulade right through in lots of places with a thin skewer. Squeeze the juice from the lemon, then drizzle it over the roulade. Dredge with icing sugar, then leave for 20 minutes or so before serving, to allow the lemon to flavour the sponge.

Cappuccino Sponges

These individual sponge puddings are delicious served with the low-fat coffee sauce. Ideal for dinner parties. they look more delicate and attractive than one large pudding.

SERVES 4

2 Tbsp polyunsaturated margarine	**FOR THE COFFEE SAUCE**
2 Tbsp granulated brown sugar	300 ml/10 fl oz skimmed milk
2 egg whites	1 Tbsp granulated brown sugar
60 g/3 oz plain flour	1 tsp coffee essence
¾ tsp baking powder	1 tsp coffee liqueur (optional)
6 Tbsp skimmed milk	2 Tbsp cornflour
1 tsp coffee essence	4 Tbsp cold water
½ tsp unsweetened cocoa powder	

Use non-stick spray to lightly grease 4 x 150-ml/5-fl oz individual pudding moulds. Cream the margarine and sugar in a bowl and add the egg whites. Sift the flour and baking powder together and fold into the creamed mixture with a metal spoon. Gradually stir in the milk, coffee essence and cocoa powder.

Spoon equal amounts of the mixture into the moulds. Cover with pleated greaseproof paper then foil and tie securely with string. Place in a double boiler or pan with sufficient boiling water to reach halfway up the sides of the moulds. Cover and cook for 30 minutes or until cooked through.

Meanwhile, place the milk, sugar, coffee essence and coffee liqueur in a pan to make the sauce. Blend the cornflour with 4 tablespoonfuls of cold water and stir into the pan. Bring to the boil, stirring until thickened. Reduce the heat and cook for a further 2 to 3 minutes.

Carefully remove the cooked puddings from the steamer. Remove the paper and foil and unmould on to individual plates. Spoon the sauce around and serve.

Steamed Coffee Pudding

Use stale cake crumbs as a basis for this dessert.

SERVES 6

375 g/12 oz dry coffee sponge cake	60 g/2 oz butter
90 g/3 oz plain chocolate	2 Tbsp vanilla sugar
150 ml/5 fl oz milky coffee	2 large eggs, separated
2 Tbsp instant coffee dissolved in 1 Tbsp hot water	

Crumble the cake into fine crumbs. Melt the chocolate in a bowl over a pan of hot, gently simmering, water. When melted, pour over the cake crumbs. Leave to stand for 30 minutes.

Cream the butter and sugar until light and fluffy; beat in the egg yolks. Then stir in the soaked crumbs and finally the coffee.

Beat the egg whites until stiff and gently fold into the chocolate and coffee mixture. Spoon into a large buttered ovenproof bowl – the mixture should only half fill it. Cover with greased foil or a double thickness of greaseproof paper. Place in a double boiler and steam for 1½ hours. Turn out the pudding on to a serving dish, dust with sugar and serve with custard, cream or chocolate sauce.

Banana Choc-chip Pudding

This scrumptious dessert makes a rich and delicious end to a warming winter's dinner.

SERVES 4 TO 5

120 g/4 oz butter or margarine

120 g/4 oz sugar

2 eggs, beaten

60 g/2 oz self-raising flour

60 g/2 oz unsweetened cocoa powder

Approx. 2 Tbsp milk

1 small banana, peeled and chopped

60 g/2 oz chocolate chips

SAUCE

60 g/2 oz soft brown sugar

25 g/1 oz butter

2 Tbsp golden syrup

4 Tbsp half or single cream at room temperature

Cream the butter or margarine and sugar together until light and fluffy. Gradually add the eggs, beating well between each addition. Sift together the flour and cocoa powder, and fold into the egg mixture. Add enough milk to give a soft dropping consistency. Stir in the banana and chocolate chips.

Turn the mixture into a greased 900-ml/1½-pt ovenproof bowl. Cover with buttered greaseproof paper and foil with a central pleat in each. Secure with string. Steam in a double boiler for about 1½ hours.

To make the sauce, put all the ingredients into a saucepan and bring to the boil, stirring constantly. Turn out pudding and serve with the warm sauce.

Magic Chocolate Dessert

The magic in this pudding refers to the delicious sauce that forms at the base of the dessert while it is cooking.

SERVES 4 TO 5

150 g/5 oz self-raising flour, sifted

60 g/2 oz sugar

2 Tbsp unsweetened cocoa powder, sifted

60 g/2 oz walnuts or pecans, chopped

60 g/2 oz butter, melted

150 ml/5 fl oz milk

Vanilla essence

SAUCE

150 g/5 oz soft brown sugar

2 Tbsp unsweetened cocoa powder, sifted

200 ml/7 fl oz boiling water

Vanilla ice cream to serve

Pre-heat the oven to 350°F/175°C/Gas 4.

To make the sponge, put the dry ingredients into a bowl. Add the butter, milk and a few drops of vanilla essence and mix to form a thick batter.

Pour the mixture into a well-buttered 18-cm/7-in ovenproof dish.

To make the sauce, mix together the brown sugar, cocoa powder and boiling water. Pour this sauce over the batter.

Bake in the oven for about 40 minutes. During cooking the chocolate sponge rises to the top, and a chocolate fudge sauce forms underneath. Serve with vanilla ice cream.

Date and Ginger Pudding

A favourite winter pudding, sweetened with dates and banana. On a totally decadent day, you could serve this with a toffee or butterscotch sauce, but whipped cream or ice cream would show a modicum of restraint! It could also be sliced when cold and served as a cake.

SERVES 6 TO 8

90 g/3 oz stoned dates, chopped roughly

2 pieces stem ginger, chopped finely

1 banana, mashed

2 Tbsp syrup from the ginger

120 g/4 oz margarine or butter

120 g/4 oz light brown sugar

2 large eggs, beaten

175 g/6 oz wholemeal flour

1½ tsp baking powder

Pinch of salt

2 Tbsp milk

Pre-heat the oven to 375°F/190°C/Gas 5, then lightly grease and line a deep, 18-cm/7-in cake tin.

Mix together the dates, ginger, banana, and ginger syrup. Cream the margarine and sugar together until pale and creamy, then beat in the eggs a little at a time. Mix together the flour, baking powder and salt, then fold them into the mixture. Fold in the date and banana mix then add a little milk to give a soft, dropping consistency.

Turn into the prepared tin and smooth the top. Bake for 30 to 35 minutes, until a skewer inserted into the centre comes out clean, and the pudding shrinks away from the sides of the tin. Serve cut into wedges.

Danish Apple Dessert Cake

This crumbly apple pudding is delicious served with whipped cream or ice cream. Sweeten the apples to taste, according to the variety used.

SERVES 4 TO 6

250 g/8 oz fresh wholemeal breadcrumbs

90 g/3 oz demerara sugar

90 g/3 oz butter

2 large cooking apples, peeled, cored and sliced

Grated rind and juice of 1 lemon

60 g/2 oz–120 g/4 oz sugar

Mix the breadcrumbs with the demerara sugar. Melt the butter in a large skillet, then add the crumb mixture and fry quickly until the crumbs are crisp, then set them to one side to use later.

Cook the apples with the lemon rind and juice, sugar to taste, and as little water as possible until soft. The apples may be cooked in a microwave because no water at all is required. Allow to cool.

Turn half the apples into a glass dish, then make a layer of half the crumbs over the apples. Repeat the layers, finishing with the remaining crumbs. Allow the pudding to cool, then chill for at least 1 hour before serving.

Chocolate Upside-down Pudding

This perennial pudding is an all-time family favourite. It's always a surprise to find the pineapple rings at the top when the pudding is turned out!

SERVES 6

120 g/4 oz granulated brown sugar

120 g/4 oz butter

4 pineapple rings

6 walnut halves

2 eggs, separated

25 g/1 oz butter, melted

120 g/4 oz soft brown sugar

250 g/8 oz self-raising flour

60 g/2 oz unsweetened cocoa powder

Pre-heat the oven to 350°F/175°C/Gas 4. Grease a 20-cm/8-in cake tin.

Cream the sugar and butter and spread over the base of the tin. Arrange the pineapple rings on the base, with a walnut in the centre of each.

Beat together the egg yolks and butter until creamy. Whisk the egg whites until stiff. fold in the sugar and egg yolks mixture. Sift together the flour and cocoa and fold in carefully.

Pour over the fruit and spread evenly. Bake for about 30 minutes.

Carefully unmould on to a serving dish and serve with custard or cream.

Individual Sticky Toffee "Pudding" Cakes

Popular with children and adults alike, these
puddings make an impressive dessert.

SERVES 4

CARAMEL-TOFFEE SAUCE	PUDDINGS
Melted butter to grease	120 g/4 oz unsalted butter, softened
5 Tbsp sugar	120 g/4 oz light brown sugar, packed
2 Tbsp water	4 eggs, separated
4 Tbsp double cream, heated	120 g/4 oz self-raising flour or 120 g/4 oz plain flour plus I tsp baking powder, sifted
	60 g/2 oz chopped dates
	Butter to grease

Prepare the caramel-toffee sauce: Butter four 300-g/ 10-oz custard cups or ramekins. Put the sugar in a saucepan and drizzle over the water to moisten. Cook over low heat until the sugar dissolves. Boil until a golden caramel forms. Remove from heat and, standing well back, add the warm cream. Return to the heat and stir until all ingredients are melted and smooth.

Prepare the pudding mixture: Pre-heat the oven to 350°F/175°C/Gas 4. Beat the butter and sugar until fluffy and lightened in colour, 2 minutes. Beat in the egg yolks one at a time, beating well after each addition. Fold all but 2 to 3 tablespoonfuls of the flour mixture into the butter-egg yolk mixture.

Beat the egg whites until soft peaks form. Stir a spoonful of whites into the mixture to lighten it, then fold in the remaining whites. Toss the dates in the reserved 2 to 3 tablespoonfuls of the flour mixture and sprinkle over the batter, then gently fold in. Divide equally between the cups or ramekins.

Cover each cup or ramekin with greased baking parchment. Secure then cover with foil. Put in a larger roasting tin and pour in enough boiling water to come halfway up the sides. Bake for 40 minutes. Unmould and spoon over sauce. Serve with custard or whipped cream.

Lemon-Scented Passover Cake

Passover cakes are probably the most uniquely Jewish of all cakes, because they are made with flour substitutes. The most popular substitutes are potato flour, very fine matzo meal and ground nuts. The end result is a light, delicate sponge cake, served here with a lemon sauce.

SERVES 6 TO 8

6 eggs, separated	Almond halves or slivered almonds for decoration
250 g/8 oz sugar	
120 g/4 oz fine matzo meal	**FOAMY LEMON SAUCE**
60 g/2 oz finely ground blanched almonds or potato flour	1 Tbsp potato flour
	150 g/5 oz sugar
	375 ml/12 fl oz water
¼ tsp ground cinnamon	Grated rind and juice of 1 lemon
Grated rind and juice of 1 lemon	2 eggs, separated

Pre-heat the oven to 350°F/175°C/Gas 4. Grease a 20–22-cm/8–9 in spring-release tin. In a large bowl, with an electric mixer, beat egg yolks with half the sugar until thick and lemon coloured and mixture forms a "ribbon" when beaters are lifted from the bowl, 3 to 5 minutes.

In another large bowl, with cleaned beaters, beat the egg whites until soft peaks form. Gradually beat in the remaining sugar, in 3 or 4 batches, beating well after each addition, until the whites form stiff peaks.

In a medium bowl, combine the matzo meal, ground almonds or potato flour, cinnamon and lemon rind. Alternately, in 3 batches, fold beaten whites and matzo-almond mixture into the beaten yolks. Fold in lemon juice.

Pour the batter into the prepared tin and press almond halves into the batter at 5-cm/2-in intervals or sprinkle with slivered almonds.

Bake until the top is golden and a skewer inserted in the centre comes out clean, 45 to 55 minutes. Remove to a wire rack to cool 10 minutes. Carefully run a sharp knife around the edge of the tin to loosen the edges, then unclip the side of the tin and remove. Cool completely; the cake may sink a little.

Prepare Foamy Lemon Sauce. In a medium saucepan, combine potato flour and sugar. Slowly stir in 375 ml/12 fl oz water and lemon rind and juice, until well blended and smooth. Beat in egg yolks.

Over medium-low heat, cook the mixture until slightly thickened, 3 to 4 minutes. Bring to the boil, then remove from the heat.

In a medium bowl, with the electric mixer, beat the egg whites until soft peaks form. Slowly fold in the yolk mixture until just blended. Cool, then refrigerate for at least 1 hour or until chilled. Serve cold with the cake.

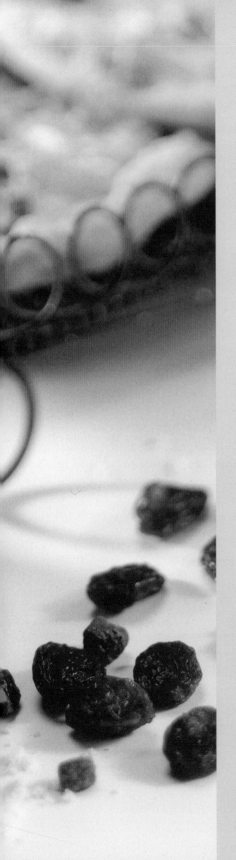

Biscuits

Everyone loves home-baked biscuits and this section is packed full of wonderful recipes. There are dropped biscuits and rolled biscuits, bar biscuits and moulded biscuits. There are old-fashioned gingerbreads and simple shortbreads as well as indulgent new variations on old favourites such as chocolate chip. The only problem with being a good biscuit baker is that they disappear so fast you always have to make more!

INTRODUCTION

Muesli biscuits, fresh from the oven – light and deliciously crumbly.

Biscuits, or cookies, were first introduced to colonial *America by the New York Dutch, who brought their* Koekjes *or "little cakes" from their homeland. Until wood-burning or coal-fired ovens were in general use, biscuit baking would have been unreliable at best. By the early 20th century, biscuits were so popular that special jars and tins were produced. Since then, there has been no looking back – biscuits are now universally popular.*

Every country seems to have its own special biscuits – chocolate chip cookies and brownies from America, galettes from Brittany, France and short-bread from Scotland – the list is endless.

Biscuits are one of life's great treats. Even the strictest of dieters and those who deny having a sweet tooth will splurge and have a biscuit with a cup of tea or coffee. And the bonus is they are almost always easy to make.

The six basic types of biscuit are generally determined by the way the dough is shaped.

Drop Biscuits

These are usually dropped or pushed from a spoon directly on to a baking sheet, leaving about a 5-cm/2-in space between each to allow for spreading.

Moulded Biscuits

These are usually shaped with the hands into balls, logs, or cylinders before placing on baking sheets; some moulded biscuits are actually baked in moulds. Moulded biscuits do not usually spread, so less space is required between them.

Refrigerator Biscuits

These are made from a rich, stiff, paste-like dough, rolled into log shapes and then sliced as required for baking. Most of these doughs can be refrigerated for several days or frozen for up to 6 months. The advantage with refrigerator biscuits is that they can be sliced and baked almost on demand.

Rolled Biscuits

These are made from a dough which is rolled out with a rolling pin, then cut into shapes using a knife or biscuit cutters, which are popular with children, being available in so many fun shapes. These biscuits are often decorated with coloured icings.

Pressed Biscuits

These are formed by pressing the dough through a piping bag and nozzle on to the baking sheet.

Biscuit Bars

These are formed by spreading a soft dough in a shallow pan, with or without a topping, then baking. After cooling they are cut into bars, squares, diamonds or triangles.

Special Biscuits

These are usually shaped by one of the above methods, and then either formed into tuiles or tulips, or fried in a moulded pancake griddle, to achieve a special effect.

Tips for Successful Biscuit Baking

Biscuit making is generally easy and requires very little equipment, but always be sure to read the recipe through before you begin. Always assemble the ingredients together before you start to cook, then put them aside or return them to their storage places as you use them, that way you'll never forget an ingredient or include it twice.

Equipment and Tins

Almost all biscuit doughs can be made by hand (originally, they were all made in that way) or with an electric mixer or in a food processor. An electric mixer is probably best, as it gives the baker more of a feel and control over the dough. Use heavy-gauge, flat, shiny aluminium baking sheets. They should be at least 5 cm/2 in smaller than your oven, so that the heat can circulate evenly. (Dark ones may cause over-browning.) Non-stick tins are ideal for certain biscuits, but may cause others to spread too much (this will be indicated in specific recipes). With practice, you will get to know which baking tins are best for your favourite biscuit recipes and can build up a supply of them.

Grease biscuit sheets only when indicated, otherwise the biscuits may spread too much or become too thin. Most butter-rich biscuit doughs do not require greased baking sheets, but a very thin layer of butter can be used as a precaution. Use a baking spray for the lightest of coatings, or a pastry brush to ensure an even coating.

Evenly space biscuits on baking sheets, and do not leave any large gaps. Arrange 2 baking sheets in the lower and upper shelves of the oven; a single baking sheet should always be placed on the middle shelf. Rotate the baking sheets from the bottom shelf to the top and from back to front, halfway through cooking time. If you do not have enough baking sheets, arrange the biscuits on sheets of heavy-duty foil, or baking parchment, cut to fit baking sheets. As soon as baked biscuits are removed from the oven, slide them off on to a rack, then slide a sheet of foil with the next batch of biscuits on to baking sheet and continue to bake immediately. *Never put biscuits directly on to a hot baking sheet.* For quick cooling, run the back of the baking sheet under cold running water and wipe dry.

Mixing and Baking

As with all baking, measure the ingredients carefully. Sweet butter is generally best as it contains less water and impurities, and large eggs. All the recipes have been tested with plain flour; it is not essential to sift the flour, but it facilitates the mixing up of the dry ingredients and ensures any lumps are eliminated. Soften the butter and cream well with the sugar, but mix in flour and dry ingredients gently or the dough may toughen.

Pre-heat the oven to the required temperature (if you are in doubt, double check with an oven thermometer). Use a kitchen timer and check several minutes before the end of the suggested baking time. Do not overbake biscuits or they may be too dry and taste stale. Because they are thin, they continue to bake even when removed from the oven. As soon as they are firm enough, transfer them to wire racks to cool.

Storing and Freezing

Most biscuits can be stored in airtight containers or tins. Store different kinds of biscuits separately, as the flavours might blend or moist biscuits might soften crisp biscuits. Delicate or sticky biscuits should be separated by sheets of greaseproof paper or foil. To crisp biscuits, re-heat for 3 to 5 minutes on a baking sheet in a 300°F/150°C/Gas 2 oven.

Most biscuit doughs can be stored in the refrigerator for several days or wrapped tightly in clingfilm or freezer bags, then frozen. To use frozen dough, thaw, wrapped, at room temperature until soft enough to handle, then shape or slice and bake. Refrigerator biscuit dough should be thawed in the refrigerator until just soft enough to slice.

Although biscuits are best freshly baked, most baked biscuits freeze well and are quick to thaw on short notice. Freeze in small quantities in heavy-duty freezer bags or small airtight containers.

Bar Biscuits

Chocolate Brownies

Low-fat Chocolate Brownies

Flapjacks

Date Flapjack

Pecan-sesame Fingers

Hermits

Apricot Muesli Bars

Grasmere Gingerbread

Houston Gingerbread

Caramel Cashew-almond Squares

Shortbread

Chocolate Peanut Butter Bars

Coffee Slices

Lemon Bars

Chocolate Chip Pecan Shortbread

Maple Macadamia Biscuits

Triple Decker Squares

Rocky Road Squares

Lebkuchen

Chocolate Brownies

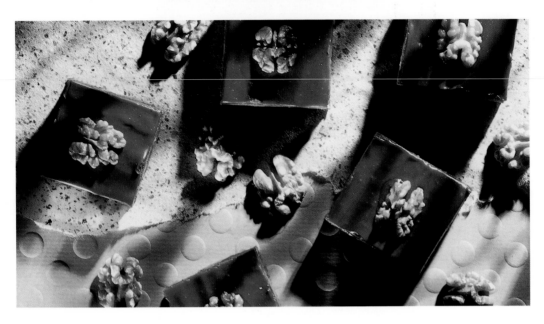

This is the classic chocolate brownie – dense, fudge-flavoured and packed with walnuts. A soft chocolate icing turns them into an elegant treat.

TIP

Mould a sheet of foil over bottom of tin, smoothing evenly around corners. Remove foil and turn tin right side up. Press foil into tin, smoothing into sides and corners. Lightly oil foil.

MAKES ABOUT 24

120 g/4 oz plain chocolate, chopped

175 g/6 oz butter or margarine, cut into pieces

400 g/14 oz sugar

3 eggs

I tsp vanilla essence

200 g/7 oz chopped walnuts or pecans

60 g/2 oz plain chocolate chips (optional)

120 g/4 oz plain flour

CHOCOLATE ICING

175 g/6 oz plain chocolate, chopped

120 ml/4 fl oz double cream

15 g/½ oz unsalted butter, cut into pieces

I tsp vanilla essence

24 walnut or pecan halves to decorate

Pre-heat the oven to 350°F/175°C/Gas 4. Prepare a 32 x 22-cm/13 x 9-in baking tin. In a medium saucepan over low heat, melt the chocolate and butter or margarine until smooth, stirring frequently. Remove from the heat, and stir in sugar until blended. Beat in eggs, one at a time, beating well after each addition. Beat in vanilla essence, nuts and chocolate chips. Stir in the flour until just blended; batter will be stiff. Spread in the prepared tin.

Bake the brownies until a skewer inserted in the centre comes out with sticky crumbs attached, 30 to 35 minutes. *Do not over-bake.* Transfer the tin to a wire rack to cool completely.

In a medium saucepan over low heat, melt the chocolate and cream until smooth, stirring frequently. Remove from the heat to cool slightly. Whisk in butter and vanilla essence. Dip 24 walnut or pecan halves halfway into the chocolate, and place on a greaseproof paper-lined baking sheet to set. Cool remaining glaze until slightly thickened and spreadable.

Using foil as a guide, remove the brownies from the tin, and invert on to a board or baking sheet. Using a metal palette knife, spread the icing over the brownies. Refrigerate until set, at least I hour.

Using a long-bladed, sharp knife, cut into 24 squares. Press a walnut or pecan half into the centre of each brownie square. Store in single layers in airtight containers.

Low-fat Chocolate Brownies

Low-fat chocolate brownies? They taste just as good as the real thing but have a slightly different texture. Store in an airtight container if you can resist them for long enough.

MAKES 16

120 g/4 oz stoned dried prunes

175 g/6 oz granulated brown sugar

3 Tbsp unsweetened cocoa powder, sifted

60 g/2 oz plain flour

1 tsp baking powder

3 egg whites

Icing sugar to dust

Grease and line a shallow 18-cm/7-in square cake tin.

Place the prunes in a food processor with 3 tablespoons of water and blend to a purée. Transfer the purée to a mixing bowl and stir in the sugar, cocoa powder, flour and baking powder. Whisk the egg whites until peaking and fold into the mixture. Pour into the prepared tin and level the surface.

Bake at 350°F/175°C/Gas 4 for 1 hour or until cooked through. Let the brownies cool in the tin for 10 minutes, then turn out on to a wire rack and cool completely. Cut into 16 squares, dust with icing sugar and serve.

Flapjacks

This is an easy-to-make, old-fashioned biscuit made from dark brown sugar or molasses and oats.

MAKES 8 TO 16

60 g/2 oz butter

1½ Tbsp golden syrup

90 g/3 oz dark brown sugar

120 g/4 oz oats

60 g/2 oz chopped walnuts, pecans or hazelnuts

¼ tsp salt

Pre-heat the oven to 350°F/175°C/Gas 4. Line a 20-cm/8-in cake tin with baking parchment or foil, lightly oiled.

In a medium saucepan, cook the butter, golden syrup and sugar over medium heat until melted and well-blended, 2 to 3 minutes. Remove from the heat, and stir in oats, chopped nuts and salt until blended. Pour into prepared tin, and smooth the top.

Bake until crisp and golden brown, 20 to 25 minutes. Remove the tin to a wire rack to cool slightly, 5 to 10 minutes. Invert on to a board, peel off paper, and, while still warm, cut into 8 or 16 equal wedges. Return to wire rack to cool completely. Store in airtight containers.

Date Flapjack

This is quick to make and bake, looks terrific and tastes delicious. It does, however, contain a lot of calories and should be saved for a treat!

SERVES 8 TO 10

300 g/10 oz dried dates, roughly chopped	90 g/3 oz butter
	250 g/8 oz rolled oats
150 ml/5 fl oz water	120 g/4 oz wholemeal flour
1 tsp vanilla essence	250 g/8 oz light brown sugar

Pre-heat the oven to 350°F/175°C/Gas 4 and line a deep 20-cm/8-in baking tin.

Place the dates and water in a pan and cook slowly until the dates are soft, the water is slightly reduced, and the mixture can be beaten into a thick purée. Add the vanilla essence then set the mixture aside until needed.

Melt the butter in a pan then stir in all the remaining ingredients. Press half the mixture into the bottom of the prepared tin, then top it with the date mixture before pressing the remaining oat mixture over the dates. Smooth the top then bake for 30 minutes.

Mark into portions while still warm then leave to cool completely before slicing. Store in an airtight container.

Pecan-sesame Fingers

The toasted sesame seeds give an unusual flavour to these biscuits.

MAKES ABOUT 36

SESAME BASE

120 g/4 oz unsalted butter, softened

120 g/4 oz soft brown sugar

1 tsp sesame oil (optional)

120 g/4 oz plain flour

120 g/4 oz sesame seeds, toasted

PECAN TOPPING

2 eggs

250 g/8 oz packed brown sugar

1 tsp vanilla essence

2 Tbsp plain flour

1 tsp baking powder

½ tsp salt

200 g/7 oz chopped pecans

120 g/4 oz sweetened flaked coconut

2–3 Tbsp sesame seeds for sprinkling

TIP

If the bar is difficult to remove from baking tin, cut into bars or squares, and store in the baking tin covered with clingfilm or foil.

Pre-heat the oven to 375°F/190°C/Gas 5. Well grease a 32 x 22-cm/13 x 9-in baking tin. In a large bowl, with electric mixer, beat butter, sugar and sesame oil, if using, until light and fluffy, 1 to 2 minutes. Beat in flour and sesame seeds until soft dough forms. Push dough evenly on to bottom of the prepared tin, smoothing the top. Bake for 10 minutes.

Meanwhile prepare the topping. In a large bowl with an electric mixer, beat eggs, brown sugar, vanilla essence, flour, baking powder and salt until light and fluffy, 1 to 2 minutes. Fold in pecans and coconut.

Remove crust to a wire rack. Pour over the egg–pecan mixture, and sprinkle with sesame seeds. Bake until the top is firm and golden, 15 to 20 minutes. Transfer the tin to a wire rack, and cool completely.

Run a sharp knife around the sides of the tin to loosen the mixture then carefully slide on to a board. Cut into 4-cm/1½-in bars.

Hermits

In New England this recipe usually contains soured cream; in this Southern version the moisture is provided by the molasses. Use any kind of dried fruit and nuts you like.

MAKES 24

120 g/4 oz plain flour

1½ tsp bicarbonate of soda

½ tsp cream of tartar

1 tsp ground cinnamon

½ tsp grated or ground nutmeg

½ tsp ground cloves

¼ tsp ground mace

¼ tsp ground allspice

120 g/4 oz raisins

120 g/4 oz chopped, stoned dates

120 g/4 oz dried apricots, chopped

120 g/4 oz butter or margarine, softened

120 g/4 oz sugar

2 eggs, lightly beaten

120 g/4 oz treacle

150 g/5 oz chopped walnuts, pecans or hazelnuts

Icing sugar to dust

Pre-heat the oven to 350°F/175°C/Gas 4. Prepare a 32 x 22-cm/13 x 9-in baking tin.

In a medium bowl, sift together flour, bicarbonate, cream of tartar, cinnamon, nutmeg, cloves, mace and allspice. Place raisins, dates and apricots in a small bowl, and toss with a quarter of flour-spice mixture.

In a large bowl with the electric mixer, cream butter and sugar until light and fluffy, 1 to 2 minutes. Gradually beat in eggs and treacle until well-blended. On low speed, beat in flour-spice mixture until blended then stir in flour-coated fruit and nuts.

Spread the mixture into the foil-lined tin. Bake until top is set, 17 to 20 minutes. Transfer the tin to a wire rack to cool completely. Remove biscuit mixture to a board, and peel off foil. Cut into bars and dust with icing sugar. Store in airtight containers with greaseproof paper between layers.

Apricot Muesli Bars

These fruit muesli bars make a substantial snack or a light meal.

MAKES 8

FILLING

150 g/5 oz dried apricots, chopped finely

Grated rind and juice of 1 orange

50 g/2 oz margarine

90 g/3 oz honey

120 g/4 oz muesli

60 g/2 oz wholemeal flour

Pre-heat the oven to 375°F/190°C/Gas 5 and lightly grease an 18-cm/7-in square cake tin.

Cook the apricots with the orange rind and juice, simmering slowly until all the orange juice has disappeared. Allow to cool until needed. Melt the margarine in a pan, add the honey and heat gently until melted into the margarine. Stir in the muesli and flour and mix well.

Press half the muesli mixture into the prepared cake tin then cover with a layer of apricots. Top with the remaining muesli mixture, pressing it down and smoothing the top with a metal spoon. Try to push any raisins into the mixture so they do not overcook.

Bake for 20 to 25 minutes, until lightly browned. Mark into bars and allow to cool in the tin. Cut through then cool completely on a wire rack. Store in an airtight container.

Grasmere Gingerbread

This is an unusual gingerbread containing candied peel. Substitute chopped dried apricots or raisins, if you prefer.

MAKES 12

250 g/8 oz self-raising flour	2 egg yolks, beaten
175 g/6 oz sugar	120 g/4 oz chopped mixed peel
1–2 tsp ground ginger	
120 g/4 oz butter or hard margarine	**TOPPING**
	Egg white
1 Tbsp golden syrup	2 Tbsp granulated sugar

 Pre-heat the oven to 325°F/160°C/Gas 3.

Put the flour, sugar and ginger into a bowl and mix together. In a pan, melt the butter or margarine and syrup. Take off the heat, cool slightly, and stir the egg yolks into the melted mixture. Gently beat the butter mixture into the flour.

Roll half the dough out to an oblong about 18 x 10 cm/ 7 x 4 in on non-stick paper. Sprinkle the peel over the dough. Press the remaining dough over the top.

Lightly whisk the egg white and brush the top of the gingerbread with the froth and sprinkle with sugar. Bake the gingerbread for 20 to 30 minutes. When cool cut into small squares and serve.

Houston Gingerbread

Very dark but light and fluffy in texture, this is a sort of gingerbread "brownie".

MAKES ABOUT 24

250 g/8 oz plain flour

2 Tbsp unsweetened cocoa powder

2 tsp bicarbonate of soda

2 tsp ground ginger

2 tsp ground cinnamon

120 g/4 oz butter or margarine

175 g/6 oz caster sugar

2 eggs, separated

300 ml/10 oz treacle

250 ml/8 fl oz buttermilk

FROSTING

200 g/7 oz plain chocolate

Pre-heat the oven to 350°F/175°C/Gas 4. Grease and line a 32 × 22-cm/13 × 9-in cake tin.

Sift the flour, cocoa powder, bicarbonate and spices into a bowl. In another larger bowl, cream the butter or margarine and sugar. Beat in the egg yolks and treacle. Alternately, fold the dry ingredients and buttermilk into the larger bowl. Whisk the egg whites until stiff and fold into the mixture.

Spread the mixture into the tin and bake for 25 to 30 minutes. Cool the cake slightly before turning out on to a wire rack to cool thoroughly.

Melt the chocolate gently in a bowl over a pan of hot water and spread over the gingerbread. When set, cut into squares to serve.

Caramel Cashew-almond Squares

This is a delicious biscuit bar with a rich, sticky topping of caramelized honey and nuts. Not for calorie counters!

MAKES 36

PASTRY BASE	CARAMEL NUT TOPPING
375 g/12 oz plain flour	175 g/6 oz unsalted butter
90 g/3 oz cornflour	120 g/4 oz dark brown sugar
½ tsp salt	120 g/4 oz honey
375 g/12 oz unsalted butter, softened	300 g/10 oz salted cashews, lightly toasted and coarsely chopped
150 g/5 oz sugar	150 g/5 oz whole blanched almonds, toasted and coarsely chopped
Grated rind of 1 lemon	2½ Tbsp whipping cream

Prepare a 32 × 22-cm/13 × 9-in baking tin (see page 219).

In a medium bowl, sift together flour, cornflour and salt. In a large bowl with an electric mixer, beat butter, sugar and lemon rind until light and fluffy, 1 to 2 minutes. On low speed, beat in flour mixture until blended and soft dough forms. Scrape down the sides of bowl, and refrigerate the dough for 10 minutes.

Turn the dough out on to a large sheet of greaseproof paper, and pat into a rectangle. Cover with another piece of greaseproof paper, and roll out to a 37 × 25-cm/15 × 10-in rectangle. Slide on to baking sheet, and refrigerate, 10 minutes.

Discard the top layer of greaseproof paper and carefully invert the pastry into the foil-lined tin or pie dish. Remove the remaining paper and press the pastry on to bottom and 2.5 cm/1 in up sides of tin, pressing into the corners. Prick the bottom of the pastry with a fork, and bake until lightly coloured, about 30 minutes, turning the tin halfway through cooking and pricking with fork if pastry puffs during baking. Remove the tin to wire rack.

In a medium saucepan over medium heat, bring the butter, sugar and honey to the boil, stirring until sugar dissolves. Then boil without stirring until mixture thickens slightly, about 1 minute. Remove from the heat and stir in cashews, almonds and cream until well-mixed.

Pour the nut mixture over the pastry, spreading evenly. Bake until sticky and bubbling, about 20 minutes. Transfer to a wire rack to cool completely. Using the foil as a guide, remove the biscuit mixture to a board. Peel off the foil, and cut into 4-cm/1½-in squares. Store in single layers in airtight containers.

Shortbread

This is a simple, classic recipe – butter, sugar and flour – and yet one of the most delicious. Perfect with a cup of tea.

MAKES 16 LARGE WEDGES OR 32 THIN WEDGES

60 g/2 oz icing sugar	175 g/6 oz unsalted butter, softened
60 g/2 oz caster sugar	
¼ tsp salt	300 g/10 oz plain flour

TIP

Shortbread is sometimes made with part rice flour (about ¼ of the total volume of flour). Rice flour, available from some specialist and health food shops, and can be substituted for part of the flour in the above proportions for an even shorter texture.

Pre-heat the oven to 275°F140°C/Gas 1. In a large bowl, sift icing sugar. Add caster sugar and salt, and mix well. Add butter and, using an electric mixer, beat butter and sugars until light and fluffy, 1 to 2 minutes. Stir in the flour until blended. On a lightly floured surface, knead the dough very lightly to ensure even blending.

Divide the dough evenly between two 20-cm/8-in loose-bottomed cake tins, and pat down in even layers. Using a fork, press 2-cm/¾-in radiating lines around the edge of the dough. Prick the surface lightly with the fork (this helps keep an even surface as well as creating the traditional pattern).

Bake until pale golden (do not brown; shortbread should be very pale), about 1 hour, rotating the tins halfway through cooking. Transfer the tins to a wire rack to cool, about 10 minutes.

Carefully remove side of each pan, and place tin base on to heatproof surface. Cut each shortbread circle into 8 wide or 16 thin wedges. This must be done while the shortbread is warm and soft, or it will break. Return the shortbread wedges on their bases to the wire racks to cool completely. Store in airtight containers.

Chocolate Peanut Butter Bars

This most popular combination of chocolate and peanut butter is wonderful as a glazed brownie filled with chocolate chips and peanuts.

MAKES ABOUT 24

120 g/4 oz smooth or chunky peanut butter, softened

90 g/3 oz butter, softened

250 g/8 oz sugar

3 eggs

1 tsp vanilla essence

120 g/4 oz plain flour

90 g/3 oz plain chocolate chips

150 g/5 oz salted peanuts, chopped

ICING

175 g/6 oz plain chocolate, chopped

2 Tbsp smooth peanut butter

2 Tbsp butter

2 Tbsp golden syrup

1 tsp vanilla essence

Pre-heat the oven to 350°F/175°C/Gas 4. Then prepare a 32 x 22-cm/13 x 9-in baking tin.

In a large bowl, beat peanut butter and butter until creamy and smooth, 30 to 60 seconds. Add sugar, eggs and vanilla essence. Stir in the flour until blended; then stir in chocolate chips and peanuts. Spread the mixture into the prepared tin, smoothing the top.

Bake until golden round the edges, 25 to 30 minutes. Transfer the tin to wire rack to cool completely.

In a medium saucepan over low heat, melt chocolate, peanut butter, butter, golden syrup and vanilla essence until smooth, stirring frequently. Remove from the heat, and cool until slightly thickened, stirring occasionally.

Using foil as a guide, remove the cooked mixture from the tin, and invert on to a board or baking sheet. Using a metal palette knife, spread the icing over the top. Refrigerate until set, about 1 hour.

Using a long-bladed, sharp knife, cut into 48 4-cm/1½-in bars. Store in single layers in airtight containers, or refrigerate in an airtight container with greaseproof paper between the layers.

Coffee Slices

There's something extra special about coffee-flavoured bakes. These slices are so simple to make, and very good to eat.

MAKES 18

120 g/4 oz butter

60 g/2 oz sugar

120 g/4 oz self-raising flour

1 Tbsp coffee essence

ICING

4 Tbsp icing sugar

1 Tbsp instant coffee

60 g/2 oz butter

Pre-heat the oven to 350°F/175°C/Gas 4.

Cream the butter and sugar until light and fluffy. Fold in the flour and coffee essence. Press into a greased Swiss roll tin and bake for 15 to 20 minutes.

Place all the icing ingredients into a saucepan and heat and stir for 2 to 3 minutes until the mixture looks like fudge. Pour the mixture on top of the shortbread. Leave to set and cut into slices.

Lemon Bars

These biscuit bars are simple to make and are quite delicious. The combination of buttery shortbread and tart lemon topping is perfect.

MAKES 30

SHORTBREAD BASE	LEMON TOPPING
175 g/6 oz plain flour	4 eggs
175 g/6 oz icing sugar	375 g/12 oz caster sugar
½ tsp salt	Grated rind of 1 lemon
175 g/6 oz cold unsalted butter, cut into small pieces	120 ml/4 fl oz fresh lemon juice
1 tsp grated lemon rind (optional)	175 ml/6 fl oz double cream
	Icing sugar to dust

Pre-heat the oven to 325°F/160°C/Gas 3. Prepare a 32 x 22-cm/13 x 9-in baking tin (see page 219).

In a large bowl, sift together the flour, sugar and salt. Sprinkle over the cut-up butter with lemon rind, if using, and, using a pastry blender or fingertips, cut in the butter until coarse crumbs form and the mixture sticks together.

Turn the crumbs into the prepared tin, and press firmly into the bottom of the tin to form a level base, smoothing the top evenly. Bake until just golden, about 20 minutes. Transfer the tin to a wire rack to cool slightly.

In a medium bowl, beat the eggs and sugar until fluffy, 3 to 5 minutes. Beat in lemon rind and juice until blended.

In another bowl with cleaned beaters, whip the cream until soft peaks form. Fold into the beaten egg mixture in 2 batches, and pour over base. Return the tin to oven, and bake until the topping is set, about 40 minutes. Transfer the tin to a wire rack to cool completely.

Using foil as a guide, remove the biscuit mixture from the tin, and set on a board. Peel off the foil, and cut into bars. Dust lightly with icing sugar. Store in single layers in airtight containers.

Chocolate Chip Pecan Shortbread

This is a rich shortbread speckled with chocolate chips and finely ground pecans. It will become a favourite cookie and is very easy to make.

MAKES 32 PIECES

150 g/5 oz pecans, toasted and cooled	250 g/8 oz unsalted butter, softened
200 g/7 oz plain flour	90 g/3 oz plain chocolate chips
25 g/1 oz cornflour	
120 g/4 oz icing sugar	45 g/1½ oz plain chocolate, melted for drizzling
¼ tsp salt	

Pre-heat the oven to 325°F160°C/Gas 3. Lightly grease two 20-cm/8-in loose-bottomed flan tins. In a food processor fitted with a metal blade, process the toasted pecans until very fine crumbs form; do not over-process or the nuts may form a paste and release oil. Pour into a large bowl.

Into the ground nuts, sift together flour, cornflour, icing sugar and salt, and mix well. Add the butter and, using a pastry blender or fingertips, blend well until the dough holds together. Stir in the chocolate chips.

Divide the dough evenly between the flan tins, and pat over the base in an even layer. Bake until the edges are golden and the surface appears slightly puffed, 20 to 25 minutes. Transfer the tins to wire racks to cool, about 5 minutes.

Carefully remove the side of each tin, and place the tin base with the shortbread on heatproof surface. Cut each shortbread circle into 16 thin wedges; this must be done while the shortbread is warm and soft, or it will break. Return the shortbread wedges on their bases to wire racks to cool completely.

Using a metal palette knife, remove the shortbread wedges to wire rack, arranging top-to-toe to fit the wedges close together on rack. Spoon melted chocolate into a paper cone or piping bag and drizzle wedges evenly. Store in airtight containers with greaseproof paper between layers.

Maple Macadamia Biscuits

These delicious biscuits combine a sweet maple
flavour with crunchy nuts.

MAKES ABOUT 24

MAPLE BASE	NUT TOPPING
120 g/4 oz unsalted butter, softened	250 g/8 oz dark brown sugar
120 g/4 oz sugar	60 g/2 oz unsalted butter
1 egg	60 ml/2 fl oz whipping cream
1 tsp natural maple flavouring or maple syrup	3 Tbsp golden syrup
175 g/6 oz plain flour	3 Tbsp natural maple syrup
	300 g/10 oz unsalted macadamia nuts

Prepare a 32 × 22-cm/13 × 9-in baking tin (see page 219). In a medium bowl, beat the butter and sugar until light and fluffy, 1 to 2 minutes. Beat in egg and maple flavouring or syrup. On low speed, beat in flour until just blended. Roll out the dough between 2 sheets of greaseproof paper to a 42 × 25-cm/14 × 10-in rectangle.

Slide on to a baking sheet, and refrigerate 10 minutes.

Preheat the oven to 350°F/175°C/Gas 4. Remove the top sheet of greaseproof paper, and invert the dough into the tin. Peel off the bottom piece of greaseproof paper. Press the pastry on to the bottom of the tin and 1 cm/½ in up the sides. Prick the dough with a fork. Line the pastry with greaseproof paper or foil, and fill with baking beans or rice. Bake for 15 minutes. Remove beans or rice and paper, and bake until set and golden, 5 to 7 minutes. Transfer the tin to a wire rack.

In a heavy-bottomed saucepan, whisk together the sugar, butter, cream, golden syrup and maple syrup. Over medium heat, bring the mixture to the boil, stirring constantly until the sugar dissolves; then boil without stirring, 1 minute. Remove from the heat; and stir in nuts until well-coated. Pour the mixture over the pastry base.

Bake until the filling is bubbling and thickened, 10 minutes. Transfer to a wire rack to cool completely. Using foil as a guide, transfer the biscuit mixture to a board. Peel off the foil, and cut into 5 × 2.5-cm/2 × 1½ in bars.

Triple Decker Squares

These rich squares are always popular with
adults and children alike. They are especially
good straight from the refrigerator.

MAKES 16

120 g/4 oz butter or margarine	2 Tbsp golden syrup
60 g/2 oz sugar	175-ml/6-fl oz tin condensed milk
175 g/6 oz plain flour	
	TOPPING
FILLING	175 g/6 oz plain chocolate
120 g/4 oz butter or margarine	2 Tbsp milk
90 g/3oz sugar	

Pre-heat the oven to 350°F/175°C/Gas 4. Cream the butter or margarine and sugar until light and fluffy. Stir in the flour. Work the dough with your hands and knead well. Roll out and press into a shallow 20-cm/8-in square tin. Prick well with a fork.

Bake for 25 to 30 minutes. Cool in the tin.

To make the filling, put all the ingredients in a pan and heat gently, stirring until the sugar has dissolved. Bring to the boil and cook, stirring, for 5 to 7 minutes until golden.

Pour the caramel over the shortbread base and leave to set.

Melt the chocolate and milk together. Spread it evenly over the caramel. Leave until quite cold before cutting into squares.

Rocky Road Squares

This combination of marshmallows, nuts and chocolate is a winner. For a delicious dessert, serve with vanilla ice cream.

MAKES ABOUT 12

200 g/7 oz plain flour	1 tsp vanilla essence
60 g/2 oz unsweetened cocoa powder	60 g/2 oz desiccated coconut
1 tsp bicarbonate of soda	175 g/6 oz plain chocolate chips
½ tsp salt	150 g/5 oz whole blanched almonds, coarsely chopped
250 g/8 oz unsalted butter, softened	90 g/3 oz mini marshmallows
250 g/8 oz light brown sugar	Icing sugar to dust
2 eggs, lightly beaten	

Pre-heat the oven to 350°F/175°C/Gas 4. Prepare a 32 x 22-cm/13 x 9-in baking tin (see page 219).

In a medium bowl, sift together flour, cocoa powder, bicarbonate and salt, In a large bowl with an electric mixer, beat the butter and brown sugar until light and fluffy, 1 to 2 minutes. Beat in the eggs and vanilla essence. On low speed, beat in the flour-cocoa mixture until blended, then stir in the coconut, 60 g/2 oz of the chocolate chips and the chopped almonds.

Turn dough into a prepared tin, and pat or spread mixture evenly over the base of the tin. Bake until set, but still moist in the middle, 15 to 17 minutes. Remove the tin from the oven, and sprinkle the top evenly with the remaining chocolate chips and mini marshmallows. Return the tin to the oven and bake until the chocolate chips and marshmallows begin to soften and blend into each other, about 4 minutes. Remove the tin to a wire rack to cool for 10 minutes.

Using the foil as a guide, remove the biscuit mixture from the tin and set on a board. Peel off the foil and, while still warm, cut into bars or squares. Cool completely on a wire rack. Dust lightly with icing sugar. Store in airtight containers with greaseproof paper between layers.

Lebkuchen

This old German recipe is equally mouth-watering warm or cold.

MAKES ABOUT 18

300 g/10 oz plain flour	120 g/4 oz caster sugar
½ tsp baking powder	250 ml/8 fl oz honey
½ tsp ground ginger	6 Tbsp milk
½ tsp ground cinnamon	
½ tsp ground cloves	**ICING**
¼ tsp ground nutmeg	175 g/6 oz icing sugar
150 g/5 oz ground almonds	½ tsp almond essence
60 g/1 oz finely chopped candied peel	1 tsp lemon juice
	Water
2 eggs	

Pre-heat the oven to 400°F/200°C/Gas 6. Line a Swiss roll tin with baking parchment, brush lightly with oil and put aside.

In a bowl, sift together the flour, baking powder and spices. Stir in the almonds and chopped peel. Break the eggs into another bowl, add the sugar and whisk until the mixture is light and thick, leaving a trail when the whisk is lifted. Whisk in the honey and milk followed by the flour mixture.

Pour the mixture into the prepared tin. Bake for 15 to 20 minutes. Cool on a wire rack for 10 minutes, then turn out. Ice while warm.

To make the icing, put the icing sugar into a bowl. Add the almond essence, lemon juice and enough water to mix to a thick consistency. Brush over the hot Lebkuchen. Cut into bars to serve.

Drop Biscuits

Peanut Butter, White Chocolate and Peanut Biscuits

These luscious biscuits should always be made with a commercially prepared peanut butter, as freshly ground or homemade peanut butters may not react the same way in the recipe.

MAKES ABOUT 18

150 g/5 oz freshly shelled peanuts	2 Tbsp sugar
120 g/4 oz plain flour	1 egg
½ tsp bicarbonate of soda	1 tsp vanilla essence
¼ tsp salt	175 g/6 oz good-quality white chocolate, coarsely chopped
120 g/4 oz chunky peanut butter	60 g/2 oz plain chocolate, melted
120 g/4 oz unsalted butter	
120 g/4 oz light brown sugar	

In a medium frying pan over medium-low heat, toast the peanuts until golden and fragrant, about 5 minutes, stirring frequently. Turn on to a plate, and allow to cool.

Pre-heat the oven to 375°F/190°C/Gas 5. In a medium bowl, sift together flour, bicarbonate and salt. In a large bowl with an electric mixer, beat the peanut butter, butter and sugars until light and fluffy, about 2 to 3 minutes. Add the egg and continue beating for 2 minutes; beat in the vanilla essence. Stir in the flour mixture until well-blended; then stir in white chocolate and toasted peanuts.

Drop heaped tablespoonfuls at least 5 cm/2 in apart on 2 large baking sheets. Flatten slightly with the back of a moistened spoon. Bake until golden-brown, about 12 to 15 minutes; do not overbake or the biscuits will be dry. Remove the baking sheets to wire racks to cool, 3 to 5 minutes. Then, using a metal spatula or palette knife, transfer the biscuits to wire racks to cool completely.

Spoon melted plain chocolate into a paper cone and drizzle over the biscuits in a zig-zag pattern. Leave to set; store biscuits in airtight containers.

Double Chocolate Chip Biscuits

This is a slightly updated version of the classic chocolate chip—more chunky than ever.

MAKES ABOUT 48

250 g/8 oz plain flour

1 tsp bicarbonate of soda

¾ tsp salt

250 g/8 oz unsalted butter or margarine, softened

250 g/8 oz light brown sugar

120 g/4 oz sugar

2 eggs

1 tsp vanilla essence

375 g/12 oz plain chocolate chips or plain chocolate chopped into small pieces

175 g/6 oz good-quality white chocolate chopped into small pieces

150 g/5 oz chopped pecans or walnuts

Pre-heat the oven to 375°F/190°C/Gas 5. Into a large bowl, sift together the flour, bicarbonate and salt. In a large bowl, with an electric mixer, beat the butter and sugars until light and fluffy. On low speed, beat in the eggs, beating well after each addition, and scraping down the sides of the bowl occasionally. Beat in the vanilla essence; then stir in the flour mixture. Mix well and stir in the chocolate chips and nuts.

Drop rounded tablespoonfuls, at least 5 cm/2 in apart, on to large ungreased baking sheets. Bake until set and golden brown, 10 to 13 minutes, rotating the baking sheets from the top to the bottom shelf and front to back halfway through the cooking time. Transfer baking sheets to wire racks to cool slightly; using a metal spatula or palette knife, transfer the biscuits to wire racks to cool completely. Repeat with the remaining biscuit dough. Store in airtight containers.

Triple Chocolate Chunk Biscuits

These biscuits are large and flat, crisp on the edge, soft in the centre and filled with chocolate – a chocolate lover's dream. For best results do not over-bake.

MAKES ABOUT 18

250 g/8 oz plain chocolate, chopped

175 g/6 oz unsalted butter, cut into pieces

3 eggs

175 g/6 oz sugar

90 g/3 oz light brown sugar

2 tsp vanilla essence

60 g/2 oz plain flour

6 Tbsp cocoa powder, sifted

1½ tsp baking powder

¼ tsp salt

300 g/10 oz plain chocolate, chopped into ½-cm/¼-in pieces or 120 g/4 oz chocolate chips

175 g/6 oz good-quality milk chocolate, chopped into ½-cm/¼-in pieces

175 g/6 oz good-quality white chocolate, chopped into ½-cm/¼-in pieces

200 g/7 oz pecans or walnuts, toasted and chopped

Pre-heat the oven to 325°F/160°C/Gas 3. Lightly grease 2 large baking sheets. In a medium saucepan over low heat, melt the plain chocolate and butter, stirring frequently until smooth. Remove from the heat to cool slightly.

In a large bowl, with an electric mixer, beat the eggs and sugars until light and fluffy, about 2 to 3 minutes. On low speed, gradually beat in the melted chocolate and vanilla essence until well-blended. Into a small bowl, sift together the flour, cocoa powder, baking powder and salt then gently stir into chocolate mixture. Stir in the unmelted chocolate pieces and nuts.

Drop heaped tablespoons, at least 10 cm/4 in apart, on to baking sheets. Moisten the bottom of a drinking glass, and flatten each dough round slightly, trying to make each biscuit about 7 cm/3 in round; you will only fit 4 to 6 biscuits on each baking sheet. Bake for 10 minutes until the tops are cracked and shiny; do not over-bake or the biscuits will break when removed from baking sheet.

Transfer the baking sheets to wire racks to cool slightly. Then, using a metal spatula or palette knife, transfer the biscuits to wire racks to cool completely. Repeat with the remaining dough. Store in airtight containers.

Triple Chocolate Chunk Biscuits ▶

Spiced Apple Biscuits

These soft, spiced biscuits are delicious. If you don't like nuts, substitute some chopped dates.

MAKES ABOUT 36

120 g/4 oz unsalted butter, softened	½ tsp salt
120 g/4 oz light brown sugar	1 tsp ground cinnamon
90 g/3 oz sugar	1 tsp ground ginger
1 egg	½ tsp ground cloves
1 cup apple sauce	150 g/5 oz sultanas
250 g/8 oz plain flour	120 g/4 oz chopped walnuts or pecans
1 tsp bicarbonate of soda	60 g/2 oz chocolate chips

Pre-heat the oven to 350°F/175°C/Gas 4. Lightly grease 2 large baking sheets. In a large bowl with an electric mixer, beat the butter until creamy, about 30 seconds. Add the sugars, and beat until light and fluffy, 1 to 2 minutes. Beat in egg, and stir in the apple sauce.

Into a medium bowl, sift together the flour, bicarbonate, salt, cinnamon, ginger and cloves. Stir into the butter-sugar mixture until well-blended then stir in the sultanas, walnuts or pecans and chocolate chips.

Drop tablespoonfuls, about 4 cm/1½ in apart, on to baking sheets. Bake until golden, 5 to 7 minutes. Transfer the baking sheets to wire racks to cool slightly. Using a metal spatula or palette knife, transfer the biscuits to wire racks to cool completely. Repeat with the remaining mixture. Store in airtight containers.

White Chocolate Macadamia Drops

The combination of white chocolate and macadamia nuts is luscious. Although macadamias are expensive, they are worth it for these biscuits.

MAKES ABOUT 48

120 g/4 oz unsalted butter, softened	2 tsp baking powder
250 g/8 oz cream cheese, softened	150 g/5 oz coarsely chopped macadamia nuts
175 g/6 oz light brown sugar	120 g/4 oz good-quality white chocolate, coarsely chopped
Grated rind of 1 lemon	
1½ tsp vanilla essence	Icing sugar to dust or melted plain chocolate to drizzle
175 g/6 oz plain flour	

In a large bowl with an electric mixer, beat the butter and cream cheese until creamy, 1 to 2 minutes, scraping the bowl occasionally. Add the sugar and continue beating until light and fluffy, 1 to 2 minutes. Beat in the lemon rind and vanilla essence.

Into a medium bowl, sift together the flour and baking powder and stir into the cream cheese mixture. Stir in the nuts and chocolate. Chill the dough until firm, 1 to 2 hours.

Pre-heat the oven to 400°F/200°C/Gas 6. Lightly grease 2 large baking sheets. Drop heaped teaspoonfuls of the mixture 5 cm/2 in apart on to baking sheets, and flatten slightly. Bake until puffed and golden, 8 to 10 minutes. Transfer the baking sheets to wire racks to cool, 5 to 8 minutes. Then, using a spatula or palette knife, transfer the biscuits to wire racks to cool completely. Repeat with remaining mixture.

When the biscuits are cool, arrange on wire racks, and drizzle over some melted chocolate in a zigzag pattern. Store in airtight containers.

Walnut Biscuits

These biscuits are delicious as they are, but could easily be coated with melted chocolate or a chocolate substitute such as carob. Use pecans if you prefer, but the slightly bitter flavour of walnuts is very good in biscuits. Place the biscuits far apart on the baking sheets or they may spread into each other.

MAKES ABOUT 30

120 g/4 oz butter, slightly softened	120 g/4 oz wholemeal flour
200 g/7 oz light brown sugar	1 tsp baking powder
1 large egg, beaten	90 g/3 oz walnut pieces, finely chopped

Pre-heat the oven to 350°F/175°C/Gas 4 then lightly grease 2 or 3 baking sheets.

Beat the butter and sugar together until pale – the mixture will be slightly sticky. Add the egg and mix well, then fold in the flour and baking powder and finally work in the nuts.

Turn the mixture out on to a lightly floured surface and knead gently to bring the dough together. Roll into a sausage shape about 30 cm/12 in long, wrap in clingfilm, and chill for at least 1 hour, until firm enough to handle.

Cut the dough into thin slices and roll them into balls about the size of a walnut. Place on the prepared baking sheets, flattening the biscuits slightly with the palm of your hand. Bake for 12 to 15 minutes, then allow to cool slightly on the baking sheet before transferring to a wire rack to cool completely.

Muesli Biscuits

These sweet biscuits are very quick to make, but they must be chilled before baking or they will spread too much in the oven. The honey binds the mixture together; no egg is used. Work the dough well to produce light biscuits.

MAKES ABOUT 20

120 g/4 oz butter or margarine

120 g/4 oz light brown sugar

60 g/2 oz honey

175 g/6 oz muesli

120 g/4 oz wholemeal flour

Cream the butter and sugar until pale and fluffy then add the honey and beat thoroughly again. Work in the muesli and flour to give a stiff dough which is only slightly sticky, then turn out on to a lightly floured surface and knead firmly until the dough is easily manageable.

Form into a sausage shape, about 30 cm/12 in long, then cover in clingfilm and chill in the refrigerator for at least 30 minutes.

Pre-heat the oven to 350°F/175°C/Gas 4 and lightly grease 2 baking sheets. Cut the biscuit dough into 20 pieces, form into balls then flatten slightly and place on the prepared baking sheets. Bake for 12 to 15 minutes, until lightly browned. Leave to cool slightly on the baking sheets until firm enough to transfer to a wire rack to cool completely.

Store in an airtight container.

Macaroons

This is the classic macaroon, made with marzipan, egg whites and sugar.

MAKES ABOUT 30

250 g/8 oz white marzipan, cut into pieces	90 g/3 oz sugar
250 g/8 oz caster sugar	2 Tbsp plain flour, sifted
3 egg whites, at room temperature	⅛ tsp salt
	2 Tbsp chopped blanched almonds

Pre-heat the oven to 300°F/150°C/Gas 2. Line 2 baking sheets with rice paper or lightly oiled baking parchment.

In a food processor fitted with a metal blade, using pulse action, process the marzipan. Gradually add the sugar and the egg whites and process until smooth. Sprinkle over icing sugar, flour and salt and, using the pulse action, process until well-blended. Scrape into a bowl and chill for 15 minutes to firm slightly.

Drop teaspoonfuls, 5 cm/2 in apart, on to prepared baking sheets, and sprinkle a few chopped almonds on to centre of each mound. Cover with a clean dish cloth, and allow to sit for 30 minutes. Bake until pale golden and set, allow 20 to 25 minutes.

Dampen 2 teatowels, and spread over 2 wire racks. Remove the baking sheets from the oven, and slide the paper linings on to the damp cloths. Leave to cool completely, then peel the macaroons off the paper.

> **TIP**
> *Marzipan, a paste of ground almonds, is available in most large supermarkets.*
> *Rice paper is an edible paper available in specialist cook shops.*

Swedish Almond Wafers

Grinding your own almonds makes all the difference to these rich, buttery, lace-like biscuits. Be sure to leave plenty of space between the biscuits as they spread considerably. Having extra baking sheets is helpful as it is necessary to bake them in small batches.

MAKES ABOUT 24

90 g/3 oz unblanched almonds	2 Tbsp plain flour
120 g/4 oz caster sugar	¼ tsp salt
120 g/4 oz unsalted butter, cut into pieces	2 Tbsp single cream

Pre-heat the oven to 350°F/175°C/Gas 4. Lightly grease 2 large baking sheets. In a food processor fitted with a metal blade, process the almonds until very finely ground. Do not overgrind or they will form a paste. Add a little sugar, and pulse again to be sure they are evenly ground.

Combine the almond mixture, remaining sugar, butter, flour, salt and cream in a heavy-based saucepan and cook over medium heat until the butter is melted and the mixture is smooth. Remove from the heat.

Drop scant teaspoonfuls, 7–10 cm/3–4 in apart, on to baking sheets (you may only get 5 to 6 on a sheet). Bake for 3 to 5 minutes, until lightly brown at the edges, but bubbling in the centre. Transfer the baking sheet to wire racks to cool slightly.

When the edges are firm enough to lift, use a thin palette knife to remove the biscuits to wire racks to cool completely. Repeat with the remaining mixture, cooling and greasing the baking sheets again between each batch. Store in airtight containers with greaseproof paper between layers. They are very fragile.

Luxury Macaroons

T he flavour of the macadamias goes very well with coconut.

MAKES 24

175 g/6 oz desiccated coconut	**1 tsp vanilla essence**
120 g/4 oz unsalted macadamia nuts, chopped	**2 egg whites**
	Pinch of salt
Flavourless vegetable oil for greasing	**175 g/6 oz white or plain chocolate, melted (optional)**
150 ml/5 fl oz condensed milk	

Pre-heat the oven to 350°F/175°C/Gas 4. Place the coconut on one large baking sheet and the macadamia nuts on another. Toast until lightly golden, 7 to 10 minutes, stirring and shaking frequently. Pour the coconut on to one plate and the nuts on to another to cool completely.

Line 2 large baking sheets with baking parchment. Brush very lightly with oil. Into a large bowl, combine the condensed milk, vanilla essence, coconut and macadamia nuts until well-blended.

In a medium bowl with an electric mixer on medium speed, beat the egg whites until foamy. Add salt and increase the speed to high. Continue beating until the whites are stiff but not dry. Fold into the coconut mixture. Drop rounded tablespoonfuls on to prepared baking sheets. Bake until golden around edges, 12 to 14 minutes. Transfer the baking sheets to wire racks to cool completely, then gently peel off the paper.

Line a large baking sheet with greaseproof paper. Dip the macaroon bottoms into melted white or plain chocolate. Place on the lined baking sheet until the chocolate sets, 15 to 20 minutes. Peel off the paper and refrigerate in airtight containers with greaseproof paper between layers.

Spiced Muesli and Nut Biscuits

These chewy biscuits are sturdy enough to send by post as a gift, or to take on a picnic. They keep well.

MAKES ABOUT 36

300 g/10 oz plain flour

2½ tsp baking powder

2 tsp ground cinnamon

½ tsp ground nutmeg

½ tsp bicarbonate of soda

½ tsp salt

120 g/4 oz unsalted butter, softened

120 g/4 oz sugar

60 ml/2 fl oz fresh orange juice

1 egg

90 g/3 oz plain muesli

90 g/3 oz raisins

60 g/2 oz chopped walnuts or almonds

60 g/2 oz quick-cooking rolled oats

Pre-heat the oven to 250°F/120°C/Gas ½. Lightly grease 2 baking sheets. Into a medium bowl, sift together flour, baking powder, cinnamon, nutmeg, bicarbonate and salt.

In a large bowl with an electric mixer, beat the butter and sugar until light and fluffy, 1 to 2 minutes. Slowly beat in the orange juice and egg. Stir in the flour mixture until well-blended; then stir in the muesli, raisins, chopped nuts and oats.

Drop rounded tablespoonfuls at least 5 cm/2 in apart on to prepared baking sheets. Smooth the tops slightly with a moistened fingertip. Bake until set and lightly browned, 15 to 18 minutes, rotating the baking sheets from the top to the bottom shelf and front to back halfway through cooking time. Transfer baking sheets to wire racks to cool slightly. Then, using a metal spatula or palette knife, transfer the biscuits to wire racks to cool completely. Repeat with the remaining dough. Store in airtight containers.

Brownie Biscuits

These chewy chocolate biscuits are like brownies. Do not over-bake or they will be dry.

MAKES ABOUT 36

90 g/3 oz plain flour

¼ tsp salt

60 g/2 oz plain chocolate, chopped

120 g/4 oz unsalted butter, softened

250 g/8 oz sugar

2 eggs, lightly beaten

1 tsp vanilla essence

90 g/3 oz walnuts, chopped

90 g/3 oz plain chocolate chips

Icing sugar to dust

Pre-heat the oven to 350°F/175°C/Gas 4. Grease 2 baking sheets. Into a small bowl, sift together the flour and salt; set aside.

In a heatproof bowl placed over a saucepan of simmering water, melt the chocolate, stirring frequently, until smooth. Remove from the heat to cool slightly. In a large bowl with an electric mixer, beat the butter until creamy, about 30 seconds. Add the sugar and beat until light and fluffy, 1 to 2 minutes. Beat in the eggs and vanilla essence then stir in walnuts and chocolate chips. Add the flour mixture and stir until just blended.

Drop tablespoonfuls, 5 cm/2 in apart, on to greased baking sheets, and bake until the tops feel set but the centres remain moist, about 10 to 12 minutes. Transfer the baking sheets to wire racks to cool until the biscuits have set and become firm enough to move, about 5 minutes. Then, using a metal spatula or palette knife, transfer the biscuits to wire racks to cool completely. Repeat with the remaining biscuit mixture.

Dust the cooled biscuits with a little icing sugar. Store in airtight containers with greaseproof paper between the layers.

New England-Style Jumbles

This is a new version of an old-fashioned American biscuit recipe, so called because the nuts were "jumbled" into the dough.

MAKES ABOUT 36

150 g/5 oz plain flour	150 g/5 oz dried cranberries
¾ tsp bicarbonate of soda	60 g/2 oz dried cherries
½ tsp ground cinnamon	120 g/4 oz unsalted butter, softened
⅛ tsp salt	175 g/6 oz sugar
90 g/3 oz plain chocolate chips	60 g/2 oz light brown sugar
90 g/3 oz walnuts, coarsely chopped	1 egg
90 g/3 oz hazelnuts, chopped	1 tsp vanilla essence
90 g/3 oz unblanched whole almonds, chopped	

Pre-heat the oven to 375°F/190°C/Gas 5. Into a medium bowl, sift together the flour, bicarbonate, cinnamon and salt. In a large bowl, stir the chocolate chips, walnuts, hazelnuts, almonds, cranberries and cherries.

In a large bowl with an electric mixer, beat the butter until creamy, 30 seconds. Add the sugars and beat until light and fluffy, 1 to 2 minutes. Beat in the egg and vanilla essence. On low speed, beat in the flour mixture until blended. Pour into the bowl of nuts and dried fruit, and stir until combined.

Drop rounded tablespoonfuls, 5 cm/2 in apart, on 2 large ungreased baking sheets. Bake until golden, 12 to 15 minutes, rotating the baking sheets from the top to the bottom shelf and from front to back halfway through the cooking time. Transfer the baking sheets to wire racks to cool slightly. Then transfer the biscuits to wire racks to cool completely. Repeat with the remaining biscuit dough.

TIP

If the dough seems soft, refrigerate for 15 minutes before dropping on to baking sheets. This will keep it from spreading too much.

Low-fat Oat and Orange Biscuits

These little biscuits are hard to resist. Rolled in oatmeal, they are crisp on the outside, and soft in the centre with a mild orange flavour.

MAKES 20

3 Tbsp polyunsaturated margarine	Grated rind of 1 orange
60 g/2 oz granulated brown sugar	150 g/5 oz self-raising flour
	90 g/3 oz oatmeal
1 egg white, lightly beaten	Strips of orange rind to decorate (optional)
2 Tbsp skimmed milk	
3 Tbsp raisins	

Pre-heat the oven to 350°F/175°C/Gas 4. Cream the margarine and sugar together until the mixture is light and fluffy. Add the egg white, milk, raisins and orange rind. Fold in the flour and bring the mixture together to form a dough then roll into 20 equal-sized balls.

Place the oatmeal in a shallow bowl, roll each dough ball in the oatmeal to coat completely, pressing gently. Place the biscuits on non-stick baking sheets, spacing well apart. Flatten each round slightly.

Bake for 15 minutes or until they are golden. Cool on a wire rack, then decorate the biscuits. Store in airtight containers.

Oatmeal Lace Biscuits

These beautiful lacy biscuits are so thin they are transparent, but simple to make.

MAKES ABOUT 24

175 g/6 oz quick-cooking rolled oats

250 g/8 oz light brown sugar

250 g/8 oz sugar

2 Tbsp plain flour

¼ tsp salt

150 g/5 oz unsalted butter, melted

1 egg, lightly beaten

1 tsp vanilla essence

60 g/2 oz mini chocolate chips

Pre-heat the oven to 350°F/175°C/Gas 4. In a large bowl, combine oats, sugars, flour and salt. Make a well in the centre. Add the melted butter, egg and vanilla essence. Stir until blended into a soft batter-like dough. Stir in the chocolate chips.

Drop half-teaspoonfuls, 7 cm/3 in apart, on ungreased baking sheets. Bake 3 to 5 minutes until the edges are lightly browned and the centres bubbling; the biscuits will spread to large circles. Transfer the sheets to wire racks.

When the edges are firm enough to lift, use a thin palette knife to remove the biscuits to wire racks to cool completely. Repeat with remaining mixture. The biscuits can be stored in airtight containers with greaseproof paper between the layers. They are crisp and fragile.

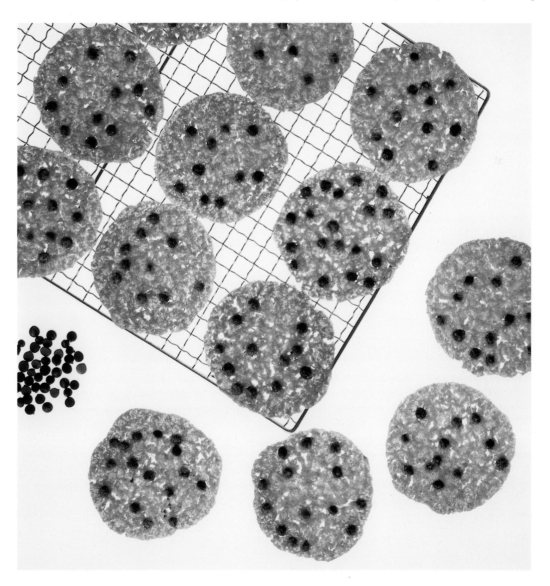

Moulded Biscuits

Chocolate Butter Biscuits · Chocolate-dipped Hazelnut Crescents

Chocolate Peanut Butter Biscuits · Austrian Crescents

Peanut Butter Biscuits · Lemon Madeleines

Mexican Wedding Cakes · Chocolate Madeleines

Grantham Ginger Biscuits · Almond and Pine Nut Biscotti

Gingernuts · Chinese Almond Biscuits

Coconut Macaroons · Poppy Seed Pistachio Puffs

Coffee Macaroons · Kourambiedes

Cinnamon Balls · Cardamom Biscuits

Chocolate Butter Biscuits

These rich chocolate butter biscuits can also be moulded into different shapes for special occasions.

MAKES ABOUT 36

175 g/6 oz flour	I egg yolk
60 g/2 oz unsweetened cocoa powder	I tsp almond or vanilla essence
¼ tsp salt	50 g/2 oz plain chocolate
175 g/6 oz unsalted butter, softened	60 g/2 oz unblanched chopped almonds, toasted
120 g/4 oz sugar	

TIP

The biscuits can be shaped into 4-cm/1¹/₂-in balls, decorated with half a glacé cherry, or dusted with sugar.

Pre-heat the oven to 375°F/190°C/Gas 5. In a medium bowl, sift together the flour, cocoa powder and salt.

In a large bowl, with an electric mixer, beat the butter until creamy, 30 seconds. Gradually add the sugar and beat until light and fluffy, 1 to 2 minutes. Add the egg yolk and almond or vanilla essence, and beat for 1 minute. Gradually stir in the flour mixture until well-blended.

Using a teaspoon to scoop the dough and also using your palms, form into 5-cm/2-in logs. Place logs 2.5 cm/1 in apart on greased baking sheets. Bake until just set, 7 to 9 minutes. Transfer the baking sheets to wire racks to cool slightly. Place the biscuits on wire racks to cool completely.

Arrange the logs on a wire rack placed over a baking sheet to catch any drips. Using a teaspoon or paper cone, drizzle with chocolate in a zigzag pattern; then sprinkle over a few chopped almonds. Leave to set. Store in airtight containers.

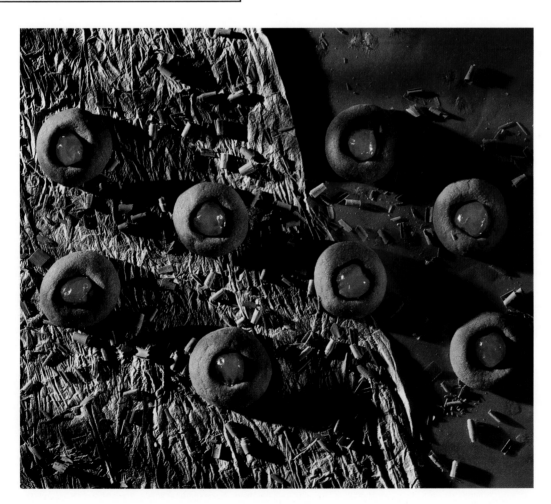

Chocolate Peanut Butter Biscuits

The combination of chocolate and peanut butter is a classic one.

MAKES ABOUT 36

120 g/4 oz plain flour	1 egg
1 tsp baking powder	1 tsp vanilla essence
¼ tsp salt	CHOCOLATE FILLING
120 g/4 oz unsalted butter, softened	375 g/12 oz plain chocolate, chopped
120 g/4 oz light brown sugar	90 g/3 oz unsalted butter, softened
60 g/2 oz sugar	
250 g/8 oz smooth peanut butter	

In a small bowl, sift together the flour, baking powder and salt. In a large mixing bowl with an electric mixer, beat butter until creamy, 30 seconds. Add the sugars and continue beating until mixture is light and fluffy. Add the peanut butter in 3 batches, beating well until mixture is well-blended. Beat in the egg and vanilla essence. Stir in flour mixture until just mixed. Refrigerate the dough until chilled, 1 hour.

Pre-heat the oven to 375°F/190°C/Gas 5. Using a tablespoon, scoop out the mixture and, with slightly moistened hands, roll between your palms to form 2.5-cm/1-in balls. Place balls 5 cm/2 in apart on 2 ungreased baking sheets. Using a finger, press down into the centre to make a hole. Bake until just set and golden, 10 to 12 minutes. Rotate the baking sheets halfway through the cooking time. Transfer the baking sheets to wire racks to cool for about 2 to 3 minutes. Then transfer the biscuits to wire racks to cool completely.

In a medium bowl over a saucepan of simmering water, melt the chocolate until smooth, stirring frequently. Remove from the heat and cool slightly. Gently beat in the butter until the mixture just thickens. Spoon into a piping bag fitted with a medium star nozzle. When the biscuits are completely cold, pipe a small amount of chocolate into the centre of each biscuit. Allow to set.

Peanut Butter Biscuits

This is a classic biscuit. If you like, add some chopped peanuts for extra crunch.

MAKES 24

120 g/4 oz plain flour	1 egg, lightly beaten
½ tsp bicarbonate of soda	1 tsp vanilla essence
½ tsp salt	250 g/8 oz crunchy peanut butter
120 g/4 oz unsalted butter, softened	90 g/3 oz peanuts, coarsely chopped
175 g/6 oz light brown sugar	

TIP

Smooth peanut butter can be used instead of crunchy. Be sure to use a commercial, not home-made, peanut butter.

In a bowl sift together the flour, bicarbonate and salt. In a large bowl with an electric mixer, beat the butter until creamy, 30 seconds. Add the sugar and continue beating until the mixture is light and fluffy, 1 to 2 minutes. Beat in the egg and vanilla essence until well-blended. Beat in the peanut butter then, on low speed, beat in the flour mixture and peanuts. Refrigerate the dough until firm, about 30 minutes.

Pre-heat the oven to 350°F/175°C/Gas 4. Lightly grease 2 large baking sheets. Use a teaspoon to scoop out the dough and form into 2.5-cm/1-in balls. Place on baking sheets 5 cm/2 in apart, and use a fork to press flat, making 5-cm/2-in rounds with a criss-cross pattern.

Bake until golden, 12 to 15 minutes. Transfer the baking sheets to wire racks to cool slightly. Then, using a metal spatula or palette knife, transfer the biscuits to wire racks to cool completely. Store in airtight containers.

Mexican Wedding Biscuits

These melt-in-the-mouth biscuits, dusted with several coats of icing sugar, resemble wedding bells and are sometimes called by that name.

MAKES ABOUT 48

90 g/3 oz pecan or walnut halves	1 tsp vanilla essence
175 g/6 oz icing sugar	¼ tsp salt
½ tsp ground cinnamon	250 g/8 oz plain flour
250 g/8 oz butter, cut into pieces, softened	Icing sugar to dust

Pre-heat the oven to 375°F/190°C/Gas 5. Place the pecans or walnuts on a baking sheet, and toast until golden, 7 to 10 minutes, turning and shaking occasionally. Pour on to a plate to cool completely. Turn off the oven.

In a food processor fitted with a metal blade, process the toasted nuts with the icing sugar and cinnamon until fine crumbs form. Add the butter to processor, and process until creamy and smooth, scraping the sides of the bowl once. Add vanilla essence, and pulse to blend. Add the salt and flour, and, using the pulse action, process until the mixture begins to stick together and form a soft dough. Scrape into a bowl, cover and refrigerate 1 to 2 hours to firm.

> **TIP**
>
> *If the biscuits have been stored, re-roll in icing sugar a few hours before serving to ensure they are well-coated.*

Pre-heat the oven to 375°F/190°C/Gas 5. Using a small scoop or tablespoon and lightly floured hands, shape the dough into 2.5-cm/1-in balls, rolling them between your palms. Place 5 cm/2 in apart on 2 large ungreased baking sheets. Bake until barely golden, 12 to 15 minutes, rotating the baking sheets from the top to the bottom shelf and from front to back halfway through the cooking time. Transfer the baking sheets to wire racks to cool, 2 minutes. Then, using a metal spatula or palette knife, transfer the biscuits to wire racks. Repeat with the remaining biscuit dough.

Place about 250 g/8 oz icing sugar in a medium bowl. While the biscuits are still warm, roll a few at a time in the sugar to coat well. Transfer to wire racks to cool completely. Roll again in icing sugar before storing in airtight containers.

Grantham Ginger Biscuits

These round, puffy gingerbread biscuits should be hollow and slightly dome-shaped.

MAKES ABOUT 30

250 g/8 oz self-raising flour

1 tsp ground ginger

120 g/4 oz butter or margarine

300 g/10 oz caster sugar

1 egg, beaten

Pre-heat the oven to 300°F/150°C/Gas 2. In one bowl, sift together the flour and the ginger. In another bowl, beat together the butter or margarine and sugar, then beat in the egg. Stir in the flour mixture and combine well. Roll the dough into walnut-sized balls.

Place the balls on greased baking sheets and bake for about 40 minutes until crisp, hollow and lightly browned.

Gingernuts

Gingernuts have become a firm favourite all over the world, and are especially enjoyable when dipped in a cup of tea.

MAKES ABOUT 20

120 g/4 oz self-raising flour

½ tsp bicarbonate of soda

1–2 tsp ground ginger

1 tsp ground cinnamon

1 Tbsp caster sugar

60 g/2 oz butter or hard margarine

5 Tbsp golden syrup

1 Tbsp treacle

Pre-heat the oven to 375°/190°C/Gas 5. Sift the flour, bicarbonate and spices into a bowl. Stir in the sugar. Melt the butter or margarine, golden syrup and treacle together, pour on to the dry ingredients, and combine thoroughly.

Roll the dough into balls. Place on greased baking sheets and flatten slightly with the palm of the hand. Bake for about 15 minutes. Store in airtight containers.

Coconut Macaroons

These Passover cookies store well and taste delicious. Macaroons are an excellent way to use up any left-over egg whites.

MAKES ABOUT 30

4 egg whites

¼ teaspoon cream of tartar

250 g/8 oz sugar

1 tsp lemon juice or white wine vinegar

1 tsp vanilla essence

250 g/8 oz desiccated coconut

In a large bowl, with an electric mixer on medium speed, beat the egg whites until frothy. Add the cream of tartar and beat on high speed until peaks form. Gradually sprinkle in the sugar, 2 tablespoons at a time, beating well after each addition until the egg whites form stiff peaks.

Sprinkle lemon juice or vinegar, vanilla essence and coconut over the egg whites. Gently fold in until just blended.

Pre-heat the oven to 300°F/150°C/Gas 2. Line 2 large baking sheets with baking parchment or foil. Drop the mixture in heaped teaspoonfuls on to the baking sheets, keeping a cone shape, about 2.5 cm/1 in apart.

Bake for 40 to 45 minutes until lightly browned; macaroons should be very slightly soft in the centre. Transfer to wire racks to cool slightly. Carefully peel off paper and cool completely. Store in an airtight container.

Coffee Macaroons

The flavour of coffee and the lightness of macaroons make a perfect combination.

MAKES ABOUT 20

Rice paper	I Tbsp cornflour
150 g/5 oz ground almonds	¼ tsp vanilla essence
175 g/6 oz sugar	I Tbsp coffee essence
2 egg whites	12 chocolate coffee beans

Pre-heat the oven to 375°F/190°C/Gas 5. Line 2 or 3 baking trays with rice paper.

Mix the ground almonds, sugar and all but one tablespoon of the egg white together. Stir until all the ingredients are evenly blended. Stir in the cornstarch, vanilla and coffee essences.

Spoon into a piping bag fitted with a 1-cm/½-in plain nozzle. Pipe the mixture on to the rice paper in large round circles. Top each one with a chocolate coffee bean. Brush with the remaining egg white.

Bake the coffee macaroons for 15 minutes or until lightly browned, risen and slightly cracked.

Cut the rice paper to fit round each coffee macaroon and leave to cool on a wire rack.

Cinnamon Balls

These cinnamon biscuits have a delicate flavour.

MAKES ABOUT 20

250 g/4 oz finely blanched and ground almonds, walnuts or pecans	2 egg whites
	⅛ tsp cream of tartar
250 g/8 oz sugar	120 g/4 oz icing sugar
I Tbsp ground cinnamon	I Tbsp ground cinnamon

> **TIP**
> If the mixture is too soft, add more ground almonds to firm it up.

Pre-heat the oven to 325°F/160°C/Gas 3. Lightly grease a large non-stick baking sheet. In a medium bowl, combine the ground nuts, 120 g/4 oz of the sugar and the cinnamon.

In a medium bowl with an electric mixer, beat egg whites until foamy. Add the cream of tartar, and continue beating until soft peaks form. Gradually add the remaining sugar, a tablespoon at a time, beating well after each addition, until the whites are stiff and glossy. Gently fold in the nut mixture.

With moistened hands, shape the mixture into walnut-size balls. Place on a baking sheet 2.5 cm/1 in apart. Bake until set and golden, about 25 to 30 minutes, rotating from the top to the bottom shelf and from front to back halfway through the cooking time. Transfer the baking sheets to a wire rack to cool slightly.

In a small bowl, combine the icing sugar and the cinnamon. Roll each warm cinnamon ball in the mixture to coat completely; then set on wire racks to cool completely. Roll the balls again when cold. Store in airtight containers.

Chocolate-dipped Hazelnut Crescents

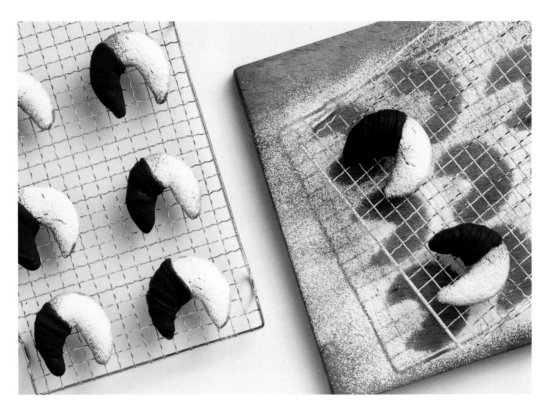

The combination of chocolate and hazelnuts is a classic one.

MAKES ABOUT 36

90 g/3 oz hazelnuts	1 tsp vanilla essence
250 g/8 oz plain flour	60 g/2 oz grated or finely chopped chocolate
¼ tsp salt	
250 g/8 oz unsalted butter, softened	Icing sugar to dust
90 g/3 oz sugar	175 g/6 oz plain chocolate, melted to dip
1 Tbsp hazelnut- or almond-flavoured liqueur, or water	

Pre-heat the oven to 375°F/190°C/Gas 5. Place the hazelnuts on a baking sheet, and toast until golden, 5 to 7 minutes, turning and shaking frequently. Cool on a plate. Reduce the oven temperature to 325°F/160°C/Gas 3. In a medium bowl, sift together the flour and salt.

In a food processor fitted with the metal blade, process the toasted hazelnuts until finely chopped but not ground; do not over-process.

In a large bowl with an electric mixer, beat the butter until creamy, about 1 minute. Add the sugar and beat until the mixture is light and fluffy, 1 to 2 minutes; beat in liqueur or water and vanilla essence. Gently stir in the flour until just blended then fold in the chopped hazelnuts and grated or finely chopped chocolate.

Using lightly floured hands, form the dough into 4-cm/1½-in balls. Then roll the balls into 2 × 1-cm/½-in crescent shapes, and place them 5 cm/2 in apart on large ungreased baking sheets. Bake until the edges are set and the biscuits are lightly golden, about 20 to 25 minutes, rotating the baking sheets from front to back halfway through the cooking time. Transfer the baking sheets to wire racks to cool for 10 minutes. Then, using a palette knife, transfer the biscuits on to wire racks to cool completely. Repeat with the remaining crescent shapes.

Arrange the crescents on a wire rack over a baking sheet to catch drips; dust with icing sugar. Using kitchen tongs, dip half of each biscuit into melted chocolate. Place on baking sheets lined with greaseproof paper, and refrigerate until set, 10 to 15 minutes. Store in airtight containers with greaseproof paper between the layers.

Austrian Crescents

This is a typical Viennese biscuit. The addition of ground almonds makes the dough very short and they melt in the mouth.

MAKES ABOUT 36

120 g/4 oz unsalted butter, softened

60 g/2 oz caster sugar

120 g/4 oz plain flour

60 g/2 oz slivered blanched almonds, finely ground

¼ tsp salt

¾ tsp almond essence

Icing sugar to dust

Pre-heat the oven to 325°F/160°C/Gas 3. Grease 2 large baking sheets.

In a large bowl, with an electric mixer, beat the butter until creamy, 30 seconds. On low speed, gradually beat in sugar, flour, ground almonds, salt and almond essence, until a soft dough forms.

Using a teaspoon, scoop out the dough and, using lightly floured fingers, shape into 4-cm/1½-in crescents. Place crescents 2.5 cm/1 in apart on baking sheets. Bake until firm and lightly golden (they should be pale), about 18 to 20 minutes, rotating from the top to the bottom shelf and from front to back halfway through cooking time.

Transfer the baking sheets to wire racks to cool slightly. Then, using a metal spatula or palette knife, transfer the biscuits to wire racks to cool completely. Arrange on wire racks, and dust lightly with icing sugar. Store in airtight containers. Dust again with icing sugar before serving.

Lemon Madeleines

Madeleines are a classic French biscuit-cake baked in special shell-shaped moulds. A madeleine tin makes 12.

MAKES ABOUT 12

2 eggs

175 g/6 oz icing sugar

Grated rind of 1 large lemon

1 Tbsp lemon juice

120 g/4 oz plain flour, sifted

1 tsp baking powder

90 g/3 oz unsalted butter, melted and cooled

Icing sugar to dust

Pre-heat the oven to 375°F/190°C/Gas 5. Butter a madeleine tin. In a large bowl with an electric mixer, beat the eggs and sugar until light and pale and a slowly falling ribbon forms when the beaters are lifted from the bowl, 5 to 7 minutes. Gently fold in the lemon rind and juice.

Add baking powder to the flour and, beginning and ending with flour, alternately gently fold in flour and butter in 4 or 5 batches. Allow the mixture to rest for 10 minutes. Spoon into prepared moulds.

Bake until a skewer inserted into the centre of a madeleine comes out clean, 12 to 15 minutes. Remove from the oven, and turn the madeleines out on to a wire rack immediately. Leave to cool completely. Dust with icing sugar. Store in airtight containers.

Chocolate Madeleines

This version of the classic madeleine is made with cocoa powder for a rich chocolate flavour.

MAKES 36

4 Tbsp unsweetened cocoa powder

3 Tbsp hot water

3 eggs

250 g/8 oz caster sugar

2 tsp vanilla essence

175 g/6 oz plain flour

¾ tsp baking powder

¼ tsp salt

175 g/6 oz unsalted butter, softened

Icing sugar to dust

Pre-heat the oven to 350°F/175°C/Gas 4. Butter a madeleine tin. In a small bowl, dissolve the cocoa powder in hot water, until completely smooth. Set aside to cool; then beat in the eggs, sugar and vanilla essence. Continue beating until the mixture is light and creamy, 2 to 3 minutes.

In a bowl, sift together the flour, baking powder and salt. Add half the chocolate-egg mixture and butter, and, on low speed, beat until well-blended. Increase the speed to medium, and beat for 1 minute until light. Fold in the remaining chocolate-egg mixture in 2 batches.

Using a small ladle or large spoon, fill the madeleine moulds almost full. Bake until a skewer inserted in the centre of a madeleine comes out clean, 10 to 12 minutes. Rotate the tin from front to back halfway through.

Transfer the tin to a wire rack and unmould the madeleines on to a rack immediately. Cool the tin and repeat with the remaining mixture. Madeleines are best eaten within a day or two of baking, as they tend to dry out when stored for too long. Store in airtight containers. Dust with icing sugar to serve.

TIP

To cool a madeleine baking sheet quickly, run the back of it under cold running water to chill. Wipe out, butter again and bake the next batch.

Lemon Madeleines ▶

Almond and Pine Nut Biscotti

These dry nutty biscuits are an Italian version of the German almond bread, *Mandelbrot*. They are delicious with coffee or dunked in a glass of Italian dessert wine. They keep for a long time.

MAKES ABOUT 48

375 g/12 oz plain flour	90 g/3 oz pine nuts, toasted
120 g/4 oz finely ground almonds or fine semolina	2 eggs, lightly beaten
1 tsp bicarbonate of soda	250 g/8 oz caster sugar
½ tsp salt	120 g/4 oz light brown sugar
½ tsp allspice	60 g/2 oz unsalted butter, melted and cooled
1 tsp cinnamon	1½ tsp almond or vanilla essence
200 g/7 oz blanched almonds, toasted and coarsely chopped	Grated rind of 1 lemon
	Milk to glaze

Pre-heat the oven to 375°F/190°C/Gas 5. Line a large baking sheet with heavy-duty foil. In a large bowl combine the flour, ground almonds or semolina, bicarbonate, salt, allspice, cinnamon, chopped almonds and pine nuts. In another bowl, whisk the eggs until foamy, then whisk in the sugars, melted butter, almond or vanilla essence and lemon rind. Gradually stir the flour mixture into the egg mixture until a dough forms.

Turn out on to a lightly floured surface, and knead gently just until the nuts are evenly distributed in the dough. Divide the dough into quarters, and form into even log-shapes, about 25 x 7 cm/10 x 3 in long.

Using a long metal palette knife, transfer each log, 5–7 cm/2–3 in apart, to a prepared baking sheet. Brush each log lightly with a little milk, and bake until golden and a skewer inserted in the centre comes out clean, 25 to 30 minutes, rotating the baking sheet from front to back halfway through the cooking time. Transfer the baking sheet to a wire rack to cool, about 10 minutes. Reduce the oven temperature to 325°F/160°C/Gas 3.

While the logs are still warm and soft, with a sharp knife, score into 1-cm/½-in wide slices. Slide the foil on to a wire rack and allow the logs to cool until beginning to turn hard. Using a sharp serrated knife, cut through the logs and arrange cut-side down, on baking sheets. You may need another large baking sheet at this point. Bake the biscotti until golden and crisp, 20 to 25 minutes, turning once halfway through the cooking time.

Transfer to wire racks to cool completely. Leave to cool thoroughly, about 2 to 3 hours, then store in airtight containers.

Chinese Almond Biscuits

These biscuits are popular in Chinese restaurants and bakeries. They were originally made with bitter almonds and lard, but you can use half butter and lard or white vegetable fat or all butter.

MAKES ABOUT 24

375 g/12 oz plain flour	120 g/4 oz sugar
¾ tsp bicarbonate of soda	2 eggs
½ tsp salt	1 tsp almond essence
120 g/4 oz unsalted butter, softened or use 90 g/3 oz butter and 25 g/1 oz white vegetable fat	1 egg yolk beaten with 1 Tbsp water
	Blanched almonds for decoration

In a medium bowl with an electric mixer, beat the butter or butter and vegetable fat until creamy, 30 seconds. Add the sugar and continue beating until fluffy, 1 to 2 minutes. Beat in the eggs and almond essence until blended. On low speed, beat in flour mixture until a dough forms. If too soft to handle, refrigerate for 15 minutes. Divide into 4 or 5 pieces.

Pre-heat the oven to 375°F/190°C/Gas 5. Lightly oil 2 large baking sheets. On a lightly floured surface, roll each piece of dough into a log shape 2.5 cm/1 in in diameter. Cut off 2.5-cm/1-in pieces and roll into small balls. Place the balls on baking sheets, and using back of an oiled spoon, flatten slightly. Brush with the egg and water, then press an almond into the centre of each biscuit.

Bake until lightly coloured, 8 to 10 minutes. Transfer the baking sheets to wire racks to cool slightly. Then, using a metal spatula, transfer the biscuits to wire racks to cool completely. Repeat with the remaining dough and almonds.

Poppy Seed Pistachio Puffs

The flavours of poppy seed and pistachio go very well together in these feather-light biscuits.

MAKES ABOUT 36

175 g/6 oz plain flour	2 egg yolks
6 Tbsp poppy seeds	Grated rind from 2 oranges
¼ tsp salt	1½ tsp vanilla essence
250 g/8 oz unsalted butter, softened	120 g/4 oz shelled fresh pistachios (or almonds)
175 g/6 oz caster sugar	

In a bowl, combine the flour, poppy seeds and salt. In a large bowl, beat the butter until creamy, 30 to 60 seconds. Add the sugar and continue beating until light and fluffy, 1 to 2 minutes. Beat in egg yolks, orange rind and vanilla essence. On low speed, gradually beat in the flour mixture until a soft dough forms. Scrape down the sides of the bowl and refrigerate, covered, until firm, about 1 hour.

Pre-heat the oven to 350°F/175°C/Gas 4. In a food processor fitted with a metal blade, process pistachios (or almonds) until very fine. Do not over-process or paste will form. Turn into a small bowl. Use a tablespoon to form the dough into 4-cm/1½-in balls. Drop each ball, as it is formed, into the nuts, and roll to coat well. Place the coated balls, 5 cm/2 in apart, on 2 large ungreased non-stick baking sheets.

Bake until the edges begin to brown, 18 to 20 minutes, rotating the baking sheets from the top to the bottom shelf and front to back, halfway through the cooking time. Transfer the baking sheets to wire racks to cool slightly. Then, using a thin metal palette knife, transfer the biscuits to wire racks to cool completely. Store in airtight containers.

Kourambiedes

These rich, tender almond biscuits are served at all festive occasions in Greece. At Christmas, a whole clove is often buried in the biscuit to symbolize the gifts the three wise men brought to the Christ-child.

MAKES ABOUT 36

60 g/2 oz blanched almonds, lightly toasted and cooled	1 small egg yolk
250 g/8 oz unsalted butter, softened	1 Tbsp brandy or orange-flavoured liqueur
2 Tbsp icing sugar	250 g/8 oz plain flour, sifted
¼ tsp salt	Icing sugar to dust

Pre-heat the oven to 450°F/225°C/Gas 8. In a food processor fitted with metal blade, process the cooled, toasted almonds until very fine crumbs form.

In a medium bowl with an electric mixer, beat the butter until creamy, 30 seconds. Gradually add the sugar and continue beating until light and fluffy, 1 to 2 minutes. Beat in the salt, egg yolk and brandy. On low speed, gradually beat in the flour and ground almonds until a soft dough forms. Scrape the bowl and refrigerate until firm, about 1 hour.

Use a tablespoon to scoop out the dough, and form into 2.5-cm/1-in balls. Place on ungreased baking sheets, and bake until set and just golden, 15 to 20 minutes. Transfer the baking sheets to wire racks to cool slightly. Then, using a metal spatula or palette knife, transfer the biscuits to wire racks to cool completely. Dust with icing sugar. Store in airtight containers.

Cardamom Biscuits

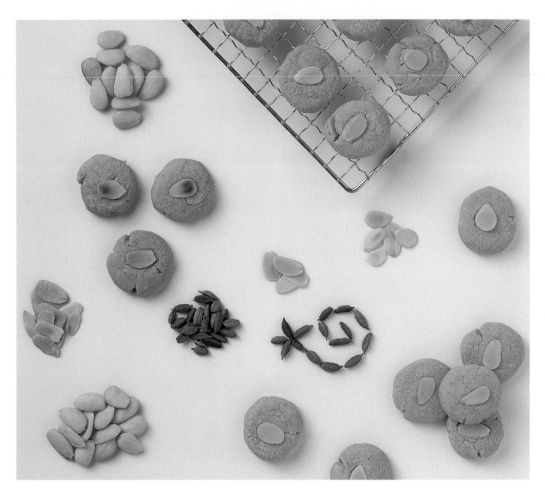

These rich butter biscuits are flavoured with cardamom, a favourite Scandinavian spice.

MAKES ABOUT 24

250 g/8 oz plain flour

4 tsp ground cardamom

¼ tsp salt

175 g/6 oz unsalted butter, softened

120 g/4 oz caster sugar

60 g/2 oz sliced or flaked almonds

90 g/3 oz icing sugar

1½ tsp cardamom

Sliced or flaked almonds

Pre-heat the oven to 375°F/190°C/Gas 5. Grease 2 large baking sheets. In a medium bowl, sift the flour, cardamom and salt.

In a large bowl with an electric mixer, beat the butter until creamy, 30 seconds. Gradually add the sugar and continue beating until light and fluffy, 1 to 2 minutes. On low speed, gradually beat in the flour mixture until well-blended then stir in the sliced or flaked almonds.

In a small bowl, sift together the icing sugar and cardamom. Using a tablespoon, scoop out the dough and roll into 4-cm/1½-in balls. Drop the balls one at a time into sugar-spice mixture, rolling to coat well. Place 4 cm/1½ in apart on baking sheets. Dip the bottom of a glass into the sugar mixture, and flatten the biscuits to 1-cm/½-in thick rounds. Press an almond on the top of each biscuit.

Bake until golden brown, 12 to 14 minutes. Transfer the baking sheets to wire racks to cool, 2 to 3 minutes. Then, using a thin metal palette knife, transfer the biscuits to wire racks to cool completely. Store in airtight containers.

Refrigerator Biscuits

Chocolate Vanilla Pinwheels

Lemon Wafers

Belgian Almond Biscuits

Cashew Butter Rounds

Poppy Seed Swirls

Chocolate-ginger Freezer Biscuits

Chocolate Vanilla Pinwheels

Be careful not to over-bake these pretty pinwheels or the colour contrast could be lost.

MAKES ABOUT 60

375 g/12 oz plain flour	2 eggs, lightly beaten
½ tsp salt	2 tsp vanilla essence
250 g/8 oz unsalted butter, softened	25 g/1 oz plain chocolate, melted and cooled
250 g/8 oz caster sugar	

In a medium bowl, sift together the flour and salt. In a large bowl with an electric mixer, beat the butter until creamy, 30 to 60 seconds. Add the sugar and continue beating until light and fluffy, 1 to 2 minutes. Beat in the eggs and vanilla essence until blended. On low speed, beat in the flour until well-blended.

Divide the dough in half, and wrap one half in clingfilm; refrigerate until firm enough to roll. Add the melted chocolate to the remaining dough in the bowl, and mix until completely blended. Wrap the chocolate dough in clingfilm and refrigerate until firm enough to roll.

On a lightly floured surface or between 2 sheets of clingfilm or greaseproof paper, roll half the vanilla dough to a ½-cm/¼-in thick, 10-cm/4-in wide rectangle. Repeat with half the chocolate dough, rolling to the same size.

If rolling between sheets of greaseproof paper, remove the top sheet and turn the chocolate dough over on to the vanilla dough; roll lightly to seal. Roll up the dough, Swiss-roll fashion, as tightly as possible. Wrap tightly in clingfilm and repeat with the remaining doughs. Refrigerate dough rolls for several hours or overnight until firm. (The dough can be prepared ahead up to 5 days or frozen.)

Pre-heat the oven to 375°F/190°C/Gas 5. Lightly grease 2 large baking sheets. Using a sharp knife, cut dough rolls into ½-cm/¼-in slices, and place 2.5 cm/1 in apart on prepared baking sheets. Bake until just beginning to colour, 7 to 10 minutes. Using a metal spatula or palette knife, transfer the biscuits to wire racks to cool.

Lemon Wafers

These thin biscuits have a delicate lemon flavour. They are perfect to serve with fruit sorbets.

MAKES ABOUT 50

175 g/6 oz plain flour	250 g/8 oz caster sugar
½ tsp baking powder	½ tsp vanilla essence
½ tsp bicarbonate of soda	¾ tsp lemon essence
¼ tsp salt	Grated rind and juice of 1 lemon
60 g/2 oz white vegetable fat, softened	Icing sugar to dust
2 Tbsp unsalted butter, softened	

In a medium bowl, sift together the flour, baking powder, bicarbonate and salt; set aside.

In a large bowl with an electric mixer, beat the white vegetable fat and butter until creamy, 30 to 60 seconds. Gradually add the sugar and continue beating until light and fluffy, 1 to 2 minutes. Beat in the vanilla and lemon essences and the grated lemon rind and juice. Stir in the flour until a soft dough forms.

Scrape the dough on to a piece of clingfilm or greaseproof paper, and, using this as a guide, form the dough into a log about 4 cm/1½ in in diameter. Wrap tightly, and refrigerate for several hours or overnight until very firm. (The dough can be made up to 5 days ahead or frozen.)

Pre-heat the oven to 350°F/175°C/Gas 4. Slice log crosswise into 3-mm/⅛-in slices, or as thin as possible, and place the dough rounds 5 cm/2 in apart on 2 large non-stick baking sheets. Bake until golden around the edges but still pale in the centre, about 8 minutes. Transfer the baking sheets to wire racks to cool slightly. Then, using a metal spatula or palette knife, transfer the biscuits to wire racks to cool completely. Before serving dust with icing sugar. Store in airtight containers.

> **TIP**
> *Do not allow the biscuits to cool on the baking sheets or they will be too crisp to remove.*

Belgian Almond Biscuits

This is a traditional Belgian recipe. The dough log is rolled in chopped almonds for an attractive effect.

MAKES ABOUT 36

50 g/2 oz unsalted butter	¼ tsp salt
60 ml/2 fl oz milk	120 g/4 oz grated or very finely chopped blanched almonds
2 Tbsp brandy	
250 g/8 oz plain flour	120 g/4 oz packed light brown sugar
½ tsp baking powder	
¾ tsp ground cinnamon	120 g/4 oz chopped blanched almonds

Melt the butter in a small saucepan over low heat. Remove from the heat and cool slightly. Stir in the milk and brandy; set aside.

In a large bowl, sift together the flour, baking powder, cinnamon and salt. Stir in the almonds and sugar. Stir into butter mixture to form a soft dough. (If the dough is too soft, add a little more flour.)

Scrape the dough on to a piece of clingfilm or greaseproof paper, and using wrap or paper as a guide, form the dough into a 5-cm/2-in roll. Chill the dough for 5 to 10 minutes. Sprinkle chopped blanched almonds on a work surface, and roll the dough log in almonds to coat, pressing the almonds into surface. Wrap the log again, and refrigerate for several hours or overnight until firm.

Pre-heat the oven to 375°F/190°C/Gas 5. Lightly grease 2 large baking sheets. Cut log crosswise into 1-cm/½-in slices, and place 2.5 cm/1 in apart on prepared baking sheets. Bake until golden, about 10 minutes. Transfer the baking sheets to wire racks to cool slightly. Then, using a metal spatula or palette knife, transfer the biscuits to wire racks to cool completely. Store in airtight containers.

Cashew Butter Rounds

These delicious biscuits are enriched by the cashew butter. A food processor is necessary to make the cashew butter, although it can be bought at some health food stores.

MAKES ABOUT 50

120 g/4 oz unsalted roasted cashews	120 g/4 oz light or dark brown sugar
2 Tbsp vegetable oil	1 egg
200 g/7 oz plain flour	2 Tbsp rum or brandy
1 tsp bicarbonate of soda	1 tsp vanilla essence
½ tsp salt	120 g/4 oz chopped roasted cashews
120 g/4 oz unsalted butter, softened	60 g/2 oz rolled oats
120 g/4 oz sugar	

TIP
Biscuit dough can be refrigerated for up to 5 days or frozen. Defrost overnight in refrigerator before using. Cut off as many slices as you require for baking at one time.

In a food processor fitted with a metal blade, process the cashews and oil until a thick, smooth paste forms, like peanut butter. In a medium bowl, sift together flour, bicarbonate and salt; set aside.

In a large bowl with an electric mixer, beat the butter until creamy, 30 seconds. Add the sugars and beat until light and fluffy, 1 to 2 minutes. Beat in the egg, cashew butter, rum or brandy and vanilla essence until well-blended.

On low speed, gradually beat in the flour mixture until a soft dough is formed. Stir in the chopped nuts and oats. On a lightly floured surface, form the dough into two 5-cm/2-in logs. Wrap each log tightly in clingfilm and then refrigerate for 4 to 6 hours, or overnight until the dough becomes very firm.

Pre-heat the oven to 350°F/175°C/Gas 4. Lightly grease 2 large baking sheets. Cut the dough log crosswise into 9-mm/⅜-in slices, and place the slices 2.5 cm/1 in apart on baking sheets. Bake until golden, 10 to 12 minutes. Transfer the baking sheets to wire racks to cool slightly. Then, using a metal spatula or palette knife, transfer the biscuits to wire racks to cool completely. Repeat with the remaining dough. Store in airtight containers.

Poppy Seed Swirls

Poppy seeds form the basis of the filling in these crisp cookie swirls.

MAKES ABOUT 48

60 g/2 oz walnut pieces, finely ground	90 g/3 oz unsalted butter, softened
60 g/2 oz poppy seeds	120 g/4 oz caster sugar
90 g/3 oz honey	1 egg, lightly beaten
½ tsp ground cinnamon	1 tsp vanilla essence
Grated rind of 1 orange	175 g/6 oz plain flour

In a small bowl, combine walnuts, poppy seeds, honey, cinnamon, orange rind and 2 tablespoons of the softened butter until the mixture forms a paste. Set aside.

In a large bowl with an electric mixer, beat the remaining butter and sugar until light and fluffy, 1 to 2 minutes. Beat in the egg and vanilla essence until well-blended then slowly beat in flour until a soft dough forms. Refrigerate the dough until firm enough to handle, 15 to 20 minutes.

On a lightly floured sheet of greaseproof paper or baking parchment, roll out the dough to a 15 × 30-cm/6 × 12-in rectangle and spread with poppy seed paste. Starting at one short side, roll up the dough Swiss-roll fashion and wrap tightly. Refrigerate for several hours or overnight until firm.

Pre-heat the oven to 375°F/190°C/Gas 5. Lightly grease 2 large non-stick baking sheets. Slice the dough roll crosswise into ½-cm/¼-in slices and place 1 cm/½ in apart on baking sheets. Bake until golden, about 10 minutes. Transfer the baking sheets to wire racks to cool slightly. Then, using a metal spatula or palette knife, transfer the biscuits to wire racks to cool completely. Repeat with the remaining slices. Store in airtight containers.

Chocolate-ginger Freezer Biscuits

The combination of chocolate and ginger is a delightful one. These biscuits use fresh root ginger and have a definite zing!

MAKES ABOUT 36

5–7-cm/2–3-in piece of fresh ginger root

175 g/6 oz plain flour

2 Tbsp unsweetened cocoa powder

120 g/4 oz wholemeal flour

½ tsp salt

¼ tsp finely ground black pepper

250 g/8 oz unsalted butter, softened

250 g/8 oz dark brown sugar

2 egg yolks

2 tsp vanilla essence

375 g/12 oz plain chocolate, chopped

Crystallized ginger to decorate

Finely grate the root ginger; set aside. In a medium bowl, sift together the plain flour and cocoa powder. Stir in the wholemeal flour, salt and pepper.

In a large bowl with an electric mixer, beat the butter until creamy, 30 seconds. Add the brown sugar and continue beating until light and fluffy, 1 to 2 minutes. Beat in egg yolks, vanilla essence and grated ginger until the mixture is smooth and well-blended. Stir in the flour mixture until blended.

Scrape out on to a piece of clingfilm and, using this as a guide, shape the dough into a 7-cm/3-in log. Wrap tightly and freeze until hard. (The dough can be frozen for up to 2 months.)

Pre-heat the oven to 350°F/175°C/Gas 4. Line 2 large baking sheets with baking parchment. Using a sharp knife, cut the frozen dough log into ½-cm/¼-in slices, and place 2.5 cm/1 in apart on baking sheets.

Bake until lightly coloured, about 15 minutes, rotating the baking sheets from the top to the bottom shelf and from front to back halfway through the cooking time. Transfer the baking sheets to a wire rack to cool, about 1 minute. then, using a metal spatula or palette knife, carefully transfer the biscuits to wire racks to cool completely.

Place the chopped chocolate in a bowl over a pan of simmering water. Stir until melted and smooth. Remove the chocolate from heat, and set aside to cool, stirring occasionally. When it reaches a spreading consistency, use a palette knife to spread a little on each biscuit. Top each biscuit with a piece of crystallized ginger, and allow to set. Store in airtight containers with greaseproof paper between layers.

> **TIP**
> A food processor is ideal for grating the fresh root ginger.

Rolled Biscuits

Chocolate-orange Hearts

Shrewsbury Biscuits

Chocolate Macadamia Windmills

Aniseed Sugar Hearts

Golden Gingerbread

Gingerbread Men and Women

Chocolate-orange Hearts

These stunning biscuits can be made in any shape – you need three cutters of the same shape: about a 7-cm/3-in, 5-cm/2-in, and a 2.5-cm/1-in.

MAKES ABOUT 30

60 g/2 oz plain chocolate, chopped	175 g/6 oz sugar
250 g/8 oz plain flour	I egg
I½ tsp baking powder	I tsp vanilla essence
¼ tsp salt	Grated rind of I orange
175 g/6 oz unsalted butter, softened	I Tbsp orange juice
	Caster sugar to sprinkle

In a small bowl over a saucepan of simmering water, melt the chocolate until smooth. Set aside to cool.

In a medium bowl, sift together the flour, baking powder and salt. In a large bowl with an electric mixer, beat the butter and sugar until light and creamy, I to 2 minutes. Beat in the egg, vanilla essence, orange rind and juice until well-blended. On low speed, beat in flour until a soft dough forms. Remove half the dough and wrap tightly in clingfilm; refrigerate until firm, about 2 hours.

With the mixer on low speed, beat melted, cooled chocolate into the dough remaining in the bowl. Wrap in clingfilm and refrigerate until firm.

Grease and flour 2 or more large baking sheets. On a lightly floured surface, using a floured rolling pin, roll out half the orange-flavoured dough 3 mm/⅛ in thick (keep the remaining dough refrigerated). With a floured, 7-cm/3-in heart-shaped cutter, cut out as many hearts as possible. Place I cm/½ in apart on a baking sheet and refrigerate. Repeat with the chocolate dough, cutting an equal number of chocolate hearts, and place on another baking sheet. Refrigerate until all cut-outs are firm.

Pre-heat the oven to 350°F/175°C/Gas 4. With a 5-cm/2-in floured heart-shaped cutter, carefully cut another heart from the centre of each 7-cm/3-in heart. Place smaller orange hearts in larger chocolate hearts and smaller chocolate hearts in larger orange hearts. With a 2.5-cm/1-in heart-shaped cutter, cut small hearts from the centre of each biscuit, and place small orange hearts into medium chocolate hearts, and small chocolate hearts into medium orange hearts.

Sprinkle the biscuits with caster sugar. Bake until golden, about 10 minutes. Cool the baking sheets slightly. Then transfer the biscuits to wire racks to cool completely.

Shrewsbury Biscuits

This traditionally English biscuit is flavoured with sherry and speckled with dried currants, then dredged with caster sugar – perfect with tea.

MAKES ABOUT 36

250 g/8 oz unsalted butter, softened	1 tsp caraway seeds, lightly crushed (optional)
250 g/8 oz caster sugar	90 g/3 oz currants
1 egg, beaten	120–175 g/4–6 oz plain flour, sifted
60 ml/2 fl oz double cream	
1 Tbsp dry sherry	Caster sugar to sprinkle

In a large bowl with an electric mixer, beat the butter and sugar until light and creamy, 1 to 2 minutes. Beat in the egg, cream, sherry, caraway seeds if using and currants. Stir in the flour until a soft dough forms.

Scrape the dough on to a piece of clingfilm or greaseproof paper and, using this as a guide, shape into a flat disc and refrigerate until firm, about 1 hour.

Pre-heat the oven to 350°F/175°C/Gas 4. Lightly grease 2 large baking sheets. On a lightly floured surface, using a floured rolling pin, roll the dough out ½ cm/¼ in thick. With a 5-cm/2-in fluted cutter, cut out as many rounds as possible. If you like, roll out the trimmings, and cut out more rounds. Place the rounds 2.5 cm/1 in apart on prepared baking sheets.

Brush the top of the biscuits with a little water, and sprinkle with a little caster sugar. Bake until crisp and golden, 15 to 20 minutes. Transfer the baking sheets to wire racks to cool slightly. Then, using a metal spatula, transfer the biscuits to wire racks to cool completely. Store in airtight containers.

TIP

Biscuit dough is easier to handle when chilled. If the dough becomes too soft to handle, return it to the refrigerator for a few minutes to firm up.

Chocolate Macadamia Windmills

These biscuits are rich, yet delicate, and easy to make.

MAKES ABOUT 36

250 g/8 oz plain flour	**120 g/4 oz caster sugar**
2 Tbsp unsweetened cocoa powder	**1 egg, lightly beaten**
	2 Tbsp golden syrup
2½ tsp baking powder	**60 g/2 oz finely chopped macadamia nuts**
½ tsp salt	
120 g/4 oz unsalted butter, softened	**90 g/3 oz plain chocolate, melted**

In a medium bowl, sift together the flour, cocoa powder, baking powder and salt.

In a large bowl with an electric mixer, beat the butter and sugar until light and creamy, 1 to 2 minutes. Beat in the egg and syrup until blended; then the flour mixture. Turn the dough on to lightly floured surface, and knead until smooth. Wrap in clingfilm or greaseproof paper, and refrigerate until firm enough to roll, about 30 minutes.

Pre-heat the oven to 350°F/175°C/Gas 4. Lightly grease 2 large baking sheets. On a lightly floured surface, using a floured rolling pin, roll out half the dough 3-mm/⅛-in thick (keep the remaining dough refrigerated). Using a floured 7-cm/3-in round or square cutter, cut as many rounds or squares as possible.

Place the cut-outs on a baking sheet. Beginning at the outside edge, make 4 radial cuts almost to the centre forming quarters (if a square cutter has been used, cut from each corner). Fold the left corner of each quarter to the centre and press to seal, forming a windmill shape. Sprinkle the centre with nuts.

Bake until firm, about 10 minutes. Transfer the baking sheets to wire racks to cool slightly. Using a metal spatula or palette knife, transfer the biscuits to wire racks to cool completely. Repeat with the remaining dough and trimmings.

Spoon the melted chocolate into paper cone and drizzle in zigzag pattern over each windmill biscuit. Leave the chocolate to set. Store in airtight containers.

Aniseed Hearts

These aniseed-flavoured biscuits can be cut into any shape.

MAKES ABOUT 24

375 g/12 oz plain flour	250 g/8 oz sugar
¾ tsp baking powder	I egg
¼ tsp salt	2 Tbsp whipping cream
1½ tsp aniseeds, finely chopped	I tsp vanilla essence
250 g/8 oz unsalted butter, softened	Icing sugar to dust

TIP

For a delicious dessert, sandwich two heart biscuits with aniseed-flavoured whipped cream, and top with a few raspberries or blueberries; dust with icing sugar.

In a medium bowl, sift together the flour, baking powder and salt. Stir in the chopped aniseed; set aside.

In a large bowl with an electric mixer, beat the butter until creamy. Add the sugar and continue beating until light and fluffy. Beat in the egg, cream and vanilla essence until blended. Stir in the flour mixture, until blended.

Scrape the dough on to a piece of clingfilm and, using this as a guide, shape into a flat round. Wrap tightly, and refrigerate until firm enough to roll out, 30 minutes.

Pre-heat the oven to 350°F/175°C/Gas 4. Lightly butter 2 large baking sheets. On a lightly floured surface, roll out half the dough about ½-cm/¼-in thick. Using a 7- or 10-cm/3- or 4-in heart-shaped floured biscuit cutter, cut out as many biscuits as possible. Transfer the hearts to prepared baking sheets 2.5 cm/1 in apart.

Bake biscuits until set and the edges are golden, about 8 minutes. Transfer the baking sheets to wire racks to cool slightly. Then transfer the biscuits to wire racks to cool. Dust the cooled biscuits with icing sugar.

Golden Gingerbread

If you prefer a darker-coloured gingerbread, replace half or all of the golden syrup with treacle. Be sure to measure the syrup or treacle accurately with measuring spoons or the dough might spread when it is baked.

SERVES 4

375 g/12 oz plain flour	120 ml/4 fl oz butter
2 tsp ground ginger	175 g/6 oz soft brown sugar
I tsp ground cinnamon	4 Tbsp dark golden syrup
½ tsp bicarbonate of soda	I egg, beaten

Pre-heat the oven to 375°F/190°C/Gas 5. Sift the flour, spices and bicarbonate into a bowl. Blend in the butter with your fingers until the mixture resembles fine crumbs.

Stir in the sugar. In a saucepan, warm the syrup to make it runny. Add the syrup and the beaten egg to the flour mixture; mix to a soft dough. If it is too sticky, add a little more flour. Knead the dough lightly until smooth.

Roll out as desired. If the dough is rolled out too thinly, a crisp texture will be obtained. If rolled out thickly, a softer texture will result. Most items will take 8 to 10 minutes to cook. Smaller items will need less time and large pieces will take slightly longer.

Gingerbread Men and Women

Everyone loves gingerbread men and women. Keep them plain and simple, or add more detail using icing.

MINI-PEOPLE GIFT BOX BISCUITS

Golden Gingerbread dough	**Red food colouring**
Royal icing, coating and piping consistency	**Tiny gingerbread people cutters**

Roll out the dough and cut out the figures with a cutter or template. Carefully remove the excess dough.

Bake for about 8 minutes. Cool completely.

Divide the royal icing in half. Colour one half of with red food colouring. Place the biscuits on a wire rack.

Coat half the biscuits with the red icing and the other half with the plain white icing. Allow to dry.

Divide the royal icing for piping in half. Colour one half of the piping icing with red food colouring. Using a small plain writing nozzle, pipe features and outline clothes in red icing on all the white figures. Using white royal icing, pipe features and outline clothes on all the red people.

Pressed and Piped Biscuits

Apricot Thumbprints

Vanilla Rings

Viennese Chocolate Biscuits

Carnival Biscuits

Chocolate Amaretti

Florentines

Ginger Snaps

Almond Tuiles

Pizzelle

Apricot Thumbprints

These biscuits get their name from the round depression in the middle, achieved by a thumbprint. The hole can be filled with any jam you like.

MAKES ABOUT 50

175 g/6 oz unsalted butter, softened	½ tsp ground cinnamon
120 g/4 oz sugar	¼ tsp salt
2 eggs, lightly beaten	250 g/8 oz plain flour
1 tsp vanilla essence	175 g/6 oz apricot jam or other favourite jam or jelly

---

TIP

For a more colourful selection, use two or more different jams, such as apricot, raspberry and cherry.

Pre-heat the oven to 400°F/200°C/Gas 6. In a large bowl with an electric mixer, beat butter until creamy, 30 seconds. Add the sugar and beat until light and fluffy, 1 to 2 minutes. Gradually beat in the eggs, vanilla essence, cinnamon and salt. Stir in the flour until soft dough forms.

Spoon the dough into a large piping bag fitted with a plain 1-cm/½-in nozzle. Pipe 4-cm/1½-in rounds, 2.5 cm/1 in apart, on 2 large ungreased baking sheets. Press a lightly floured thumb into the centre of each round, making a deep depression.

Bake biscuits until golden, 7 to 10 minutes. Transfer the baking sheets to wire racks to cool slightly. Then, using a metal spatula, transfer the biscuits to wire racks to cool completely.

In a small saucepan over low heat, heat the apricot jam until just beginning to bubble. Using a small teaspoon, spoon a little apricot jam into each indentation while the biscuits are still warm. Allow biscuits and jam to set and cool completely. Store in airtight containers in single layers.

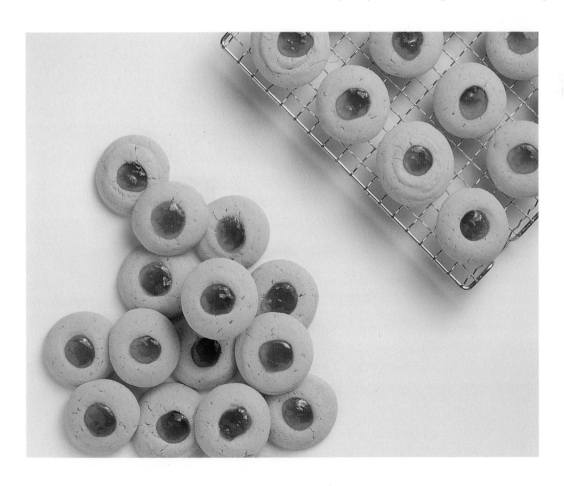

Vanilla Rings

Danish biscuits, pastries and cakes are both rich and artistic. They deserve a place of honour on the tea table.

MAKES 20

120 g/4 oz butter	2 tsp vanilla essence
250 g/8 oz sugar	175 g/6 oz ground almonds
1 egg	375 g/12 oz plain flour

Pre-heat the oven to 350°F/175°C/Gas 4. Cream the butter and sugar in a bowl, or use a food processor on a low speed, until light and fluffy. Beat in the egg, then the vanilla essence, almonds and flour.

Put the mixture into a piping bag fitted with a star nozzle. Pipe 5-cm/2-in rings on to a greased baking sheet. Bake for 8 to 9 minutes.

Viennese Chocolate Biscuits

These elegant little biscuits originate from Vienna, where they would be served with coffee.

MAKES ABOUT 20

250 g/8 oz butter or margarine	2 Tbsp unsweetened cocoa powder
120 g/4 oz icing sugar, sifted	3 Tbsp cornflour
250 g/8 oz plain flour	120 g/4 oz plain chocolate
	Icing sugar to dust

Pre-heat the oven to 350°F/175°C/Gas 4. Cream the butter or margarine and sugar until light and fluffy. Work in the flour, cocoa powder and cornflour.

Put the mixture into a piping bag fitted with a large star nozzle. Pipe in fingers, shells, or "s" shapes on to greased baking sheets. Bake for 20 to 25 minutes. Cool on a wire rack.

Melt the chocolate. Dip half of each biscuit into the chocolate and leave to set on greaseproof paper.

Dust the uncoated halves of the biscuits with icing sugar.

VARIATION

To make chocolate stars pipe the mixture into small individual star shapes. Bake for about half the time. Place a chocolate button in the centre of each one while still hot.

Carnival Biscuits

In Scandinavia May Day is carnival time, and celebrations start on 30 April. Lots of singing and balloons signal the arrival of spring.

MAKES 20–30

2 eggs	1–2 tsp vanilla essence
2 tsp sugar	250 ml/8 fl oz vegetable or coconut oil for frying
1 tsp salt	
250 ml/8 fl oz milk	Icing sugar to dust
400 g/14 oz plain flour	

⚘ Gently mix the eggs and sugar together. Add all the remaining ingredients, and stir until the mixture is smooth. Put the mixture into a piping bag fitted with a small nozzle. Heat the oil in a heavy pan. Pipe some of the mixture into the pan of hot oil, making a nest-like shape. Use a metal ring in the pan, if possible, to keep the shape better during cooking. Remove the biscuits when they are golden brown. Drain and cool on kitchen paper. When cold, dust with icing sugar.

Chocolate Amaretti

These delicious macaroon-like biscuits combine the flavours of chocolate and almond. They are surprisingly easy to make, and ideal with an after-dinner coffee.

MAKES ABOUT 24

120 g/4 oz blanched whole almonds	2 egg whites
120 g/4 oz sugar	⅛ tsp cream of tartar
1 Tbsp unsweetened cocoa powder	½ tsp vanilla essence
2 Tbsp icing sugar	½ tsp almond essence
	Icing sugar to dust

Pre-heat the oven to 350°F/175°C/Gas 4. Spread the almonds on a small baking sheet, and toast until golden, 7 to 10 minutes. Cool completely. Reduce the oven temperature to 325°F/160°C/Gas 3. Line a large baking sheet with baking parchment or lightly greased foil.

In a food processor fitted with a metal blade, process the almonds with 2 tablespoons of the caster sugar until finely ground, but not oily. Add the cocoa powder and icing sugar, and, using the pulse action, process to blend well.

In a medium bowl, beat the egg whites, until foamy. Add cream of tartar and continue beating until stiff peaks form. Sprinkle in the remaining caster sugar, a tablespoon at a time, beating well after each addition until whites are stiff and glossy. Beat in the vanilla and almond essences; gently fold in almond-cocoa mixture until just blended.

Spoon the mixture into a large piping bag fitted with a plain 1-cm/½-in nozzle. Pipe 4-cm/1½-in mounds 2.5 cm/1 in apart on prepared baking sheets.

Bake until firm on top when touched with a fingertip and the surface is slightly crisp, 12 to 15 minutes. Transfer the baking sheets to wire racks to cool slightly. Using a spatula, transfer the biscuits to wire racks to cool completely. Dust with icing sugar and store in airtight containers.

Florentines

Austrian bakers usually get the credit for inventing these biscuits, despite their Italian name. Whatever their origin, they're utterly delicious.

MAKES ABOUT 8–10

60 g/2 oz butter	2 Tbsp raisins, chopped
60 g/2 oz sugar	1½ Tbsp glacé cherries, washed and chopped
4 Tbsp plain flour, sifted	
90 g/3 oz almonds, blanched and chopped	Grated rind of ½ lemon
	120 g/4 oz plain chocolate
60 g/2 oz candied peel, chopped	

Pre-heat the oven to 350°F/175°C/Gas 4. Line 2 baking trays with baking parchment.

Gently heat the butter and sugar in a pan until melted. Remove the pan from the heat and stir in the flour. Add the almonds, peel, raisins, cherries and lemon rind. Stir well.

Put teaspoonfuls of the mixture well apart on the baking sheets. Bake in the oven for about 10 minutes or until golden brown.

While still warm press the edges of the biscuits back into a neat shape. Leave to cool on the baking sheets until set. Carefully transfer the florentines to a wire rack.

Melt the chocolate. Spread over the smooth sides of the florentines. As the chocolate begins to set, mark into wavy lines with a fork. Leave to set.

Ginger Snaps

This is a regional variation of the more commonly known "Brandy Snap".

MAKES ABOUT 48

150 g/5 oz plain flour	60 g/2 oz butter
1 tsp ground ginger	175 ml/6 fl oz golden syrup
1 tsp ground cinnamon	3 Tbsp treacle
½ tsp ground mace	250 g/8 oz caster sugar
Grated rind ½ lemon	

Pre-heat the oven to 350°F/175°C/Gas 4. Sift the flour and spices into a bowl. Stir in the lemon rind. Melt the butter, golden syrup, treacle and sugar together in a pan. Pour the liquid into the flour mixture and blend until it is a soft dropping consistency.

Drop teaspoonfuls of the mixture on to a greased baking sheet. Leave room between the biscuits to allow for spreading.

Bake for about 7 to 10 minutes. Allow to cool for 1 to 2 minutes, then loosen with a thin metal palette knife. Roll the still soft "pancakes" around a greased wooden spoon handle. Leave until set into shape, then twist the ginger snaps gently to remove.

If the biscuits cool too much while still on the sheet, return to the oven for a moment to soften them. Serve filled with whipped cream.

Almond Tuiles

These are one of the most popular French biscuits—tuiles aux amandes—so called because they resemble the curved roof tiles seen all over France.

MAKES ABOUT 30

60 g/2 oz whole blanched almonds, lightly toasted	2 egg whites
120 g/4 oz caster sugar	½ tsp almond essence
50 g/2 oz unsalted butter, softened	25 g/1 oz plain, sifted
	120 g/4 oz flaked almonds

In a food processor fitted with a metal blade, process the toasted almonds with 2 tablespoons of the sugar until fine crumbs form. Pour into a small bowl; set aside.

Pre-heat the oven to 400°F/200°C/Gas 6. Butter 2 baking sheets. In a medium bowl with an electric mixer, beat butter until creamy, 30 seconds. Add the remaining sugar and beat until light and fluffy, 1 minute. Gradually beat in the egg whites and almond essence until well-blended. Sift in the already sifted flour, and fold into the butter mixture; then fold in the reserved almond-sugar mixture.

Begin by working in batches of 4 tuiles on each sheet. Drop tablespoonfuls of mixture about 15 cm/6 in apart on a baking sheet. With the back of a moistened spoon, spread each mound of mixture into very thin 7-cm/3-in rounds. Each round should be transparent. If you make a few holes, the mixture will spread and fill them in. Sprinkle the tops with some flaked almonds.

Bake, one sheet at a time, until the edges are browned and centres just golden, 4 to 5 minutes. Transfer the baking sheet to a wire rack and, working quickly, use a thin-bladed metal palette knife to loosen the edge of a hot tuile and transfer to a rolling pin or glass tumbler. Gently press the sides down to shape each biscuit.

If the biscuits become too firm to transfer, return the baking sheet to the oven for 30 seconds to soften, then proceed as above. When cool, transfer immediately to airtight containers in single layers. These biscuits are fragile.

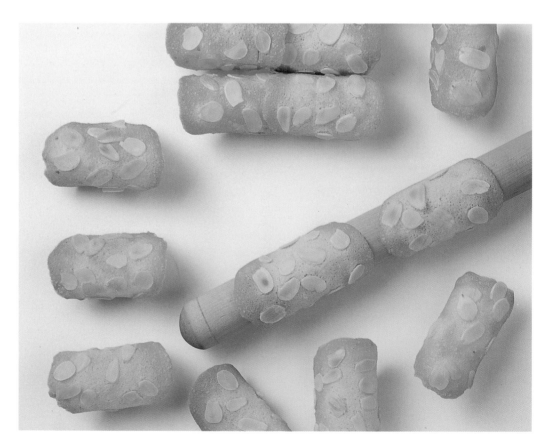

Pizzelle

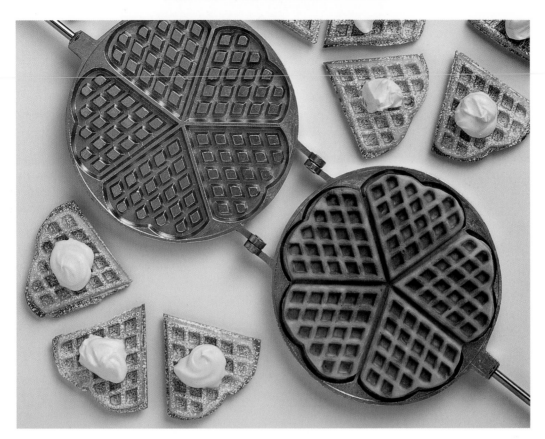

These Italian biscuits are like little waffles. Use any shape of waffle iron or griddle you like, but a heart shape is prettiest.

MAKES ABOUT 48

200 g/ 7 oz plain flour	120 g/4 oz unsalted butter, melted
2 tsp baking powder	
½ tsp salt	2 Tbsp vanilla essence
3 eggs, lightly beaten	Icing sugar to dust
175 g/6 oz sugar	

Pre-heat an 18-cm/7-in electric waffle iron following the manufacturer's instructions. In a large bowl, sift together the flour, baking powder and salt.

Make a well in the centre of the flour mixture and pour in the eggs, sugar, melted butter and vanilla essence. With the mixer on low speed, beat the liquid ingredients until blended, then slowly incorporate the flour from edge of well until it is all blended and mixture is smooth. (If the mixture is too thick, thin with a little milk or water.)

Using a small ladle, pour about 2 tablespoons of the mixture into the centre of the waffle iron or griddle. Pull down the cover and cook, without lifting the cover, for the manufacturer's specified time.

Lift the cover, and use a metal palette knife or fork to lift the edge of the pizzelle. Slide on to a wire rack to cool completely. Repeat with the remaining mixture. Dust pizzelle with icing sugar. Store in airtight containers. Alternatively, keep pizzelle warm in a 250°F/120°C/Gas ½ oven, and serve dusted with icing sugar and with a little jam or maple syrup.

TIP

Griddles and waffle irons are available in electric and non-electric models and in different shapes and sizes. Be sure to follow the manufacturer's instructions for use and cooking times.

Meringues and Soufflés

This section is about the wonderful baking properties of whisked egg whites. Meringues combine the egg white with sugar to make a powdery light biscuit or a foamy topping for tarts, deceptively simple but wickedly good. Some believe that soufflés are difficult to make, but once the principles are explained, they are easily mastered. They make excellent family meals or equally may be served to impress at dinner parties.

INTRODUCTION

Egg Whites

The chief joy of the egg white is that it will hold amazing quantities of air (8 times its own volume) when whisked. As it is practically tasteless, it is ideal for both sweet and savoury dishes.

Whisking and Folding

The best way to obtain the maximum volume of air into egg whites is to use a steel balloon whisk in a copper bowl. The copper reacts with the egg white (especially if a little vinegar or lemon juice is added – which is why copper bowls are often wiped out with a cut lemon before whisking) and a mass of chains or tunnels of small stable air bubbles are produced. An electric whisk works faster, but produces bigger bubbles that burst and disintegrate faster. The difference is not vital – perfectly good whisked egg white can be produced by machine, and in commercial kitchens today copper bowls are not used as much as chefs and catering colleges would have us believe. Apart from being very hard work, copper bowls have another disadvantage – the egg white frequently discolours as a result of the contact with the copper, and even when the bowl is assiduously cleaned beforehand the egg whites will often look greenish grey. But this colour disappears on cooking, and is nothing to worry about.

If using an electric machine, hand whisk or mixer, a metal bowl with the machine running at half pace produces the best results. Rapidly whisked white produced in a glass or ceramic bowl will be the least voluminous, and the least likely to hold their air for any length of time. But even whites whisked like this, if they are immediately incorporated into soufflés, cakes or mousses, are perfectly adequate.

Raw egg whites are used in cooking at all stages from unwhisked to whisked until stiff and dry.
Unwhisked As they come from the shell. Used to paint rose or geranium petals if making crystallized petals. The egg white must not be at all frothy or the coating will be bubbly. Unblemished dry fresh petals are painted on both sides with egg white. The petal

Frothy egg whites – the first stage of the whisking process.

Egg whites whisked until soft peaks form.

is then dusted lightly on both sides with caster sugar and left on a sheet of greaseproof paper in a warm room (or above the boiler or heater) for about 24 hours until dry and brittle, when they can be stored in an airtight container or used at once for cake or pudding decoration. They must be fully dried out before storing or they will soften and go mouldy.

Frothy Whisked, usually with a fork, just enough to mix them and prevent them plopping out of the jug separately. This makes them easier to add gradually to mixtures.

Soft peak Whisked until the egg white will just hold its shape when the whisk is lifted, the points that are dragged up by the rising action are flopping over softly. Used to add to fairly liquid mixtures such as batters or whipped cream.

Medium peak Whisked until the egg white will stand in peaks when the whisk is lifted, but with the tips of the peaks just flopping over like wilted leaves. For incorporating in soft mixtures such as soufflés, creams and sorbets. The idea is to have the two mixtures combining as close to each other in consistency as possible. It can be difficult to add over-whisked (too stiff and too dry) egg whites to a very soft chocolate mousse mixture – the egg whites break up into islands of foam and by the time the cook has stirred and struggled to get the mixture mixed most of that carefully incorporated air has been knocked out.

Stiff peak Whisked until the egg white will stand up in rigid peaks (not floppy) peaks when the whisk is lifted. Used mainly for meringues, at which point the sugar is added.

Holding egg whites If stiffly whisked, egg whites must be left before being folded into the mixture, liquefication can be delayed by excluding the air which causes the disintegration, either by wrapping clingfilm across the bowl or turning the bowl right over on the surface (the whisked whites will stick to the bowl). Alternatively, if sugar is to form part of the mixture, as in meringue or sweet puddings, some, or all of it folded into the whites will keep them stable for 15 minutes or so.

The Folding Technique

Egg whites, and other mixtures into which air has been carefully incorporated (such as sifted flour, creamed sugar-and-butter mixtures, whipped cream) are often "folded" into something else. The difference between folding and simple mixing is that, with folding, great care is taken to preserve the trapped air in the mixture. Simple stirring or vigorous beating could easily break the bubbles and

let out the air. The technique of folding is easier to learn than to describe, but the essential points are laid out below:

How to Fold

- Use a bowl rather than a flat-bottomed container. Make sure the bowl is large enough to hold the completed mixture comfortably. (Working in a small bowl is awkward and leads to lumps of egg white spilling out.) Add first a spoonful of egg white to the base mixture, beating it in to soften the mixture. Then tip in the rest of the egg whites and fold.

- Use a large metal cook's spoon, not a wooden spoon and not an ordinary tablespoon. It should be metal because that will cut neatly and cleanly through the mixture with as little disturbance of the air bubbles as possible. A wooden spoon is too clumsy, does not cut through cleanly, and has not a big enough head to lift sufficient mixture.

- Hold the spoon near the head, not halfway up the handle.

- Do not stir round and round but using the spoon edge like a knife, cut down to the bottom of the bowl, then turn the spoon to lift up the maximum amount of mixture from the bottom and bring it to the top. Turn the spoon over to drop the mixture when it comes to the top, and repeat the action in various parts of the bowl, always lifting the mass, bottom to top. Many cooks develop a "figure of eight" motion, and it is helpful to use the non-folding hand to turn the bowl.

- Do not over-beat. As the mixture is tipped into a soufflé dish or bowl, patches can be broken up with a spatula or spoon.

Meringue

Meringue is whisked egg white with sugar added (to the proportion of 50 g/2 oz sugar to each egg white). Sometimes a few drops of vinegar are added to encourage volume on whisking. Meringue is used in countless ways, and there are three main types, which can be folded into various mousses, ice creams and desserts, or baked in the oven as pie toppings or crisp meringue.

Swiss Meringue

Swiss Meringue is probably the nicest meringue to eat – light, airy, crumbly and crisp. It also makes the lightest meringue topping for pies etc.

- **Whisk the egg whites to stiff peaks but take care not to over-beat as the whites can break down and lose their volume.**
- **Fold in 1 teaspoon sugar per egg white and whisk again until the eggs have become rather shiny. Half the sugar can be beaten in using a strong electric mixer, but beating whites and sugar to the correct solid consistency by hand is almost impossible. The mixture at this point should not be at all runny and should form a solid bridge between whisk and bowl if the whisk is held 2.5–5 cm/ 1–2 in above the mixture.**
- **Fold the rest of the sugar into the mixture until combined. Do not let it stand about because, after about 15 minutes it will begin to "weep".**
- **Swiss meringue can take 3 hours in a cool oven to cook and ends up pale biscuit-coloured with a slightly toffee-like centre.**
- **A good variation of Swiss meringue is made by substituting brown sugar for half of the caster sugar. The resulting meringue is caramel-flavoured.**

The Soufflé

There is a certain amount of myth and mystique about soufflés but they are actually quite easy to make. They are satisfyingly untemperamental. They rise because the air inside them expands but will sink fast if the mixture cools while still uncooked. To stay up permanently they must be rigid and over-cooked. Chefs have solved this problem. They over-cook the soufflé, then serve a sauce with it.

To Make a Perfect Soufflé

Make the base: this can be done in advance, but should be warmed before folding in the egg whites or it will be too stiff. It should be of not-quite-

The final stage of the whisking process.

Brush out the soufflé dish with melted butter and dust with breadcrumbs before adding the soufflé mixture.

A super-light coffee soufflé, one of the many varieties you can try.

pouring consistency. If it is too solid it will take too vigorous stirring, as opposed to light folding, to incorporate the whites and much air will be lost resulting in a too-heavy soufflé. If it is too liquid the mixture will rise unevenly, not dry out satisfactorily and sink. Soufflé bases almost always include egg yolks, so stir the base over a low heat when reheating to prevent scrambling. Stop when the mixture is warm and soft. Season and flavour the base very well.

Pre-heat the oven. Most soufflés are cooked at 375˚F/190˚C/Gas 5. Put a baking sheet on the middle shelf to heat too. When the soufflé is put on this will give the bottom a good burst of heat. Make sure there is no shelf above the one to be used.

Brush out the soufflé dish with butter and dust with dried breadcrumbs. This helps the mixture glide easily up the sides and gives a crisp crust at the finish. For an impressively straight-sided soufflé tie a collar of greaseproof paper round the dish and grease that too. It is not strictly necessary – a well-made soufflé will rise above the rim anyway, but it helps even rising if the oven is at all uneven or draughty. Whisk the whites to medium peak.

If necessary, briskly stir a single spoonful of the whites into the base to further loosen and soften it. Using a spatula scrape all the egg white into the base mixture and fold in with a metal spoon. Pour the mixture into the soufflé dish. It should not be more than three-quarters full. Smooth the top. Give the whole dish a sharp crack on the table top. This will burst any over-large air bubbles.

Bake, without opening the door until 5 minutes before the estimated end of the cooking time. To check it is cooked, give the dish a sharp shove. If the soufflé wobbles easily it should be left in the oven. If it is rock solid, it is too dry. A slight tremble is best – it means a just moist centre. Remove the paper collar. Serve as quickly as is feasible.

Chocolate-Nut Meringue

This is a delicious combination of meringue and nut layers (almonds or hazelnuts), with chocolate icing. It makes a perfect after-dinner dessert and may be frozen for up to 2 months.

SERVES 4–6

250 g/8 oz ground toasted hazelnuts	120 g/4 oz sugar
300 g/10 oz caster sugar	60 g/2 oz plain chocolate
2 Tbsp plain flour	1 Tbsp milk
6 egg whites	½ tsp vanilla essence
2 Tbsp vanilla sugar	250 g/8 oz icing sugar
FILLING	1 whole toasted hazelnut for decoration
90 g/3 oz butter	

Pre-heat the oven to 300°F/150°/Gas 2. Line three baking sheets with baking parchment. Draw the chosen shape on each.

Mix together two-thirds of hazelnuts and half sugar and flour; set aside. Whisk egg whites in a large bowl until they hold firm peaks. Beat in rest of sugar and vanilla sugar until mixture is firm and glossy. Using a large metal spoon, lightly fold in the nut, sugar and flour mixture.

Divide the mixture evenly between the three baking sheets and level out, taking care not to break down the delicate aerated structure. Because of the nut content the meringue bases rise little.

Bake until lightly coloured; they will feel slightly soft to the touch while warm but become crisp and brittle as they cool. Leave on the parchment to cool on wire racks.

To make the filling melt over low heat the butter, sugar and chocolate. Stir in the milk and vanilla essence. Add the icing sugar and beat until the icing is of spreading consistency.

To assemble the cake trim the meringue bases to the same size. Place one on a wire rack. Spread one-third of the icing over it and cover with the second layer. Smooth over half the remaining icing and place the last meringue on top. Cover the top and sides of the cake with the remaining icing. Press the last of the hazelnuts all round the side of the cake. Place one whole hazelnut in the centre. Transfer to a serving dish and chill for at least 3 to 4 hours or, if possible, overnight.

The top may be piped with a chocolate icing decoration if wished.

Lemon Meringue Pie

Lemon meringue pie is a much loved classic. It has that unbeatable contrast of textures, and sweet and tangy flavours.

SERVES 4

20–22-cm/8–9-in pastry shell, baked blind	2 eggs
	3 egg whites
LEMON CURD	¼ tsp cream of tartar
Grated rind and juice of 3 lemons	6 Tbsp caster sugar
375 g/12 oz granulated sugar	Caster sugar to dredge
175 g/6 oz unsalted butter, chilled and cubed	

Using a wooden spoon, crush the lemon rind and sugar in a heatproof bowl. Strain in the lemon juice and add the butter cubes. Set the bowl over a pan of simmering water and leave the butter to melt and the sugar to dissolve. Meanwhile whisk the 2 eggs in a separate bowl until frothy and strain them into the lemon mixture. Blend all the ingredients carefully and cook slowly, stirring often, until the mixture thickens to a creamy consistency. Remove from the heat, lightly rub a little butter over the surface to prevent a skin forming and set aside to allow it to cool.

Pre-heat the oven to 350°F/175°/Gas 4. Pour the lemon curd into the cooled pastry shell and level out. Place the pie in the heated oven to warm and set the filling.

Reduce the temperature to 300°F/150°C/Gas 2. Make the meringue. Beat the egg whites and cream of tartar until foamy. Beat in sugar, 1 tablespoon at a time; continue beating until stiff and glossy. Lift the pie out of the oven and reduce the temperature of the oven. Quickly spoon the meringue on to the lemon filling and dredge with caster sugar. Return the pie to the oven and bake until the meringue peaks are crisp and have turned a golden brown colour. Serve warm or cold.

Mocha Meringue Stars

These unusual little meringues are made with cocoa and coffee powder for a sophisticated mocha flavour.

MAKES ABOUT 36

250 g/8 oz icing sugar, sifted

1½ tsp unsweetened cocoa powder

1 tsp instant espresso powder (not granules)

4 egg whites

¼ tsp cream of tartar

1 tsp vanilla essence

TIP

For even-sized stars, use a star-cutter as a guide; place cutter on foil and gently make a mark at each tip in rows on the foil.

Line 2 large baking sheets with foil. Into a small bowl, sift together 60 g/2 oz of the icing sugar, and the cocoa and espresso powders; set aside.

Pre-heat the oven to 225°F/110°C/Gas ¼. In a large bowl with electric mixer, beat egg whites on low speed until foamy. Add the cream of tartar and continue beating until soft peaks form. Gradually add the remaining icing sugar, a tablespoon at a time, beating well after each addition, until the whites are stiff and glossy, 10 to 14 minutes. Beat in the vanilla essence. Add the sugar-cocoa mixture, and fold into the whites until just blended.

Spoon meringue mixture into a large piping bag fitted with a medium star nozzle. Pipe 6-cm/2½-in star shapes, 4 cm/1½ in apart, on to the baking sheets. Bake for 1 hour. Turn off the oven, but leave meringues in oven 1 hour more to continue drying. Remove the baking sheets from the oven and peel the foil off the meringues. Cool completely on wire racks. Store in airtight containers.

Meringue Swirls

The grated chocolate cuts the sweetness of these speckled meringues. Dipping in chocolate adds a sophisticated effect.

MAKES ABOUT 36

60 g/2 oz plain chocolate, chopped

90 g/3 oz icing sugar, sifted

4 egg whites

¼ tsp cream of tartar

300 g/10 oz caster sugar

1 tsp vanilla essence

Cocoa powder to dust

Line 2 large baking sheets with foil. In a food processor fitted with a metal blade, process the chocolate with icing sugar very finely. Pour into a small bowl and refrigerate until ready to add to meringues.

In a large bowl with an electric mixer on low speed, beat egg whites until foamy. Add cream of tartar, and beat on high speed until soft peaks form. Gradually add the caster sugar, a tablespoon at a time, beating well after each addition until the whites are stiff and glossy, 10 to 15 minutes. Gently fold in the chocolate mixture until just blended.

Pre-heat the oven to 225°/110°C/Gas ¼. Spoon the mixture into a large piping bag fitted with a medium star nozzle. Pipe 6-cm/3-in "S" shapes 4 cm/1½ in apart on the prepared baking sheets.

Bake for 1 hour. Turn off the oven but leave the meringues in the oven 1 hour more. Remove the baking sheets from the oven and peel off the foil. Arrange on wire racks to cool completely. Dust with cocoa if you like.

In a small bowl set over a saucepan of simmering water, melt the chocolate until smooth, stirring frequently. Remove from the heat. Dip one end of each meringue into melted chocolate and place on a greaseproof paper-lined baking sheet. Allow to set until firm, about 1 hour. Store in airtight containers with greaseproof paper between the layers.

Meringue Swirls ▶

Chocolate-nut Divinity

These meringue biscuits are delicious with tea or coffee, and make delicious after-dinner petits fours.

MAKES ABOUT 24

4 egg whites, at room temperature

¼ tsp cream of tartar

250 g/8 oz caster sugar

1 tsp cornflour

2 tsp vanilla essence

120 g/4 oz hazelnuts, toasted and coarsely chopped

90 g/3 oz plain chocolate chips

Pre-heat the oven to 225°F/110°C/Gas ¼. Line 2 large baking sheets with foil, shiny side up.

In a large bowl with an electric mixer, beat the egg whites on low speed until foamy. Add cream of tartar, increase speed to medium-high, and continue beating until the whites are stiff. Combine 2 tablespoons sugar with cornflour; set aside. Add the remaining sugar to the egg whites a tablespoon at a time, beating well after each addition, until the sugar is completely dissolved and the whites are stiff and glossy, 15 to 20 minutes. Fold in the reserved sugar-cornflour mixture; then fold in the vanilla essence, nuts and chocolate chips.

Using a tablespoon, scoop up a mound of meringue; then use another tablespoon to scrape the mound on to the baking sheet. Make each meringue with tall rough peaks to form a large spectacular shape.

Bake for 2 hours, rotating the baking sheets from top to bottom shelf and front to back halfway through the cooking time. Turn off the heat but do not open the oven for 1 hour. The meringues should be completely dry, but not coloured. Remove the baking sheets from oven, and peel the meringues off the foil. Store in single layers in airtight containers.

Hazelnut and Lemon Bites

These meringue-like biscuits are crisp on the outside but nutty and chewy on the inside.

MAKES ABOUT 16

4 egg whites, at room temperature	150 g/5 oz diced candied citron peel
175 g/6 oz caster sugar	Candied citron peel to decorate
300 g/10 oz chopped hazelnuts	

Pre-heat the oven to 250°F/120°C/Gas ½. Line a large baking sheet with rice paper. Place egg whites and sugar in top of a double boiler, or in a heatproof bowl over a saucepan of simmering water.

With a hand-held electric mixer, beat the whites until stiff and glossy, 4 to 6 minutes. Remove the top of the double boiler or bowl from water, and continue beating until the meringue mixture is completely cold. Fold in the chopped nuts and diced citron peel.

Using a teaspoon, scoop up balls of meringue and transfer them off with another teaspoon on to the baking sheet, 5 cm/2 in apart. Press a piece of candied citron peel on to top of each mound. Bake until the meringue is set, but pale, 12 to 15 minutes; they should remain white. Transfer the baking sheets to a wire rack to cool then slide the paper with the biscuits on to a rack to cool completely. When cool, gently peel off from the paper. Store in airtight containers.

TIP

Rice paper is an edible paper which is available in specialist cook shops. If you cannot find it, use baking parchment, brushed very lightly with a flavourless vegetable oil.

Tropical Slice

Juicy fresh pineapple and shredded coconut give this meringue dish a tropical flavour.

SERVES 8

4 egg whites	150 g/5 oz double cream
250 g/8 oz sugar	1 small fresh pineapple, peeled, cored and chopped into pieces
2 Tbsp instant coffee powder	
150 g/5 oz ground almonds	120 g/4 oz desiccated coconut
50 g/2 oz slivered toasted almonds	

Pre-heat the oven to 225°F/110°C/Gas ¼. Draw two rectangles 30 x 10 cm/12 x 4 in on to sheets of baking parchment. Place upside down on baking sheets.

Beat the egg whites until stiff and whisk in 4 tablespoons of sugar and the coffee. Continue whisking until the meringue forms stiff peaks. Fold in the remaining sugar and ground almonds.

Spoon the meringue into a piping bag fitted with a 1-cm/½-in plain nozzle. Pipe in lines across the width of each rectangle. Sprinkle one rectangle with the toasted almonds. Bake for 2 hours and leave to cool.

Whip the cream until thick and soft and spread over the meringue base without almonds. Cover with the pineapple pieces and sprinkle over the coconut. Top with the second meringue layer. Refrigerate for 2 hours.

Meringue Mushrooms

These little meringues never fail to please. In France they are used to decorate the Christmas log, *Bûche de Noël*.

MAKES ABOUT 36

3 egg whites	60 g/2 oz plain chocolate, melted
⅛ tsp cream of tartar	
250 g/8 oz icing sugar	Unsweetened cocoa powder to dust

1 Line a large baking sheet with foil. In a large bowl with an electric mixer on low speed, beat the egg whites until foamy. Add cream of tartar, increase speed, and beat until soft peaks form. Gradually add sugar, a tablespoon at a time, and beat well until stiff and glossy.

2 Spoon into a large piping bag fitted with a 1-cm/½-in plain nozzle. Pipe about 30 4-cm/1½-in rounds, resembling mushroom caps, 4 cm/1½ in apart on prepared baking sheets. Pipe the remaining mixture between rounds into an equal number of 2- to 2.5-cm/¾- to 1-in high cone shapes. Leave for 1 hour to dry slightly.

3 Pre-heat the oven to 225°F/110°C/Gas ¼. Bake for 1 hour, rotating baking sheet from front to back halfway through the cooking time. Turn off the oven, but leave the meringues in oven 1 hour more to continue drying. Transfer the baking sheet to a wire rack and peel the foil off mushroom caps and stems. With tip of small sharp knife, make a small hole in the underside of each cap.

4 With a small palette knife or round-bladed kitchen knife, spread a little melted chocolate on the underside of a "mushroom cap", and gently push the pointed end of a cone shape into the hole to form the stem. Allow to set at least 1 hour. Dust with cocoa powder.

TIP

Do not be tempted to add the sugar to the whites too quickly. This can make the meringues weep and stick.

Coffee and Almond Pavlova

An impressive dessert, meringue topped with coffee and toasted almond cream, then drizzled with chocolate. The best pavlovas are crisp on the outside and sticky in the middle. I don't add sugar to the cream as the meringue base is very sweet, but you may sweeten it slightly if you wish.

SERVES 8 TO 10

300 g/10 oz caster sugar, plus extra for sprinkling	1 tsp white wine vinegar
90 g/3 oz ground almonds	2 Tbsp coarsely ground high-roast coffee
1 tsp cream of tartar	90 ml/3 fl oz hot water
1 Tbsp cornflour	25 g/1 oz blanched almonds
4 egg whites	300 ml/10 fl oz double cream
Pinch of salt	25 g/1 oz roughly chopped plain chocolate
½ tsp almond essence	

Pre-heat the oven to 300°F/150°C/Gas 2. Cover a baking sheet with baking parchment and mark out a 25-cm/10-in circle. Scatter a little caster sugar over the parchment to prevent the pavlova from sticking to the paper.

Toast the ground almonds under a medium grill until golden, stirring them once or twice, then leave to cool. Mix together the sugar, cream of tartar and cornflour in a small bowl.

Whisk the egg whites with the salt until stiff. The mixture should remain firm in the bowl when tipped upside down. Add the almond essence and whisk again. Gradually add the sugar mixture, and stop whisking as soon as it is combined. Quickly fold in the vinegar and the cold toasted almonds using a wire whisk. (Do not attempt to add the almonds with an electric whisk as the fat from them will oil the mixture and the meringue will collapse.)

Pile the meringue on to the baking sheet, spreading it lightly over the marked circle, then fork up the edges into soft peaks. Bake for 2 hours, until crisp on the outside and a pale golden colour.

Prepare the coffee while the meringue is cooking. Pour the hot water over the grounds then leave for 15 minutes. Strain through a fine sieve, then leave until completely cold. Toast the blanched almonds for 3 to 4 minutes under a medium grill until browned, stirring and turning them once or twice, then leave them to cool. Chop the almonds roughly.

Turn off the oven and leave the cooked meringue to stand for about 10 minutes, then lift it carefully on to a wire rack and leave until completely cold.

Whip the cream until thick and soft, then add the cold coffee – you should have 3 to 4 tablespoons. Continue whipping until soft peaks form, then fold in the chopped toasted almonds. Carefully peel away the paper from the meringue base, then gently place it on a large serving plate. Spoon the coffee and almond cream on to the meringue. Spread it over the centre and fork it up gently into tiny peaks.

Melt the chocolate pieces in a bowl over a pan of hot water, or in a microwave. Spoon the melted chocolate into a greaseproof paper piping bag, snip off the end, then drizzle the chocolate over the pavlova. Leave for a few minutes before serving, to allow the chocolate to set.

Spinach Soufflé

Cheese and spinach make a nutritious combination. The addition of mustard and cayenne brings out the flavours.

SERVES 4

120 g/4 oz sorrel	Pinch of cayenne
375 g/12 oz spinach	½ tsp mustard
Salt and pepper	½ cup grated mature Cheddar or Gruyère cheese
60 g/2 oz butter	
Dried white breadcrumbs	4 eggs
60 g/2 oz plain flour	1 Tbsp grated Parmesan cheese
300 ml/10 fl oz milk	

To prepare the sorrel and spinach, remove the stalks and wash the leaves very carefully. Place in a pan of boiling salted water for 2 minutes. Drain very well, squeezing water out through a colander or sieve or between two plates. Chop finely.

Pre-heat the oven to 400°F/200°C/Gas 6. Lightly butter a 15-cm/6-in soufflé dish or 4 large ramekins. Coat the sides lightly with breadcrumbs.

Melt the butter in a pan and stir in the flour. Add the milk and bring to the boil, stirring continuously. Boil for one minute. Take the sauce off the heat, stir in the salt and pepper, cayenne, mustard, cheese, spinach and sorrel. Cool slightly.

Separate the eggs, adding the yolks to the spinach mixture. Whisk the egg whites until stiff but not dry, and mix a spoonful thoroughly into the spinach mixture. Then gently fold in the rest. Spoon into the dish and bake for about 40 minutes, until set.

Serve with a tomato sauce or with anchovy butter, and sprinkle with grated Parmesan.

Coffee Soufflé

A wonderfully light soufflé, ideal to serve after a rich main course or on a summer's evening in the garden with a glass of chilled dessert wine.

SERVES 8

150 ml/5 fl oz hot water

4 Tbsp coarsely ground high-roast coffee

4 eggs, separated

120 g/4 oz caster sugar

1 Tbsp powdered gelatine

3 Tbsp boiling water

300 ml/10 fl oz double cream, whisked until thick

DECORATION

150 ml/5 fl oz double cream

10 to 12 coffee beans, or chocolate-coated coffee beans

Pour the hot water over the ground coffee then leave to infuse for 10 to 15 minutes. Meanwhile, place a 900-ml/ 1½-pint soufflé dish on a baking sheet (which makes it easier to handle) and tie a double thickness collar of greaseproof paper or baking parchment around the dish, to stand about 4 cm/1½ in above the top.

Strain the coffee through a fine sieve into a large bowl, then add the egg yolks and sugar. Whisk in a food processor for about 10 minutes, until very thick, and the beaters leave a ribbon trail when lifted. If whisking by hand, place the bowl over a pan of hot water as the heat will help to thicken the mixture.

Sprinkle the gelatine over the boiling water in a small bowl and stir, then leave to stand for 2 to 3 minutes. Stir again to make certain that the gelatine has dissolved. If necessary, heat the bowl for 30 to 60 seconds in a shallow pan of hot water or in the microwave, until the gelatine has completely dissolved.

Stir a spoonful of the coffee mixture into the gelatine, then whisk it all into the mixture, and fold in the whipped cream. Chill in the refrigerator for 20 minutes, or until starting to set and thicken around the edges of the bowl.

Whisk the egg whites until stiff, then fold them into the soufflé mixture using a wire whisk. Turn into the prepared soufflé dish, then chill in the refrigerator for 2 to 3 hours.

To decorate the soufflé, carefully loosen the paper from the top with a sharp, thin-bladed knife and peel away from around the dish. Whip the cream until stiff, then pipe it into rosettes either around the top of the soufflé or around the base of the dish on a serving plate. Top each rosette with a coffee bean.

Twice-Baked Soufflé

These individual soufflés are baked once, then turned upside down, sprinkled with cheese and baked again before serving.

SERVES 4

300 ml/10 fl oz milk	175 g/6 oz grated strong Cheddar cheese
Slice of onion	
Pinch of nutmeg	4 whole eggs plus 1 egg white
Knob of butter	
60 g/2 oz butter	Salt and freshly ground black pepper
60 g/2 oz flour	375 ml/12 fl oz double cream
Pinch of dry English mustard	

Heat the milk slowly with the onion and nutmeg.

Pre-heat the oven to 350°F/175°C/Gas 4. Butter 6 small teacups.

Melt the butter, add the flour and mustard. Cook for 30 seconds. Remove from the heat and leave to cool for one minute. Strain in the milk. Stir well and return to the heat. Bring gradually to the boil and simmer, stirring continuously for 30 seconds. Then add three quarters of the cheese.

Separate each of the eggs. Add the egg yolks to the cheese sauce. Taste and season as necessary.

Whisk the egg whites until stiff: put the egg whites into a clean, dry bowl and with a large dry balloon whisk, whisk the whites until stiff but not dry. Whisk slowly to begin with and gradually build up speed. Do not stop whisking or leave the whites sitting around – they will liquefy and not re-whisk.

Fold the egg whites into the soufflé base mixture: mix a spoonful of the egg whites into the base. Mix it in thoroughly, to "loosen" the mixture. With a large metal spoon held near the bowl, not at the end, fold in the remaining egg whites in. Be gentle but firm to ensure that they are completely incorporated without knocking out all the air. Think of it as drawing a three-dimensional figure of eight as you cut and fold. Do not forget to take your spoon right down to the bottom of the bowl.

Spoon into the cups, which the mixture should fill to two-thirds at the most. Stand the cups in a roasting tin of boiling water and bake for 15 minutes or until the mixture is risen and set. Allow to sink and cool.

Butter a shallow ovenproof serving dish. Run a knife round the soufflés to loosen them. Turn them out on to your hand, giving the cups a sharp jerk. Put them, upside down, on the dish.

Twenty minutes before serving, set the oven to 425°F/220°C/Gas 7. Sprinkle remaining cheese on top.

Season the cream with the salt and pepper and pour all over the soufflés, coating them completely. Bake for 10 minutes until a pale gold. Serve at once.

TIP

If egg and cheese soufflés soaked in double cream seem excessively rich, a simple béchamel sauce can be used instead of the cream, or cream and béchamel could be mixed together.

Spiced Pumpkin Soufflé

Many people worry about preparing soufflés, but they are actually very easy to make – it's just that they don't stay all light, puffy and fluffy for very long, so rounding up your guests at the appropriate time is actually more important than your cooking technique!

SERVES 3

2 Tbsp butter

1 Tbsp fine wholemeal flour

1 tsp ground cumin

1 tsp ground ginger

150 ml/5 fl oz milk

175 g/6 oz thick pumpkin purée

1 tsp Dijon mustard

3 large eggs, separated

Salt and freshly ground black pepper

Pre-heat the oven to 350°F/175°C/Gas 4, and lightly butter a 15–18-cm/6–7-in soufflé dish.

Heat the butter in a small pan, then stir in the flour with the spices and salt and pepper, and cook briefly for 1 minute, stirring all the time. Gradually beat in the milk, off the heat, then bring slowly to the boil, stirring all the time. Cook for 1 minute, then stir in the pumpkin, mustard and egg yolks and blend well.

Whisk the egg whites until stiff then fold them into the pumpkin mixture. Scrape the soufflé into the prepared dish, then bake for 30 to 40 minutes, until set. Serve immediately with a salad garnish.

Batter

A simple batter can be transformed into
pancakes, crêpes, waffles or even baked into
a rugged Toad in the Hole. Batters are
versatile – griddle pancakes and soured
cream waffles make excellent breakfast
foods, Persian pancakes, latkes, and apple
pancakes make good snacks, while stuffed
crêpes accompanied by a side salad are an
excellent dinner dish.

INTRODUCTION

Batter has many uses and is very versatile.

Batter is a versatile mixture of flour and liquid – usually milk and sometimes beaten egg – used to make pancakes, dropped biscuits and waffles, and also to give a protective coating to many foods which are deep-fried.

Pancakes

Thin Pancakes

Thin pancakes, or French crêpes, are made by pouring a thin layer of pancake batter into a hot greased frying pan about 20 cm/8 in in diameter, tipping to spread the batter evenly and pouring out the excess. The pancake is cooked fast to brown one side, turned to brown the other and when ready, wrapped around sweet or savoury fillings, or served simply with sugar and lemon juice.

Batter for Thicker Pancakes

Batter for thicker pancakes, sometimes called griddle pancakes, is mixed with baking powder or yeast. The rising agent causes the butter to rise in the pan to form thickish pancakes which spread out only a little as they are fried on a greased hot griddle or in a large skillet. They are best eaten warm with butter. Blinis are an example of a yeasted batter.

Waffles

Waffles are also made from raised batter and cooked in a special iron device which holds the batter and gives the cooked waffles a thin, flat, indented shape on both sides. The waffle iron is heated on the hob if of the hand-held variety, or electrically if a table-top one, before the batter is poured in. This ensures that the waffles are crisp on the outside and soft on the inside, while the raised batter makes them light. As with the coating on deep-fried foods, waffles must be eaten quickly.

Making Batter

The following recipes are examples of the main uses of batters. If the cook successfully manages these, no batter recipe should really present any problems in the future.

- ● Sift the flour into a large, wide bowl ensuring there are no lumps. Sprinkle the salt (or sugar or other dry ingredients) on top.
- ● Using either a wooden spoon or your hand, make a well in the flour to expose the bottom of the bowl. The hole should be wide enough to mix in liquid ingredients (say, two eggs and a little milk) without bringing in too much of the surrounding flour.
- ● Using a fork, whisk, wooden spoon or the fingertips of one hand, mix and stir the central liquid ingredients to a smooth paste.

- ● Gradually incorporate the surrounding flour. With practice, the stirring action flips the liquid over the banks of flour and; as it runs back into the central well, it brings with it a thin film of flour. Pour more liquid into the centre as the batter gets thicker. The idea is to keep it at the consistency of heavy cream – easier to keep lump-free than a runny mixture. Once all the flour is incorporated and the batter is absolutely smooth, beat in the remaining liquid.
- ● Leave for 30 minutes, if possible, to allow time for the starch cells to swell, giving a less doughy final product. If the mixture is left for more than an hour it might separate, but it is easily remixed. Do not make batter more than 12 hours in advance. It ferments easily.

Food Processor or Blender Method

With a food processor, making batter takes much less effort. Put any eggs and other liquid ingredients into the processor fitted with a metal blade or a blender, and spoon the flour and other dry ingredients on top. Blend for a second or two – just enough to combine the mixture without creating too many bubbles.

Classic Crêpes

T his is the traditional French pancake made with the thinnest of batters.

MAKES ABOUT 12

120 g/4 oz flour	300 ml/10 fl oz milk or milk and water mixed
Pinch of salt	
I egg	I Tbsp oil
I egg yolk	Oil for frying
	Caster sugar
	Lemon juice

Sift the flour and salt into a bowl and make a well in the centre exposing the bottom of the bowl. Place the egg and egg yolk with a little of the milk into this well.

Using a wooden spoon or whisk mix the egg and milk and then gradually draw in the flour from the sides as you mix.

When the mixture reaches the consistency of thick cream beat well and stir in the oil. Add the rest of the milk – the consistency should now be that of thin cream. (Batter can also be made by placing all the ingredients together in a blender or food processor for a few seconds, but take care not to over-whizz or the mixture will be bubbly.)

Cover the bowl and refrigerate for about 30 minutes. This is done so that the starch cells will swell, giving a lighter result.

Prepare a pancake or omelette pan by heating well and wiping out with oil. Crêpes are not fried in fat like most foods – the purpose of the oil is simply to prevent sticking. When the pan is ready, pour in about 1 tablespoon batter and swirl about the pan until evenly spread across the bottom. Place over heat and, after 1 minute, using a thin palette knife and your fingers, turn the crêpe over and cook again until brown. (Crêpes should be extremely thin, so if the first one is too thick, add a little extra milk. The first crêpe is unlikely to be perfect, and is often discarded.)

Make up all the crêpes, turning them out on to a plate. Lay the crêpes mottled-side (the second side to be fried) up, sprinkle them with a little sugar and lemon juice and roll up. Serve warm.

NOTE

Crêpes can be kept warm in a folded teacloth, on a plate over a saucepan of simmering water, in the oven, or in a warmer. They freeze well, but should be separated by pieces of greaseproof paper. They may also be refrigerated.

Toad in the Hole

This unattractively named dish is a delicious and inexpensive recipe. It is particularly good if served with meat gravy so is traditionally cooked the day after a roast dinner, when a little left-over gravy is available.

SERVES 8

	BATTER
500 g/1 lb pork sausages	120 g/4 oz plain flour
4 Tbsp lard, meat fat or sunflower oil	Good pinch of salt
	2 eggs
	150 ml/5 fl oz water mixed together with 150 ml/ 5 fl oz milk

Sift the flour and salt into a large wide bowl. Make a well or hollow in the centre of the flour and break the eggs into it.

With a whisk or wooden spoon mix the eggs to a paste and very gradually draw in the surrounding flour, adding just enough milk and water to the eggs to keep the central mixture a fairly thin paste. When all the flour is incorporated, stir in the rest of the liquid. The batter can be made more speedily by putting all the ingredients together in a blender or food processor for a few seconds, but take care not to over-whisk or the mixture will be bubbly. Leave to "rest" at room temperature for 30 minutes before use. This allows the starch cells to swell, giving a lighter, less doughy final product.

Pre-heat the oven to 425°F/220°C/Gas 7. Heat 1 tablespoon fat or sunflower oil in a frying pan and in it fry the sausages until evenly browned all over, but do not cook them through.

Heat the rest of the fat or oil in an ovenproof shallow metal dish or roasting tin until smoking hot, either in the oven or over direct heat. Add the sausages to it and pour in the batter. Bake for 40 minutes or until the Toad in the Hole is risen and brown. Serve with hot gravy.

Banana Fritters

Bananas and batter are made for each other. Try this recipe once and you'll be hooked for life!

MAKES 8

	BATTER
8 small bananas	120 g/4 oz plain flour
Oil for shallow-frying	Pinch of salt
Icing sugar	2 eggs
	300 ml/10 fl oz milk
	1 Tbsp oil
	60 g/2 oz sugar

> **NOTE**
>
> *This batter can be speedily made in a blender. Simply put all the ingredients, except the egg white, into the machine and whizz briefly.*

Sift the flour with the salt into a bowl. Make a well in the centre, exposing the bottom of the bowl. Put one whole egg and one yolk into the well and mix with a wooden spoon or whisk until smooth, gradually incorporating the surrounding flour and the milk. A thick creamy consistency should be reached. As the mixture thickens gradually add the milk to retain the creamy consistency. Add the oil and sugar. Allow to rest for 30 minutes.

Whisk the egg white and fold into the batter with a metal spoon just before using.

Peel the bananas and cut in half lengthwise and dip immediately into the prepared batter.

Heat ½ cm/¼ in of oil in a frying pan and when hot fry the fritters for about 2 minutes on each side until golden brown. Drain well and dredge with icing sugar.

Waffles

This is a thick batter with plenty of rising agent (baking powder) to make it puff up. The outside will be crisp, while the inside remains soft. Waffles can be served with jam, maple syrup or honey, with or without cream or, alternatively, topped with crisp grilled bacon or fried egg. Here they are served with a heavy dusting of icing sugar.

MAKES 10

2 eggs	300 ml/10 fl oz milk
175 g/6 oz plain flour	60 g/2 oz butter, melted
Pinch of salt	Vanilla essence
3 tsp baking powder	Extra melted butter
2 Tbsp caster sugar	Icing sugar

Separate the eggs. Sift the flour, salt, baking powder and sugar together. Make a well in the centre and drop in the egg yolks. Stir the yolks, gradually drawing in the flour from the edges and adding the milk and melted butter until you have a thin batter. Add the vanilla essence.

Grease a waffle iron and heat it.

Whisk the egg whites until stiff but not dry and fold into the batter.

Add a little melted butter to the hot waffle iron, pour in about 4 tablespoons of the mixture, close and cook for 1 minute per side. Do not worry if the first waffle sticks to the iron. It always does. Throw it away. The second one will come away cleanly. Serve the waffles heavily dredged with icing sugar.

Soured Cream Waffles

These waffles are delicious served on their own, or with jam, cream or a dusting of sugar.

SERVES 6

5 eggs	175 ml/6 fl oz soured cream
120 g/4 oz sugar	60 g/2 oz butter
120 g/4 oz flour	
1 tsp ground cardamom or ginger	

Mix the eggs and sugar for about 5 minutes until fluffy. Whisk in the flour, cardamom or ginger and soured cream. Whisk until smooth and creamy. Melt the butter and stir it into the mixture. Set aside for 10 minutes.

Cook in a waffle iron according to the manufacturers' instructions. Serve with jam, cream or sugar.

Sour Cream Waffles ▶

Potato Scones 1

There are many versions of potato scones. Here are two.

SERVES 4–6

90 g/3 oz butter

175 g/6 oz self-raising flour

Salt and pepper

300 g/10 oz freshly mashed potatoes

A little milk

Butter

Bacon

Pre-heat the oven to 425°F/220°C/Gas 7. Cut the butter into the flour, with a pinch of salt and pepper. Mix with the mashed potato and enough milk to make a soft dough.

Roll out on to a floured board and cut into circles or triangles. Place on a lightly oiled baking tray and bake for 25 minutes. Serve hot split with butter and bacon.

Potato Scones 2

This plainer version is no less delicious, served hot and dripping with butter.

SERVES 4–6

60 g/2 oz butter

120 g/4 oz plain flour

½ tsp salt

½ tsp baking powder

300 g/10 oz freshly mashed potatoes

Butter

Cut the butter into the flour. Add the salt and baking powder and mix well. Mix in the potatoes and knead for a few minutes.

Roll out on to a well-floured board with a floured rolling pin. Cut into circles or triangles. Cook on a dry griddle or pan until brown on both sides. Serve hot.

Cheese Blintzes with Strawberries

Blintzes are a symbol of Jewish cooking around the world, with the name coming from the Yiddish for pancake. It is a simple crêpe or pancake filled with cheese or fruits or fillings such as potato and mushroom, chicken livers or meat.

SERVES 6–8

3 large eggs	**FILLING**
½ tsp salt	1 480-g/16-oz tub cottage cheese
½ tsp sugar	2 120-g/4-oz packets cream cheese, softened
2 Tbsp butter or margarine, melted	60 g/2 oz sugar
375 ml/12 fl oz milk or water	1 tsp vanilla essence
90 g/3 oz plain flour	500 g/1 lb strawberries
Butter or margarine for baking or frying, melted	Sugar
	Juice and grated rind of 1 lemon

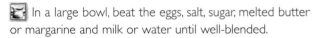 In a large bowl, beat the eggs, salt, sugar, melted butter or margarine and milk or water until well-blended.

Sift the flour into a medium bowl and make a well in the centre. Using a wire whisk, gradually stir the beaten egg mixture into flour, drawing in the flour from the edges until all the egg mixture is added. Whisk until smooth. Strain into a 1-litre/1¾-pt measure. Cover and refrigerate about 1 hour. (The batter may thicken; add milk or water to thin if necessary.)

Over medium heat, heat an 18-cm/7-in pancake or omelette pan. Brush the pan with a little melted butter. Pour 3 to 4 tablespoons batter into the pan, tilting the pan to coat with batter. Cook until the top looks set and the bottom is lightly browned, about 2 minutes. Using a metal spatula, loosen the edges and flip the blintze, then cook for 10 seconds. Slip the cooked blintze on to a piece of greaseproof paper. Repeat until all the batter is used, stacking blintzes between sheets of greaseproof paper. (Blintzes can be used immediately or stored in the refrigerator or frozen.)

Pre-heat the oven to 350°F/175°C/Gas 4. Brush a 30 × 25-cm/15 × 10 in Swiss-roll pan with melted butter or margarine.

Make the filling. In a medium bowl, with a mixer at medium speed, beat the cottage cheese, cream cheese, sugar and vanilla essence until smooth.

NOTE

For Passover, the blintze batter can be made with potato flour and water. The mixture will be slightly thinner and will make crisper blintzes.

On a clean work surface, spread 1 heaped tablespoon of cheese mixture down the centre of each blintze. Fold the sides towards the centre, so each side covers about half the filling. Roll up the blintze. Arrange seam-side down on a buttered dish. Brush each folded blintze with a little butter and bake for about 10 minutes.

Reserve 6 to 8 strawberries and hull the remainder. Slice each in half lengthwise and set aside. Place half the remaining strawberries into a food processor, fitted with a metal blade. Add sugar to taste and lemon juice and grated rind. Process until smooth and pour into a small bowl. Chop the remaining strawberries and add to the purée. Add more sugar if necessary.

To serve, place 2 blintzes on a plate, spoon over a little strawberry sauce and garnish with a strawberry half.

Blinis with Smoked Salmon and Soured Cream

Blinis are Russian pancakes made with buckwheat flour. They have a nutty flavour which is complemented by smoked salmon and soured cream or caviar. A less extravagant presentation can be offered with chopped radishes and cucumber, spring onions and capers.

SERVES 6

60 ml/2 fl oz lukewarm water	120 g/4 oz smoked salmon, thinly sliced
1½ tsp active dried yeast	
60 g/2 oz plain flour	4 spring onions, thinly sliced on the diagonal
90 g/3 oz buckwheat flour	
½ tsp salt	2 Tbsp soured cream
250 ml/8 fl oz milk	Snipped fresh chives to garnish
2 eggs, separated	
60 g/2 oz butter or margarine	
120 ml/4 fl oz soured cream	

Pour the lukewarm water into a small bowl and sprinkle over the yeast. Leave to stand until the yeast becomes foamy and bubbly, 5 minutes.

Into a large bowl, sift the plain flour, buckwheat flour and salt; make a well in the centre. Heat 175 ml/6 fl oz of the milk to lukewarm and add it to the well with the yeast mixture, stirring with a wire whisk and drawing in the flour little by little to form a smooth batter. Cover the bowl with a clean teatowel and leave in a warm place until the batter becomes light and bubbly, 2 to 3 hours.

Beat remaining 60 ml/2 fl oz milk into batter; beat the egg yolks and stir into the batter with half the butter, melted, and the sour cream.

In another bowl, with a hand-held mixer at medium speed, beat the egg whites until stiff peaks form (do not over-beat). Fold them into the blini batter until just blended. (Do not over-blend; a few white lumps will cook out.)

In a large frying pan or on a griddle, over medium-high heat, melt the remaining butter. Using a small ladle, pour batter into pan or griddle to form small pancakes. Cook until the undersides are lightly browned and the tops are covered with bubbles, about 2 minutes. Turn the blinis over and cook for 1 to 2 minutes longer. Continue until all the batter is used, adding more butter if necessary. (Keep the blinis warm in a 300°F/150°C/Gas 2 oven if necessary.)

Arrange on a serving dish. Divide the smoked salmon on the blinis. Top with a few sliced spring onions and a spoonful of soured cream. Sprinkle with chives. Serve.

Orange-flavoured French Toast

Challah bread is used in this recipe, but any good white bread could be used. Serve with maple syrup or dust with icing sugar.

SERVES 6

4 eggs, well beaten	12 slices challah bread, each about 2 cm/¾ in thick
½ tsp salt	
2 Tbsp sugar	Butter for frying, melted
250 ml/8 fl oz orange juice	Maple syrup or icing sugar to serve
½ tsp vanilla essence	
120–250 ml/4–8 fl oz milk	Orange slices to garnish (optional)

In a large shallow baking dish, beat the eggs with the salt, sugar, orange juice, vanilla essence and 120 ml/4 fl oz milk. (Depending on the size of the bread, you may need to add a little more milk.)

Lay the bread slices in the egg mixture and leave to stand for 2 minutes. Turn over and leave to soak until the egg is completely absorbed, about 5 minutes longer.

In a large frying pan, over medium heat, melt 3 tablespoons butter. Add the bread and cook until the underside is golden. Using a spatula, turn slices and fry until brown. Serve immediately.

Potato Latkes

Latkes are a popular vegetable dish in the Jewish culinary repertoire. Cooked in oil, these potato pancakes are traditionally served at Hanukah. They are delicious with poultry, but can also be eaten on their own sprinkled with sugar or topped with apple sauce or sour cream.

SERVES 6 TO 8

6 medium potatoes, peeled	I tsp salt
I onion	Pinch of ground white pepper
2 eggs, lightly beaten	Vegetable oil for frying
60 g/2 oz fine matzo meal, or plain flour	Apple sauce or soured cream to serve

Grate the potatoes and onion. Drain in a colander, pressing to squeeze out as much liquid as possible. Place in a large bowl and beat in remaining ingredients except oil and accompaniments. (Work as quickly as possible so the potatoes do not turn brown.)

In a large heavy frying pan, over medium-high heat, heat about 2.5 cm/1 in vegetable oil or just enough to cover the pancakes. Drop tablespoonfuls of the batter into hot oil and cook until the underside is browned, 2 minutes. Turn and cook the other side until browned, 1 to 2 minutes longer.

Remove to a serving platter and keep warm in a 300°F/150°C/Gas 2 oven. Continue until all the batter is used, adding a little more oil if necessary. Serve immediately with apple sauce or soured cream.

Persian Pancakes with Yogurt

These delicious "green" pancakes are like a fritter. They can be eaten on their own with yogurt or cream cheese, or as an accompaniment to spicy curries.

SERVES 4

- 250 g/8 oz chopped spinach, Swiss chard or watercress
- 2 large sprigs each fresh coriander, parsley and dill
- 2 small leeks, or 4 large spring onions, thinly sliced
- 6 eggs, beaten
- Salt
- Freshly ground black pepper
- ¼ tsp grated nutmeg
- 120 g/4 oz matzo meal
- Vegetable oil for frying
- Yogurt, soured cream or cream cheese to serve
- Fresh coriander or dill to garnish

In a food processor fitted with the metal blade, process the spinach, Swiss chard or watercress, herbs and leeks or spring onions until smooth. Turn into a large bowl. Add the beaten eggs, salt and pepper to taste and nutmeg. Stir in matzo meal. The batter should be quite thick but pourable.

In a large frying pan, over high heat, heat 2 tablespoons oil. Drop heaped tablespoonfuls of batter into the pan. Cook until the undersides are lightly browned, about 2 minutes, then turn over and cook 2 minutes longer. Place on kitchen paper to drain; keep warm. Continue until all the batter is used, adding more oil to the pan as needed. (Keep warm in a 300°F/150°C/Gas 2 oven until all batter is used.) Serve hot with yogurt, soured cream or cream cheese, garnished with coriander or dill.

Baking with Yeast

Home-baked breads are a real treat.
Although they take hours to make, most of
that time they need simply to sit in a warm
place while you get on with other things,
and the results are definitely worth the
effort. Whether you are making a simple
bread, a special breakfast bake, a fruit bread,
or a bagel, you will find the recipes in this
section along with a comprehensive
introduction that will dispel all the mysteries
of that wonderful substance, yeast.

INTRODUCTION

All types of bread supply carbohydrate, protein and B vitamins to the diet.

Wholemeal and brown breads provide more dietary fibre than white bread. Bread also supplies calcium, phosphorus and iron. Flour with an extraction rate of 80 per cent or less of the bran and wheatgerm is fortified with the B vitamins thiamine (B1) and nicotinic acid and iron to compensate for milling losses. Brown and white flours also contain added calcium. The varieties of bread are numerous and display a wide spectrum of textures and flavours, plain and enriched, sweet and savoury. The home baker is able to cater for special requirements such as salt-free bread, gluten-free bread, milk- and wheat-free breads and breads, buns and fruit loaves free of artificial colouring and flavouring. There is a growing consumer preference today for wholemeal breads: some 25 per cent of the bread consumed in English-speaking countries is a variety other than white.

Bread-Making Ingredients

Flour

The flour most commonly used in bread-making is wheat. Bread may be made from a single flour or a mixture of two or more flours, but wheat is prized for its fine baking qualities. Wholemeal flour contains all of the wheat grain with nothing added or taken away, an extraction rate of 100 per cent; and white flour contains about 75 per cent of the wheat grain. Most of the bran (ie the outer fibrous layers of the grain) and the wheatgerm are removed in the milling process. The term stoneground, sometimes applied to flours, means that the flour is ground between two stones instead of being milled by the modern steel-roller-mill process.

Gluten is composed of insoluble proteins which absorb water and produce a fine network of elastic strands. Carbon dioxide is produced by yeast fermentation and this raises the bread. The gluten stretches to give the loaf its bold volume. Flour used in yeast cookery should be plain and not the chemically aerated self-raising type. Strong white flour gives best results because of its higher gluten content. The texture of loaves made from wholemeal and brown flours is closer than that of white bread. The volume is also usually less in the wholemeal and brown bread types because of the effect of the higher bran content on gluten elasticity.

As wholemeal and rye flours produce a very heavy result, it is best to mix them with plain flour, but remember that even the same brand of flour can vary from region to region, or from season to season, depending on the level of humidity and how long it has been stored, so the amount of liquid needed in the dough may vary.

Liquids Used in Dough-Making

The liquid in a dough usually consists of water or milk (which may be skimmed or whole, dried or fresh). Some baking-powder breads utilize sour milk and buttermilk which react with the raising agent for a lighter dough. Less commonly, wort (a yeasty liquid made from hops), beer and even blood provide the liquid ingredient as in some Scandinavian breads, for instance. Liquids for yeast doughs are usually added when lukewarm.

Eggs

Eggs are added to doughs to enrich them nutritionally. They also improve the keeping properties and colour of the baked product.

Raising Agents

Compressed baker's yeast consists of unicellular organisms which, under suitable conditions of temperature, moisture, and food supply, break

Fresh yeast is moist, and grey-cream in colour.

down the sugar in dough, forming carbon dioxide and alcohol. Fresh yeast is moist, grey-cream in colour and free from a dry, brown covering of dead cells. Yeast works best at blood heat. It is unnecessary to add sugar when blending compressed yeast with liquid. Cold temperatures slow down yeast activity as do doughs containing a lot of fat, sugar and salt. Slow proving is often desirable, as it improves the flavour and texture of the bread; it may be achieved by placing the dough in a refrigerator for several hours at a time. Suitably

wrapped fresh yeast (in amounts most frequently used) may be stored in the refrigerator for about three weeks or in a freezer for up to six weeks. If too much yeast is used in a dough, it produces a sour, yeasty flavour and a smell of alcohol. The bread goes stale quickly and is crumbly in texture. Compressed yeast is usually sold by weight.

Dried Yeast

Dried yeast is convenient to store – up to four months in an airtight container. Check the date stamp when purchasing it. Dried yeast has a shelf life of 4 to 6 months. Reconstitute dried yeast with some of the warm dough liquid and a small quantity of "starter" sugar or follow the manufacturers' instructions if they are different. Leave in a warm place until the yeast dissolves and the mixture becomes frothy. Easy-blend dried yeast is mixed directly with the flour. The instructions will also tell you how much dried yeast will prove what amount of flour. Follow the manufacturers' instructions if these conflict with the recipe.

The Sponge Technique

This method is applied to enrich yeast doughs where the amounts of fat, eggs and sugar slow down the fermentation process. The use of a sponge helps to overcome the slowness.

Prepare the sponge by adding the yeast (and a little sugar in the case of dried yeast) to warm liquid. Stir in a small amount of the flour to make a batter. If dried yeast is used, allow some 5 to 10 minutes for the yeast to foam before adding flour.

Set the batter aside in a warm place for about 20 minutes to enable the yeast to ferment. The fat, eggs and sugar are then added to the foaming batter and mixed to a soft dough.

Sourdough

Sourdough is a fermentation agent used in American bread recipes; although not frequently found in home-baking today. It is made from dough which has been allowed to lie and ferment naturally, thereby producing yeast cells and lactic acid bacteria. The final product flavour results from normal yeast activity combined with the sour lactic acid taste. Nowadays sourdough starter is usually made under laboratory conditions, to prevent impurities entering the bread.

Chemical Substances

Chemical substances used to lighten doughs include bicarbonate of soda which needs to combine with an acidic ingredient such as sour milk or buttermilk, as in Irish soda bread.

Baking Equipment

Measuring cups in various sizes.

Loaf tins – useful for shaped loaves.

Sieve, rolling pin, wooden spoons, whisk and baking sheet.

The equipment for baking consists of a large glass, porcelain, or stainless steel bowl, a wooden fork and mixing spoon, a rubber or plastic spatula, a rolling pin, plastic sheeting, 2 pastry brushes, oven gloves, wire racks and baking sheets, loaf tins, weighing scales and a set of measuring spoons, a sieve for icing sugar and a grater for citrus rinds.

Loaf tins and flowerpots are useful for shaped loaves. They should be prepared before use to prevent sticking. Grease tins and baking sheets with white vegetable fat or dust thoroughly with flour. The greased pans may also be dusted with cracked wheat, semolina or bran flakes. Non-stick tins are ready for use without greasing.

Earthenware (not plastic) flowerpots need to be washed thoroughly and dried. Coat them with white vegetable fat, inside and out, and then bake in a hot oven for 5 to 10 minutes. Allow to cool and repeat the process 3 or 4 times. The pots are then ready for use. Grease prior to half-filling with dough. Wipe with damp kitchen paper after use. Electric food mixers with a dough hook accessory are available on the market to facilitate dough-kneading.

Storage

Breads vary in their keeping properties. Crusty loaves are best eaten freshly baked. Enriched breads, milk, malt and rye breads keep fresh for several days. The storage life depends on the recipe formula and the storage conditions.

Unwrapped bread is best stored at room temperature in a clean, airy, dry container such as a bread crock or bin. The container should not be airtight. Bins and crocks should be cleaned and dried weekly, or crusts and crumbs may promote mould growth. Unsliced bread may be put into a clean, dry, plastic bag for storage. Wrapped bread should be left in its wrapper. Leave the wrapper loosely folded.

Bread can go stale rapidly if refrigerated, since moisture may be lost. Freezer storage of wrapped bread is very successful. Plain breads may be kept in a freezer for about 6 months, enriched loaves for 4 months. Crusty loaves may shed their crusts after a few days. Frozen bread may be thawed in a microwave oven and sliced bread may be toasted directly from the freezer.

Stale bread loaves and rolls may be refreshed by wrapping in foil and heating for 5 to 10 minutes in a pre-heated oven at 450°F/230°C/Gas 8. Allow to cool in the foil. Don't cover crusty varieties; place them in a hot oven for 5 to 10 minutes. Stale bread is better than fresh bread for use in cooking.

Baking Techniques and Methods

Fermented Doughs

Cream the yeast, fresh or dried, with the warm dough liquid. Add the yeast liquid to the flour and mix by hand or with a wooden dough fork.

Kneading

Knead the dough with the heel of the right hand on a lightly floured board, folding the dough in half toward you, then pushing it down and away from you. Using the fingertips of the left hand, give the dough a quarter turn and repeat the folding and pushing movements with the heel of the right hand. The soft, sticky dough gradually becomes smooth and elastic and loses its stickiness. White doughs require about 10 minutes' kneading, wholemeal and brown doughs only about 4 minutes (even less for quick brown doughs).

Kneading may also be done using a food mixer or processor according to the manufacturer's instructions. If the dough is very soft, beat it with a wooden spatula, or in a food mixer, until smooth and elastic.

The kneaded dough is left to prove until doubled in size. Normally the dough is left to rise twice, first after kneading and then after shaping. Quick methods of bread-making cut out this first proving stage and reduce the overall time to 1¾ hours. The method involves the use of vitamin C in the dough: 25 mg vitamin C is added to 1½ lb all-purpose flour. It is added to the liquid. Dough which is left to prove must be covered. The traditional floured cloth is replaced nowadays with oiled plastic. The dough may be placed in a large, oiled plastic bag or the dough bowl may be covered with a sheet of oiled plastic. The speed at which the dough rises depends upon the surrounding temperature. Suitable places include a warm place such as a kitchen or hot cupboard to the cool of the refrigerator. Dough may need only one hour to rise in a warm place, 1½ to 2 hours at room temperature, 3½ to 4 hours in cool conditions and up to 12 hours in a refrigerator. Reduce by half the quantity of yeast used if rising takes place in the refrigerator or the dough will be difficult to handle and the product will taste yeasty when served. However warm the environment, if the atmosphere is too damp this can affect the proving.

Before the final stages of dough-handling, ensure that the oven is pre-heated to the correct temperature. Plain doughs require an oven temperature of 450°F/230°C/Gas 8 and enriched doughs 400°F/200°C/Gas 6.

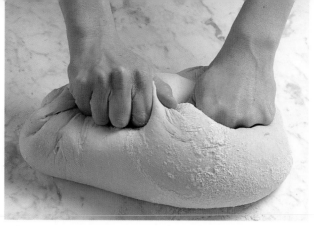

Punching down – the second part of the kneading process.

Knead the dough with the heel of your right hand.

Punching Down

The second kneading process is known as punching down. The aim is to obtain a product with good, even texture. Punching down ensures that large air bubbles are broken up and the air redistributed. Nutrients for the yeast cells are also redistributed and made more readily available. Knead the dough as before and then shape into loaves or rolls, as required.

The shaped items (on baking sheets, in baking tins or flowerpots) are lightly covered with oiled heavy plastic sheeting and set aside to prove for ½ to 1 hour (according to the volume of the items to be baked). The dough becomes light and doubles in size.

Baking

Bake in a very hot oven in order to kill the yeast cells. The loaves, rolls or buns should rise well, look brown and crisp and feel light. Loaves tapped on the base should sound hollow. Bread may be tested by inserting a skewer into it. If the skewer is dry when withdrawn, the bread is baked. Loaves may be removed from their tins some 5 minutes before the end of baking if crisp results are needed.

Dough Mixes

Products for preparing yeasted wheat doughs (including pizza-base mixes) and soda breads, using both white and wholemeal flours, are obtainable. Always follow the instructions on the packet.

Prepared doughs of various kinds are obtainable frozen, ready to put into the oven. They may even be ready meals, frozen or chilled, such as pizzas, with a yeast dough base. Thawing may be carried out in a microwave oven, but baking results are usually best using a conventional oven.

Handy Hints for Yeast Breads

- **Prepare the tins in advance.**
- **Use a thermometer to check the liquids before adding yeast; choose a warm place for proving the dough.**
- **To check if the bread is cooked, tap the bottom of the loaf with your knuckles; it should sound hollow.**
- **Dough textures vary and can range from soft and slightly sticky to firm, smooth doughs. Doughs for firm bread should be very firm, while medium-firm doughs are fine for savoury breads. Most sweet-yeast bread doughs are soft and some can even be quite sticky.**
- **For kneading, fold the dough, then push down and away from you with the heel of your hand, slightly curving your fingers over the edge. Turn the dough and repeat.**
- **To prove the dough, place in an oiled bowl, and turn to coat the dough with oil; this prevents a crust from forming over the surface. Alternatively, slide the dough in its bowl into a large, plastic bag, and seal tightly, allowing room for expansion.**
- **To check if the dough has doubled in volume, press a finger into the dough. If the hole remains, the dough is ready to be punched down.**
- **To punch down the dough, push your first into the centre of the dough, pulling the edges to the centre, knead once or twice. Alternatively, turn the dough on to a lightly floured surface; it will automatically deflate. Knead once or twice.**

Bread-Making Machines

With a bread machine, baking bread becomes one of the easiest tasks in the kitchen, yet it produces spectacular results. You don't have to worry that the water will be too cold to activate yeast, or so hot that it kills it: the bread machine regulates the temperature. You won't be kneading dough until your muscles ache: the bread machine will do all the kneading for you.

With a bread machine, you can create an infinite variety of loaves to suit your tastes, your store cupboard and the season. Substitute dried cranberries for raisins in a Christmas bread, add cracked wheat to a favourite bread to give it more fibre, or decorate a plaited loaf with the slivered almonds left over from another baking project. You no longer have to settle for ordinary bread.

Mastering bread-machine baking is like getting to know the quirks and idiosyncracies of any new piece of equipment. Some machines knead longer than others or allow a longer proving time. Some bread tins have different capacities than others, although they are labelled as the same size. Some models require a little more liquid or yeast than others. Flour absorbs varying amounts of liquid depending on the weather. The dough reacts differently to water that is highly acidic or alkaline.

To get accustomed to a new machine, start with a simple recipe, such as basic white bread, and see how it comes out. With a little experience you will soon be able to adapt conventional recipes for use in the machine.

Before you start, assemble all the ingredients. Be sure that the yeast is fresh. All ingredients should be at room temperature. Cold liquids and butter can be heated in the microwave.

Be sure the kneading paddle is well seated in the bottom of the tin. Add the ingredients in the order suggested by the manufacturer's instructions. This may vary from one machine to the next. If you are using a timer, the order may change. Fix the bread tin securely into the bread machine. Select settings on the control panel according to the manufacturer's instructions and press Start.

To check the dough while the bread is kneading, look for it to form a fairly smooth ball that is a bit sticky to the touch and settles only slightly when the paddle stops kneading. If, after the ingredients are mixed, the imprint of the

The kneading paddle should be well seated in the bottom of the bread pan.

Add ingredients in the order suggested by the manufacturer.

The bread tin should be securely positioned inside the machine.

paddle remains in the dough and the edges look a little jagged, add more liquid. Start with one tablespoon, then add more liquid one teaspoon at a time, giving the dough time to absorb the liquid before adding more. If the dough is so soft that it loses its shape as soon as the paddle pauses, add more flour, one tablespoon at a time. Although these instructions suit most breads, some breads are designed to have dough that is a little stiffer or softer.

Don't be shy about lifting the lid and watching at this stage. It is only when the bread is in the proving and baking stages that an open lid will interfere with temperature controls.

When the bread is cooked, remove it from the machine and the baking tin immediately. Otherwise, the steam released by the bread will condense in the tin, making the bread soggy on the outside. The bread should be allowed to cool for 20 to 30 minutes before slicing.

Instead of putting the dough into a bread tin it may be shaped in various ways as loaves or rolls.

Round Loaf

Shape the dough into a large ball. Flatten it slightly and place on a greased baking sheet. Slash the top of the dough with a sharp knife to make a cross. Cover and leave to prove for about 45 minutes in a warm place. Bake for 30 to 40 minutes.

Rolls

Baking time for rolls is 10 to 15 minutes after shaping, rising and glazing.

Cottage Rolls

Cut off one-third of each 60 g/2 oz piece of dough. Shape each piece into a ball. Place the large ball on a baking sheet and put the smaller one on top. Push a floured wooden spoon handle through both pieces of dough.

Dinner Rolls

Shape each 60-g/2-oz dough piece into a ball or sausage shape. Place on a baking sheet.

Clover Leaf Rolls

Divide each 60-g/2-oz piece of dough into 3 equal parts. Shape into 3 balls. Place on the baking sheet in the shape of a clover leaf and press lightly together.

Knot Rolls

Roll 60-g/2-oz pieces of dough into a thick 15-cm/ 6-in strand. Tie into a simple knot.

Plait

Divide the dough into three equal pieces. Roll each piece into a strand 30 x 35 cm/12 x 14 in long. Pinch together one end of the three strands and then plait them. Pinch the remaining ends together and lift the plait on to a greased baking sheet. Cover, leave to prove and glaze. Decorate with poppy seeds, if desired. Bake for 25 to 30 minutes.

Three-Strand Plaited Rolls

Cut off 60-g/2-oz pieces of risen dough. Divide and roll each piece into three 10-cm/4-in strands. Plait as above.

Two-Strand Plaited Rolls

Divide the 60-g/2-oz dough pieces in half. Roll each piece into a strand 20-cm/8-in long. Place the strands in the form of a cross on the work surface. Take the two ends of the lower strand and cross them over the middle of the upper strand so that they lie side by side. Repeat this with the remaining strand and repeat alternately until all the dough has been used. Pinch the ends firmly together. Place on the baking sheet, glaze and decorate, cover, prove and bake.

Plaited Loaf

1 Cut dough into 3 equal pieces. Roll each piece to a long sausage shape, tapering the ends. Lie the shapes next to each other. Beginning in the centre and, working towards one end, plait shapes together.

2 Pinch the ends together and tuck them under the plait. Turn dough and continue plaiting the other end, pinching ends and tucking under. Transfer to a baking tray, keeping ends tucked under.

The finished plaited loaf.

Simple Yeast Breads

White Bread · Lemon Poppyseed Plait

Quick White Bread · Pumpernickel

Wholemeal Bread · Potato Bread

Oatmeal Bread · Muesli Bread

Old-fashioned Rye Bread · Seed Bread

Challah · Sourdough Starter

Cheese Bread · San Francisco Sourdough Bread

Onion Bread · Milk Bread

Focaccia ·

White Bread

This recipe is the cornerstone of yeast baking.

MAKES 3 LARGE LOAVES

30 g/1 oz fresh yeast or 2 Tbsp dried yeast and 1 tsp sugar	2 to 3 tsp salt
	1 Tbsp sugar
900 ml/1½ pt warm water	90 g/3 oz butter or margarine
1.5 kg/3 lb strong white or plain flour	

BREAD MACHINE METHOD – MAKES 1 500-G/1-LB LOAF

½ cup water	1 tsp salt
¼ cup milk	2 cups bread flour
1 Tbsp butter	2 tsp yeast
1 Tbsp sugar	

● Put all ingredients in the bread tin in the order suggested by your bread machine instructions. Set for white bread, medium crust. Press start.

Grease three large bread tins. Stir the yeast with a few tablespoons of the water adding the teaspoon of sugar if dried yeast is used. Put the bowl of dried yeast liquid aside for 10 minutes until frothy.

Mix the flour and salt together. Add the sugar, blend in the fat, stir in the yeast liquid and the rest of the warm water to make a soft dough. Turn the dough on to a lightly floured board and knead until it becomes smooth, elastic and not sticky. Return the dough to the bowl, cover it with oiled plastic and leave to prove until doubled in size, about 1¼ hours.

Punch back the dough and divide it into 3 portions. Knead and shape into loaves to fit into the three bread tins. Cover the bread tins with oiled plastic. Allow to rise until doubled in size, about 45 minutes. Remove plastic and bake loaves for 45 to 50 minutes. Cool on a wire rack.

Quick White Bread

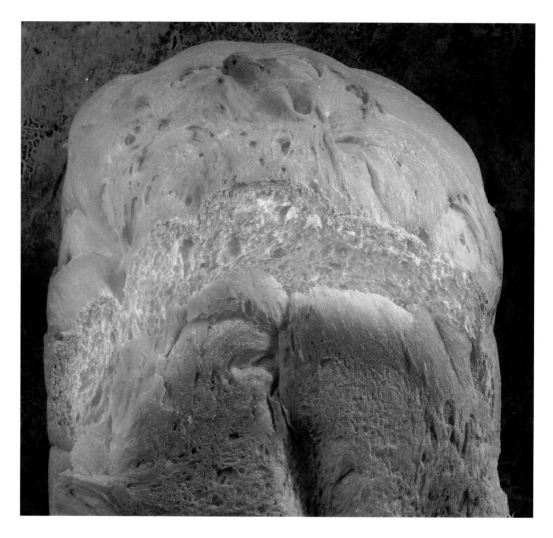

A quick bread because the rising process is accelerated by the addition of citric acid in the form of vitamin C.

MAKES 2 LARGE (OR 4 SMALL) LOAVES

60 g/2 oz fresh yeast or 4 Tbsp dried yeast and ½ tsp sugar	1.5 kg/3 lb strong white or plain flour
900 ml/1½ pt warm water	2 tsp salt
2 25-mg pills vitamin C	2 Tbsp sugar
	60 g/2 oz butter or margarine

Grease two large (or four small) loaf tins. Mix the yeast with a few tablespoons of the water adding the teaspoon of sugar if dried yeast is used. Set the dried yeast liquid aside for 10 minutes until frothy. Crush the vitamin C pills in a little water and add to the yeast liquid.

Mix the flour and salt together in a large warm bowl. Add the sugar and blend in the fat. Stir in the yeast liquid and the rest of the warm water and mix to a soft dough. Turn on to a lightly floured board and knead the dough until it is smooth, elastic and no longer sticky. Divide the dough in half, shape into 2 or 4 loaves and put them into the tins. Cover the tins with oiled plastic and allow to rise until doubled in size, about 1 hour.

Pre-heat the oven to 450°F/230°C/Gas 8. Remove the plastic and bake the loaves for about 45 minutes (30 to 35 minutes for small loaves). Cool the bread on a wire rack.

Wholemeal Bread

This bread has a dense texture as it uses only wholemeal flour. To lighten use half plain and half wholemeal flours.

MAKES 3 LARGE LOAVES

15 g/½ oz fresh yeast or 3 Tbsp dried yeast and 1 tsp sugar	60 g/2 oz butter or margarine or 4 Tbsp vegetable oil
900 ml/1½ pt warm water	Beaten egg, milk or salted water for glazing
1.5 kg/3 lb wholemeal flour	
2 to 3 tsp salt	Cracked wheat, bran, or buckwheat to decorate (optional)
1 Tbsp sugar	

TIP

Proving takes some 15 to 30 minutes longer if carried out at room temperature.

Grease three large 22 x 13-cm/9 x 5-in loaf tins. Stir the yeast into a few tablespoons of warm water, adding the teaspoon of sugar if dried yeast is used. Set the dried yeast liquid aside for 10 minutes until frothy. Put the wholemeal flour into a large mixing bowl and add the salt and sugar. Blend in the fat and stir in the yeast liquid and the rest of the warm water. Mix well and turn on to a floured board. Knead the dough until it is no longer sticky. Return the dough to the bowl, cover it with oiled plastic and leave it to prove in a warm place for about 1¼ hours, until doubled in size.

Punch down the dough. Divide it into 3 portions and shape into loaves to fit into the tins. Cover the tins with oiled plastic and leave them to prove in a warm place for about 40 to 45 minutes, until doubled in size.

Pre-heat the oven to 450°F/230°C/Gas 8. Remove the plastic and brush the tops of the loaves with the selected glaze. Sprinkle the loaves with grain if desired.

Bake for 45 to 59 minutes. Cool on a wire rack.

Oatmeal Bread

A delicious home-baked bread with a distinctive flavour.

MAKES 2 SMALL LOAVES

30 g/1 oz fresh yeast or 1 sachet (1 Tbsp) dried yeast and 1 tsp brown sugar	250 g/8 oz fine oatmeal
	4 Tbsp wheatgerm
500 ml/1 pt warm water	4 Tbsp soya flour
2 Tbsp brown sugar	2 Tbsp vegetable oil
600 g/1¼ lb mixed flour (½ wholemeal, ½ white flour)	1½ tsp salt

BREAD MACHINE METHOD – MAKES 1 500-G/1-LB LOAF

60 g/2 oz rolled oats (not quick oatmeal)	1 tsp salt
90 ml/3 fl oz very hot water	½ tsp bicarbonate of soda
	2 Tbsp wheatgerm
⅝ cup buttermilk	500 g/1 lb strong white flour
15 g/½ oz butter	1½ tsp yeast
2 Tbsp sugar	

● Put oats in a loaf tin. Pour very hot or boiling water over the oats and stir. Leave for at least 15 minutes. Put the remaining ingredients in the tin in the order suggested in the instructions. Set for white bread, medium crust. Press Start.

Grease two small loaf tins. Put the yeast into a bowl (with the sugar, if dried yeast is used) and stir with 120 ml/4 fl oz of the warm water. Set aside for up to 10 minutes until foamy. Add the sugar and half the mixed flours to the rest of the water and beat well for 5 minutes. Add the yeast liquid and beat thoroughly. Stir in the rolled oats and set the mixture aside in a warm place for about 30 minutes to make a sponge.

Add the wheatgerm, soya flour, oil, salt and the rest of the mixed flours to the sponge. Turn out on to a floured board and knead well until smooth. Return the dough to the bowl and cover with oiled plastic. Set aside in a warm place until doubled in size, about 30 minutes.

Punch down the dough on a floured board and divide into 2 pieces. Shape into loaves and place them in the tins. Cover with oiled plastic and leave to prove until doubled in size again. Bake for about 1 hour. Cool on a wire rack.

Old-fashioned Rye Bread

Rye flour is very low in gluten, so white flour is needed to lighten the texture and give the bread more body. It does make the dough more difficult to work with, so an electric mixer is helpful unless you are an expert bread maker.

MAKES 2 LOAVES

600 g/1¼ lb plain flour	2 Tbsp caraway seeds
375 g/12 oz rye flour	90 ml/3 fl oz vegetable oil
2 tsp salt	600 ml/1 pt lukewarm water
2 sachets (2 Tbsp) dried yeast	1 egg, beaten or 25 g/1 oz butter or margarine, melted, for glaze
2 tsp sugar	

BREAD MACHINE METHOD – MAKES 1 500-G/1-LB LOAF

175 ml/6 fl oz water	175 g/6 oz strong white flour
1 Tbsp vegetable oil	90 g/3 oz rye flour
4 tsp treacle	2 tsp yeast
1 tsp salt	
2 tsp caraway seeds	

● Put all the ingredients in the tin in the order suggested in the instructions. Set for wholemeal bread, medium crust. Press start.
● For oven-baked bread, set the machine for dough stage. When the dough is ready, remove it from the machine and press down. Shape into a large ball and flatten slightly or roll it into a fat baguette. Place on a baking sheet that has been sprinkled with cornmeal. Cover the bread loosely, set it in a warm place and leave to prove until doubled in volume, about 1 hour.
● Make a glaze of 1 egg lightly beaten with 1 tablespoon of milk. Gently brush the egg glaze over the top and sides of the loaf. Bake in a pre-heated 375°F/190°C/Gas 5 oven until the top and bottom are crusty and sound hollow when tapped – about 35 minutes.

In a large bowl, combine the flours and salt. Set aside. In the bowl of an electric mixer fitted with the dough hook, combine the yeast, sugar and caraway seeds. Add the oil and 250 ml/8 fl oz lukewarm water and stir. Sprinkle with a little flour. Cover the bowl with a clean teatowel and leave until the mixture looks frothy, 10 to 12 minutes.

With the mixer on low speed, pour in 375 ml/12 fl oz lukewarm water and beat until combined. Gradually add the flours; when completely incorporated the dough will be sticky. You may have some flour mixture left over.

Increase the speed to medium and knead dough until it forms a soft ball around the dough hook and leaves the sides of bowl, 5 to 7 minutes. If the dough remains very sticky, add a little more plain flour and continue to knead 2 minutes longer. (Do not add too much more flour or bread will be tough.)

Lightly grease a bowl and place dough in it; turn dough to coat with oil. (This prevents a crust from forming on surface.) Cover bowl with a teatowel and leave to prove until doubled in bulk, 1½ to 2 hours, in a warm, draught-free place.

Lightly grease a large baking sheet. Turn the dough on to a lightly floured work surface and punch down. Knead lightly, cut the dough in half and shape each half into a smooth round ball. Place each loaf on opposite corners of the baking sheet, flatten slightly and cover with a teatowel. Leave to prove until almost doubled in bulk, 1 hour.

Pre-heat the oven to 350°F/175°C/Gas 4. Brush the loaves with egg glaze or melted butter or margarine. With a sharp knife, slash the top of each loaf 2 or 3 times. Bake until well-browned and hollow-sounding when tapped, 35 to 40 minutes. Transfer to a wire rack to cool.

Challah

Challah is a traditional, plaited Jewish egg bread. This popular bread is very versatile because its soft, cake-like texture goes well with most foods.

MAKES 2 LOAVES

1 sachet (1 Tbsp) dried yeast	3 eggs, lightly beaten
1 Tbsp sugar	500 g/1 lb plain flour, sifted
90 ml/3 fl oz lukewarm water	1 egg, beaten with a pinch of salt and pinch of sugar, to glaze
1 tsp salt	
250 ml/8 fl oz milk, scalded	Sesame or poppy seeds
6 Tbsp vegetable oil	

VARIATION

To form a spiral-shaped Challah, prepare the dough as above but roll each half into 1 long sausage about 60 cm/24 in long and 2.5 cm/1 in in diameter. Hold one end against the surface and using it as the centre, begin coiling the spiral. Place on a baking sheet and tuck one end under the loaf. Repeat with the second piece and bake as for plaited loaves.

In the bowl of an electric mixer with the dough hook fitted, combine yeast and sugar. Stir in the water. Sprinkle with a little flour to cover. Cover with a clean teatowel and leave until the mixture looks frothy, 10 to 12 minutes.

With the mixer on low speed, beat in the salt, milk, oil and eggs until well-mixed. Gradually add the flour; when completely incorporated, the dough will be slightly sticky. Increase the speed to medium and knead until the dough forms a ball around the hook and leaves the sides of the bowl, 5 to 7 minutes. If the dough remains sticky, add a little more flour and knead for 2 minutes longer. (Do not add too much flour; a softer dough yields a moister loaf.)

Lightly grease a large bowl. Place the dough in it and turn the dough to coat with oiled plastic. Cover with a clean teatowel and leave to prove until doubled in bulk, 1½ to 2 hours, in a moderately warm, draught-free place; do not leave to prove in too warm a place or the texture may be uneven.

BREAD MACHINE METHOD – MAKES 1 500-G/1-LB LOAF

	GLAZE
2 eggs	
60 ml/2 fl oz water	1 egg yolk
15 g/½ oz butter	1 tsp water
2 Tbsp sugar	1–2 tsp poppy seeds
1 tsp salt	
250 g/8 oz strong white flour	
2 tsp yeast	

● Put the ingredients in the tin in the order suggested in the instructions. Set for white bread, dough stage. Press start.
● When the dough is ready, remove and punch down. Cut into three equal parts. Roll each piece into a rope about 30 cm/12 in long. Plait the three ropes together. Pinch the ends together and turn them under. Cover the loaf and set it in a warm place to prove until doubled in volume, 45 minutes to 1 hour.
● Pre-heat the oven to 350°F/175°C/Gas 4. Make a glaze by beating egg yolk and water with fork. Brush lightly over the loaf. Sprinkle with poppy seeds.
● Bake until is nicely browned, 30 to 35 minutes.

Turn the dough on to a lightly floured work surface and knead gently. Return to the bowl, cover tightly and refrigerate for 6 to 8 hours or overnight to prove slowly a second time. (The slow proving provides a light, even texture.)

Turn the dough on to a lightly floured work surface and knead gently. Shape into a ball and cut into 2 even-sized pieces.

Lightly grease a large baking sheet. Working with one half at a time, cut each dough half into 3 even-sized pieces; roll into balls. Roll each ball into long sausage shapes about 18 inches long and 1 inch wide. Plait the 3 sausage shapes together and place on one side of the baking sheet, tucking the ends neatly underneath loaf. Repeat with the remaining dough to form a second loaf.

Cover the loaves with a clean teatowel and leave in a warm place to prove until almost doubled in size, 1 hour. Pre-heat the oven to 375°F/190°C/Gas 5.

Brush each loaf with egg glaze and sprinkle with sesame or poppy seeds. Bake the loaves for 40 minutes until they are well-browned and sound hollow when tapped on the bottom. Transfer to a wire rack to cool.

Cheese Bread

Perfect to accompany soups or salads. The dough may also be used as a pizza base.

15 g/½ oz fresh yeast or 1 sachet (1 Tbsp) dried yeast and ½ tsp sugar

300 ml/10 fl oz warm water

500 g/1 lb plain flour

1 tsp salt

¼ tsp cayenne pepper

2 Tbsp chopped chives

½ tsp dry mustard powder or 2 tsp creamed horseradish

15 g/½ oz butter or margarine

120 g/4 oz finely grated Cheddar cheese

Beaten egg or milk to glaze

1–2 Tbsp grated cheese to decorate (optional)

Grease one large or two small loaf tins. Stir the yeast into the warm water, adding sugar if dried yeast is used. Stand the dried yeast liquid for 10 minutes to become frothy.

Put the flour, salt, cayenne pepper, mustard and chives into a bowl and blend in the fat. Stir in the cheese and then the yeast liquid (and horseradish if used). Work together to make a dough. Turn the dough on to a floured board and knead until smooth and no longer sticky.

Return to the bowl, cover with oiled plastic and leave to prove for 1 hour until doubled in size. Punch down the dough and shape into 1 large or 2 small loaves. Place the

BREAD MACHINE METHOD – MAKES 1 500-G/1-LB LOAF

150 ml/5 fl oz water

2 Tbsp olive oil

1 Tbsp sugar

½ tsp dried thyme

1 tsp salt

250 g/8 oz strong white flour

1½ tsp yeast

90 g/3 oz crumbled feta cheese

60 g/2 oz coarsely chopped green olives

2 Tbsp chopped sun-dried tomatoes

2 Tbsp strong white flour

● Put the first seven ingredients in the tin in the order suggested in the instructions. Set for white bread, medium crust. Press start. Toss the remaining ingredients with flour, then add them to the dough after first kneading or at the beeper.

● To bake in the oven, set the bread machine for dough stage. When dough is ready, remove and punch down. Shape into a round loaf. Put on a baking sheet that has been sprinkled with cornmeal. Cover loosely and put in a warm place to prove until doubled in volume. Brush the surface with a glaze of 1 egg mixed with 1 tablespoon water, and bake in a pre-heated oven at 350°C/175°C/Gas 4 until golden, about 25 minutes.

shaped dough in the tin(s). Brush the dough with beaten egg or milk. Cover the tin(s) with oiled plastic and leave to prove in a warm place for about 45 minutes.

Sprinkle the bread dough with grated cheese if desired. Bake for about 40 minutes until brown. Turn out and cool on a wire rack.

Onion Bread

Serve this savoury bread hot or cold.

¼ quantity White Bread dough (see page 328)

2 onions, sliced

60 g/2 oz butter or margarine

2 Tbsp plain or strong white flour

150 ml/5 fl oz milk

¼ tsp salt or garlic salt

Pinch of freshly ground black pepper

1 tsp poppy or sesame seeds

Grease and flour a 20-cm/8-in round cake tin. Roll out the dough to fit the tin. Put the dough into the tin, cover with oiled plastic and leave to prove until doubled in size, about 30 minutes.

Pre-heat the oven to 375°F/190°C/Gas 5. Cook the onions in the fat in a heavy pan until transparent and softened. Stir in the flour and cook for a couple of minutes. Add the milk, stirring constantly. Bring to the boil and simmer for another minute. Add the salt and pepper. Spread the onion mixture over the dough and sprinkle with the seeds. Bake for 30 minutes.

Focaccia

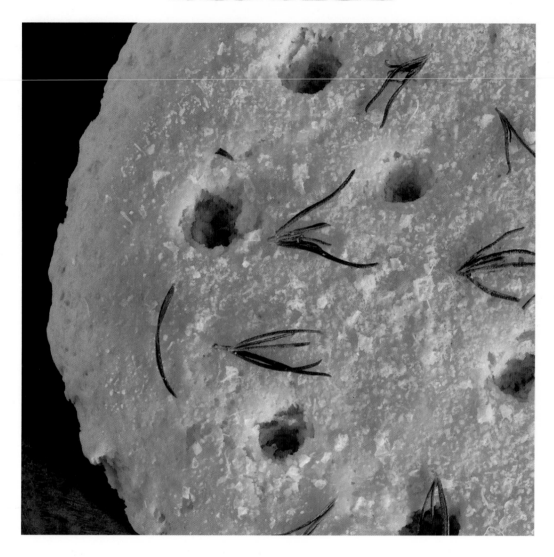

S erve wedges of this hearty bread as an appetizer or with a meal instead of garlic bread. Instead of butter, dip pieces in high-quality olive oil. This bread is best served warm.

BREAD MACHINE RECIPE – MAKES 1 500-G/1-LB LOAF

150 ml/5 fl oz water	1 or 2 garlic cloves, crushed
2 Tbsp olive oil	1 tsp dried rosemary
1 tsp salt	1 tsp coarse salt
250 g/8 oz strong white flour	2 Tbsp olive oil
1¼ tsp yeast	2 tsp grated Parmesan cheese

Put first five ingredients in a loaf tin in the order suggested in the instructions. Set for white bread, dough stage. Press start.

Pre-heat the oven to 400°F/200°C/Gas 6. Lightly sprinkle cornmeal on a baking sheet.

Remove the dough and punch down. Leave to rest about for 5 minutes. On a lightly floured surface, roll dough into a round, about 1 cm/½ in thick. Place on a baking sheet. Sprinkle the garlic, rosemary and coarse salt over the top, then lightly press it into the dough. With your fingertips, make shallow indentations all over the top of the round. Pour the remaining olive oil over the top, letting it pool in the indentations. Sprinkle Parmesan over the top.

Bake until lightly browned, about 20 minutes.

Lemon Poppyseed Plait

Slightly sweet, flavoured with lemon, and full of poppy seeds, this plaited bread makes an impressive addition to the tea table.

BREAD MACHINE RECIPE – MAKES 1 500-G/1-LB LOAF

1 egg	1 tsp salt
120 ml/4 fl oz lemon yogurt	250 g/8 oz strong white flour
40 g/1½ oz butter	1½ tsp yeast
3 Tbsp sugar	
3 Tbsp poppy seeds	**GLAZE**
2 tsp grated lemon rind	1 egg white beaten with 2 tsp water

Put all the dough ingredients in the bread machine tin. Set for white or sweet bread, dough stage. Press start.

When the dough is ready, remove from the tin and punch down. Cut into three equal pieces. Leave to rest for 5 minutes. Butter a baking sheet. Roll each piece of dough into a rope, about 35 cm/14 in long. Plait three ropes together and tuck the ends underneath. Cover and put in a warm place to prove until doubled, 45 minutes to 1 hour.

Brush the dough with egg-water glaze. Bake in a pre-heated oven at 350°F/175°C/Gas 4 until golden, 25 to 30 minutes.

Pumpernickel

Pumpernickel is an eastern European bread which keeps well. Serve with butter and cheese or cured meats.

MAKES 2 LARGE LOAVES

30 g/1 oz fresh yeast or 2 sachets (2 Tbsp) dried yeast and 1 tsp brown sugar	90 g/3 oz buckwheat flour
	60 g/2 oz cornmeal
1¼ 1/2 pt warm water	2 tsp salt
900 g/1½ lb wholemeal flour	1 cup cooked mashed potatoes
1 Tbsp treacle	1 tsp caraway seeds
120 g/4 oz dark rye flour	120 g/4 oz wholemeal flour (if needed)

Grease two large loaf tins. Stir the yeast into 250 ml/ 8 fl oz of the warm water, with the brown sugar if dried yeast is used. Set the dried yeast liquid aside for 10 minutes until frothy.

Mix the wholemeal flour, treacle, yeast liquid and the rest of the warm water to make a very wet dough. Beat well and knead in the bowl until it becomes smooth and less sticky. Add the rest of the ingredients and mix well. Turn on to a floured board and knead, working in the last 120 g/4 oz wholemeal flour if required. Knead until the dough is smooth and elastic. Return it to the bowl and cover with a sheet of oiled plastic. Leave to prove in a warm place until doubled in size, 1¼ to 1½ hours.

BREAD MACHINE METHOD – MAKES 1 500-G/1-LB LOAF

175 ml/6 fl oz milk	30 g/1 oz strong white flour
1 Tbsp vegetable oil	
2 Tbsp molasses	120 g/4 oz rye flour
½ tsp salt	60 g/2 oz wholemealt flour
2 Tbsp cocoa powder	2 Tbsp cornmeal
2 tsp caraway seeds	2 tsp yeast

● Put the ingredients in the bread tin in the order suggested in the instructions. Set for wholemeal bread, medium crust. Press start.

● Alternatively, to make baguettes, remove the dough from the bread machine after first kneading and punch down. Cut into two equal parts. Roll each part into a thick rope, about 20 cm/ 8 in long. Put the baguettes on a baking sheet that has been sprinkled with cornmeal. Put in a warm place and cover loosely. Prove until doubled in volume. Bake in a pre-heated oven at 350°F/175°C/Gas 4 for about 25 minutes, or until loaves are crusty and sound hollow.

Punch down the dough and divide it into 2 pieces. Shape into loaves and put the dough into the tins. Cover the pans with oiled plastic and leave to prove until doubled in size, about 1 hour.

Pre-heat the oven to 375°F/190°C/Gas 5. Bake for 1 hour, remove the loaves from the tins and bake for a further 10 to 15 minutes. Cool on a wire rack. Keep the bread for 1 to 2 days before slicing.

Potato Bread

This is a nutritious bread containing potato, egg and soured cream. It is delicious toasted and spread with jam.

MAKES 3 LOAVES

1 (250-g/8-oz) large raw potato, peeled	1 kg/2 lb flour
	2 tsp salt
500 ml/1 pt milk	1 egg
30 g/1 oz fresh yeast or 1 sachet (1 Tbsp) dried yeast and 1 tsp sugar	3 Tbsp soured cream

Grease three small loaf tins. Finely grate the potato. Bring the milk to the boil and pour over the potato in a bowl. Cool until lukewarm and add fresh yeast. If dried yeast is used stir it, with the sugar, into 3 tablespoons warm milk or water. Leave for 8 to 10 minutes until frothy. Add the dried yeast mixture to potato–milk mix. Beat in half the flour until well mixed. Add the salt, egg, soured cream and the remaining flour. Beat thoroughly.

Cover bowl with oiled plastic. Set aside in a warm place for 2 to 2½ hours. Knead and divide between 3 loaf tins. Leave to prove again, covered, for 40 minutes. Pre-heat oven to 350°F/175°C/Gas 4. Bake 45 minutes.

Muesli Bread

This recipe calls for unsweetened muesli so the only sweetness comes from the raisins. This is an ideal breakfast bread.

MAKES 3 LARGE LOAVES

Cracked wheat or bran	500 g/1 lb wholemeal flour
15 g/½ oz fresh yeast or 1 sachet (1 Tbsp) dried yeast and 1 tsp sugar or honey	2 tsp salt
	30 g/1 oz margarine
900 ml/1½ pt warm water	175 g/6 oz unsweetened muesli
900 g/1½ lb plain or strong white flour	

BREAD MACHINE METHOD – MAKES 1 500-G/1-LB LOAF

120 ml/4 fl oz water	150 g/5 oz strong white flour
60 ml/2 fl oz milk	
2 Tbsp vegetable oil	90 g/3 oz wholemeal flour
2 Tbsp honey	1½ tsp yeast
1 tsp salt	120 g/4 oz mixed seeds and dried fruit

● Put all ingredients except the seeds and dried fruit in the tin in the order suggested in the instructions. Set for wholemeal bread, medium crust. Press start. Add the seeds and dried fruit at the beeper or after first kneading.

● For the seeds and dried fruit, try a selection of raisins and sunflower seeds, chopped dates, apricots, cherries, pecans or cashews. Coarsely chop whole nuts such as almonds.

Grease three large flowerpots or three large loaf tins and sprinkle them with cracked wheat or bran.

Stir the yeast into the water, adding the sugar or honey if dried yeast is used. Set aside for about 10 minutes until frothy. Mix the white and wholemeal flours together with the salt (and sugar, if used). Blend in the margarine. Pour in the yeast liquid and mix thoroughly. Turn the dough on to a floured board and knead until smooth and elastic. Cover the dough in the bowl using a sheet of oiled plastic and leave to prove in a warm place until doubled in size (1 to 1¼ hours). Turn the dough on to the floured board and punch down after working in the muesli.

Divide the dough into 3 portions and shape them to fit the flowerpots or tins. Brush with milk and cover with oiled plastic. Leave to prove for 40 to 50 minutes until doubled in size.

Pre-heat the oven to 425°F/220°C/Gas 7. Bake for about 45 to 50 minutes. Cool on wire racks.

Seed Bread

The seeds in this loaf add flavour and texture to the bread. It is divided into six portions which are simply broken off for serving.

MAKES 1 LOAF

1 sachet (1 Tbsp) dried yeast	25 g/1 oz polyunsaturated margarine
500 g/1 lb wholemeal flour	
2 tsp granulated sugar	2 tsp fennel seeds
2 tsp salt	2 tsp sesame seeds
2 tsp caraway seeds	1 egg white

BREAD MACHINE METHOD – MAKES 1 500-G/1-LB LOAF

120 ml/4 fl oz buttermilk	60 g/2 oz wholemeal flour
90 ml/3 fl oz water	175 g/6 oz strong white flour
1 Tbsp vegetable oil	
1 Tbsp sugar	1½ tsp yeast
¼ tsp bicarbonate of soda	3 Tbsp raw, shelled sunflower seeds
1 tsp salt	
2 Tbsp toasted wheatgerm	1 Tbsp toasted sesame seeds

● Put all the ingredients except seeds in the tin in the order suggested in the instructions. Set for wholemeal bread, medium crust. Press start. Add the seeds after the first kneading or when machine beeps to add nuts.
● To toast the wheatgerm and sesame seeds, put each in a small, ungreased pan over medium heat. Shake the pan occasionally so they do not scorch. Cook until lightly brown. Leave to cool before adding them to the dough.

Place the yeast, flour, sugar and salt in a large bowl. Rub in the margarine and add half of each of the seeds. Stir in 300 ml/10 fl oz warm water and mix well. Bring the mixture together to form a soft dough. Knead the dough for 5 minutes on a lightly floured surface and break into six equal pieces.

Lightly grease a deep 15-cm/6-in round cake tin. Shape each of the dough pieces into a round. Place five pieces around the edge of the tin and one in the centre. Cover and leave to prove in a warm place for 1 hour or until doubled in size.

Whisk the egg white and brush over the top of the dough. Sprinkle the remaining seeds on to the top of the dough, alternating the different types on each section of the loaf.

Bake at 400°F/200°C/Gas 6 for 30 minutes or until cooked through. The loaf should sound hollow when tapped on the base. Cool slightly and serve.

Sourdough Starter

Sourdough is the product of fermentation in dough that has been allowed to sit out for days and gather wild yeasts from the air. In ancient times, it was the only leavening known to bread bakers, and much effort was made to disguise its sour taste. It came back into common usage in mining camps during the California Gold Rush of 1849, then hit a new wave of popularity in the middle of the 20th century.

Making and maintaining your own sourdough starter is not difficult. A pot of starter takes at least a few days to ferment and develop a sour flavour before you add it to the first loaf, but after that, it can be used and replenished daily.

MAKES ONE POT SOURDOUGH STARTER

250 ml/8 fl oz semi-skimmed milk, scalded

250 ml/8 fl oz hot water

1 Tbsp sugar

2¼ tsp dried yeast

60 g/2 oz plain or strong white flour

Mix the milk, water and sugar. When cooled add the yeast. Leave the yeast to become frothy, about 5 to 10 minutes. Then add it to the flour and mix well.

Put the bowl in a warm draught-free place, such as the back of the stove. Loosely cover the bowl so that air will still circulate and the starter will gather airborne yeasts. Within 24 hours, it should be bubbly and have the beginnings of a sour smell. Stir it once or twice a day. The starter may separate into a thick, curd-like mixture on the bottom and grey watery liquids on the top. This is normal, as long as it does not turn green or pink. (If it does, throw it away and start again.) The mixture is ready to use when it develops a good sour smell, usually 3 to 5 days.

To bake sourdough bread, you need to prepare a sponge at least six hours in advance. Mix some starter with a portion of flour and liquid, as directed by the recipe. Replenish the starter with amounts of flour and water equal to the amount you removed. For instance, if the recipe calls for 120 g/4 oz of sourdough starter, replenish the starter with 120 ml/4 fl oz water and 60 g/ 2 oz flour. Both the sponge and the replenished starter should be put in a warm place, covered loosely, and left to ferment at least 6 hours, until bubbly.

If you use the sourdough on an almost daily basis, you can leave the starter pot at the back of the stove, replenishing it after each use. If you are only an occasional baker, replenish it, leave it out for 6 to 24 hours, then put it in the refrigerator. The starter pot should be tightly covered when it is in the refrigerator. If you do not bake at least once a week, refresh the starter every week or two. Remove 250 g/8 oz of starter and discard the rest. Add 250 ml/8 fl oz of water and 120 g/4 oz of flour and return it to the refrigerator.

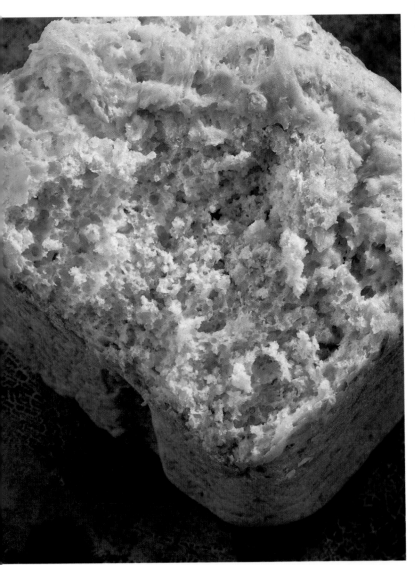

San Francisco Sourdough Bread

San Francisco is famous for its sourdough bread.

MAKES 2 LOAVES

1 sachet (1 Tbsp) dried yeast	½ tsp salt
1 Tbsp sugar	2 Tbsp vinegar
375 ml/12 fl oz warm water	600 g/1¼ lb plain or strong white flour
250 g/8 oz sourdough starter	½ tsp bicarbonate of soda

Stir the yeast and sugar into the water and set aside for 15 minutes, or until foamy. Stir in the starter, salt and vinegar and 375 g/12 oz of the flour. Cover with oiled plastic and leave to prove until doubled in size.

Punch down the dough and combine with remaining flour and bicarbonate of soda. Knead on a floured surface until smooth, elastic and no longer sticky. Divide the mixture in two and form into long loaves. Place on large greased and floured baking sheets. Cover with oiled plastic and leave to prove until doubled in size, about 1 hour.

Pre-heat the oven to 450°F/230°C/Gas 8. Place a tray of water in the oven. Spray the loaf with water and bake for 10 minutes. Reduce the heat to 400°/200°C/Gas 6, remove the water and bake for a further 35 minutes, misting the loaves with water twice more to ensure a hard crust. Turn out on to a wire rack.

Milk Bread

Using milk instead of water gives this bread additional richness of flavour.

MAKES 3 SMALL LOAVES OR 1 LARGE AND 1 SMALL LOAF

15 g/½ oz fresh yeast or 1 sachet (1 Tbsp) dried yeast and ½ tsp sugar	1½ tsp salt
	1½ tsp sugar
16 fl oz/1 pt warm skimmed milk or full-cream milk and water mixed	90 g/3 oz butter or margarine
750 g/1½ lb flour	Beaten egg or milk to glaze

Grease three small loaf tins (or 1 large and 1 small). Stir the yeast into the liquid, adding sugar if dried yeast is used. Leave for 15 minutes in a warm place until frothy.

Mix the flour, salt and sugar and blend in the butter or margarine. Stir in the yeast liquid and mix to a soft dough. Turn the dough on to a lightly floured board and knead until it becomes smooth and loses its stickiness. Return the dough to the warm mixing bowl and cover it with oiled plastic. Leave to prove until doubled in size, 1½ hours.

Punch down the dough, divide it into three (or 1 large and 1 small piece) and shape to fit the tins. Brush with beaten egg or milk. Cover the tins with oiled plastic and leave to prove until doubled in size, about 1 hour.

Pre-heat the oven to 400°F/200°C/Gas 6 and bake for about 50 minutes. Cool on a wire rack.

VARIATION: OLIVE BREAD

Omit the 1½ tsp sugar and stir in 5 to 6 tablespoons olive oil instead of blending in the butter or margarine. Add 150 g/5 oz stoned, sliced black olives to the dough with the dough liquid. The olive loaves may be shaped into 2 or 3 rounds and baked on greased baking sheets instead of being baked in loaf tins, if preferred.

Pizza

Basic Pizza Dough

Pizza Primavera

Wholemeal Pizza Dough

Corn Bread Pizza Dough

Pizza with Caramelized Onions

Deep-pan Creole Pizza

Basic Pizza Dough

Basic pizza dough works well with just about any topping you like. This is the recipe for the classic Italian base.

MAKES 2 30-CM/12-IN THIN-CRUST PIZZAS
OR 1 DEEP-PAN PIZZA

1 sachet (1 Tbsp) dried yeast	**2 Tbsp olive oil**
250 ml/8 fl oz warm water	**½ tsp salt**
375 g/12 oz plain flour	

Combine the yeast, warm water and 375 g/12 oz of the flour. Mix well to blend. Add the oil, salt and remaining flour and stir until the dough sticks together (1).

Place the dough on a lightly floured surface. Dust your hands with flour and knead the dough until it is smooth and elastic, above 5 minutes. If the dough gets sticky, sprinkle it with a little flour (2).

Roll the dough into a ball. Cover with a teacloth and set in a warm, but not hot, place to prove until doubled in volume, about 1 hour (3).

When the dough has proved, roll it into a ball to make one deep-pan pizza or divide it in two balls to make two 30-cm/12-in thin-crust pizzas. Before rolling out and topping the pizza, allow the dough to rest for 20 minutes (4).

When ready to bake, place the dough in the centre of lightly oiled baking sheet.

Wholemeal Pizza Dough

Wholemeal flour adds a robust flavour to the dough, but this recipe also calls for plain flour. On its own, wholemeal flour is too heavy to make a proper base. It, too, goes well with most toppings.

MAKES 2 30-CM/12-IN THIN-CRUST PIZZAS
OR 1 DEEP-PAN PIZZA

1 sachet (1 Tbsp) dried yeast	2 Tbsp olive oil
250 ml/8 fl oz warm water	½ tsp salt
300 g/10 oz plain flour	150 g/5 oz wholemeal flour

In a large bowl, combine the yeast, warm water and white flour. Mix well to blend. Add the oil, salt and wholemeal flour and stir until the dough sticks together. Place the dough on a lightly floured surface. Dust your hands with flour and then knead the dough until it is smooth and elastic, about 5 minutes. If the dough gets sticky, sprinkle it with a little more flour.

Roll the dough into a ball and place it in a lightly oiled bowl. Cover the bowl with a teacloth and set in a warm, not hot, place to prove until doubled in volume, about 1 hour.

When the dough has proved, roll it into a ball to make one 30-cm/12-in deep-pan pizza or divide it in two balls to make two 30-cm/12-in thin-crust pizzas. Before rolling out and topping the pizza, allow the dough to rest for 20 minutes.

When ready to bake, place the dough in the centre of a lightly oiled tin. Roll outward toward the edges with the palm of your hand until the dough fills the tin evenly.

VARIATION

To make Wholemeal Cheese Pizza Dough, follow the instructions for Wholemeal Pizza Dough, but add 60 g/ 2 oz grated Parmesan cheese to the oil and salt which will then be added to the yeast mixture.

Corn Bread Pizza Dough

Cornmeal makes an interesting variation on ordinary flour. It complements tomato-based sauces and Mexican-style toppings. It also goes well with cheeses.

MAKES 1 30-CM/12-IN THIN-CRUST PIZZA

250 ml/8 fl oz warm water	¼ tsp salt
1 sachet (1 Tbsp) dried yeast	1 tsp sugar
375 g/12 oz plain flour	2 Tbsp corn oil
250 g/8 oz yellow cornmeal	

In a large bowl, combine the warm water, yeast, 250 g/ 8 oz white flour and half of the cornmeal. Stir to mix thoroughly. Add the remaining ingredients, stirring with a wooden spoon until mixed. Place the dough on a floured surface. Dust your hands with white flour and knead the dough for 5 minutes, dusting with additional flour if necessary to keep it from sticking. The dough should be smooth and elastic.

Place the dough in a clean bowl, cover with a teacloth, and set in a warm place to prove for about 1 hour or until doubled in size.

When the dough is ready, roll into a ball and leave to rest for 20 minutes before topping and baking.

Pizza Primavera

T his pizza combines a selection of delicious vegetables with a cream and cheese sauce.

MAKES 1 30-CM/12-IN DEEP-PAN PIZZA

1 quantity Wholemeal Pizza Dough (see page 346)	2 spring onions, chopped
3 tsp olive oil	60 g/2 oz Parmesan cheese
3 tsp flour	250 g/8 oz fresh asparagus, chopped
250 ml/8 fl oz double cream	½ large red pepper
1 handful basil leaves, finely chopped	1 small onion
2 cloves garlic, crushed	1 small courgette

Pre-heat the oven to 500°F/260°C/Gas 10. Bake the pizza dough for 3 minutes and remove from the oven.

To make the sauce, heat the olive oil in a pan and add the flour, stirring to blend. Cook for 2 or 3 minutes until bubbling. Slowly add the cream, stirring to mix. When the flour mixture is smooth, add the basil, garlic and spring onions. Bring to the boil and then simmer over low heat for 5 minutes, stirring frequently. Remove from the heat and stir in the Parmesan cheese.

Wash the asparagus and trim off the ends, then chop on the diagonal into 5-cm/2-in pieces. Seed and chop the pepper into 5-cm/2-in squares. Chop the onion and courgette into fairly small pieces. Toss the vegetables in a bowl and mix.

To assemble the pizza, spread the vegetables on the pre-baked base. Pour the sauce over the vegetables, spreading it with a back of a spoon if necessary. Bake for 7 to 8 minutes.

Pizza with Caramelized Onions

aramelized onions are cooked slowly in oil until they are golden brown and very soft. They have a wonderful flavour that goes well on a pizza. Make them ahead of time and store them in the refrigerator until ready to use.

MAKES 1 30-CM/12-IN DEEP-PAN PIZZA

1 quantity Basic or Wholemeal Pizza Dough (see pages 345 and 346)	½ tsp salt
	2 tsp red wine vinegar
2 large onions	175 g/6 oz grated fontina cheese
3 Tbsp olive oil	

SAUCE

1 800-g/28-oz tin passata	1 tsp basil
1 bay leaf	1 tsp thyme
1 tsp oregano	½ tsp marjoram

Slice both ends off the onions but do not peel. Cut the onions in quarters. Place them skin-side down in a roasting tin. Liberally brush each onion with 1 tablespoon oil and sprinkle with salt. Cover the tin with foil and bake for 30 minutes, remove the foil and brush the onion with the remaining oil. Sprinkle with vinegar. Turn the onion quarters on one side and return to the oven for one hour. Occasionally turn the onions and baste with the oil from the tin. When cooked, leave to cool or store in refrigerator for later use.

Pre-heat the oven to 500°F/260°C/Gas 10.

To make the sauce, place ingredients in a pan and bring to the boil. Reduce the heat, cover loosely and simmer for 30 minutes, stirring occasionally.

To assemble the pizza, slice the onion quarters into strips. Spread the pizza sauce over the pizza dough. Spread sliced onion over the sauce and top with cheese. Bake for 10 minutes.

Deep-pan Creole Pizza

Creole dishes tend to be spicy tomato and vegetable mixtures, and this pizza is no exception. Okra exudes a sticky substance when cut, which adds a viscous texture to the topping.

MAKES I 22 X 32-CM/9 X 13-IN DEEP-PAN PIZZA

1 quantity Basic Wholemeal Pizza Dough (see page 346)	1 tsp thyme
	½ tsp basil
120 g/4 oz okra	½ tsp cayenne pepper
2 400-g/14-oz tins chopped tomatoes	2 cloves garlic, crushed
	2 sticks celery, chopped
1 tsp oregano	1 small onion, chopped

Pre-heat the oven to 500°F/260°C/Gas 10.

Place the dough in the centre of a lightly oiled 32 x 22 x 5-cm/13 x 9 x 2-in tin.

Using your fingers, gently spread the dough until it covers the bottom of the tin evenly and goes halfway up the sides.

Boil the okra until tender then chop. Put the tomatoes into a colander to drain and discard the liquid but retain the thick sauce. Place the tomatoes and sauce in a bowl. Add the spices and garlic. Chop the celery and onion into small pieces and add them to the bowl. Finally, add the okra and stir gently to mix.

To assemble, spread the tomato and okra mixture on to the pizza dough and bake for 20 minutes.

Sweet Breads and Yeasted Cakes for Coffee

Sweet-potato Bread

In a small saucepan over low heat, heat the water and 1 tablespoon of the sugar until very warm. Pour into the bowl of a heavy-duty electric mixer, and sprinkle over the yeast and 1 tablespoon of the flour. Leave to stand until frothy, about 15 minutes.

Fit the mixer with the dough hook and beat in the salt, 1 teaspoon of the mixed spice, the dried milk, mashed sweet potato or pumpkin, 120 g/4 oz of the sugar, half the butter, the grated orange rind and 250 g/8 oz of the flour until well-blended.

On low speed, gradually beat in the remaining flour. Continue to beat on medium speed until a rough dough forms. Turn the dough on to a lightly floured surface and knead until smooth, 10 to 12 times. Place the dough in a greased bowl, turning to grease the top. Cover with a clean teatowel and leave to prove in a warm, draught-free place until doubled in volume, about 1 to 1½ hours.

Punch down the dough and turn on to a lightly floured surface; knead lightly 2 to 3 times. Cut the dough into 3 equal pieces, and roll each into a cylinder about 45 cm/18 in long. Cut each cylinder into 18 pieces, and roll each piece into a ball.

Generously grease a 25-cm/10-in ring tin. Combine the remaining sugar and mixed spice in a small bowl. Roll the dough balls in the remaining butter and then into the sugar mixture. Arrange the balls in the bottom of the prepared tin, and sprinkle over half of the chopped nuts. Arrange the remaining balls over the first layer, pushing into the creases and pressing together to fit. Sprinkle over the remaining nuts. Cover with the teatowel and leave in a warm place until just doubled, about 45 minutes.

Pre-heat the oven to 350°F/175°C/Gas 4. Bake until risen and well coloured, about 1 hour. Transfer to a wire rack to cool, for 10 to 15 minutes, then unmould on to the wire rack to cool, top-side up, until just warm. Serve with butter.

This warm, well-coloured bread is perfect for a winter brunch or coffee morning.

SERVES 12–14

250 ml/8 fl oz water

300 g/10 oz sugar

2 sachets (2 Tbsp) dried yeast

600 g/1¼ lb plain flour

1 tsp salt

2 tsp mixed spice

120 ml/4 fl oz instant, fat-free dried milk

250 g/8 oz sweet potato or pumpkin, cooked and mashed

120 g/4 oz butter, melted and cooled

Grated rind of 1 orange

60 g/2 oz chopped walnuts or pecans

Malt Loaf

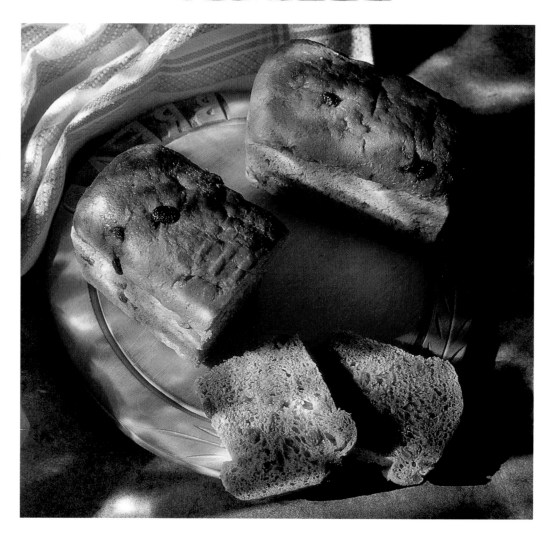

This sticky bread studded with golden raisins is excellent for breakfast spread with honey.

MAKES 2 SMALL LOAVES

30 g/1 oz compressed yeast or 2 tsp dried yeast and 1 tsp sugar	1 Tbsp honey or golden syrup
600 ml/1 pt warm water	2 Tbsp vegetable oil
1 tsp salt	120 g/4 oz sultanas
2 Tbsp malt	500 g/1 lb wholemeal flour
	Honey or syrup to glaze

Grease two small loaf tins. Mix the yeast (and sugar) in the warm water.

Add the malt, honey, oil and sultanas to the warmed flour. Stir in the yeast liquid and mix thoroughly. Put the mixture into the tins.

Set aside for 1 hour in a warm place, covered with oiled plastic. Pre-heat oven to 400°F/200°C/Gas 6. Bake for 15 minutes then lower the temperature to 350°F/175°C/Gas 4 and bake for a further 20 minutes until cooked. A skewer inserted into the centre of the loaf should emerge clean.

Place the loaves on a wire rack. Warm a little honey or syrup and brush the tops of the loaves while they are still hot.

Swedish Limpa

For an even richer flavour use half golden syrup and half treacle.

MAKES 3 LOAVES

60 g/2 oz compressed yeast or 4 Tbsp dried yeast and 1 tsp sugar	5 Tbsp dark corn syrup
	2 to 4 tsp ground star anise or fennel or 2 tsp ground star anise, 2 tsp ground fennel, and 1 tsp bitter orange rind, finely chopped
500 ml/1 pt warm milk	
60–90 g/2–3 oz butter, melted and cooled	
	670 g/1 lb 6 oz rye flour
1 tsp salt	250 g/8 oz flour

BREAD MACHINE METHOD
MAKES 1 500 G/ 1 LB LOAF

180 ml/6 fl oz water	½ tsp caraway seeds
1 Tbsp vegetable oil	1 Tbsp grated orange rind
2 Tbsp honey	175 g/6 oz strong white flour
1 tsp salt	90 g/3 oz rye flour
½ tsp ground anise	1½ tsp yeast

● Put the ingredients in the tin in order suggested in the instructions. Set for whole-wheat bread, medium crust. Press start.

Grease a large baking sheet. Put the yeast into a mixing bowl and beat it with a little of the milk. Add the teaspoon of sugar if dried yeast is used and set it aside for 10 minutes until frothy. Mix the melted fat with the milk, pour it on to the yeast and add the salt, golden syrup and spices. Stir in half the rye flour. Add the rest gradually and the strong white flour.

Work the dough until smooth. Cover it with oiled plastic and prove until doubled in size, 40 to 50 minutes.

Punch it down then put it on a lightly floured board and knead thoroughly. Divide the dough into 3 and roll into smooth loaves. Put them side by side on the baking sheet with a piece of oiled foil between loaves. Cover the loaves with oiled plastic and leave to rise.

Pre-heat the oven to 400°F/200°C/Gas 6. Prick the loaves with a skewer. Bake for about 30 minutes. Brush them with water twice during and after baking. Wrap the loaves in a clean towel and cool on a rack.

Kubaneh

This soft, semi-steamed Yemenite sweet bread can be eaten with jam or as the Yemenites do, with a hot chutney-type relish or *zhoug*, a chilli-flavoured dip. Kubaneh can be baked in the oven or on top of the hob in a heavy-bottomed saucepan.

SERVES 8

1 sachet (1 Tbsp) dried yeast	½ tsp ground cinnamon or ginger
6 Tbsp sugar	
500 ml/1 pt lukewarm water	Margarine or butter, softened to grease
375 g/12 oz plain flour	
1 tsp salt	

In the bowl of an electric mixer fitted with dough hook, combine the yeast, 1 teaspoonful sugar and 120 ml/4 fl oz lukewarm water. Stir until the yeast is almost dissolved, 1 to 2 minutes. Leave the yeast mixture to stand until it looks frothy, 5 to 7 minutes.

In a large bowl, combine the flour, salt and cinnamon or ginger. With the mixer on low speed, beat in 375 ml/ 12 fl oz lukewarm water until well blended.

With the machine on low speed, gradually add the flour mixture and beat until mixture forms a soft dough. If the mixture is very sticky, add a little more flour, but the dough should be soft. Increase the speed to medium and knead until the dough is very smooth but still soft, 5 to 7 minutes.

Lightly oil a bowl. Place dough in bowl and turn to coat with oil. Cover with a clean teatowel and leave in a warm place to prove until doubled in bulk, 1½ to 2 hours.

Turn the dough on to a lightly floured surface and punch down. Return to the bowl, re-cover and leave to prove again in a warm place, about 1 hour longer.

Pre-heat the oven to 325°F/160°C/Gas 3. Heavily coat a 25-cm/10-in ring tin with 3 to 4 tablespoonfuls softened margarine or butter. Turn the dough on to lightly floured surface and punch down. Divide the dough into 8 pieces. Roll each piece into a ball. Place the balls into the base of the tin just touching each other. Cover the tin and leave in a warm place to prove again until the balls form a ring, 30 minutes.

Heavily grease a piece of foil large enough to cover the tin; cover the tin tightly. Bake until the bread leaves the sides of the tin, 1¼ to 1½ hours. Carefully remove the foil, lifting an edge facing away from you to allow steam to escape. If you like, continue baking, uncovered, to brown the top, 15 to 20 minutes. Serve warm.

Bara Brith

This Welsh currant bread has an attractive speckled appearance.

MAKES 1 LARGE LOAF

30 g/1 oz fresh yeast or 1 sachet (1 Tbsp) dried yeast plus 1 tsp sugar	90 g/3 oz butter or margarine
250 ml/8 fl oz warm milk	375 g/12 oz soft brown sugar
500 g/1 lb plain or strong white flour	1 egg, beaten
1 tsp salt	375 g/12 oz mixed dried fruit (currants, sultanas, raisins, candied peel)
1 tsp mixed spice	Warm milk and honey to glaze

Stir the yeast into the warm milk. If the yeast is dried, add the sugar and set aside for about 10 minutes until frothy. Add 60 g/2 oz of the flour and beat well. Set the bowl aside in a warm place for 20 minutes to produce a foamy batter.

Mix together the rest of the flour with the salt and spice. Blend in the fat and add the brown sugar. Add the flour mixture and the beaten egg to the yeast batter and knead the dough, first in the bowl and then turned on to a floured board. Knead until the dough is smooth. Return the dough to the bowl. Cover it with a sheet of oiled plastic and leave to prove for 1½ hours in a warm place.

Work the dried fruit into the dough, knead and shape to fit into a large loaf tin. Brush the dough with warm milk and honey and cover with oiled plastic. Leave to prove for a further 1 to 1¼ hours, until doubled in size.

Pre-heat the oven to 425°F/220°C/Gas 7. Bake for 15 minutes. Reduce the heat to 350°F/175°C/Gas 4, then bake for a further 45 minutes at the lower temperature. Turn the loaf on to a wire rack to cool. Serve with butter.

Sally Lunn

These little cakes are named after Sally Lunn, the woman who first made them in Bath, in the 18th century.

MAKES 2 CAKES

15 g/½ oz fresh yeast or 2 tsp dried yeast and 1 tsp sugar	2 eggs, beaten
	60 g/2 oz butter or margarine, melted and cooled
300 g/10 oz warm milk	
500 g/1 lb flour	TO GLAZE
1 tsp salt	2 Tbsp sugar
	2 Tbsp water

BREAD MACHINE METHOD – MAKES 1 500-G/1-LB LOAF

90 ml/3 fl oz milk	½ tsp salt
2 eggs	250 g/8 oz strong white flour
60 g/2 oz butter	
3 Tbsp sugar	1½ tsp yeast

● Put all the ingredients in the bread tin in the order suggested in the instructions. Set for wholemeal bread, medium crust. Press start.

Grease two 15-cm/6-in cake tins. Stir the fresh yeast (or dried yeast and sugar) into the warm milk. If dried yeast is used, set the bowl aside for 10 minutes until frothy.

Mix in 120 g/4 oz of the flour and leave in a warm place for about 20 minutes until the yeast batter is frothy.

Mix the remaining flour with the salt and stir into the yeast with the eggs and melted butter. Beat well until a smooth batter is produced. Pour the batter into the cake tins, cover them with oiled plastic and leave in a warm place for about 1½ hours until doubled in size.

Bake for about 20 minutes until nicely browned. Turn the cakes on to a wire rack and brush them with the hot glaze made by boiling the sugar and water together. Allow to cool a little before serving warm with whipped cream or butter.

Swedish Saffron Bread

This bread is served for the Santa Lucia festival in Sweden (December 13).

MAKES 2 OR 3 LOAVES

60 g/2 oz fresh yeast or
  4 Tbsp dried yeast and
  I tsp sugar

550 ml/2.2 pt warm milk

175 g/6 oz butter or
  margarine, melted and
  cooled

I tsp powdered saffron

½ tsp salt

250 g/8 oz sugar

700 g/1½ lb plain or strong
  white flour

I egg

60 g/2 oz almonds, blanched
  and chopped

90 g/3 oz raisins

60 g/2 oz mixed candied peel,
  chopped

Egg to glaze

Crushed sugar cubes and
  chopped almonds or raisins
  to decorate

Grease two baking sheets. Put the yeast into a mixing bowl with a few tablespoons of the warm milk. If dried yeast is used add the teaspoon of sugar and set aside in a warm place for 10 minutes until frothy.

Add the fat and the rest of the milk to the yeast liquid. Stir in the saffron, salt, sugar, half the flour, the egg, nuts and dried fruit. Add the rest of the flour gradually and work the dough until it becomes smooth and shiny and no longer sticky. Cover the dough with oiled plastic and leave to prove until doubled in size, about I hour. Knead the dough in the bowl then turn it on to a lightly floured board and knead thoroughly until smooth.

Divide the dough into 2 or 3 rounds and place them on the baking sheets. Cover with oiled plastic and allow to rise, about 40 minutes. Brush with egg and sprinkle with sugar and almonds or decorate with raisins.

Pre-heat the oven to 400°F/200°C/Gas 6. Bake for 20 to 25 minutes. Cool on a wire rack.

Lemon Brioche Loaf

Rich and buttery, classic French brioche is a favourite breakfast treat. It can be baked in a loaf tin, but use the traditional moulds if you like; be sure to start the dough the night before you want the loaf.

MAKES 1 LARGE LOAF OR 12 BUNS

2 Tbsp sugar	¼ tsp salt
3 Tbsp water	Grated rind of 1 lemon
1 sachet (1 Tbsp) dried yeast	90 g/3 oz unsalted butter, cut into small pieces, softened
2 eggs, lightly beaten	
120–175 g/4–6 oz plain flour	1 egg yolk, beaten with 1 Tbsp water, to glaze

Put 1 tablespoon of the sugar in a small saucepan with the water, and heat over low heat until very warm, stirring to dissolve the sugar. Sprinkle over the yeast and allow to stand until yeast is frothy, about 5 to 10 minutes. Stir to dissolve, then beat in the eggs.

Put the flour, salt, grated lemon rind and remaining sugar in a food processor fitted with a metal blade, and blend. With the machine running, slowly pour the yeast-egg mixture through the feed tube; a dough will form immediately. Scrape down the side of the bowl, and process the dough until very well kneaded, 2 to 3 minutes. Sprinkle over the softened butter pieces, and pulse in the butter until just blended, about 12 times.

Scrape the dough into a large, greased bowl, turning to grease the top. Cover with a clean teatowel and leave to prove in a warm, draught-free place until dough doubles in volume, about 1½ hours. (At this point the dough can be refrigerated overnight to rise very slowly.)

Butter a 22 x 13-cm/9 x 5-in loaf tin. Punch down the dough and turn on to a lightly floured surface; knead lightly 2 to 3 times. Divide the dough into 8 or 9 pieces, and shape into balls. Arrange the dough balls in the tin, pushing them together to fit. Cover and leave to prove in a warm place until just doubled in volume, about 40 minutes.

Pre-heat the oven to 400°F/200°C/Gas 6. Brush the top of the risen loaf with the egg glaze and bake until well risen and deep-golden brown, about 30 minutes. Transfer to a wire rack, and unmould immediately, top-side up, to cool. Serve warm with butter and jam.

Savarin

Is it a cake, a bread, or a dessert? However you choose to serve it, savarin is delicious soaked as it is in syrup and fruit.

MAKES 1 SAVARIN

15 g/½ oz fresh yeast or 1 sachet (1 Tbsp) dried yeast and ½ tsp sugar	**SYRUP**
	6 Tbsp honey
5 Tbsp warm milk	6 Tbsp golden syrup
175 g/6 oz plain or strong white flour	150 ml/5 fl oz water
¼ tsp salt	3 Tbsp rum
1 Tbsp caster sugar	
90 g/3 oz butter	
3 eggs, beaten	

Grease a 20-cm/8-in ring tin. Stir the yeast into the warm milk, adding the sugar if dried yeast is used. Stand the dried yeast mixture in a warm place for 5 to 10 minutes until frothy. Add 4 tablespoonfuls of the flour to the yeast liquid and set aside in a warm place for 20 to 25 minutes until the batter is foamy. Mix together the rest of the flour with the salt and sugar. Blend in the butter. Stir this mixture into the eggs and yeast batter. Beat thoroughly with a wooden spoon or fork.

Put the savarin mixture into the tin. Cover with oiled plastic and leave to prove in a warm place for 30 to 40 minutes.

Pre-heat the oven to 400°F/200°C/Gas 6. Uncover the tin, place it on a baking sheet and bake for 20 minutes until browned and cooked. Turn the savarin on to a wire rack standing on a large plate.

Combine the syrup ingredients in a saucepan and heat them. Prick the savarin with a thin skewer. Pour the hot syrup over the savarin. Serve with whipped cream. Fruit may be piled into the centre of the savarin if you like.

Swedish Tea Ring

This tea ring is moist and delicious, a perfect, refreshing accompaniment to a cup of tea.

MAKES 1

15 g/½ oz fresh yeast or 1 sachet (1 Tbsp) dried yeast and ½ tsp sugar

6 Tbsp warm milk

250 g/8 oz plain or strong white flour

½ tsp salt

2 Tbsp sugar

2 Tbsp butter or margarine

1 egg, beaten

1 Tbsp melted butter

4 Tbsp coarse sugar crystals or demerara sugar mixed with 2 tsp ground cinnamon or 4 Tbsp sweetened apple sauce and 1 Tbsp slivered almonds

250 g/8 oz icing sugar

2 Tbsp water

A few red and green glacé cherries

Grease a baking sheet. Stir the yeast (and sugar if dried yeast is used) into the warm milk. Set aside the dried yeast for 10 minutes until frothy. Add one-quarter of the flour to the yeast liquid and leave in a warm place for about 20 minutes.

Mix the rest of the flour with the salt and sugar and rub in the fat. Add the egg and stir the mixture into the yeast batter to make a soft dough. Turn the dough on to a floured board and knead until smooth, elastic, and no longer sticky. Return the dough to the warm bowl. Cover with oiled plastic and leave to prove for about 1 hour, until doubled in size.

Roll out the lightly kneaded dough on a floured board into a rectangular strip 25 x 37 cm/10 x 15 in. Brush the dough with the melted butter and sprinkle the cinnamon sugar over the dough (or spread the apple sauce over the dough and sprinkle on the flaked almonds). Roll up the dough like a Swiss roll, starting at the longer side. Transfer the roll to the baking sheet and form into a circle. Moisten the ends of the dough with milk and pinch them together. Clip the dough with scissors at 2.5-cm/1-in intervals but without cutting right through. Turn the corners backwards and bend them downwards to make a decorative pattern. Cover the ring with oiled plastic and leave to prove for about 45 minutes.

Pre-heat the oven to 400°F/200°C/Gas 6. Uncover and bake for 20 to 25 minutes. Transfer the ring to a wire rack to cool.

Mix the icing sugar and water and frost the ring. Decorate with cherries.

Honey-walnut Bread

This dense, nutty, slightly sweet bread is delicious for breakfast especially when eaten with soft cheese.

MAKES 1 LOAF

300 ml/½ pt water	Water
1 Tbsp sugar	1 sachet (1 Tbsp) dried yeast
250 g/8 oz wholemeal flour	120 g/4 oz walnut halves, chopped, plus extra walnut halves for decoration (optional)
175 g/6 oz plain flour	
2½ tsp salt	
2 Tbsp honey	1 egg, lightly beaten, to glaze

In a small saucepan over low heat, heat the water and sugar until very warm. In a large bowl, stir the wholemeal flour, plain flour and salt together until well-blended, and make a well in the centre. Stir the honey into warm water and pour into the well. Sprinkle the yeast over it and allow to stand until foamy, about 15 minutes.

Pour in the remaining water, and slowly incorporate the flour from the edge of the well into the liquid with an electric mixer on low speed or a wooden spoon, mixing to form a smooth dough. If the dough is very sticky, sprinkle in a little more flour.

Turn the dough on to a lightly floured surface and knead until smooth and elastic, about 5 minutes. Place the dough in a greased bowl, turning to grease the top. Cover with a clean teatowel and leave to prove in a warm, draught-free place until doubled in volume, about 1½ hours.

Grease a large baking sheet. Punch down the dough and turn on to a lightly floured surface. Sprinkle over the chopped walnuts, and knead into the dough until evenly distributed. Shape the dough into a round or oval, and place on the baking sheet. Cover with a teatowel and leave in a warm place to prove again until just doubled in volume, about ½ hour.

Pre-heat the oven to 425°F/220°C/Gas 7. Brush the loaf with the egg glaze. With a sharp knife, slash the top of the dough in 3 to 4 places and bake for 15 minutes. Reduce the oven temperature to 375°F/190°C/Gas 5, and bake until the loaf is deep-golden brown, about 40 minutes more. Transfer to a wire rack..

German Plum Cake

There are many variations on this recipe – you can scatter a Streusel crumb mixture on top or serve it with whipped cream. The genuine traditional German "Zwetschkenkuchen", however, should consist of a yeast dough base with fresh ripe plums baked in a large rectangular tin.

MAKES 1 30-CM/12-IN CAKE

25 g/¾ oz fresh yeast or 1½ Tbsp dried yeast plus 1½ tsp sugar	2 eggs
	2 tsp grated lemon rind
150 ml/5 fl oz warm milk	Pinch of salt
90 g/3 oz sugar	1 kg/2 lb plums
300 g/10 oz plain or strong white flour	2 Tbsp ground hazelnuts or almonds or toasted breadcrumbs
5 Tbsp butter	

Crumble the yeast into the warm milk, add a teaspoon of sugar and 120 g/4 oz flour taken from the main quantity. Beat well. Cover and leave to ferment for 10 minutes.

Beat the butter and sugar until pale and fluffy and mix in the eggs one at a time. Add the lemon rind. Sift the flour and salt two or three times, finally into a large bowl. Make a well in the centre and put in the egg mixture, scatter over a little of the flour then add the yeast batter. Combine well, then knead hard in the bowl or on a floured worktop until the dough starts to roll cleanly off the sides of the bowl or board and becomes very elastic and forms air bubbles. Replace in the bowl and cover with oiled plastic. Leave the dough to prove in a warm place until it has doubled in bulk.

Grease two cake tins about 20 x 30 x 4 cm/8 x 12 x 1½ in, and dust with flour. Divide the dough in two. Keep one half covered and roll out the other half on a floured board to fit the cake pan approximately. Use to line the tin, gently easing it into place and pushing the dough up the sides a little. Stand it uncovered in a warm place for about 20 minutes to rise again. Repeat with the remaining dough.

Prepare the fruit; wash, dry and split almost in half. Remove the stones. Lightly brush the risen dough with melted butter and scatter over the ground nuts or toasted breadcrumbs. Pack in the prepared fruits close together in straight rows; they should not be opened out but left closed so that the layer of fruit is rich and juicy when it is baked.

Pre-heat the oven to 400°F/200°C/Gas 6 and bake for 35 minutes. This cake is best served while it is still slightly warm. Dredge the slices generously with caster sugar as you serve them.

Crumb Cake

Like German Plum Cake (see page 362), this is another German classic. Here the yeast dough base is covered with a thick cinnamon and almond crumb covering. Streusel is made like pastry, and here are two simple ways of making it.

MAKES I 30-CM/12-IN CAKE

DOUGH	STREUSEL
(see German Plum Cake, on page 362)	250 g/8 oz unsalted butter
	375 g/12 oz plain flour, sifted
	120 g/4 oz ground almonds
	2 tsp ground cinnamon
	I tsp grated lemon rind
	250 g/8 oz sugar
	Icing sugar to serve

Prepare the yeast dough and line two baking tins as for German Plum Cake. Leave to prove.

Using a food processor. Gently melt the butter and leave to cool. Drop the flour, almonds, cinnamon, lemon rind, and sugar into the processor bowl and switch on for 2 to 3 seconds to mix well. Then quickly pour the cooled butter through the tube on to the mixture with the machine switched on. Stop the motor as soon as a crumb texture is reached.

By hand. Cut the chilled butter pieces into the sifted flour and blend to fine crumbs. Use a knife to blend in the rest of the ingredients and make a coarse crumb texture. Roll into a ball, wrap and chill for I hour until hardened. Rub the dough through a coarse grater and dust lightly with flour to prevent it from sticking together.

Pre-heat the oven to 400°F/200°C/Gas 6. Finish the cakes by brushing the risen dough with melted butter; scatter the crumb mixture generously on top. Bake until well risen and golden, about 35 minutes. Cool in the tins, set on a wire rack. Dust with icing sugar before serving and cut in slices.

Currant Loaf

A simple fruit bread, which is good with butter, and especially good toasted.

MAKES 2 LOAVES

30 g/I oz fresh yeast or I sachet (I Tbsp) dried yeast and I tsp sugar	2 Tbsp sugar
	I tsp salt
300 ml/10 fl oz warm skimmed milk (or warm milk and water)	60 g/2 oz butter or margarine
	90 g/3 oz currants
500 g/I lb plain flour	Warm honey to glaze

Grease two small loaf tins. Stir the yeast into the warm milk (add the spoonful of sugar if the yeast is dried). Leave until frothy, about 10 minutes in the case of dried yeast. Mix the flour, sugar and salt together and blend in the butter. Add the currants and pour on the yeast liquid. Work to a firm dough which no longer clings to the bowl.

Turn the dough on to a lightly floured board and knead until smooth and elastic, about 5 minutes.

Put the dough back into the bowl, cover it with oiled plastic and leave to prove for about 45 minutes or more, until doubled in size.

Punch down the dough on a lightly floured board. Divide the dough into 2 halves. Roll out each piece into an oblong shape, then roll it up Swiss-roll fashion. Place each roll into a loaf tin. Cover them with oiled plastic, then leave to prove for I to 1¼ hours until doubled in size. Bake the uncovered loaves for 40 to 45 minutes.

Turn the loaves out on to a wire rack and brush the tops of the bread with warmed honey. Cool and serve with butter.

Chocolate Poppy-seed Plait

This sweet-yeast dough is filled with a rich, poppy-seed and chocolate-chip mixture before being plaited.

MAKES 1 LARGE LOAF

60 ml/2 fl oz water	CHOCOLATE POPPY-SEED FILLING
60 g/2 oz sugar	
1 sachet (1 Tbsp) dried yeast	60 g/2 oz poppy seeds
60 ml/2 fl oz lukewarm milk	60 g/2 oz sugar
½ tsp salt	60 g/2 oz raisins
1 egg, lightly beaten	½ tsp ground cinnamon
60 g/2 oz butter, softened	Grated rind of ½ orange
375 g/12 oz plain flour	60 ml/2 fl oz soured cream
1 egg yolk, beaten with 1 Tbsp milk, to glaze	1 Tbsp marmalade or apricot jam
	60 g/2 oz plain chocolate chips

In a small saucepan over low heat, heat the water and 1 tablespoonful sugar until very warm. Pour into the bowl of a heavy-duty electric mixer, and sprinkle over the yeast. Allow to stand until frothy, about 15 minutes.

Fit the mixer with the dough hook and beat in the warm milk, the remaining sugar, salt, egg and butter. On low speed, gradually beat in 300 g/10 oz of the flour until a soft dough forms. If the dough is sticky, add more flour. Beat until the dough comes together and becomes elastic.

Turn the dough on to a lightly floured surface, and knead until smooth and elastic, 2 to 3 minutes, adding a little more flour if necessary. Place the dough in a greased bowl, turning to grease the top. Cover with a clean teatowel, and leave to prove in a warm, draught-free place until doubled in volume, about 1½ hours.

Meanwhile, prepare the filling. Put all the ingredients except the chocolate chips in the bowl of a food processor fitted with the metal blade, and process using the pulse button, until just well blended, but not completely smooth. Grease a large baking sheet.

Punch down the dough and turn on to a lightly floured surface, kneading 2 to 3 times. With a lightly floured rolling pin, roll into a rectangle about 37 × 25 cm/ 15 × 10 in. To transfer to the baking sheet, roll the dough around the rolling pin and carefully unroll on to the baking sheet, stretching gently to keep the shape. Spread the filling down the centre third of the dough, to within about 5 cm/ 2 in from each end.

With a sharp knife, cut 8 to 10 diagonal slashes from both sides of the filling to both edges of the dough, cutting about 1 cm/½ in from the filling. Beginning at one end, fold the end over the bottom edge of the filling, then fold over all the strips from alternate sides, and tuck the ends of the strips under the plait. Cover with the teatowel. Leave in a warm place to prove again until almost doubled in size.

Pre-heat the oven to 375°F/190°C/Gas 5. Brush the braid with the egg glaze, and bake until golden and well browned, about 30 minutes. Remove the baking sheet to a wire rack to cool, 15 to 20 minutes, then carefully transfer the braid on to the rack to cool until just warm.

Butter Kuchen

K uchen are Austrian-German-style cakes which are traditionally served with coffee.

SERVES 10 TO 12

2 sachets (2 Tbsp) dried yeast

175 g/6 oz sugar

60 ml/2 fl oz lukewarm milk

175 g/6 oz unsalted butter or margarine, softened

3 eggs, lightly beaten

250 ml/8 fl oz soured cream

Grated rind of I lemon

I tsp vanilla essence

550 g/1¼ lb plain flour

I tsp salt

FILLING

3 Tbsp butter or margarine, melted

I tbsp ground cinnamon

175 g/6 oz sugar

120 g/4 oz sultanas

60 g/2 oz candied lemon peel

GLAZE

3 to 4 Tbsp icing sugar

2 Tbsp water

1–2 tsp lemon juice

In a small bowl, combine the yeast, 2 tbsp sugar and the lukewarm milk. Stir until the yeast begins to dissolve, I minute. Leave to stand until bubbles form on the surface and the mixture looks frothy, 7 to 10 minutes.

In the bowl of an electric mixer fitted with beaters, cream the butter or margarine and remaining sugar until well-blended and smooth, 2 to 3 minutes. Beat in the eggs, soured cream, lemon rind, vanilla essence and yeast mixture.

Scrape the beaters and replace with the dough hook. On low speed, slowly add the flour and salt and beat until well blended and a soft dough forms. Increase the speed to medium and knead the dough until dough is smooth and elastic, 5 to 7 minutes.

Lightly grease a bowl. Place the dough in the bowl and turn to coat. Cover bowl with a damp teatowel and leave in a warm place until doubled in bulk, 2 to 2½ hours. (Alternatively, cover the bowl with the teatowel and refrigerate overnight to allow the dough to prove slowly.)

Lightly grease a large baking sheet. Turn the dough on to lightly floured surface and roll into a rectangle I cm/½ in thick at least 60 cm/24 in long; brush with melted butter for filling. In a small bowl, combine the cinnamon and sugar then sprinkle over the dough. Sprinkle with sultanas and candied lemon peel.

Starting at one long end, roll up the dough Swiss-roll fashion and bring the ends together. Pinch the ends to form a ring and place on the baking sheet. With a sharp knife slash the ring diagonally from the outer edge halfway to the centre edge at 7-cm/3-in intervals. (This allows the dough to rise more evenly, shows the filling and forms a decorative shape.) Cover with a teatowel and leave in a warm place until doubled in bulk, 1½ to 2 hours.

Pre-heat the oven to 375°F/190°C/Gas 5. Bake until golden brown, 40 to 45 minutes. Remove the Kuchen to wire rack to cool.

Sift the icing sugar into a small bowl. Stir in 2 tbsp water and lemon juice to form a glaze. Thin with a little more water if necessary. Drizzle over the warm Kuchen and slide on to serving plate. Serve warm.

Small Yeast Bakes

Crisp Breadsticks

These thin breadsticks, made in the bread machine, will keep for several days if they are stored in an airtight container.

BREAD MACHNE RECIPE – MAKES 24

150 ml/5 fl oz water	2 tsp yeast
60 ml/2 fl oz vegetable oil	About 2 Tbsp vegetable oil
2 tsp sugar	1 egg white
1 tsp salt	2 Tbsp water
250 g/8 oz strong white flour	Sesame or poppy seeds or coarse salt (optional)

Put all but last three ingredients in the bread tin in the order suggested in the instructions. Set for white bread, dough stage. Press start.

Grease 2–3 baking sheets.

When the dough is ready, remove from the bread tin and punch down. Cut into 24 pieces. Roll each piece between your palms to form a very skinny rope, about 20 cm/8 in long. Place bread sticks 2.5 cm/1 in apart on baking sheets. Brush lightly with oil. Cover loosely and set in a warm place to prove 20 to 25 minutes.

Pre-heat the oven to 350°F/175°C/Gas 4. Make a glaze with egg white and 2 tbsp water. Brush the glaze lightly over the bread sticks. Sprinkle with seeds or salt, if desired. Bake until golden brown, about 25 minutes.

Soft Breadsticks

These soft breadsticks do not keep well, but are delicious served warm from the oven. Sprinkle them with sesame with poppy seeds or coarse salt.

BREAD MACHINE RECIPE – MAKES 20

1 egg, separated	250 g/8 oz flour
120 ml/4 fl oz water	1½ tsp yeast
2 Tbsp vegetable oil	2 Tbsp water
2 tsp sugar	Sesame or poppy seeds or coarse salt (optional)
1 tsp salt	

Separate the egg and put the yolk in the bread tin. Save the white for glazing. Put the remaining ingredients except the last 2 tbsp water and seeds in the bread tin in the order suggested in the instructions. Set for white bread, dough stage. Press start.

Grease 2 or 3 baking sheets. Make a glaze with the egg white and 2 tbsp water. Pre-heat the oven to 350°F/175°C/Gas 4.

When the dough is ready, remove from the bread machine and punch down. Cut the dough into 20 pieces. Roll each piece between your palms to form a rope about 15 cm/6 in long. Place the breadsticks on baking sheet about 4 cm/1½ in apart. Brush with egg glaze. Sprinkle with seeds or salt, if desired.

Bake the breadsticks until golden, 20 to 25 minutes.

Cinnamon Buns

These sweet, sticky buns can be assembled in advance and refrigerated overnight. In the morning, they will have to finish their second proving before you bake them.

BREAD MACHINE RECIPE – MAKES 15

120 ml/4 fl oz milk	FILLING
1 egg	90 g/3 oz brown sugar
40 g/1½ oz butter	1 tsp cinnamon
60 g/2 oz sugar	2 Tbsp very soft butter
½ tsp salt	
250 g/8 oz strong white flour	SYRUP
2 tsp yeast	3 Tbsp butter
	120 g/4 oz brown sugar
	2 Tbsp water
	30 pecan halves

Put the dough ingredients in the bread tin in the order suggested in the instructions. Set for white or sweet bread, dough stage. Press start.

Remove the dough from the bread machine and punch down. Let it rest for 5 minutes to make it easier to roll out. Meanwhile, mix the brown sugar and cinnamon to make the filling. Roll the dough into a rectangle 18–20 cm/7 to 8 in wide and about 40 cm/16 in long. Spread the soft butter over the surface of the dough. Thickly sprinkle brown sugar and cinnamon over the surface, spreading to edges. Roll dough into a long cylinder. Slicing crosswise through the cylinder, cut into 15 pieces.

The buns can be baked together in baking tins or separately in bun tins. The bun-tin buns are neater and crusty on the outside. If you cook them in baking tins, they will be softer. A 20-cm/8-in square baking tin is the perfect size for nine buns; a 22 × 32-cm/9 × 13-in tin should easily hold 15 buns.

Make the syrup by combining the butter, brown sugar and water in a small pan. Heat until the butter is melted and the sugar dissolved. Stir well, then pour the syrup into the bottoms of the baking tin or bun tin. Place two pecan halves in the bottom of each bun tin section, or on the top of each bun if you are using a baking tin. Place rolls in the bun tin, or turn them upside down (so pecans are on the bottom) in a baking tin. Cover loosely, set them in a warm place, and leave to prove until doubled, 45 minutes to 1 hour.

Bake the buns in a pre-heated oven at 350°F/175°C/Gas 4 until they are nicely browned, 17 to 22 minutes in a bun tin, 20 to 25 minutes in a baking tin. The buns must be removed from the tin immediately, or the sugar syrup will harden. Keeping in mind that excess sugar syrup will run off, invert the tin or bun tin over a large plate or baking sheet. Remember to let the buns cool slightly, otherwise the hot sugar will burn your mouth.

Almond Croissants

These tender, flaky croissants are filled with a homemade almond paste for an extra-luxurious treat. Making them is well worth the effort.

MAKES 24

375 ml/12 fl oz milk	**ALMOND PASTE**
2 Tbsp sugar	90 g/3 oz blanched almonds
1 sachet (1 Tbsp) dried yeast	1 Tbsp plain flour
375–400 g/12–14 oz plain flour	1 Tbsp cornflour
	120 g/4 oz sugar
1½ tsp salt	25 g/1 oz unsalted butter, cut
250 g/8 oz unsalted butter	into pieces, softened
1 egg, with 1 tsp water, to glaze	1 egg
	1 egg yolk
Slivered almonds for sprinkling	½ tsp almond essence
Icing sugar to dust (optional)	

In a small saucepan, heat the milk and half of the sugar over low heat until very warm. Pour into the bowl of an electric mixer, and sprinkle over the yeast and 1 tablespoonful of the flour. Allow to stand until frothy, about 15 minutes. With a hand whisk, beat in 1 cup of the flour, the salt, and the remaining sugar.

Fit the mixer with the dough hook, and gradually beat in 250 g/8 oz flour on low speed. Beat on high until the dough comes together and begins to leave the sides of the bowl; if the dough is very wet, sprinkle in a little more flour. Beat until smooth. Scrape the dough into a greased bowl. Cover and leave to prove in a warm, draught-free place until dough doubles in volume, about 1½ hours.

Punch down the dough and turn on to a lightly floured surface; knead lightly until smooth, 4 to 5 times. Wrap in a teatowel and refrigerate about 10 minutes, while preparing the butter.

Put the butter between 2 sheets of clingfilm, and roll the butter into a rectangular shape. Fold the butter in half and roll out again. Repeat until butter is smooth and pliable, but still cold. Flatten to form a 15 × 10-cm/6 × 4-in rectangle.

Roll the dough to a 45 × 20-cm/18 × 8-in rectangle on a lightly floured surface, keeping the centre third thicker than the two outer ends. Put the butter rectangle on the thicker centre of the dough, and fold the bottom third of the dough over the butter. Fold the top third of the dough over the bottom to enclose the butter; with the rolling pin press down the "open edges" to seal the dough and create a neat dough "package."

Turn the dough "package" so that the short "open edge" faces you, the folded edge is on the left and it resembles a closed book. Gently roll the dough to a rectangle about 45 cm/18 in long, keeping the edges straight; do not press out the butter. Fold the rectangle in thirds, as for enclosing the butter, and press down the edges to seal. Press your index finger into one corner to mark the first turn clearly. Wrap the dough in clingfilm, and refrigerate for 30 minutes.

Repeat the rolling and folding, or "turns," twice more, wrapping, marking and chilling the dough between each turn. After the third turn, wrap and refrigerate the dough for at least 2 hours.

Meanwhile, prepare the almond paste. Put the blanched almonds, flour, cornflour and sugar in the bowl of a food processor, and process until very fine crumbs form. Sprinkle over the butter, the egg, egg yolk, and almond essence, and process until a smooth paste forms. If not using immediately, cover and refrigerate.

Lightly spray 2 large baking sheets. Soften the dough at room temperature, 5 to 10 minutes, for easier rolling. Roll the dough to a 3-mm/⅛-in thick rectangle about 32 cm/13 in wide on a lightly floured surface. Trim the edges straight. Cut the rectangle in half to form 2 long, narrow strips. Cut each strip into triangles, 15 cm/6 in high and 10 cm/4 in wide at the base. Using the rolling pin, roll gently from the base to the point, stretching each triangle lengthwise.

Place a tablespoonful of almond paste about 2.5 cm/1 in up from the base of each triangle. Pulling the base slightly to widen it, roll up the dough from the base to the point. Arrange point-side down on the baking sheets, curving the ends to form a crescent shape. Brush each croissant with a little egg glaze; cover and leave to prove in a warm place until almost tripled in volume, about 2 hours. (At this point, the shaped croissants can be refrigerated overnight and baked the next day.) Refrigerate the egg glaze until ready to bake the croissants.

Pre-heat the oven to 475°F/240°C/Gas 9. Brush each croissant again with the egg glaze. Sprinkle each with a few flaked almonds. Bake for 2 minutes, then reduce the oven temperature to 375°F/190°C/Gas 5 and bake until golden, about 10 minutes more. Remove to a wire rack and transfer the croissants to the wire rack to cool. Dust lightly with icing sugar, and serve warm.

TIP

In Step 6, if the butter squeezes out of the package, or the dough becomes sticky at any time, slide it on to a baking sheet and chill until it is easier to handle.

Chocolate Croissants

A variation on the preceding recipe, chocolate croissants make a wonderful sweet treat.

MAKES ABOUT 24

1 quantity Croissants (see page 372)	1 egg, beaten
	2 tsp water
90 g/3 oz chocolate chips	1 tsp sugar

Make the croissants as in the previous recipe.

Put a little pile of chocolate chips at the base end of each triangle.

Beat together the egg, water and sugar. Brush over the edges of each croissant.

Roll up each croissant loosely starting at the base and finishing with the tip underneath.

Put on to a baking sheet and shape as in the previous recipe. Cover and leave to prove for 20 to 30 minutes. Brush with glaze.

Pre-heat the oven to 475°F/240°C/Gas 9 and bake for 2 minutes, then reduce the oven temperature to 375°F/190°C/Gas 5 and bake until golden. Cool on a wire rack and serve warm.

Danish Pastries

A breakfast classic. Danish pastries can be filled with a variety of ingredients from cream cheese to spiced nuts. Here, almonds and chocolate are used.

MAKES ABOUT 16

45 g/1½ oz fresh yeast

150 ml/5 fl oz lukewarm water

500 g/1 lb plain flour

Pinch of salt

4 Tbsp white vegetable fat

2 tbsp sugar

2 eggs, beaten

300 g/10 oz butter

FILLING

60 g/2 oz butter

175 g/6 oz icing sugar, sifted

90 g/3 oz plain chocolate, melted

1½ Tbsp toasted almonds, finely chopped

Few drops of almond essence

GLAZE

1 egg, beaten

Honey

Blend the yeast and water together. Sift the flour and salt into a bowl and blend in the white vegetable fat. Stir in the sugar. Add the yeast liquid and eggs to the flour and mix to a smooth elastic dough. Knead lightly until smooth. Put into a lightly-oiled bowl and cover with oiled plastic. Chill for 10 minutes.

Soften the butter and shape into a flat oblong on greaseproof paper. Roll out the dough on a floured surface to a rectangle three times the size of the butter. Place the butter in the centre of the dough and fold the dough over to enclose it. Press the rolling pin firmly along the open sides. Give the dough a quarter turn and roll out to a rectangle three times as long as it is wide. Fold into three. Wrap in clingfilm and chill for 10 minutes. Repeat the rolling and folding three more times.

To make the filling, beat together the butter and icing sugar. Beat in the chocolate, almonds and essence. Chill.

Roll out the dough thinly and cut into 7-cm/3-in squares. Put a rounded teaspoonful of filling on to the centre of each square. Bring two opposite corners of the dough to the centre. Either seal with beaten egg or secure with a wooden cocktail stick.

Place on a greased baking sheet. Cover with greased clingfilm and leave to prove for about 30 minutes.

Pre-heat the oven to 425°F/220°C/Gas 7. Brush with beaten egg. Bake for about 20 minutes. Brush with a little honey while still warm.

Hot Cross Buns

Hot Cross Buns, traditionally eaten at Easter, make delicious breakfast rolls at any time.

BREAD MACHINE RECIPE – MAKES 12–16

I egg	½ tsp salt
120 ml/4 fl oz milk	250 g/8 oz strong white flour
60 g/2 oz butter	2 tsp yeast
60 g/2 oz sugar	60 g/2 oz currants or raisins
I tsp grated lemon rind	**GLAZE**
½ tsp ground cinnamon	120 g/4 oz icing sugar
¼ tsp nutmeg	I Tbsp milk or cream
⅛ tsp ground cloves	½ tsp lemon juice

Put all ingredients except the currants or raisins in the bread tin in order suggested in the instructions. Set for white bread, dough stage. Press start. Add the currants and raisins after the first kneading or when the machine signals it's time to add fruit.

Lightly oil a 22-cm/9-in square tin or a 25-cm/10-in round tin.

When the dough is ready, remove from the bread machine and punch down. Cut into 12 to 16 equal pieces. Roll each piece into a ball. Place balls about I cm/½ in apart in the baking tin. Cover loosely and leave in a warm place to prove until doubled, 45 minutes to I hour.

Pre-heat the oven to 375°F/190°C/Gas 5. With a sharp knife or razor blade, cut a cross in the top of each bun. Bake 12 to 15 minutes, until a skewer inserted in a bun comes out clean.

Make the glaze, adding sugar or milk if necessary to give it a consistency that will allow you to drizzle it over the buns without it being runny. Let buns cool slightly but not completely. Drizzle the glaze in a cross, following the cuts in the top.

Crumpets

Traditional crumpets are full of tiny holes into which melted butter drips when served hot.

MAKES ABOUT 20

15 g I½ oz fresh yeast or I sachet (I Tbsp) dried yeast and ½ tsp sugar	½ tsp bicarbonate of soda
	Up to 250 ml/8 fl oz warm milk (more, if required, to make a pouring batter)
300 ml/10 fl oz warm water	
375 g/12 oz plain flour	
I tsp salt	

Heat a greased griddle or frying pan. When ready to cook the batter, grease egg-poaching rings or plain biscuit cutters 7 cm/3 in in diameter. Stir the yeast into the water, adding the sugar if dried yeast is used.

Let the dried yeast liquid stand for 5 to 10 minutes until frothy. Mix in half the flour and beat well. Set the batter aside in a warm place for about 30 minutes until it becomes foamy.

Add the rest of the ingredients to the batter, stirring thoroughly. Beat well, adjusting the milk quantity if necessary.

Place the crumpet rings on the heated griddle and pour 2 tablespoonfuls of the batter into each ring. Cook until set underneath and holes appear on the upper surface. Take away the rings and turn the crumpets with a spatula. Lightly cook the second side. Cool the crumpets stacked on a wire rack. Serve freshly made with butter or toast them on both sides, serving them hot with butter.

Swiss Buns

These simple, colourful little buns are very popular with children.

MAKES 8

15 g/½ oz fresh yeast or 1 sachet (1 Tbsp) dried yeast and 1 tsp sugar

150 ml/5 fl oz warm milk

250 g/8 oz plain flour

2 tsp sugar

½ tsp salt

30 g/1 oz butter or margarine

GLACÉ ICING

175 g/6 oz icing sugar

3 Tbsp water

Food colouring (optional)

Grease one large or two small baking sheets. Stir the yeast with the milk, adding 1 teaspoonful of sugar in the case of the dried yeast. If the latter, allow the yeast liquid to stand for 10 minutes or so until frothy.

Mix the flour with the sugar and salt and blend in the fat. Stir in the yeast liquid and mix to a soft dough. Turn on to a lightly floured board and knead thoroughly until the dough is smooth and no longer sticky. Return the dough to the warm bowl, cover with oiled plastic and leave to prove until doubled in size, about 1 hour.

Punch down the dough, divide it into 8 pieces and shape each piece into an oblong 13 cm/5 in long.

Place the buns on the greased baking sheet(s). Cover with oiled plastic and leave to prove in a warm place for about 20 minutes.

Pre-heat the oven to 425°F/220°C/Gas 7. Uncover the buns and bake for about 15 minutes until browned. Lift on to a wire rack to cool. Combine the icing ingredients and use to ice the buns.

Bagels

Dense and chewy, bagels are a delight when they are split and toasted and served with butter or cream cheese. They also made delicious sandwiches. You can experiment by adding chopped sautéed onions, or raisins and cinnamon, to the dough.

BREAD MACHINE RECIPE – MAKES 8 TO 10

1 egg	2 tsp yeast
120 ml/4 fl oz milk	1 Tbsp sugar
1 Tbsp vegetable oil	1 egg white
2 tsp sugar	2 tsp water
½ tsp salt	Sesame or poppy seeds or coarse salt
250 g/8 oz strong white flour	

Put all but the last four ingredients in the bread tin in the order suggested in the instructions. Set for white bread, dough stage. Press start.

When the dough is ready, remove from the bread machine and punch down. Cut into 8 to 10 equal pieces. Roll each piece between your palms to form a thin rope, about 20 cm/8 in long with tapered ends. Bring the ends together to form a circle, with the tapered ends overlapping. With moistened fingers, pinch or lightly knead the joined ends so the circle is securely fastened.

Set the bagels in a warm place to rise and cover them loosely. They should prove for 15 minutes. Pre-heat the oven to 400°F/200°C/Gas 6. While they are proving, bring about 2 1/3¼ pt of water to the boil in a saucepan.

Add 1 tablespoonful sugar. When the bagels have risen for 15 minutes, drop one or two at a time into the boiling water, handling them as gently as possible so they do not deflate. They will rise to the surface of the water and swell up. Cook for 1 minute, then turn them over and let them cook 3 minutes longer.

Remove the bagels, drain over the water, and place on an ungreased baking sheet. Beat the egg white with water and brush over the bagels. Sprinkle with sesame or poppy seeds or coarse salt. Bake until golden, 20 to 25 minutes.

VARIATIONS

Poppy Seed Bagels: Sprinkle the bagels generously with poppy seeds after they have been glazed.

Sesame Seed Bagels: Sprinkle the bagels generously with sesame seeds after they have been glazed.

Onion Bagels: Heat 3 tablespoonfuls vegetable oil in a large frying pan and add 2 large, finely chopped onions. Cook for about 10 minutes or until golden brown. Drain. Place a little of the fried onion on the top of the bagels after they have been glazed.

Cinnamon and Raisin Bagels: Substitute 120 g/4 oz of the strong white flour with wholemeal flour and add 90 g/3 oz raisins and 1 Tbsp ground cinnamon to the dry ingredients. Stir well and continue following the recipe.

Carnival Buns

On the Monday before Shrove Tuesday, Danish children wake up their parents early by traditionally beating them with birchwood twigs. In the afternoon they play a game called "beating a cat off the barrel," and dress up for a party afterwards, when these buns are served.

MAKES 8 TO 10

1 sachet (1 Tbsp) dried yeast	175 ml/6 fl oz milk
60 ml/2 fl oz lukewarm water	500 g/1 lb plain flour, sifted
2 Tbsp sugar	
1 egg	**FILLING**
1 egg yolk	120 g/4 oz finely chopped marzipan (almond paste)
½ tsp salt	2 Tbsp candied peel
1 tsp ground cardamom	Icing sugar to dust
500 g/1 lb butter	

Dissolve the yeast in the lukewarm water. Mix the sugar, egg, egg yolk, salt, cardamom and two-thirds of the butter. Add to the dissolved yeast. Warm the milk. Add the lukewarm milk to the mixture. Mix in the flour and the rest of the butter. Knead the dough until smooth and pliable. Add the marzipan and peel. Chill for 10 minutes.

Roll out the chilled dough to a ½-cm/¼-in thickness. Then cut into 5–7-cm/2–3-in squares, and put on to a greased baking tray.

Cover with oiled plastic and leave to prove until doubled in size. Pre-heat the oven to 425°F/220°C/Gas 7. Bake for 12 minutes, until golden brown. Sprinkle with sifted icing sugar.

Wholemeal Morning Rolls

This is an overnight dough for creamy, soft breakfast rolls. There is nothing better than waking up to the smell of freshly baking bread.

MAKES 18

OVERNIGHT DOUGH

600 ml/1 pt warm water

375 g/12 oz wholemeal bread flour

1 Tbsp salt

1 sachet (1 Tbsp) easy-blend dried yeast

MORNING DOUGH

1 sachet (1 Tbsp) easy-blend dried yeast

175 ml/6 fl oz warm water

375 g/12 oz strong wholemeal flour

60 g/2 oz margarine, at room temperature

1 tsp light brown sugar

BREAD MACHINE METHOD – MAKES 12–16

60 g/2 oz mashed potatoes

1 egg

60 ml/2 fl oz milk

1 Tbsp vegetable oil

1 Tbsp sugar

1 tsp salt

150 g/5 oz strong white flour

90 g/3 oz wholemeal flour

2 tsp yeast

About 3 Tbsp melted butter

● Put all the ingredients except melted butter in the bread tin in the order suggested in the instructions. Set for wholemeal bread, dough stage. Press start.
● Lightly oil 1–2 bun tins.
● When the dough is ready, remove it from the bread machine and punch down. Cut into 12 to 16 equal pieces. Cut each piece into thirds. Roll each piece into a tiny ball and dip in the melted butter. Place three tiny balls in each bun tin. Cover loosely and leave in a warm place to prove until doubled, 45 minutes to 1 hour.
● Pre-heat the oven to 375°F/190°C/Gas 5. Lightly brush the tops of rolls with the remaining melted butter. Bake for 15–20 minutes, until golden brown.

Place the water for the overnight dough in a large bowl. Add the flour, salt and yeast and mix lightly – do not beat or knead. Cover with oiled plastic and leave overnight at room temperature.

In the morning, add all the remaining ingredients to the bowl and mix to a manageable dough; the margarine will be incorporated during the mixing. Turn out on to a floured surface and knead well for about 10 minutes until smooth and elastic.

Divide the dough into 18 pieces and shape them into rolls. Place them on lightly greased baking sheets, quite close together so that they grow into each other and form a broken crust. Cover with oiled plastic and leave in a warm place for 30 minutes to rise.

Pre-heat the oven to 425°F/220°C/Gas 7. Bake the rolls for about 20 minutes. The bases will sound hollow when tapped, but the tops will only brown slightly and remain soft. Cool on a wire rack.

Wholemeal Cheese Baps

Baps are almost inextricably linked with hamburgers – a soft roll for serving with meat and salad. They also make excellent sandwich rolls, being soft in texture and able to take more filling than the typical bread roll. Adding some white flour makes the dough soft and silky and the cheese gives an interesting flavour.

MAKES 8

50 g/2 oz white vegetable fat	250 ml/8 fl oz warm milk and water, mixed
300 g/10 oz strong wholemeal flour	60 g/2 oz sunflower seeds
120 g/4 oz plain flour	60 g/2 oz grated Cheddar cheese
1 tsp salt	
1 sachet easy-blend dried yeast	

Blend the white vegetable fat into the flours and salt in a large bowl. Stir in the yeast then mix to a manageable dough with the warm liquid, adding a little extra if necessary. Knead thoroughly on a lightly floured surface until soft and elastic, then return the dough to the bowl, cover, and leave in a warm place for about 1½ hours, until doubled in size.

Punch the dough down. Add the sunflower seeds and knead lightly to incorporate the seeds, then divide the dough into 8 balls. Shape into rolls, then roll out until 1 cm/½ in thick. Place the baps on lightly greased baking sheets, then cover with oiled plastic and leave to prove in a warm place for a further 30 to 40 minutes.

Pre-heat the oven to 400°F/200°C/Gas 6. Scatter the cheese over the baps then bake for 15 to 20 minutes. Transfer to a wire rack to cool.

Hamburger Buns and Hot Dog Rolls

Baking your own hamburger buns or hot dog rolls in the bread machine is as easy as making simple dinner rolls.

BREAD MACHINE RECIPE – MAKES 6

1 egg	250 g/8 oz strong white flour
120 ml/4 fl oz milk	2 tsp yeast
3 Tbsp butter	2 Tbsp milk
2 Tbsp sugar	Sesame seeds, optional
½ tsp salt	

Put all ingredients except 2 or 3 tablespoonfuls milk and sesame seeds in bread tin in order suggested in instructions. Set for white bread, dough stage. Press start.

When the dough is ready, remove it from bread machine and punch down. Cut into 6 equal pieces. Leave the dough to rest for 5 minutes while you butter one or two baking sheets. For hamburger buns, roll each piece into a ball and flatten it to form a patty about 7 cm/3 in wide and 1 cm/½ in thick. For hot dog buns, roll each piece into a 15-cm/6-in rope and flatten to a 1-cm/½-in thickness. Place the rolls on a baking sheet. Cover loosely and set in a warm place to rise for 20 minutes. Pre-heat the oven to 400°F/200°C/Gas 6.

Lightly brush the tops of rolls with milk and sprinkle with sesame seeds, if desired. Bake for 12 to 15 minutes, until a skewer inserted in a roll comes out clean.

Garlic-herb Bread

In this pull-apart bread small balls of garlic-flavoured dough are dipped in melted butter seasoned with garlic and herbs, and layered in a baking tin. Serve hot, with savoury dishes.

BREAD MACHINE RECIPE – MAKES A I LB LOAF

175 ml/6 fl oz milk	I½ tsp yeast
2 Tbsp vegetable oil	60 g/2 oz butter
I tsp sugar	2 cloves garlic, pressed
I tsp salt	¼ tsp dried sage
I clove garlic, pressed	¼ tsp dried rosemary, crushed
175 g/6 oz strong white flour	½ tsp dried basil
60 g/2 oz wholemeal flour	

Put the first eight ingredients in the bread tin in the order suggested in the instructions. Set for wholemeal bread, dough stage. Press start.

A few minutes before the dough is ready, melt the butter in a small frying pan. Add the garlic and herbs. Sauté for 2 minutes. If the garlic or herbs brown too quickly, remove the pan from the heat and let the mixture continue cooking in its own heat. The garlic will give the bread a bitter flavour if it burns. Lightly oil a baking tin or dish.

Remove the dough from the bread machine and punch down. Roll dough into a thick log and cut out into 20 to 24 pieces. Roll pieces of dough into balls (they do not need to be perfectly round). Dip each ball in the butter-herb mixture and layer in the baking tin. The pieces in the first layer should be close but not touching to give them room to rise. On each succeeding layer, place the balls so they overlap empty spaces on the layer beneath. Drizzle any remaining butter over the dough in the tin.

Cover the dough loosely and put it in a warm place to prove. When doubled in volume, about 30 to 40 minutes, put it in the oven pre-heated to 350°F/175°C/Gas 4. Bake until bread is lightly browned and a skewer inserted comes out clean, about 25 to 30 minutes. Invert on to a serving plate, remove the tin and serve.

If you need more time to coincide the baking with serving a meal, you can slow down the rising by putting the assembled bread in the refrigerator, then letting it return to room temperature before baking. Monkey bread is traditionally baked in a tube pan, 7 or 8 inches across. However, it looks impressive and tastes just as good when baked in round casserole dishes, about 1 inch smaller in diameter than the tube pan.

English Muffins

These crisp muffins have a fresh flavour. The easiest way to make them is with a 7 cm/3-in round biscuit cutter and a griddle.

½ Tbsp bicarbonate of soda	½ tsp salt
60 ml/2 fl oz water	250 g/8 oz strong white flour
120 ml/4 fl oz milk	2 tsp yeast
2 Tbsp vegetable oil	Cornmeal
2 tsp sugar	

Dissolve the bicarbonate in the water. Put the water and remaining ingredients except the cornmeal in the bread tin in the order suggested in the instructions. Set for white bread, dough stage. Press start.

Sprinkle cornmeal on a baking sheet or large platter. When the dough is ready, remove it and punch it down and cut it in half. Let it rest for 5 minutes. Then on a lightly floured surface, roll out the first half to 9 mm/⅜ in thick. With the biscuit cutter, cut out 7-cm/3-in rounds. Put the rounds on the cornmeal-covered baking sheet, then turn to coat both sides. Repeat with the second half. If you wish, you may roll up the scraps, knead them a little, let the dough rest for a few minutes, then roll it out and cut a few more muffins. Don't reroll – the muffins will be tough.

Cover the muffins and leave to prove, 45 minutes.

If you have a griddle, set it for moderate heat. If not, place a frying pan – preferably non-stick – over moderate heat. If the griddle or pan is well-seasoned, it will not require oil. If not, use just the barest trace of oil to cook. Cook until muffin bottoms are nicely browned, then turn and cook the other side. The cooking time will vary from 6 to 10 minutes.

Doughnuts

Doughnuts are always welcome. This recipe is for the classic doughnut.

MAKES 28 DOUGHNUTS

15 g/½ oz fresh yeast	90 g/3 oz butter
250 ml/8 fl oz milk, warmed to blood heat	½ tsp salt
400 g/14 oz plain flour, sifted	Raspberry jam for the filling
2 Tbsp sugar	Vegetable oil for deep-frying
2 egg yolks, lightly beaten	Caster sugar to dredge

BREAD MACHINE METHOD

120 ml/4 fl oz milk	CHOICE OF SUGAR COATINGS
1 egg	Icing sugar
2 Tbsp butter	Granulated cinnamon and
60 g/2 oz sugar	sugar
½ tsp salt	Sugar glaze (see below)
250 g/8 oz bread flour	SUGAR GLAZE
1½ tsp yeast	90 g/3 oz icing sugar
Oil for frying	½ tsp vanilla essence
	1 Tbsp warm milk

● Put all the ingredients except the oil and sugar coating in the bread tin in the order suggested in the instructions. Set for white bread, dough stage. Press start.

● When the dough is ready, punch down. Let it rest for 5 minutes. On a lightly floured surface, roll into a rectangle about 9 mm/⅜ in thick. Using a doughnut cutter or a 7-cm/3-in biscuit cutter, cut out doughnuts. If you are not using a doughnut cutter, cut out a 1-cm/½-in hole in the centre. Knead scraps together and let rest 5 minutes. Reroll the dough and cut out more doughnuts. Place the doughnuts on ungreased baking sheets. Cover loosely and put them in a warm place to rise 45 minutes to 1 hour, until doubled.

● About 15 minutes before the doughnuts finish proving, pour oil at least 7 cm/3 in deep into a deep frying pan. Heat oil to 360°F/180°C. Watch the oil temperature carefully, as it can climb quickly. Slide two or three doughnuts into the hot oil. Do not crowd them. Cook until golden on the bottom, 1½ to 2½ minutes. Then turn and cook the other side.

● When golden, remove the doughnuts from the oil, letting them drain for a few moments over the oil. Place them on several layers of kitchen paper. Make sure the oil temperature returns to 360°F/180°C before you add the next batch of doughnuts.

● Put icing sugar on a mixture of cinnamon and granulated sugar in a paper bag with two doughnuts. Shake until they are coated. Remove and repeat until all doughnuts are coated.

● Alternatively, mix the ingredients for the sugar glaze together and drizzle it over the tops of the doughnuts.

Mix the yeast with 90 ml/3 fl oz milk, 120 g/4 oz flour, and 1 teaspoonful of sugar. Beat well. Set aside until frothy. Mix half remaining milk with egg yolks and set aside. Melt butter in rest of milk. Cool to lukewarm.

Sift together the rest of the flour with the salt into a large bowl and make a well in the centre. Stir in the rest of the sugar, the yeast and the milk mixture. Blend all together and beat well until the dough thickens and continue beating until the dough is smooth and shiny. It should drop off a spoon. Take out half the mixture and cover the bowl with a warm teatowel while you prepare the first batch of doughnuts.

Dust the worktop well with flour and drop the mixture on to it. Dredge with just a little flour and gently roll it out to about 1 cm/½ in thick. Using a floured glass or biscuit cutter about 5 cm/2 in diameter, lightly press circles into half the dough, but do not actually cut it. Place a small teaspoonful of jam in the centre of each. Cut out the same number of circles from the other half of the dough, and turn the top, unfloured sides over on to the jam circles.

Stick the doughnut edges well together (the jam must not leak out as they cook) and gently press around the edges with the end of a teaspoon handle. Cut out each pastry with a slightly smaller cutter. Turn over the finished doughnuts and place them well apart on a floured board, covering lightly with a teatowel. Leave the doughnuts to rise in a warm place and turn them over when they have risen on one side so that the other side may rise. Assemble the left-over scraps and beat them into the remaining dough with 2 spoonfuls of warm milk and finish in the same way.

A light and well-risen doughnut should have a pale ring around its middle. The wider the ring, the lighter the pastry will be. Cook only four or five doughnuts at a time and always start by cooking the side that has risen first.

Heat the vegetable oil to 350–360°F/175–180°C. Using a large slotted spoon, gently lower each doughnut into the hot oil at 4-second intervals. Watch them all the time as they brown very quickly. As soon as they have coloured well, which takes about 2 minutes, flip each one over and cook the other side until it is golden brown.

Lift the doughnuts out of the oil, drain on kitchen paper for a minute or two and roll them in caster sugar. Serve the doughnuts while they are still warm.

Chelsea Buns

An old-fashioned sticky cake, ever-popular and delicious.

MAKES 9

15 g/½ oz fresh yeast or
   1 tsp dried yeast and
   ½ tsp sugar

90 ml/3 fl oz warm milk

250 g/8 oz plain flour

½ tsp salt

2 Tbsp margarine

1 egg, beaten

30 g/1 oz butter, melted

60 g/2 oz currants or raisins

3 Tbsp mixed candied peel

60 g/2 oz soft brown sugar

Warm honey

Grease an 18-cm/7-in-square baking tin. Stir the fresh yeast into the warm milk. If dried yeast is used, also add the sugar and set aside for 10 minutes in a warm place until frothy.

Put one-quarter of the flour into a warmed bowl, stir in the yeast mixture and leave in a warm place for about 20 minutes until the batter is foamy.

Mix the remaining flour with the salt. Blend in the margarine. Stir this flour mixture and the egg into the yeast batter and mix to a soft dough. Turn on to a lightly floured board and knead until smooth. Place the dough in a bowl, cover with a lightly oiled sheet of clingfilm or a plastic bag and leave in a warm place until doubled in size, about 1½ hours.

Roll out to an oblong strip 30 x 22 cm/12 x 9 in. Brush the dough with melted butter and sprinkle with the dried fruit, candied peel and brown sugar. Starting from the longer side, roll up the dough like a Swiss roll. Cut into nine slices and place them close together, cut side down, in the baking tin. Cover and leave for about 40 minutes until the buns have doubled in size and joined together.

Pre-heat the oven to 425°F/220°C/Gas 7. Bake for about 25 minutes, until golden brown. Transfer the buns to a wire rack and brush with warm honey while they are hot. Separate the buns when cool.

Brioches

These light egg-based buns have a delicate texture.

MAKES 12

15 g/½ oz fresh yeast or 1 sachet (1 Tbsp) dried yeast and ½ tsp sugar

3 Tbsp warm milk

175 g/6 oz plain flour

1 tsp sugar

½ tsp salt

60 g/2 oz butter

2 eggs, beaten

BREAD MACHINE METHOD – MAKES 1 500-G/1-LB LOAF

60 ml/2 fl oz water	½ tsp salt
2 eggs	250 g/8 oz strong white
90 g/3 oz butter	flour
1 Tbsp sugar	1½ tsp yeast

● Put the ingredients in the bread tin in the order suggested in the instructions. It is crucial that the butter is softened to room temperature – not melted – when it is added to the other ingredients. Set for white bread, medium crust. Press start.

Grease 12 brioche tins 7 cm/3 in in diameter.

Stir the yeast into the milk, adding the sugar if dried yeast is used. Leave the dried yeast to stand in a warm place for about 5 minutes.

Stir in 30 g/1 oz flour and the teaspoon of sugar and leave the mixture in a warm place for about 20 minutes.

Mix together the rest of the flour with the salt and blend in the butter. Beat the eggs into the yeast liquid. Stir in the dry flour mixture and mix to a soft dough. Turn on to a lightly floured board and knead until smooth and no longer sticky. Return the dough to the warm bowl, cover with oiled plastic and leave to rise until doubled in size, 1 to 1½ hours.

Punch down the risen dough. Divide the dough into 12 pieces. Cut off a quarter of each piece. Shape the larger part of each piece into a ball and place it into brioche tins. Press the centre of each ball to make a hole into which the small piece of dough is placed like a marble. Brush the tops with beaten egg. Cover with oiled plastic and set aside to prove for about 40 minutes. Bake for about 20 minutes and cool on a wire rack.

Pitta Bread

Pitta bread is of Middle Eastern origin and is readily available in many food shops nowadays. Pitta can be made with white or wholemeal flour. Serve hot.

15 g/½ oz fresh yeast or	1 tsp salt
1 sachet (1 Tbsp) dried	
yeast and ½ tsp sugar	500 g/1 lb plain flour

300 ml/10 fl oz warm water

Grease two baking sheets. Stir the yeast into the warm water, adding the sugar if dried yeast is used. Leave dried yeast for about 10 minutes in a warm place to become frothy.

Stir the salt into the flour and mix to a dough with the yeast liquid. Knead thoroughly on a lightly floured board for about 10 minutes until the dough is smooth, elastic and no longer sticky. Return the dough to the warm bowl and cover with oiled plastic. Leave to prove in a warm place until doubled in size, about 1¼ hours.

Punch down the dough. When thoroughly kneaded, divide into 8 pieces. Roll each portion into an oval shape 25 x 13 cm/10 x 5 in. Put the 8 pittas on baking sheets. Cover with oiled plastic and set aside to rest for 5 to 8 minutes. Bake for 6 to 8 minutes. (Do not overbrown as, if not eaten freshly baked, pittas are always re-heated before serving.) Wrap the pittas in a clean teatowel to cool to make them soft and pliable.

BREAD MACHINE METHOD – MAKES 6

175 ml/6 fl oz water	150 g/5 oz strong white
1 Tbsp olive oil	flour
1 tsp sugar	90 g/3 oz wholemeal flour
1 tsp salt	1½ tsp yeast

● Put the ingredients in bread tin in the order suggested in the instructions and set for wholemeal, dough stage. Press start.
● Punch down the dough and cut into 6 equal pieces. Roll each piece between your hands to form a ball. Flatten slightly and let the dough rest about 10 minutes. This will make the dough stretch more readily when you roll it out, rather than bouncing back. On a lightly floured surface, roll out each circle of dough to a diameter of about 15 cm/6 in. Use flour sparingly, as too much flour will interfere with the moisture that creates steam and causes the dough to puff up. Cover the dough with clingfilm or a barely damp teatowel, and let the dough prove for about 30 minutes, until it is puffy.
● Pre-heat the oven to 475°F/240°C/Gas 9. Lightly sprinkle cornmeal on a baking sheet. When the dough is ready, carefully transfer the rounds to the baking sheet. Bake until dough puffs up and is lightly browned, 5 to 6 minutes, then turn and bake until other side is lightly browned, about 2 minutes.

Naan

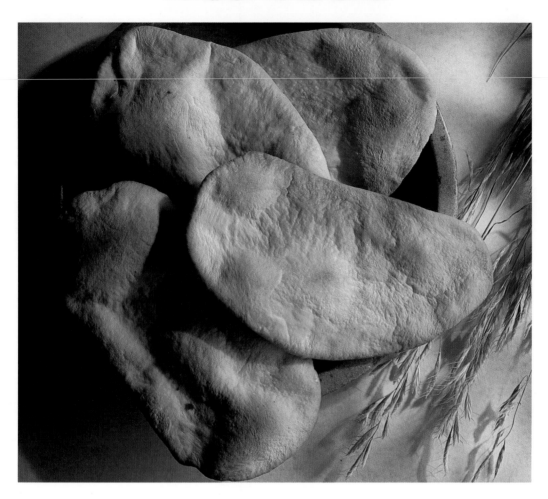

This Indian bread is served with tandoori dishes. As with pitta, naan is a yeast-risen flat bread which puffs up on cooking under a very hot grill, because this creates an air pocket inside the bread.

MAKES 6

15 g/½ oz fresh yeast or 1 sachet dried yeast and ½ tsp sugar	1½ tsp sugar
	1 tsp baking powder
250 ml/8 fl oz warm milk	2 Tbsp vegetable oil
500 g/1 lb plain flour	4 Tbsp plain yogurt
½ tsp salt	

Stir the yeast into the warm milk, adding sugar if using dried yeast. Leave the dried yeast mixture about 10 minutes in a warm place to become frothy.

Mix the remaining dry ingredients in a large bowl. Stir in the oil, yogurt and yeast liquid. Work into a dough. Turn out on to a lightly floured board and knead for about 10 minutes until the dough is smooth, elastic, and no longer sticky. Return the dough to the warm bowl, cover with oiled plastic and leave to prove for about 1 hour in a warm place, until doubled in size. Punch down the dough and, when thoroughly kneaded, divide the dough into 6 pieces. Roll into oval shapes 25 x 10 cm/10 x 4 in and place them on the baking sheets.

Pre-heat the grill a few minutes before baking the naan. Grease two baking sheets.

Cook each naan bread under the hot grill, 2 to 3 minutes on each side, until brown and well puffed.

Quick Breads

No-yeast Cakes for Coffee, Muffins and Biscuits

This section contains a range of breads that requires no proving, from cornbreads and soda breads to ethnic specialities such as Mexican tortillas and Indian chapatis. There are delicious cakes for coffee featuring such delights as blueberries, apples, and polenta. Finally a wonderful range of muffins and biscuits featuring chocolate, oranges, cranberries and even Parmesan, Roquefort and goat's cheese.

INTRODUCTION

Equipment

Most of the recipes in this book can be produced with the basic baking utensils found in the average kitchen. If you like muffins, it is worth investing in non-stick bakeware as only minimal greasing is required. It is best to use a vegetable cooking spray, as it is quick and easy. Alternatively, use a pastry brush to butter or grease the bakeware. Paper and foil liners also eliminate mess, and using various colours and designs will make pretty "packaging".

Most teabreads are baked in 22 x 13 x 15-cm/9 x 5 x 3-in or 20 x 10 x 6-cm/8 x 4 x 2½-in loaf tins; non-stick tins are a good choice. Build up a supply of loaf tins in different sizes, and always have plenty of baking sheets and bun tins.

Paper liners eliminate fussy clean-up

Methods

Quick breads are quick and easy to prepare.

Pre-heat the Oven

Always pre-heat the oven as indicated. Most baked goods and breads require a quick blast of heat at the start of the rising action; the temperature can be reduced for recipes that require longer baking times. For even results, bake on the middle shelf. Prepare any bakeware as directed before you start so the batter or dough can be baked immediately, then assemble all the ingredients and prepare any that need it beforehand.

Measuring

As with all baking, accurate measuring is essential. The "scoop-and-sweep" method for dry ingredients such as flour, sugar, cocoa powder and icing sugar is recommended. Lightly spoon the dry ingredients into the weighing scales or a metal or plastic measuring spoon, then, with the back of a knife blade or other straight edge, sweep off the excess. For baking powder, bicarbonate of soda, salt and spices, it is important to use proper tablespoon and teaspoon measures, not a spoon from your kitchen drawer; fill and sweep off the excess as for dry ingredients. Use a clean measuring jug for liquids, and check the amount at eye level for accuracy.

Mixing

Combining the ingredients for all baked goods is very important, as it determines the texture of the end result. Muffins and quick breads should be mixed lightly only until the flour is just incorporated. Although the consistency of different batters might vary, the texture should be slightly lumpy. If over-mixed until completely smooth, the texture will be slightly dry and tough. Scones should never be over-mixed or over-kneaded, as they will be dense and tough-textured. Mix the dough until it just holds together, and then knead lightly until the dough is well combined, but not smooth and elastic.

Filling the Tins

Batter should be spooned lightly into bun tins and loaf tins; let the mixture drop gently from the spoon, or scoop it into the tin, and remember not to pat down or smooth the tops of muffins. Try to spoon quick bread mixtures evenly into the tins so the tops do not require much handling. Most baking should be done in single layers on the middle shelf, as this allows the air to circulate evenly. Baking times are a guide; it is a good idea to begin checking to see if it is done after the minimum time.

Is it Ready?

There are many ways to judge if baked goods are cooked; they will usually smell good, and will have just begun to shrink from the side of the tin. For

It's worth investing in non-stick bakeware

temperature. For really quick, "freezer-to-table" muffins, line a bun tin with paper or foil liners. Fill with the batter and freeze immediately. When frozen, remove the filled cups to a plastic freezer bag or container, label them, and mark the baking time and temperature. When ready to bake, just drop the frozen muffins into the tin and bake, adding about five minutes to the baking time.

Hot Tips for Quick Breads, Cakes for Coffee and Muffins

Remember the following tips to help you make successful muffins, scones, biscuits and quick breads every time:

- **DO NOT OVER-MIX** – This tip cannot be over-emphasized. If you stir until the batter is smooth, you will get a tough, dry result with tunnels or holes. Stir wet and dry ingredients together just until combined; the batter is meant to be slightly lumpy.
- Unless specified, have all your ingredients ready and at room temperature before you start, especially butter and eggs.
- Shiny baking tins reflect heat, while dark, dull pans absorb it. Bake all cakes and breads in a single layer on the middle shelf.
- For an evenly rounded muffin top, only grease the bottom and 1 cm/½ in up side of cup.
- Bake muffins and quick breads as soon as they are mixed, since both baking powder and bicarbonate begin to rise as soon as they are moistened.
- To avoid soggy sides and bottoms, remove the muffins from the tin almost immediately after removing them from the oven. Cool quick breads for slightly longer.
- Begin checking after the minimum baking time indicated.
- Day-old muffins, scones and biscuits can be split and toasted, then served with butter or jam for a delicious breakfast treat.
- For "instant muffins", mix the dry ingredients and liquid ingredients separately (liquid ingredients should not be mixed more than 2 to 3 hours ahead) and grease the tin. When ready, pre-heat the oven, mix and bake.
- Never over-knead biscuit or scone dough. Lightly folding and pressing between 8 to 12 times is enough to distribute the ingredients.
- For soft-sided biscuits, bake close together. Arrange the shapes at least 5 cm/2 in apart for a crisper, crustier finish.

plain mixtures, a cake tester or cocktail stick inserted into the centre of the muffin, loaf or cake should come out clean. Other mixtures may have ingredients that will contain moisture or solid ingredients such as dried or chopped fresh fruit or vegetables, which make testing more difficult. These are best tested by pressing with a fingertip. If the surface springs back lightly, it should be done; however, it is preferable to under-bake slightly than over-bake, and baked goods will generally continue to cook for a few minutes after being removed from the oven. Rolls and cakes for coffee are usually fully done when risen and golden.

Most muffins and quick breads can be unmoulded or removed from the tin very quickly after baking. Muffins and quick breads will become damp and soggy if left in the tin too long. Muffins can be removed immediately, although leaving them to cool for about two minutes will ensure that they are set. Quick breads should be left for a few minutes before unmoulding. Some cakes for coffee can be treated like quick breads, but because many have toppings, they are best cooled in their tins, or as directed, before being carefully turned out.

Muffins, scones and biscuits are best eaten immediately or on the same day. Most quick breads benefit from complete cooling and storing overnight, which helps to develop their flavour, and makes for easier slicing. Before storing, cool all baked goods, then wrap in clingfilm or foil. To freeze, place in freezer bags, label and store in freezer. To thaw, transfer to the refrigerator for several hours before serving, or thaw for 2 to 3 hours at room

Quick Breads

Cranberry-apricot-banana Bread
with cranberry-apricot compote

The flavours of this moist, delicious teabread are accentuated by the Cranberry-apricot Compote.

MAKES 1 MEDIUM LOAF

175 g/6 oz plain flour	2 eggs
1½ tsp baking powder	120 ml/4 fl oz sunflower or vegetable oil
½ tsp freshly grated or ground nutmeg	1 tsp vanilla essence
60 g/2 oz rolled oats	2 ripe bananas, mashed
250 g/8 oz light brown sugar	**ICING (OPTIONAL)**
60 g/2 oz dried cranberries	30 g/1 oz sugar
60 g/2 oz dried apricots, chopped	2 to 3 Tbsp lemon juice or water

Pre-heat the oven to 350°F/175°C/Gas 7. Lightly grease and flour a 20 x 16-cm/8 x 4-in loaf tin. Sift the flour, baking powder and nutmeg into a bowl. Stir in the oats, brown sugar, cranberries and apricots until well-blended, and make a well in the centre.

Using an electric mixer in a medium bowl, beat the eggs, oil, vanilla essence and mashed bananas until well-blended. Pour into the well and stir until well combined. Scrape the batter into the prepared tin and smooth the top evenly.

Bake until well risen and golden brown, and a cake tester inserted in the centre comes out with just a crumb or two attached, about 1 hour. Transfer to a wire rack to cool, about 10 minutes, then unmould top-side up on to the rack to cool completely.

If icing, in a small bowl, stir the icing sugar and 2–3 tbsp lemon juice until it reaches a pouring consistency. Add a little more lemon juice or water if necessary. Drizzle over the top of the teabread and leave to set. Alternatively, dust with icing sugar. Serve sliced with the Cranberry-apricot Compote.

Cranberry-apricot Compote

MAKES ABOUT 250 G/8 OZ

60 g/2 oz fresh or frozen cranberries	1 cinnamon stick
60 g/2 oz dried cranberries	Grated rind and juice of 1 orange
10 to 12 oz dried, "no-soak" apricots, chopped	2 Tbsp ruby port
120 g/4 oz sugar	1 tsp vanilla essence

Put the dried fruits, sugar, cinnamon stick, grated orange rind and juice in a medium heavy-based, non-corrosive saucepan. Add enough water to cover the fruit. Place over medium heat, and bring to the boil. Simmer over low heat until the cranberries pop, the fruit is tender and almost all the liquid is absorbed. Remove from the heat, discard the cinnamon stick and stir in the port and vanilla essence. Pour into a bowl and serve warm, or refrigerate, covered, until ready to serve.

Chocolate-chip and Peanut Butter Bread

This is a moist, dense bread with a good, peanut flavour.

MAKES I LARGE LOAF

250 g/8 oz plain flour	I tsp vanilla essence
2 tsp baking powder	**FOR THE CHOCOLATE-CRUMB TOPPING**
¼ tsp salt	
90 g/3 oz chocolate chips	120 g/4 oz sugar
60 g/2 oz smooth or chunky peanut butter, at room temperature	60 g/2 oz cocoa powder
	3 Tbsp unsalted butter, cut into pieces
I Tbsp sugar	2 Tbsp finely chopped, dry-roasted peanuts
I egg, lightly beaten	
250 ml/8 fl oz milk	

Pre-heat the oven to 350°F/175°C/Gas 4. Lightly grease or spray a 22 x 13-cm/9 x 5-in loaf tin. Sift the flour, baking powder and salt into a large bowl. Stir in the chocolate chips and make a well in the centre.

Put the peanut butter in another bowl, and beat with an electric mixer to break up and soften. Gradually beat in the sugar, the egg, milk and vanilla essence. Pour into the well and lightly stir with a fork until combined.

Combine the crumb-topping ingredients in a small bowl. Spoon half the batter into the prepared tin and smooth, sprinkling with half of the crumb mixture. Spoon the remaining batter into the tin and gently smooth the top. Sprinkle with the remaining crumb mixture. Using a round-bladed knife or spoon handle, gently draw through the batter in a zigzag to marbleize the mixture slightly.

Bake until risen and golden, and a cake tester inserted in the centre comes out moist, but with no uncooked crumbs attached, 50 to 55 minutes. Transfer to a wire rack to cool, about 25 minutes, then carefully unmould on to a wire rack, top-side up. Cool completely, then wrap and store for I day before serving.

Bran Teabread

A teabread is a moist loaf that is usually served sliced and buttered, although seldom with jam or honey. For extra moistness, soak the fruit, although this is not essential. The mixture is very wet when it goes into the oven and is usually frothing. Don't worry – this is how it should be.

MAKES I LOAF

120 g/4 oz mixed dried fruit	I tsp baking powder
250 ml/8 If oz cold tea	I tsp bicarbonate of soda
120 g/4 oz light brown sugar	I tsp mixed spice
60 g/2 oz margarine	Pinch of salt
60 g/2 oz orange marmalade	60 g/2 oz bran cereal
120 g/4 oz wholemeal flour	I egg, beaten

Pre-heat the oven to 350°F/175°C/Gas 4 and lightly grease a large loaf tin. Place the fruit, tea, sugar, margarine and marmalade in a pan and heat gently until the sugar has dissolved and the margarine melted, then leave to cool.

Mix the dry ingredients together in a large bowl and make a well in the centre. Beat the egg and add it to the fruit mixture, then pour into the dry ingredients and mix thoroughly and quickly. Pour immediately into the prepared loaf tin. Bake in the pre-heated oven for 50 to 60 minutes, until a cocktail stick inserted into the loaf comes out clean.

Cool the teabread on a wire rack. Serve sliced and lightly buttered.

Banana-pecan-chocolate Chip Loaf

This delicious quick bread is great while the chocolate is still soft and melty, but keeps really well wrapped in clingfilm or foil.

MAKES I LARGE LOAF

90 g/3 oz flour	2 eggs, lightly beaten
I tsp bicarbonate of soda	5 Tbsp just boiling water
½ tsp salt	120 g/4 oz chopped pecans
I tsp ground cinnamon	90 g/3 oz semi-sweet
½ tsp ground ginger	chocolate chips
90 g/3 oz wholemeal flour	
120 g/4 oz butter, softened	**FOR THE ICING**
200 g/7 oz sugar	60 g/2 oz icing sugar
2 large ripe bananas, mashed	2 to 3 Tbsp lemon juice

Pre-heat the oven to 325°F/160°C/Gas 3. Grease and flour a 22 x 13-cm/9 x 5-in loaf tin. Sift the flour, bicarbonate, salt, cinnamon and ginger into a medium bowl and stir in the wholemeal flour; set aside.

In a large bowl with an electric mixer, beat the butter until light and creamy, 1 to 2 minutes. Gradually beat in the sugar until light and fluffy. On low speed, beat in the mashed bananas and then the eggs; do not worry if the mixture looks curdled. Stir in the flour alternately in batches with the hot water until just combined. Stir in the pecans and chocolate chips.

Scrape the mixture into the prepared tin, smoothing the top evenly. Bake until well risen and dark-golden brown, about 1 hour 10 minutes. Because this is a very moist loaf, a cake tester or skewer will not come out clean. Transfer the tin to a wire rack to cool for about ½ hour, then unmould on to the rack top-side up. To ice, stir the icing sugar and lemon juice together until smooth. Drizzle over the loaf and allow to set completely.

Cornbread

This basic cornbread is a staple in the American South and it is very simple to prepare.

MAKES 16 2 INCH SQUARES

120 g/4 oz wholemeal flour

175 g/6 oz cornmeal

½ tsp salt

1 tsp bicarbonate of soda

¾ tsp cream of tartar

375 ml/12 fl oz buttermilk or half yogurt, half skimmed milk

3 Tbsp sunflower oil

2 eggs, beaten

1 Tbsp brown sugar or honey

Pre-heat the oven to 425°F/220°C/Gas 7. Grease a 20-cm/ 8-in square cake tin.

Mix together the flour, cornmeal, salt, bicarbonate and cream of tartar. Stir the buttermilk with the oil, eggs and sugar or honey. Pour the liquid ingredients into the dry mixture and stir together.

Put the mixture into the tin and bake for about 35 minutes. Cut into 5-cm/2-in squares and serve warm.

Light Cornbread

This lighter version is also delicious, and ideal for calorie-counting.

MAKES 9 SQUARES

120 g/4 oz rice flour

60 g/2 oz sugar

4 tsp baking powder

½ tsp salt

175 g/6 oz cornmeal

2 medium eggs, lightly beaten

60 g/2 oz margarine, softened

250 ml/8 fl oz skimmed milk

Pre-heat the oven to 425°F/220°C/Gas 7. Grease a 22-cm/9-in square cake tin.

Sift together the rice flour, sugar, baking powder and salt. Stir in the cornmeal. Mix together the eggs and softened margarine. Stir in the milk and add the liquid mixture to the dry ingredients. Beat them together thoroughly.

Pour the mixture into the prepared tin and bake for 20 minutes. Cool on a wire rack and cool in the tin for 5 minutes.

Cut the cornbread into 7-cm/3-in squares – it can be served either warm or cold.

Fiesta Buttermilk Cornbread

This delicious cornbread is flecked with colourful spring onions, red pepper, sweetcorn and even chillies. A delicious accompaniment to Chilli con Carne and other Tex-Mex-style dishes.

SERVES 8

90 g/3 oz unsalted butter	250 ml/8 fl oz buttermilk
175 g/6 oz cornmeal	2 to 3 spring onions, finely chopped
120 g/4 oz plain flour	1 small red pepper, deseeded and chopped
1½ tsp baking powder	
½ tsp bicarbonate of soda	250 ml/8 fl oz fresh, frozen (thawed) or tinned sweetcorn, drained
2 Tbsp sugar	
½ tsp dried sage or oregano	1 small green chilli, deseeded and chopped
2 eggs	

Pre-heat the oven to 400°F/200°C/Gas 6. Put the butter in a 22-cm/9-in black iron frying pan or heavy 22-cm/9-in cake tin and place the tin on the middle shelf of the oven until butter is melted. Keep the tin warm.

In a large bowl, stir together the cornmeal, flour, baking powder, becarbonate, sugar and sage or oregano, and make a well in the centre.

Using a fork, beat the eggs with the buttermilk in a small bowl until well-blended. Pour into the well, add all but 2 tbsp of the melted butter from the tin, and stir lightly until just combined. Fold in the spring onions, sweetcorn and chilli, until just blended.

Pour the mixture into the hot tin and spread evenly. Bake until risen and golden, and a cake tester inserted into the centre comes out with just a few crumbs attached, about 30 minutes. (Do not over-bake or the cornbread will be dry.) Transfer to a wire rack and cool in the tin, 10 minutes. Serve hot or warm from the tin with lots of butter, on its own, or as an accompaniment to Chilli con Carne and similar dishes.

Almond Bread

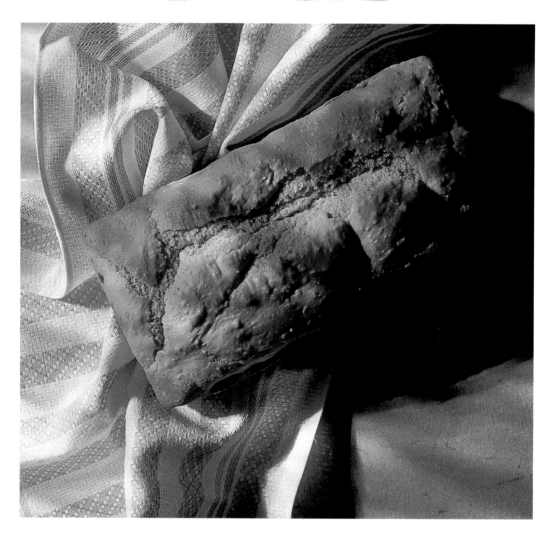

This delicious quick bread combines the tang of citrus with the crunchy texture of almonds.

MAKES 42–48 SLICES

375 g/12 oz plain flour

2 tsp baking powder

¼ tsp salt

2 large eggs

120 ml/8 fl oz sunflower oil

5–6 Tbsp honey or brown sugar

2 tsp grated orange or tangerine rind

2 tsp almond essence

90 g/3 oz chopped almonds

Pre-heat the oven to 350°F/175°C/Gas 4. Sift together the flour, baking powder and salt. Beat together in an electric blender or a bowl the eggs, oil, honey, orange or tangerine rind, and almond essence. Transfer mixture into a large bowl. Beat in the flour mixture a little at a time.

Stir the almonds into the stiff dough then divide it into six oblong rolls about 5 cm/2 in wide. Place the rolls well apart on a foil-covered baking sheet and bake for 20 minutes. Lift out the baking sheet and cut each roll into seven or eight slices 1 cm/½ in thick. Return the slices to the oven on the baking sheet and bake for a further 15 to 20 minutes until brown. Cool on a wire rack, then store in an airtight container.

Yogurt Bread

This bread, which is quick and easy to prepare, goes well with sweet or savoury accompaniments.

MAKES 1 LARGE LOAF

400 g/14 oz of two or more mixed flours (wheat, rye, barley, millet)

3 Tbsp wheatgerm

2 tsp bicarbonate of soda

1 tsp baking powder

250 ml/8 fl oz plain yogurt

250 ml/8 fl oz skimmed milk or water

1 tsp salt

120 ml/8 fl oz honey

Pre-heat the oven to 300°F/150°C/Gas 2. Grease a large loaf tin. Mix all the ingredients in a large cool bowl. Scrape the mixture into the prepared tin. Bake slowly for about 1 hour 40 minutes.

Cool the loaf on a wire rack.

Pumpkin-oatmeal-nut Loaf
with orange-lemon butter

This teabread has a sweet, fresh flavour and lots of texture. Serve with Orange-lemon Butter, or on its own.

MAKES 2 LARGE LOAVES

375 g/12 oz flour

2 tsp bicarbonate of soda

1 tsp ground cinnamon

½ tsp ground ginger

½ tsp freshly grated or ground nutmeg

¼ tsp ground cloves

½ tsp salt

60 g/2 oz porridge oats

120 g/4 oz chopped walnuts or pecans, lightly toasted

500 g/1 lb fresh or tinned pumpkin

3 eggs, lightly beaten

300 g/10 oz caster sugar

300 g/10 oz light brown sugar

120 ml/4 fl oz sunflower or vegetable oil

120 ml/4 fl oz milk

120 ml/4 fl oz evaporated milk

Orange-lemon Butter

MAKES ABOUT 1 CUP

250 g/8 oz unsalted butter, softened

Grated rind of 1 orange

1–2 Tbsp orange juice

Grated rind of 1 lemon

1 Tbsp lemon juice

½ tsp vanilla essence

90 g/3 oz caster sugar (or to taste)

Beat all the ingredients together in a medium bowl, using an electric mixer, until light and fluffy. Scrape on to a piece of clingfilm or greaseproof paper, and shape into a log. Wrap tightly and refrigerate until firm, about 1 to 2 hours. Slice into rounds and serve.

Pre-heat the oven to 350°F/175°C/Gas 4. Grease and flour two 22 x 13-cm/9 x 5-in loaf tins. Sift the flour, bicarbonate, cinnamon, ginger, nutmeg, cloves and salt into a large bowl. Stir in the oats and chopped nuts into the mixture.

Put the pumpkin flesh in a large bowl and beat on low speed to break up with an electric mixer. Gradually beat in the eggs until smooth. Beat in the sugars, oil and milks until smooth. On low speed, beat the flour mixture into the pumpkin-egg mixture until just blended.

Divide the mixture equally between the two tins, smoothing the tops evenly. Bake until risen, dark golden and a cake tester inserted in the centre comes out clean. Transfer the tins to a wire rack to cool, about 15 minutes, then unmould, top-side up, on to the wire rack to cool completely. Wrap well, and leave to stand overnight for the flavours to develop. Serve with Orange-lemon Butter.

Brown Soda Bread

With soda bread, there is no waiting for it to prove, nor does it involve endless kneading. The less soda bread is handled the better it will be.

MAKES 2 LARGE LOAVES

750 g/1½ lb wholemeal flour	Good pinch of salt
375 g/12 oz plain or strong white flour	2 eggs
1 heaped tsp bicarbonate of soda	Approx 600 ml/1 pt plain yoghurt mixed with water to the consistency of buttermilk

Pre-heat the oven to 375°F/190°C/Gas 5. Place all the dry ingredients in a large mixing bowl. Combine well using your fingers.

In another bowl mix the eggs with the yogurt and water.

Make a well in the dry mixture and slowly pour on the yogurt and water. Mix with your hands until you get a nice soft dough – not too wet. A dough that is too wet or too stiff will result in a hard and heavy bread.

Lightly flour a work surface or a pastry board. Divide the dough in half. Make 2 flat rounds of bread on the board.

Cut a deep cross in the middle of each loaf. Place in the pre-heated oven for 10 minutes, then reduce the heat to 350°F/175°C/Gas 4. Bake until the base of the bread sounds hollow when tapped. This takes about 30 minutes.

Irish Soda Bread

Irish soda bread is one of the best breads in the world. It is traditionally baked with a cross scored on the top, which people believed would scare away the devil.

MAKES I LARGE LOAF

500 g/I lb plain flour	I½ tsp cream of tartar
I tsp salt	2 Tbsp white vegetable fat
2 tsp bicarbonate of soda	300 ml/10 fl oz buttermilk

Pre-heat the oven to 425°F/220°C/Gas 7. Sift the flour, salt, bicarbonate and cream of tartar into a bowl. Rub in the white vegetable fat and add enough buttermilk to make a soft dough. Turn the mixture on to a lightly floured board and knead for a minute. Shape into a round and place on the baking sheet. Mark with the traditional cross, cutting deep into the dough.

Bake for 40 to 50 minutes, until lightly browned and firm when tapped on the base. Cool on a wire rack.

VARIATION

You can use plain milk instead of buttermilk, but if you do, double the quantity of cream of tartar.

Oatcakes

Oatcakes make a satisfying, nutritious snack, and are delicious with cheese.

MAKES 12

60 g/2 oz oatmeal	Hot water
Pinch of salt	Rolled oats
Pinch of bicarbonate of soda	30 g/I oz plain flour
I Tbsp melted bacon fat	

Mix the dry ingredients in a bowl, make a well in the centre and pour in the melted fat. Add enough hot water to make a stiff paste.

Scatter your work surface or board liberally with rolled oats and transfer the paste to the board, pressing with the hands. (Cover your hands with flour as the oatmeal is very sticky at this stage.)

Roll to about ½-cm/¼-in thickness and cut into 20-cm/8-in circles. Sprinkle with more rolled oats, then cut into quarters.

Place on a hot griddle – a heavy frying pan will do – and cook until the edges curl a little. Turn them over and cook on the other side, or finish them under a warm grill.

The oatcakes may also be baked at 350°F/175°C/Gas 4 for about 20 minutes.

Wholemeal Soya Bread with Orange and Prunes

This soya bread is brimming over with good things – oranges and prunes give it a dense, chewy texture.

MAKES 1 LARGE LOAF

175 g/6 oz wholemeal flour	1 Tbsp grated orange rind
60 g/2 oz soya flour, sifted	90 g/3 oz cooked, chopped, pitted prunes
2 tsp baking powder	
¼ tsp salt	60 g/2 oz chopped hazelnuts
120 g/4 oz brown sugar	1 large egg, beaten
½ tsp ground star anise	175 ml/6 fl oz milk
2 Tbsp margarine	

Pre-heat the oven to 350°F/175°C/Gas 4. Grease a 22 x 13 x 7-cm/9 x 5 x 3-in loaf tin.

Mix together the flours, baking powder, salt, sugar and ground star anis. Rub the margarine into the dry mix. Add the orange rind, prunes and nuts. Beat the egg and milk together and add to the flour mixture. Turn into the prepared pan.

Bake for about 1 hour until a skewer comes out clean. Place the tin on a wire rack and turn out the loaf after 10 minutes. Allow to cool before slicing.

Eliopita

This Cypriot bread is scented with rosemary and studded with olives.

MAKES 1 LOAF

375 g/12 oz plain flour

60 g/2 oz wholemeal flour

1 tsp bicarbonate of soda

1 Tbsp dried mint

1 Tbsp fresh rosemary, chopped

120 ml/4 fl oz extra-virgin olive oil

250 ml/8 fl oz warm water

1 onion, chopped

Approximately 20 olives, pitted and cut into quarters or small pieces

Combine the two flours with the bicarbonate and the mint, and set aside.

Combine the rosemary, olive oil and warm water, and stir into the flour mixture, then stir in the onion and olives. Work only until the mixture has the consistency of a thick batter.

Pour the batter into a lightly oiled, 22 x 32-cm/ 9 x 13-in or 30 x 37-cm/12 x 15-in baking tin, and bake at 350°F/175°C/Gas 4 for 30 to 40 minutes, or until evenly browned and firm. Though it is traditionally served hot, it is also excellent cool after it has set a while. When hot, it has a tendency to be a bit soft inside.

Wholemeal Coffee Teabread

Coffee adds an interesting flavour to this delicious teabread.

MAKES 1 LOAF

175 g/6 oz flour

120 g/4 oz wholemeal flour

3 Tbsp dark brown sugar

3 Tbsp sultanas

60 g/2 oz chopped candied peel

2 Tbsp coffee essence

120 g/4 oz butter

120 g/4 oz golden syrup

120 g/4 oz treacle

1 tsp bicarbonate of soda

300 ml/10 fl oz strong milky coffee

1 egg, beaten

2 Tbsp chopped hazelnuts

Pre-heat the oven to 350°F/175°C/Gas 4. Grease and line a 15 x 22-cm/6 x 9-in oblong tin.

Mix together the plain flour, wholemeal flour, dark brown sugar, sultanas and candied peel. In a large tin, melt together the coffee essence, butter, golden syrup and treacle. Add to the flour and beat well.

Dissolve the bicarbonate in the milky coffee and beat in the egg.

Pour into the prepared mixture and beat to form a smooth batter. Pour the mixture into the tin. Scatter the hazelnuts over the top.

Bake in the centre of the oven for 40 to 45 minutes until well risen and springy to the touch.

Leave to cool for 15 minutes and turn out to cool further on a wire rack. When cold, wrap in foil without removing the lining paper.

Wholemeal Scotch Pancakes

Sometimes called drop scones, these are quick to make and delicious served with butter and jam or honey. Serve them cold or keep them warm in a clean teatowel while cooking the remaining mixture. Wholemeal drop scones are more substantial than those made with white flour.

MAKES ABOUT 12

90 g/3 oz wholemeal flour

1 tsp baking powder

Pinch of salt

1 large egg, beaten

150 ml/5 fl oz milk, or milk and water mixed

Mix the flour, baking powder and salt together in a bowl and make a well in the centre. Beat the egg with the milk, add it to the flour and beat to a smooth, thick batter.

Heat a heavy non-stick frying pan until evenly hot then drop dessertspoonfuls of the mixture on to the surface, allowing room for them to spread slightly. Turn the scones after a minute or so, when bubbles begin to rise to the surface. Cook for a further 1 to 2 minutes then serve.

Quick Onion and Nut Loaf

Quick breads are often very like scone doughs but this one, being more highly seasoned than most, makes a very good loaf to serve with soups. It may also be baked in a flat, round tin, in which case reduce the cooking time to about 30 minutes.

MAKES 1 LOAF

250 g/8 oz wholemeal flour

2 tsp baking powder

½ tsp salt

1 Tbsp margarine

2 Tbsp roughly chopped parsley

1 small onion, coarsely grated

60 g/2 oz pecan nuts, chopped roughly

1 large egg, beaten

1 tsp Dijon or yellow mustard

250 ml/8 fl oz milk

Pre-heat the oven to 375°F/190°C/Gas 5 and lightly grease a small loaf tin.

Mix all the dry ingredients together in a bowl, then blend in the margarine. Stir in the parsley, onion and pecans. Beat the egg with the mustard then add to the milk. Pour the liquid into the flour and mix to a stiff, wet batter. Pile the mixture into the prepared loaf tin – it will almost fill it – and smooth the top.

Bake for 45 to 50 minutes, until set and lightly browned. Cool for a few minutes in the tin then turn out on to a wire rack to cool.

Low-fat Raisin and Honey Bread

T his loaf contains a high proportion of yogurt which gives it a white, light centre.

MAKES 1 LOAF

300 g/10 oz plain flour	**2 egg whites**
1½ tsp baking powder	**60 g/2 oz raisins**
½ tsp bicarbonate of soda	**2 Tbsp honey**
½ tsp salt	**Butter for greasing**
300 ml/10 fl oz plain yogurt	

Pre-heat the oven to 425°F/220°C/Gas 7. Mix the flour, baking powder, bicarbonate and salt in a large bowl. Whisk together the yogurt and egg whites and fold into the flour mixture with the raisins and honey.

Grease a large loaf tin and spoon in the mixture. Bake for 20 minutes until golden. Cool slightly and turn out of the tin. Serve warm.

Corn Tortillas
Tortillas de Maiz

Mexican tortillas are the cornerstone of Mexican and Tex-mex cooking. They are eaten as a staple or integrated into many of their cooked dishes.

MAKES ABOUT 30

500 g/1 lb maize flour

175 g/6 oz plain flour

600 ml/1 pt hot water

Mix the maize and plain flours together. Slowly add the hot water. Knead as you would for bread for 10 to 15 minutes, or knead in the food processor for 2 minutes. If you place a small ball of the dough into a glass of cold water and it does not dissolve, the dough is the right consistency. Flours vary, so if the mixture is too wet, add a little more flour, if too dry, add more water.

Take one heaped tablespoon of the dough and roll it into a small ball. Place the ball inside a new plastic food bag which has been split down one side and, using a tortilla press, press down hard. If you do not have a tortilla press, roll out using a rolling pin, although you will not get such a thin tortilla.

Cook on a hot griddle or in a non-stick frying pan for a few seconds until they are speckled golden brown and puff up. Store in a clean damp cloth in the refrigerator and warm when needed by returning to the hot griddle or frying pan for 30 seconds on each side.

Flour Tortillas
Tortillas de Harina

Flour Tortillas are lighter than their corn cousins, and are good with dips.

MAKES ABOUT 10–15

500 g/1 lb plain flour

1 Tbsp salt

90 g/3 oz lard or white vegetable fat

300 ml/10 fl oz warm water

Sieve the flour with the salt and blend in the fat until it resembles crumbs, as you would for pastry. Slowly add the warm water until you have a manageable dough.

On a well-floured surface, knead the dough until it is no longer sticky. Keep the dough covered with a damp cloth or with clingfilm.

Take a golfball-sized piece of dough and knead individually for about a minute. Roll into a ball and roll out with a well-floured rolling pin until the dough is almost transparent. Cut around a 22-cm/9-in plate.

Heat a griddle or non-stick frying pan so that a drop of water sizzles. Then cook the tortilla for 30 seconds on each side.

To store the tortillas, put a sheet of greaseproof paper between each one, wrap in a dry cloth or clingfilm and refrigerate.

Reheat the tortilla on a hot griddle or non-stick frying pan for about 30 seconds on each side, or, fry in a little sunflower oil and leave to cool.

Flour Tortillas ▶

Norwegian Crackers

Two Scandinavian crisp bread recipes. Both are great with dips and soft cheeses.

MAKES 20 CRACKERS

250 g/8 oz oatmeal flour	250 g/8 oz plain flour
250 g/8 oz barley flour	½ tsp salt
250 g/8 oz rye flour	¾ pint water

Lightly grease a griddle or hot plate. Mix the flours and salt well together. Add the water and work into a pliable dough. Roll the dough out thinly, cut into oblong pieces and cook on a well-heated griddle until crisp. Cool on a wire rack and store in a tin or wrapped in foil in a cool place.

Crispbread

Healthy and light, you can vary this crispbread by sprinkling the rolled-out dough with sesame seeds or cumin.

MAKES 20

375 g/12 oz plain flour	30 g/1 oz unsalted butter
120 g/4 oz wholemeal flour	Approx. 250 ml/8 fl oz boiling water
2 tsp salt	

Grease two baking sheets. Put the flours and salt into a mixing bowl. Add the butter in pats, pour the boiling water into the mixture and stir vigorously to make a firm dough, adding more water if required. Allow the dough to get cold, put it into the refrigerator and chill for 20 minutes. Knead thoroughly. Divide into 20 pieces and roll each one out thinly. Place on the baking sheets and bake for about 15 minutes. The bread should be dry but not browned. It will keep indefinitely in a dry place.

Chapatis

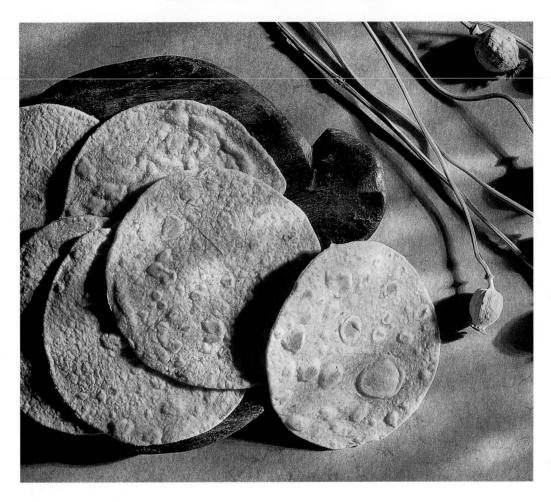

An unleavened wholemeal bread, the traditional accompaniment to curries and various vegetable dishes.

MAKES 15

375 g/12 oz flour	2 Tbsp vegetable oil
1 tsp salt	250 ml/8 fl oz water

Heat a lightly-greased griddle or large non-stick frying pan. Mix the flour and salt in a bowl. Add the oil and sufficient water to make a soft dough. Knead the dough on a lightly floured board until smooth and pliable, 5 to 10 minutes. Put the dough into a lightly oiled plastic bag and leave to rest for an hour. Divide the dough into about 15 pieces. Roll out each piece into paper-thin circles about 18 cm/7 in in diameter. Put each chapati in the plastic bag as soon as it is ready, to prevent drying out.

Use a pastry brush to remove surplus flour from the chapatis. Cook the chapatis on the griddle for about ½ minute on the first side, and 1½ to 2 minutes on the reverse side, until lightly browned. Turn the chapati back to the first side and cook for a further minute. The chapati should puff up.

Pile the chapatis in a stack, wrapped in a clean, dry teatowel. Serve hot, each one folded in four.

No-yeast
Cakes for Coffee

Lemon Crumble Coffeecake

Apple Cake

Prune Coffeecake

Blueberry Streusel Coffeecake

Polenta Cake

Rhubarb Streusel Cake

Lemon Crumble Coffeecake

T his moist cake has a rich, lemon flavour, with a crumbly topping.

SERVES 10-12

CRUMBLE TOPPING

120 g/4 oz sugar

30 g/1 oz flour

Grated rind of 1 lemon

3 Tbsp butter, cut into small pieces

CAKE

250 g/8 oz plain flour

1½ tsp baking powder

½ tsp bicarbonate of soda

¼ tsp salt

60 g/2 oz finely chopped candied lemon peel

120 g/4 oz unsalted butter

30 g/1 oz sugar

250 ml/8 fl oz plain yogurt or buttermilk

2 eggs, lightly beaten

Grated rind of 1 lemon

1 tsp vanilla essence

Pre-heat the oven to 350°F/175°C/Gas 4. Grease and lightly flour a 22 x 13-cm/9 x 5-in loaf tin. Combine the crumble topping ingredients in a small bowl and rub in the butter using your fingertips, until the mixture resembles coarse crumbs; set aside.

Sift the flour, baking powder, bicarbonate and salt into a large bowl. Stir in the candied lemon peel and make a well in the centre.

Put the butter in a saucepan and set over low heat until melted, stirring occasionally. Remove from the heat and whisk in the sugar, yogurt, eggs, grated lemon rind and vanilla essence. Pour into the well and stir with a fork until just blended.

Spoon half the mixture into the prepared tin, smoothing the top and pushing into the corners. Sprinkle over half the crumb topping. Drop spoonfuls of the remaining mixture over the topping, and spread as evenly as possible, then sprinkle with the remaining topping.

Bake until the cake is risen and golden, and a cake tester inserted in the centre comes out clean, about 1 hour. Transfer to a wire rack to cool for at least 30 minutes. Run a thin-bladed knife between the cake and the sides of the tin to loosen it, then carefully unmould on to the rack, top-side up, to cool. This cake is best made a day ahead and wrapped tightly until ready to serve.

Apple Cake

$\mathbf{A}$pple cake made with oil is more moist than if made with butter. These layers of tangy apples baked in a sweet, lemon-scented batter will make this a favourite recipe.

MAKES 16–20 SLICES

APPLE FILLING

1 kg/2 lb tart cooking apples, peeled, cored and thinly sliced

4 Tbsp sugar

1 tsp ground cinnamon

Grated rind and juice of 1 lemon

CAKE

4 eggs

250 g/8 oz caster sugar

250 ml/8 fl oz vegetable oil

250 g/8 oz self-raising flour, or 250 g/8 oz plain flour plus 2 tsp baking powder

1 tsp vanilla essence

2 Tbsp sugar to sprinkle

a Pre-heat the oven to 350°F/175°C/Gas 4. Grease a 22 x 32-cm/9 x 13-in cake tin. In a large bowl, toss the apple slices with the sugar, cinnamon, lemon rind and juice.

b In a large bowl, with the electric mixer on medium speed, beat the eggs with the sugar until thick and pale and the mixture forms a "ribbon" trail when the beaters are lifted from the bowl, 3 to 5 minutes. Beat in the oil until well-blended. Stir in the flour and vanilla essence just until well-mixed and smooth.

c Pour half the mixture into prepared tin. Spoon half the apple slices over the batter. Cover the apple slices with the remaining batter; top with the remaining apple mixture. Sprinkle with sugar.

d Bake until the apples are tender and cake is golden brown and puffed and top springs back when gently pressed with a finger, 1¼ to 1½ hours. Cover with foil during baking if the top browns too quickly. Transfer to wire rack to cool. Cut into squares and serve at room temperature.

Prune Coffeecake

A Polish recipe, usually served with mid-morning coffee. The chocolate-honey-icing makes this cake extra special.

MAKES 10–12 SLICES

375 g/12 oz plain flour

1½ tsp bicarbonate of soda

1 tsp baking powder

250 g/8 oz unsalted butter, cut into pieces

Grated rind of 1 orange

250 g/8 oz sugar

1 Tbsp vanilla or rum essence

¼ tsp salt

500 ml/1 pt soured cream

3 eggs, lightly beaten

175 g/6 oz prune purée*

60 g/2 oz chopped walnuts or pecans

2 Tbsp cocoa powder, sifted

1 tsp ground cinnamon

CHOCOLATE-HONEY ICING

90 g/3 oz plain chocolate, chopped

40 g/1½ oz unsalted butter

1½ Tbsp honey

NOTE

Prune purée, sometimes called lekvar, is used in Eastern European and Jewish baking. It can be found in many large supermarkets or delicatessens. To make your own, simmer 120 g/4 oz dried prunes with 120 ml/4 fl oz water, a little grated orange rind, and about 2 tbsp orange juice until all the liquid is absorbed and the prunes form a mushy purée. Blend in a food processor. Store, covered, in the refrigerator.

Pre-heat the oven to 350°F/175°C/Gas 4. Grease and flour a heavy 10-inch, non-stick ring tin. Sift the flour, bicarbonate and baking powder.

Melt the butter in a saucepan. Stir in the orange rind and remove the from heat. Immediately stir in the sugar, vanilla or rum essence, salt, soured cream and eggs, then beat in all the flour mixture until blended.

Spoon about half the mixture into the tin. Stir the prune purée and drop heaped tablespoonfuls over the centre of the mixture. Sprinkle the walnuts or pecans, cocoa powder and ground cinnamon over the top of the prune purée.

Spoon the remaining mixture over the prune purée and nut mixture and smooth the top evenly. Draw a palette knife through the mixture creating a swirling pattern. Bake for 50 minutes. Cool in the tin for 10 minutes.

Invert the cake on to a wire rack to cool completely. Melt the chocolate, butter and honey. Drizzle over the cake and leave to set.

Blueberry Streusel Coffeecake

This luscious coffeecake, with a cream cheese filling, is a cross between a blueberry muffin and old-fashioned cheesecake.

MAKES 10–12 SLICES

STREUSEL TOPPING

120 g/4 oz unsalted butter, softened

150 g/5 oz sugar

30 g/1 oz firmly packed, brown sugar

90 g/3 oz plain flour

60 g/2 oz chopped, toasted hazelnuts

1½ tsp ground cinnamon

½ tsp ground nutmeg

¼ tsp salt

CREAM-CHEESE FILLING

375 g/12 oz cream cheese

90 g/3 oz sugar

1 egg

Grated rind of 1 lemon

1 Tbsp lemon juice

1 tsp almond essence

CAKE

500 g/1 lb plain flour

4 tsp baking powder

1 tsp salt

120 g/4 oz unsalted butter, softened

300 g/10 oz sugar

2 eggs, lightly beaten

1 tsp almond essence

300 ml/10 fl oz milk

750 g/1½ lb fresh blueberries

TIP

Be sure to use an ovenproof glass dish, as the blueberries could react with metal. (A porcelain dish would not allow the cake to cook completely.)

Pre-heat the oven to 375°F/190°C/Gas 5. Generously butter a 32 x 22-cm/13 x 9-in glass baking dish. To prepare the topping, rub together all the ingredients with your fingertips or a pastry blender in a medium bowl, until well-blended, and large crumbs form. Set aside.

To prepare the filling: Soften the cream cheese and beat with the sugar until creamy in a medium bowl using an electric mixer, scraping down the side of the bowl occasionally. Beat in the egg, grated lemon rind and juice and almond essence until smooth. Set aside.

To prepare the cake: Sift the flour, baking powder and salt into a bowl. In another bowl, with an electric mixer, beat the butter and sugar until light and fluffy, about 2 to 3 minutes. Gradually beat in the eggs until very light and smooth. Beat in the almond essence. Beat in the flour mixture on low speed, alternating with the milk, and ending with the flour mixture, until well-blended. If the mixture is too stiff, add a little more milk. Gently fold in the blueberries.

Spread slightly less than half the cake mixture on the bottom of the dish, smoothing the surface and pushing into corners. Gently spread the cream-cheese filling over the cake mixture and lightly sprinkle about one quarter of the Streusel topping over the filling. Drop spoonfuls of the remaining batter over the top and spread evenly, trying not to mix the layers. Sprinkle the remaining topping evenly over the surface.

Bake until the topping is crisp and golden brown, and a skewer inserted into the centre comes out with just a few crumbs attached, about 1 hour. Transfer to a wire rack and cool until the cake is just warm. Cut into squares, and serve slightly warm or at room temperature.

Polenta Cake
with caramelized apples

Many versions of this cake are found all over Italy.

SERVES 6–8

70 g/3 oz plain flour

65 g/2½ oz polenta or cornmeal

1 tsp baking powder

Grated rind of 1 lemon

¼ tsp salt

2 eggs

175 g/6 oz sugar

5 Tbsp milk

½ tsp almond essence

40 g/1½ oz currants or raisins, soaked in hot water for 20 minutes and drained

75 g/3 oz unsalted butter, softened

2 apples, peeled, cored and thinly sliced

25 g/1 oz slivered almonds

3 to 4 Tbsp apricot jam

1 to 2 Tbsp water

Whipped cream, soured cream or ice cream to serve (optional)

TIP

Be sure to stir or sift together the dry ingredients (including any grated or ground spices) until they are completely blended. Most liquid ingredients can be beaten until well blended with a hand whisk or fork. Heavier mixtures that include mashed bananas, pumpkin or sweet potato might require a hand-held electric mixer.

Pre-heat the oven to 375°F/190°C/Gas 5. Generously butter a 22-cm/9-in spring-release tin, then dust the pan lightly with flour. Stir the flour, polenta or cornmeal, baking powder, grated lemon rind and salt together in a bowl.

Beat the eggs and 120 g/4 oz of the sugar in another bowl with an electric mixer until foamy; gradually beat in the milk and almond essence. Stir in the drained currants or raisins. Beat in the dry ingredients on low speed, adding half the softened butter.

Spoon into the prepared tin and smooth the top evenly. Arrange the apple slices in concentric circles over the top, and sprinkle with the slivered almonds. In a small saucepan, melt the remaining butter over low heat, and drizzle over the apples. Sprinkle with the remaining sugar.

Bake until the cake is puffed and golden, and the apples are lightly caramelized, about 45 minutes. Transfer to a wire rack to cool, about 20 minutes. Run a thin knife blade around the cake, then unclip the tin and carefully remove. Heat the apricot jam with 1 to 2 tablespoonfuls of water in a small saucepan until melted and smooth. Carefully brush or spoon over the top of the apples to glaze. Allow to cool to room temperature, and serve with whipped cream, soured cream or ice cream, as preferred.

Rhubarb Streusel Cake

This may be served as either a cake or a pudding, or cold as a cake. The crumb topping gives a delicious crunch in contrast to the rhubarb, which softens into the cake mix. Apples and gooseberries are good alternatives to the rhubarb.

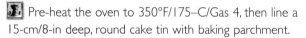
MAKES I LARGE CAKE

STREUSEL TOPPING	CAKE
90 g/3 oz butter	120 g/4 oz butter or margarine
120 g/4 oz wholemeal flour	150 g/5 oz light brown sugar
½ tsp baking powder	2 large eggs, beaten
120 g/4 oz demerera sugar	120 g/4 oz wholemeal flour
	I tsp baking powder
	½ tsp ground cinnamon
	I Tbsp milk
	175 g/6 oz rhubarb pieces, in 5-cm/2-in lengths, fresh or tinned

Pre-heat the oven to 350°F/175–C/Gas 4, then line a 15-cm/8-in deep, round cake tin with baking parchment.

First prepare the topping. Blend the butter into the flour, baking powder and sugar until evenly distributed, then set aside. Cream the butter and sugar until pale and fluffy then gradually add the beaten eggs. Mix together the flour, baking powder and cinnamon, then fold them into the mixture, adding the milk to give a soft dropping consistency.

Spoon the cake mixture into the prepared tin and roughly smooth the top. Arrange the rhubarb over the sponge then cover with the topping mixture, spreading it evenly.

Bake for I hour, or until a cocktail stick inserted into the cake comes out clean. Leave in the tin for 2 to 3 minutes, then remove the cake carefully, peel off the paper, and leave to cool completely on a wire rack.

Muffins and Scones

Soured Cream and Cherry Muffins

Double Chocolate-chip Muffins

Ginger, Pear and Pecan Muffins

Warm Orange Muffins

Very Blue-blueberry Muffins

Parmesan and Pine Nut Mini Muffins

Cheese and Bacon Muffins

Oatmeal-raisin Muffins

Cheese and Walnut Scone Round

Scones

Cranberry-orange Scones

Goat's Cheese and Sun-dried Tomato Scones

Sesame Roquefort Crescents

Sweet-potato Pinwheels

Sour Cream and Cherry Muffins
with cherry compote

The<u>hese delicious muffins are moist, crumbly and delicately flavoured, and are enhanced by the intense flavour of the cherry compote.</u>

MAKES 12

60 g/2 oz semi-dried cherries	½ tsp ground cardamom
200 g/7 oz plain flour	120 g/4 oz sugar
1 tsp baking powder	1 egg
½ tsp bicarbonate of soda	250 ml/8 fl oz soured cream
½ tsp salt	½ tsp vanilla essence

Put the cherries in a small bowl, and pour over enough boiling water to cover them. Leave to stand for about 15 minutes to soften. Drain and pat dry with kitchen paper.

Pre-heat the oven to 400°F/200°C/Gas 6. Grease or spray a 12-cup bun tin or line with paper cases. Sift the flour, baking powder, bicarbonate, salt and ground cardamom into a large bowl. Stir in the sugar then the cherries, ensuring they are coated with the flour mixture, and make a well in the centre.

Beat the egg and soured cream in another bowl until well-blended; beat in the vanilla essence. Pour into the well and stir lightly until just combined. Do not over-mix; the mixture should be slightly lumpy.

Spoon the mixture into the prepared bun tin, filling each about ¾ full. Bake until risen and golden, about 20 minutes. Transfer the tin to a wire rack to cool, about 2 minutes, then transfer muffins to the wire rack to cool until just warm. Serve with the Cherry Compote.

Cherry Compote

500 g/1 lb black or red cherries, pitted	120 g/4 oz sugar
250 g/8 oz dried cherries	1 tsp cornflour or arrowroot, dissolved in 2 tsp cold water
1 vanilla pod, split	
4–6 cardamom pods, crushed	

Put the first five ingredients in a large, non-corrosive saucepan and add just enough water to cover the fruit. Place over medium heat and bring to the boil, stirring to dissolve the sugar. Simmer for about 5 minutes, until the cherries are just tender. Stir the dissolved cornflour or arrowroot, and then stir into the simmering cherry liquid. Bring to the boil, and cook for 1 to 2 minutes, until the juices are thickened and clear. Remove from the heat to cool, stirring occasionally. Pour into a bowl and refrigerate, covered, until ready to serve.

Double Chocolate-chip Muffins

These rich, chocolate muffins make a great morning snack with a cup of *cappuccino*.

MAKES 10

200 g/7 oz flour

60 g/2 oz cocoa powder

1 Tbsp baking powder

½ tsp salt

120 g/4 oz sugar

60 g/2 oz plain chocolate chips and 30 g/1 oz white-chocolate chips

2 eggs

120 ml/4 fl oz sunflower or vegetable oil

250 ml/8 fl oz milk

1 tsp vanilla essence

Pre-heat the oven to 400°F/200°C/Gas 6. Line a muffin tin with 10 pieces of foil or double paper cases. Sift the flour, cocoa powder, baking powder and salt into a large bowl. Stir in the sugar and chocolate chips, and make a well in the centre.

In another bowl, beat the eggs with the oil until foamy. Gradually beat in the milk and vanilla essence. Pour into the well and stir until just combined. Do not over-mix; the mixture should be slightly lumpy.

Spoon the mixture into the prepared cases, filling each about ¾ full. Bake until risen, golden and springy when pressed with your fingertip, about 20 minutes. Transfer the tin to a wire rack to cool, about 2 minutes, then transfer the muffins to the wire rack to cool. Serve warm or at room temperature.

Ginger, Pear, and Pecan Muffins

Ginger and pear go well together, and the combination of spicy root ginger and sweet, crystallized ginger create an interesting contrast.

MAKES 18

250 g/8 oz plain flour

2 tsp baking powder

½ tsp salt

¼ tsp ground cinnamon

60 g/2 oz sugar

2 eggs

120 ml/4 fl oz sunflower or other vegetable oil

2 Tbsp milk

1 tsp grated root ginger

250 g/8 oz peeled, cored and chopped pears

60 g/2 oz chopped pecans

Crystallized ginger, chopped

Pre-heat the oven to 375°F/190°C/Gas 5. Lightly grease or spray bun tins or line with paper cases. Sift the flour, baking powder, salt and ground cinnamon into a large bowl, then stir in the sugar, and make a well in the centre.

Beat the eggs, oil, milk and grated root ginger in another bowl until well-blended. Pour into the well. Using a fork, lightly stir until just combined. Do not over-mix; the mixture should be slightly lumpy. Gently fold in the pears, pecans and crystallized ginger.

Spoon the mixture into the prepared bun tin, filling each just over ⅔ full. Bake until risen and golden, and a cake tester inserted in the centre comes out clean, 20 to 25 minutes. Transfer the muffins to the wire rack to cool, about 2 minutes. Serve warm with the Honey-and-Ginger Butter.

Honey and Ginger Butter

250 g/8 oz unsalted butter, softened

1–2 Tbsp honey

½ tsp ground ginger

¼ tsp ground cinnamon

Beat the butter in a medium-sized bowl until light and creamy, about 1 to 2 minutes. Add the honey, ginger and cinnamon, and beat until well-blended. Spoon into a bowl and refrigerate, covered, until ready to serve. Soften for a few minutes at room temperature for easier spreading.

TIP

Chopped nuts, fruit or chocolate chips can be added at various stages. Tossing them in the dry ingredients before mixing with the liquids helps to even out their distribution, but they can be folded in just before the mixture is completed.

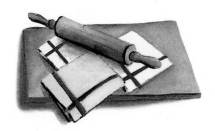

Warm Orange Muffins
with dried fruit salad

These warm, delicate muffins make a perfect accompaniment to a salad of dried fruits. Serve with whipped cream or crème fraîche for a winter breakfast or brunch.

MAKES 12

175 g/6 oz plain flour	1 egg
2 tsp baking powder	Grated rind of 1 orange
½ tsp salt	½ tsp vanilla essence
120 g/4 oz sugar	120 ml/4 fl oz buttermilk
60 g/2 oz candied orange peel, chopped	60 g/2 oz butter or margarine, melted and cooled

Pre-heat the oven to 400°F/200°C/Gas 6. Grease or spray a bun tin or line with 12 paper cases. Sift the flour, baking powder and salt into a large bowl, then stir in the sugar and chopped orange peel, and make a well in the centre.

Beat the egg, orange rind and vanilla essence in another bowl until foamy. Beat in the buttermilk and melted butter. Pour into the well, and lightly stir until just combined. Do not over-mix; the mixture should be slightly lumpy.

Spoon the mixture into the prepared cases, filling each about three-quarters full. Bake until risen and golden, and a skewer inserted in the centre comes out clean, about 20 minutes. Transfer the tin to a wire rack to cool, about 2 minutes, then transfer the muffins to the wire rack to cool slightly. Serve warm with the Dried Fruit Salad.

Dried Fruit Salad

250 g/8 oz large, pitted prunes	1 orange
175 g/6 oz dried, no-soak apricots	1 tsp vanilla essence
175 g/6 oz dried, no-soak pears	1 cinnamon stick
90 g/3 oz dried, no-soak peaches	2–3 cloves
60 g/2 oz sultanas or raisins	2–3 Tbsp sugar or honey, or to taste
	Boiling water

Put the prunes, apricots, pears and peaches in a large bowl, then sprinkle in the raisins. Using a swivel-bladed vegetable peeler, peel the orange rind in long, thin strips, and add to the fruit. Cut the orange in half and squeeze the juice over the fruit, removing any seeds. Add the vanilla essence, cinnamon stick, cloves and the sugar or honey to taste. Pour over enough boiling water to cover the fruit by 1 inch, then cover and leave to stand for at least 1 hour until the fruit is plump and tender. Stir to blend in the flavours (remove the cinnamon stick and cloves if you like), and serve at room temperature or refrigerate to serve chilled.

Very Blue-blueberry Muffins

These muffins are bursting with blueberries; mashing some of the berries releases more flavour into the mixture.

MAKES 12

250 g/8 oz plain flour

2½ tsp baking powder

½ tsp salt

¼ tsp freshly grated or ground nutmeg

60 g/2 oz sugar

2 eggs

60 ml/2 fl oz milk

120 g/4 oz butter or margarine, melted and cooled

Grated rind of ½ orange

1 tsp vanilla essence

60 g/2 oz fresh blueberries, mashed

500 g/1 lb fresh blueberries

60 g/2 oz demerara sugar, mixed with ¼ tsp freshly grated nutmeg to sprinkle

TIP

Muffin bun tins can vary in size. Your mixture may not completely fill each case; if so, it doesn't really matter. Whatever the size, make sure to fill the cases about one-quarter full.

Pre-heat the oven to 375°F/190°C/Gas 5. Lightly grease or spray a bun tin or line with 12 paper cases. Sift the flour, baking powder, salt and nutmeg into a large bowl; stir in the sugar, and make a well in the centre.

In another bowl, beat the eggs, milk, melted butter or margarine, grated orange rind and vanilla essence; then stir in the mashed blueberries. Pour into the well and lightly stir using a fork, until blended in. Do not over-mix. Lightly fold in the remaining blueberries.

Spoon the mixture into the prepared cases, filling each to almost full. Sprinkle each with the sugar-nutmeg mixture, and bake until risen and golden (a skewer inserted in the centre should come out with a few crumbs attached), 25 to 30 minutes. Transfer the tin to a wire rack to cool, about 2 minutes, then transfer the muffins to the wire rack to cool. Serve warm or at room temperature.

Parmesan and Pine Nut Mini-muffins
with sun-dried tomato butter

These delicious mini-muffins have an unusual, versatile flavor. Served with a sun-dried tomato butter, they make a great savoury snack or appetizer; when served with a sweetened honey or cinnamon butter, they have a much sweeter taste.

MAKES 24

175 g/6 oz flour	60 g/2 oz pine nuts, lightly toasted, plus extra to sprinkle
2 tsp baking powder	
¼ tsp salt	120 g/4 oz freshly grated Parmesan cheese
½ tsp dried basil leaves, crumbled	
	I egg
90 g/3 oz sugar	175 ml/6 fl oz milk
60 g/2 oz sultanas	60 g/2 oz butter, melted and cooled

Pre-heat the oven to 375°F/190°C/Gas 5. Grease or spray 24 mini paper cases or foil liners. Sift the flour, baking powder and salt into a large bowl. Stir in the dried basil, sugar, raisins, pine nuts and Parmesan until well-mixed, and make a well in the centre.

Whisk the egg with the milk in another bowl until well-blended and foamy, then whisk in the melted butter. Pour into the well and lightly fold together until combined. Do not over-mix; the mixture should be slightly lumpy.

Spoon the mixture into the prepared cases, filling each to almost full. Sprinkle each with a few pine nuts. Bake until risen, golden and springy when pressed, about 15 minutes. Transfer to a wire rack to cool, I to 2 minutes, then transfer muffins to the wire rack to cool until just warm. Serve warm with the Sun-dried Tomato Butter. Alternatively, cool to room temperature then split each muffin crosswise, spread the bottom halves with the butter and close with the tops.

Sun-dried Tomato Butter

175g/6 oz unsalted butter, softened	Freshly ground black pepper
60 g/2 oz sun-dried tomatoes, packed in oil, drained and chopped	

In a medium bowl, beat the butter until smooth and creamy. Add the sun-dried tomatoes and season with pepper to taste. Stir gently until well blended. Scrape into a serving bowl, and refrigerate, covered, until ready to serve. Soften for a few minutes at room temperature for easier spreading.

> **TIP**
> If you prefer larger muffins, bake the batter in a 12-cup bun tin prepared as above for about 20 minutes.

Cheese and Bacon Muffins

These savoury muffins are delicious served for breakfast. Vary the cheese to your taste.

MAKES 12 MUFFINS

6 rashers bacon

Vegetable oil

175 g/6 oz flour

2 tsp baking powder

½ tsp salt

2 tsp sugar

120 g/4 oz grated Gruyère, Cheddar or other cheese

3 to 4 spring onions, finely chopped

1 egg

60 ml/2 fl oz milk

1 Tbsp French mustard

Pre-heat the oven to 400°F/200°C/Gas 6. Grease or spray a bun tin, or line with paper cases. Put the bacon in a large frying pan and fry over medium heat, turning once, until crisp and brown on both sides. Drain on kitchen paper, and pour the remaining fat into a cup. Add extra oil, if necessary, to make 60 ml/2 fl oz. When cool, crumble the bacon into small pieces.

Meanwhile, sift the flour, baking powder and salt into a large bowl. Stir in the sugar, cheese and spring onions, tossing lightly to mix. Add the crumbled bacon and mix again, and make a well in the centre.

Beat the egg with the milk in another bowl until well-blended. Beat in the mustard and the reserved bacon fat. Pour into the well and stir lightly until just combined. Do not over-mix; the batter should be slightly lumpy.

Spoon the mixture into the prepared bun tin, and bake until risen, golden, and springy when pressed, 15 to 20 minutes. Transfer to a wire rack to cool, about 2 minutes, then transfer the muffins to the rack to cool until just warm. Serve warm with butter or cream cheese.

Oatmeal-raisin Muffins

These dark, moist muffins have a chewy texture. Substitute dried cranberries for raisins, if you like.

MAKES 12

120 g/4 oz porridge oats	2 eggs
120 g/4 oz plain flour	60 g/2 oz dark brown sugar
2 tsp baking powder	60 ml/2 fl oz milk
½ tsp ground cinnamon	60 g/2 oz butter or margarine, melted and cooled
½ tsp salt	
60 g/2 oz raisins	½ tsp vanilla essence
60 g/2 oz wholemeal flour	

Pre-heat the oven to 400°F/200°C/Gas 6. Grease or spray a 12-cup bun tin or line with double paper cases. Put the oats in a large bowl and sift in the plain flour, baking powder, cinnamon and salt. Stir in the raisins and wholemeal flour, and make a well in the centre.

Using an electric mixer, beat the eggs and brown sugar in another bowl until foamy. Gradually beat in the milk, melted butter or margarine and vanilla essence until well-blended. Pour into the well, and stir until combined. Do not over-mix; the mixture should be slightly lumpy.

Spoon the mixture into the prepared bun tin, filling about ¾ full. Bake until risen, golden and springy when pressed with your fingertip, about 20 minutes. Transfer the tin to a wire rack to cool, then transfer the muffins to the rack, about 2 minutes. If you like, serve them with salted butter or a flavoured butter.

Cheese and Walnut Biscuit Round

Biscuits are quick and easy to make, the perfect accompaniment to soups, stews or a bedtime drink. This mixture is baked in one large round, cutting the preparation time to an absolute minimum.

SERVES 4 TO 8

120 g/4 oz butter	120 g/4 oz grated Cheddar cheese
250 g/8 oz wholemeal flour	
2 tsp baking powder	1 large egg, beaten
Pinch of salt	120 ml/4 fl oz milk
60 g/2 oz walnuts, roughly chopped	

Pre-heat the oven to 425°F/220°C/Gas 7 and lightly oil a baking sheet.

Blend the butter into the flour, baking powder and salt, then stir in the nuts and cheese. Beat the egg with the milk then use to mix to a soft but manageable dough.

Turn on to a lightly floured surface then knead lightly until smooth. Shape the dough into a round about 2.5 cm/ 1 in thick, and mark into eight. Bake on the baking sheet for 20 to 25 minutes. Cool for at least 10 minutes before eating to avoid indigestion!

Scones

This is a classic tea-time treat. Often made with double cream, this recipe uses buttermilk, which makes the scones soft and fluffy, with a smooth texture.

MAKES ABOUT 15

375 g/12 oz flour	1 egg, lightly beaten
1½ tsp bicarbonate of soda	300 ml/10 fl oz buttermilk
½ tsp salt	2 Tbsp milk
3 Tbsp sugar	Clotted cream or lightly whipped double cream to serve
90 g/3 oz unsalted butter, cut into pieces	
30 g/1 oz currants or seedless raisins	Jam to serve

Pre-heat the oven to 425°F/220°C/Gas 7. Lightly flour a large baking sheet. Sift the flour, bicarbonate and salt into a large bowl, then stir in the sugar.

Sprinkle the butter pieces over the flour mixture and rub in the butter until the mixture resembles crumbs. Blend in the currants or raisins, and then make a well in the centre.

Beat the egg with 175 ml/6 fl oz of the buttermilk in a small bowl, and pour into the well. Stir the flour mixture into the liquid with a fork until it is combined. Do not over-mix. Form the dough into a rough ball, and place on a lightly floured surface: knead lightly 8 to 10 times until blended.

Roll or pat the dough into a 2-cm/¾-in-thick round. Use a floured 6-cm/2½-in-wide, round cutter to cut out as many rounds as possible. Transfer to the baking sheet, arranging them about 2.5 cm/1 inch apart. Press the trimmings together and shape into another 2-cm/¾-in-thick round, then cut out as many 6-cm/2½-in thick rounds as possible. Transfer these to the baking sheet.

Brush the tops of the scones with a little milk, and bake until risen and golden, about 15 minutes. Transfer the scones to a wire rack to cool slightly. Serve warm with fresh, whipped cream and strawberry or raspberry jam.

TIP

When cutting out the scones, cut straight down. Do not twist the cutter, or the scones will rise unevenly.

Cranberry-orange Scones
with cranberry-raspberry butter

These delicious, orange-flavoured scones are filled with dried cranberries. If you like, use dried cherries instead, and serve with cherry compote (see page 425).

MAKES ABOUT 10 SCONES

375 g/12 oz plain flour	90 g/3 oz dried cranberries
1 Tbsp baking powder	2 eggs
½ tsp salt	120–150 ml/4–5 fl oz double cream, plus extra to glaze
2 Tbsp sugar, plus extra to sprinkle	½ tsp vanilla essence
Grated rind of 1 orange	2 Tbsp milk
60 g/2 oz unsalted butter, cut into pieces	2 Tbsp light brown sugar

Pre-heat the oven to 425°F/220°C/Gas 7. Lightly flour a large baking sheet. Sift the flour, baking powder and salt into a large bowl; stir in the sugar and the grated rind.

Sprinkle the butter pieces over the flour mixture, and rub in the butter using a pastry blender or your fingertips, until the mixture resembles medium crumbs. Stir in the dried cranberries and make a well in the centre.

In a small bowl, beat the eggs and 120 ml/4 fl oz of the cream until blended; beat in the vanilla essence and pour into the well. Using a fork, stir the flour mixture into the liquid just until it begins to combine; do not over-mix. Form the dough into a rough ball, and place on a lightly floured surface. Knead 6 to 8 times until blended. Pat the dough into a 2-cm/¾-in-thick round and cut out as many rounds as possible using a 6-cm/2½-in floured cutter. Transfer to the baking sheet, arranging them about 2.5 cm/1 in apart. Press the trimmings together and roll or pat to another 2-cm/¾-in-thick round, then cut out as many rounds as possible, and transfer to the baking sheet.

Brush the top of the scones with a little more cream or milk, and sprinkle with sugar. Bake until risen and golden, about 12 minutes. Transfer to a wire rack to cool, about 3 to 4 minutes, then transfer the scones to the wire rack to cool until just warm. Serve with Cranberry-raspberry Butter.

Cranberry-raspberry Butter

MAKES ABOUT 1½ CUPS

1½ sticks unsalted butter, softened	1 Tbsp raspberry jam
	1 Tbsp orange juice
1 Tbsp cranberry sauce	½ tsp ground cinnamon

Beat the butter until smooth and creamy in a small bowl. Beat in the cranberry sauce, raspberry jam, orange juice and ground cinnamon until well blended. Scrape into a serving bowl and refrigerate, covered, until ready to serve.

> **TIP**
> *If the cranberries are very dry, plump them up by covering with boiling water; soak for 5 minutes, then drain and lastly pat dry with kitchen paper.*

Goat's Cheese and Sun-dried Tomato Scones

Serve these delicious scones instead of bread with salads or pasta dishes.

MAKES 10 TO 12 BISCUITS

250 g/8 oz flour	**60 g/2 oz chopped, sun-dried tomatoes, packed in oil, drained**
2 tsp baking powder	
¼ tsp bicarbonate of soda	**120 g/4 oz soft goat's cheese, crumbled or diced**
¼ tsp salt	
Freshly ground black pepper	**1 egg**
1–2 spring onions, finely chopped	**120–150 ml/4–5 fl oz buttermilk**

Pre-heat the oven to 400°F/200°C/Gas 6. Lightly flour a large baking sheet. Sift the flour, baking powder, bicarbonate and salt into a large bowl. Add a few grinds of black pepper, the spring onions, sun-dried tomatoes and goat's cheese and stir well, being sure to coat the tomatoes and cheese, and make a well in the centre.

In a small bowl beat the egg with 120 ml/4 fl oz buttermilk and pour into the well. Using a fork, stir lightly until just combined, adding a little more buttermilk if necessary. Form into a rough ball and turn on to a lightly floured surface. Knead lightly 6 to 8 times until just smooth.

Roll or pat dough into a 2-cm/¾-in-thick circle about 25 cm/10 in in diameter. Transfer to a baking sheet and using a long-bladed, sharp, floured knife, score deeply into 10 or 12 wedges. Do not drag the knife through the dough or it will not rise evenly.

Dust lightly with a little flour and bake until risen and golden, 15 to 18 minutes. Transfer to a wire rack to cool 2 to 3 minutes, then slide the scones on to the wire rack to cool until just warm. Serve warm with either salted or flavoured butter.

Sesame Roquefort Crescents

These unusual biscuits are shaped like a croissant, and make a delicious alternative to sweeter choices.

MAKES 12

250 g/8 oz plain flour	175 ml/6 fl oz buttermilk
2 tsp baking powder	2 Tbsp butter, melted
½ tsp salt	60 g/2 oz Roquefort or other strong blue cheese, crumbled
¼ tsp bicarbonate of soda	
¼ tsp ground ginger	2 Tbsp freshly chopped parsley
60 g/2 oz white vegetable fat	
	Sesame seeds to sprinkle

Pre-heat the oven to 425°F/220°C/Gas 7. Lightly grease a large non-stick baking sheet. Sift the flour, baking powder, salt, bicarbonate, and ground ginger into a large bowl. Add the white vegetable fat and using a pastry blender or your fingertips, rub into the flour until the mixture resembles coarse crumbs, and make a well in the centre.

Pour in the buttermilk and stir lightly with a fork until just moistened. Form into a rough ball and place on a lightly floured surface. Gently knead 8 to 10 times until just smooth. Using a lightly floured rolling pin, roll into a ½-cm/ ¼-in-thick round, about 30 cm/12 in in diameter. Brush the dough with half the melted butter, and sprinkle with the crumbled cheese and chopped parsley. Using a sharp knife, cut into 12 wedges. Starting from each wide end, roll the dough towards the point.

Arrange the crescents, with their points tucked under, on the baking sheet, about 2 inches apart, pulling the ends towards the centre to form a crescent shape. Sprinkle with the sesame seeds. Bake until puffed and golden, 15 to 20 minutes. Transfer to a wire rack and cool for 2 to 3 minutes, then transfer the crescents to the wire rack to cool until just warm.

Sweet-potato Pinwheels
with cinnamon, nuts and raisins

These delicious biscuits are a cross between a coffeecake and a slightly sticky, sweet bun, and are great served with morning coffee. The nuts and raisins add a crunchy texture to the warm, spiced biscuits.

MAKES 10 TO 12

175 g/6 oz flour	90–120 ml/3–4 fl oz milk
2½ tsp baking powder	2 Tbsp butter, melted
½ tsp salt	**FILLING**
1 tsp ground cinnamon	60 g/2 oz brown sugar
90 g/3 oz butter, cut into squares	60 g/2 oz chopped pecans or walnuts
1–2 Tbsp brown sugar	60 g/2 oz chopped raisins
90 g/3 oz cooked, mashed sweet potato	½ tsp cinnamon

Pre-heat the oven to 425°F/220°C/Gas 6. Lightly grease a large baking sheet. Sift the flour, baking powder, salt and cinnamon into a large bowl. Sprinkle over the butter pieces, and rub in using a pastry blender until the mixture resembles coarse crumbs. Stir in the brown sugar and make a well in the centre.

Put the sweet potato in a small bowl, and whisk in the milk until smooth. Pour into the well, stirring lightly until a soft dough forms. Form into a rough ball.

Place on a lightly floured surface and knead lightly 8 to 10 times. Using a lightly floured rolling pin, roll the dough to a ½-cm/¼-in-thick rectangle about 25–30 cm/10–12 in wide, and brush with the melted butter. Combine the filling ingredients in a small bowl, and sprinkle over the dough. Starting at one long end, roll the dough, Swiss-roll style. Cut into 2.5-cm/1-in slices and arrange cut-side down on the baking sheet, about 1 cm/½ in apart.

Bake until puffed and golden, about 12 minutes. Transfer to a wire rack to cool slightly, then transfer the pinwheels to the wire rack to cool. Serve warm.

QUICK BREADS 439

Baking for Christmas

This is the season when even the most
reluctant cook takes to the kitchen. Here is
a range of traditional Christmas specialities.
There is the Yule Log from France, Stollen
from Germany, Lemańce from Poland, and
Panettone from Italy. These wonderful treats
should not just be lavished upon the family
– make up a batch and give them as
presents as well.

Yule Log

This classic cake from France, where it is called *Bûche de Noël*, will help you celebrate Christmas in style.

4 eggs, separated	175 g/6 oz unsalted butter
120 g/4 oz sugar	90 g/3 oz plain chocolate, melted
120 g/4 oz plain flour	1–2 tsp dark rum
ICING	**DECORATION**
90 g/3 oz sugar	Meringue Mushrooms
6 Tbsp water	Marzipan holly leaves and berries
4 egg yolks	

Pre-heat the oven to 450°F/230°C/Gas 8. Grease a 22 x 32-cm/9 x 13-in Swiss roll tin and line with baking parchment.

Put the egg yolks and sugar into a mixing bowl and whisk until the mixture falls in a thick trail.

Whisk the egg whites until stiff. Fold the egg whites and flour alternately into the egg yolk mixture. Pour into the tin and bake for about 10 minutes until golden brown.

Put a sheet of greaseproof paper on top of a dampened teatowel and sprinkle with caster sugar. Turn the sponge out on to the sugared paper.

Peel off the lining paper and quickly trim the edges of the sponge. Make a shallow groove across one short side of the cake 2.5 cm/1 in from the edge. Fold the sponge over at the groove. Using the teatowel to support the cake, roll up the sponge with the paper inside. Cover with the damp cloth until cold.

To make the icing, put the sugar and water into a small pan. Dissolve the sugar and then bring to a boil and boil to the "thread" stage (230°F/110°C).

Whisk the egg yolks in a bowl until thick and creamy. Slowly pour the hot syrup on the egg yolks in a steady stream, making sure you beat constantly until the mixture is light and fluffy.

Beat the butter until soft. Add the egg mixture a little at a time until the mixture is firm and shiny. Stir in the chocolate and rum.

Carefully unroll the sponge and remove the greaseproof paper. Spread a little butter icing over the sponge and roll up again.

Transfer the cake on a serving dish. Spoon the remaining butter icing into a piping bag fitted with a star nozzle. Pipe lines lengthwise down the cake. Add an occasional swirl to represent a "knot" on a log. Decorate with Meringue Mushrooms together with marzipan holly leaves and berries.

Christmas Pear and Nut Bread

This bread bears some resemblance to a Christmas cake, but a yeast batter is used as the basis. Bake 3 to 4 weeks before Christmas, wrap in foil and store in a cool place.

MAKES 2 SMALL LOAVES

300 g/10 oz dried pears

120 g/4 oz dried prunes

120 g/4 oz dried figs, chopped small

120 g/4 oz dried or fresh dates, without stones

60 g/2 oz candied orange and lemon peel, chopped

90 g/3 oz raisins

90 g/3 oz sultanas

1 Tbsp pine kernels

90 g/3 oz hazelnuts, toasted and chopped coarsely

90 g/3 oz walnuts, chopped coarsely

1 tsp grated lemon rind

2 tsp grated orange rind

2 Tbsp Kirsch or rum

BREAD DOUGH

20 g/¾ oz fresh yeast or 1½ sachets dried yeast

250 g/8 oz plain flour

5 Tbsp caster sugar

Pinch of salt

1½ tsp ground cinnamon

Large pinch of cloves

½ tsp star anise or allspice

5-cm/2-in vanilla pod, split

ICING

2 Tbsp granulated sugar

1 Tbsp cornflour

2 Tbsp Kirsch or rum

Carefully wash the pears and prunes. Place them in a pan and just cover with water. Leave to soften for 2 to 3 hours. Then, bring to the boil and simmer gently for about 20 minutes. Drain the fruit, reserving the juice, and leave to cool. Chop the figs.

Place the figs, dates, orange and lemon rind, raisins, sultanas, pine nuts, hazelnuts, walnuts and the lemon and orange rinds in a large bowl. Toss well together to mix and pour on the Kirsch. Chop up the cooled fruit roughly. Add to the fruit-and-nut mixture.

Combine 60 ml/2 fl oz of the reserved fruit syrup, warmed to blood head, yeast, 60 g/2 oz flour and 1 tsp sugar taken from the main quantity. Cover and set aside to prove and double in bulk.

Meanwhile, sift the remaining flour with the salt and spices in a large bowl. Make a well in the centre, pour in the yeast batter and draw in a little of the flour. Scoop in the seeds of the split vanilla pod and sugar. Combine well together and moisten with about 120 ml/4 fl oz of the fruit syrup. Knead the dough very thoroughly until it becomes less sticky and starts to roll off the sides of the bowl. When it is very elastic and large air-bubbles have started to form, gather into a large ball and place on the floured surface.

Pull the dough out and gradually knead in the fruit and nut mixture until all has been used. Roll into a large ball and lay in the large flour-dusted bowl. Dredge with a little more flour and cover with a clean teatowel. Set aside in a cool place to rise overnight.

Pre-heat the oven to 350°F/175°C/Gas 4. The next day, break off pieces of dough and form into hand-sized 4–5-cm/1½–2-in rolls, or make two larger loaves 15 × 10-cm/6 × 4-in loaf tins, according to your choice. Lay small rolls, well apart, on greased baking sheets. Leave to rest and prove a little for 15 to 20 minutes, then bake until golden and well risen, about 1 hour.

Make the Kirsch icing for the warm loaves. Heat 250 ml/8 fl oz fruit syrup with 2 tablespoonfuls granulated sugar and bring to the boil. Stir in 1 tablespoon cornflour and cook until thickened. Remove from the heat and stir in 2 tablespoonfuls Kirsch. Brush on the warm loaves, press in a few almond halves for decoration, and leave to cool. Serve cut in thin slices with coffee or tea or a glass of mulled wine. It also tastes good spread with butter.

Czech Christmas Bread

This is a plaited loaf, seasoned with ginger and nutmeg and packed with fruit and nuts. It takes a bit of effort to knead in the fruit and to make the elegant plaits but the result is well worth it. This recipe will happily fit both a 500-g/1-lb and 750-g/1½-lb tin.

BREAD MACHINE RECIPE – MAKES 1 SMALL LOAF

150 ml/5 fl oz milk	1 Tbsp yeast
1 egg	60 g/2 oz slivered blanched almonds
60 g/2 oz butter	
60 g/2 oz sugar	60 g/2 oz sultanas
1 tsp salt	1 Tbsp candied orange peel
¼ tsp ground ginger	1 egg yolk beaten with 1 Tbsp water to glaze
¼ tsp ground nutmeg	
1 tsp grated lemon rind	2 Tbsp sliced almonds
375 g/12 oz strong white flour	Icing sugar

Put the milk, egg, butter, sugar, salt, spices, lemon rind, flour and yeast in the bread tin in the order suggested in the instructions. Set for white or sweet bread, dough stage. Press start. You may add the almonds when the machine signals time to add fruit, but do not add the raisins and candied orange peel at this stage because the additional sugar in an already sweet bread could interfere with the yeast's rising action.

Oil a baking sheet at least 35 cm/14 in long. When the dough is ready, remove and punch down. Knead in the fruit and nuts. Cut the dough into four equal parts. Take three and roll each to form a rope about 45 cm/18 in long. Plait the ropes, pinch the ends together and place on the baking sheet.

Cut the remaining piece into four equal parts. Again, take three and roll each between your hands to form a thin rope about 45 cm/18 in long. Plait the ropes and centre the plait on top of the fat plait. Run dampened fingers along the underside of the thin plait, then lightly press it on to the fat plait. Pinch the ends together and press them under the ends of the fat plait.

Cut the remaining piece into two equal parts. Roll each into a thin rope about 40 cm/16 in long. Twist the two ropes together. Centre the twist on the thin plait. Wet your fingers and run them lightly on the underside of the twist, then lightly press on to the thin plait. Pinch the ends together and turn them under. Use four or five cocktail sticks to skewer the plaits in place or the top plaits may slip off as the dough rises. Cover the bread loosely, put in a warm place and leave to prove until the dough has almost doubled in bulk, about an hour.

Pre-heat the oven to 375°F/190°C/Gas 5. Lightly brush with the egg glaze, then sprinkle the sliced almonds over the top and press a few into the sides. Bake until brown and a skewer inserted in a thick part comes out clean. Sprinkle with icing sugar while warm.

Mince Pies

Christmas wouldn't be Christmas without mince pies. They can be enjoyed just as they are, or eaten as a dessert with brandy butter or cream.

MAKES ABOUT 18

375 g/12 oz Rich Shortcrust Pastry (Pâte Brisée Riche) (see page 13)	1 Tbsp milk
1 egg	500 g/1 lb mincemeat
	Icing sugar

Begin by making the pastry and refrigerating it for half an hour. Roll out half of the pastry on a well-floured surface with a floured rolling pin. Using a 7-cm/3-in circular biscuit cutter, cut out 18 rounds. Put the spare ones back in the refrigerator if you only have one bun tin. Repeat the rolling process using the other half of the pastry and a 5-cm/2-in biscuit cutter.

Pre-heat the oven to 400°F/200°C/Gas 6. Beat the egg and milk together and set aside. Grease the bun tin and fill with the 7-cm/3-in pastry rounds. Using a heaped teaspoon of mincemeat, fill the pies. Brush the edges of the pies with a little of the egg and milk so to seal the pies and place the smaller rounds of pastry on the top pushing down lightly around the edges. Brush over the top of each pie with the egg mixture and prick with a fork.

Place the mince pies in the oven and bake for 20 to 25 minutes or until golden brown. Cool on a wire rack and dust with icing sugar. Serve warm.

Cinnamon Stars

Another Christmas speciality, decorative and delicious at the same time.

MAKES 30

2 egg whites	250 g/8 oz unblanched almonds, coarsely ground
250 g/8 oz caster sugar	1 Tbsp ground cinnamon
	1½ Tbsp kirsch

Beat the egg whites until stiff, then mix in the sugar and beat for about 10 minutes by machine (20 minutes by hand) until the mixture is very thick, white and glossy. Reserve about 6 tablespoonfuls of the mixture. Mix the almonds, spice, and kirsch into the rest of the meringue.

Gather into a ball, cover and chill for 30 minutes. Roll the dough out on a sugared board to 1 cm/⅜ in thick, and cut out star shapes with a biscuit cutter. Pre-heat the oven to 400°F/200°C/Gas 6.

Transfer the biscuits to a lightly buttered baking sheet lined with baking parchment and smooth some of the reserved meringue on top of each. Bake for 15 minutes. Cool on a wire rack. These biscuits will keep for several weeks stored in an airtight container.

Cinnamon stars are often used as Christmas tree decorations. Use a cocktail stick or skewer to pierce a hole in the top of each biscuit before baking.

◀ *Mince Pies*

Stollen

Full of fruit, peel and nuts, this yeast bread freezes well so can be made a month before Christmas. Stollen makes an excellent gift so it is worth baking several.

MAKES 2 LARGE OR 4 SMALL STOLLEN

60 g/2 oz fresh yeast or 4 Tbsp dried yeast, 1 tsp sugar and 3 Tbsp warm water	175–250 g/6–8 oz raisins
	90 g/3 oz currants
250 ml/8 fl oz single cream	90 g/3 oz chopped, candied orange peel
375 g/12 oz flour	90 g/3 oz mixed candied peel, chopped
300 g/10 oz butter or margarine	60 g/2 oz almonds, blanched and chopped
6 Tbsp sugar	
½ tsp salt	Melted butter or margarine to glaze
1 tsp grated lemon rind	120 g/4 oz sugar mixed with 1 Tbsp vanilla sugar for decoration
1 tsp ground cardamom	
Pinch of ground nutmeg	

Grease one or two baking sheets, depending on size. Crumble the yeast in the mixing bowl and dissolve it in a few tablespoonfuls of the cream. (Dissolve dried yeast with the teaspoon of sugar in the warm water. Set aside for 10 minutes until frothy.)

Warm the rest of the cream and pour it on to the yeast. Stir in the flour, a little at a time and work the dough until it is smooth. Sprinkle a little flour on top, cover with oiled plastic and leave the dough to prove until it has doubled in size, about 1¼ hours.

Beat together the fat and sugar until fluffy and add the salt, lemon rind, cardamom and nutmeg. Work the mixture into the yeast dough and add the dried fruit and almonds. Extra flour may be beaten in if necessary, the dough should be fairly stiff. Leave to prove once again, for 30–40 minutes, covered with oiled plastic.

Knead the dough and divide it into 2 or 4. Shape each part into round balls, flatten them a little and then fold them in the middle to make half-moons. Place the shaped dough on to the baking sheets, cover with oiled plastic and leave to prove for about 40 minutes. Pre-heat the oven to 400°F/200°C/Gas 6 and bake for 20 to 30 minutes until browned and cooked when tested with a skewer. Brush the Stollen with melted butter as soon as they are baked.

Leave them to cool slightly on the baking sheet(s). Dip the tops of the Stollen into the icing sugar so that they are completely covered. The bread surface is then sealed by the butter-and-sugar coatings and the Stollen keeps well.

Swedish Christmas Bread

This is a dark, dense rye bread made with stout, flavoured with orange peel and treacle, and studded with candied orange peel. It is best eaten simply with butter.

BREAD MACHINE RECIPE – MAKES 1 500-G/1-LB LOAF

175 ml/6 fl oz stout	175 g/6 oz rye flour
1 Tbsp vegetable oil	1 Tbsp grated orange peel
3 Tbsp treacle	2 tsp yeast
½ tsp salt	2 Tbsp candied orange peel
90 g/3 oz strong white flour	

Put all ingredients except the candied orange peel in the bread tin in the order suggested in the instructions. Set for wholemeal bread, medium crust. Add the candied orange peel after the first kneading, or when the beeper indicates it is time to add the fruit.

Pulla

Pulla is a Finnish sweet bread seasoned with cardamom, a spice widely used in Scandinavian cooking. It is an everyday bread in Finland, often dressed up with raisins and candied orange peel for holiday celebrations.

BREAD MACHINE RECIPE—MAKES 1 500-G/1-LB LOAF

1 egg	**GLAZE**
120 ml/4 fl oz milk	1 egg white beaten with 2 tsp water
25 g/1 oz butter	
3 Tbsp sugar	2 Tbsp sliced or slivered almonds
½ tsp salt	
1 tsp ground cardamom	1–2 Tbsp sugar
250 g/8 oz strong white flour	
2 tsp yeast	

Put all dough ingredients in the bread tin. Set for white or sweet bread, dough stage. Press start.

When the dough is ready, take it out and punch down. Cut into three equal pieces. Leave it to rest for 5 minutes. Butter a baking sheet. Roll each piece into a rope, about 40 cm/16 in long. Plait the ropes, tucking the ends under. Cover dough and put in a warm place to prove until doubled. Pre-heat the oven to 375°F/190°C/Gas 5.

Brush the dough with egg-water glaze. Sprinkle with almonds and then with sugar. Bake until golden, about 35 minutes.

Kolache

Kolaches are individual Czech pastries with fruit or cheese fillings, often eaten at Easter or Christmas. Below are recipes for two fillings, or you can use your favourite recipe for other fruit, nut or poppyseed fillings. For special occasions, serve a variety of fillings.

BREAD MACHINE RECIPE—MAKES 16

1 egg	**APRICOT FILLING**
120 ml/4 fl oz milk	**(Makes enough for 16 kolaches)**
60 g/2 oz butter	60 g/2 oz chopped dried apricots
60 g/2 oz sugar	
½ tsp salt	90 g/3 oz sugar
250 g/8 oz strong white flour	2 Tbsp apricot brandy, orange liqueur or orange juice
1½ tsp yeast	**CHEESE FILLING**
Icing sugar	**(Makes enough for 24 kolaches)**
	90 g/3 oz cream cheese, softened
	200 g/7 oz ricotta cheese, drained
	1 egg yolk
	3 Tbsp sugar
	½ tsp lemon juice

Put all the ingredients in the bread tin in the order suggested in the instructions. Set for white bread, dough stage. Press start.

Lightly oil two baking sheets.

When the dough is ready, remove from the bread machine and punch down. Cut into 16 equal pieces. Roll each piece into a ball and flatten slightly. Place the balls about 2.5 cm/1 in apart on a baking sheet. Cover loosely and set in a warm place to rise until doubled, about 45 minutes.

Make the fillings. For the apricot filling, put the apricots in a pan, cover with water and bring to the boil. Simmer until the water evaporates. Add sugar and liqueur and heat for 1 minute to dissolve the sugar. Cool slightly then purée in a blender or food processor. For the cheese filling, beat all the ingredients together until smooth.

Pre-heat the oven to 375°F/190°C/Gas 5. Gently use one finger to make an indentation in the top of each kolache, taking care not to deflate the roll. Gently widen the hole with your finger. Put about 1 tablespoonful of filling in each kolache. Bake until golden brown, 15 to 20 minutes. Sprinkle with icing sugar while still warm.

Cranberry Star Biscuits

Thesse beautiful biscuits are big enough to be a dessert.

MAKES ABOUT 20

250 g/8 oz plain flour

1½ tsp baking powder

½ tsp ground cinnamon

¼ tsp salt

175 g/6 oz unsalted butter, softened

120 g/4 oz sugar

60 g/2 oz light brown sugar

1 egg, lightly beaten

2 tsp vanilla essence

Grated rind of 1 lemon

120 g/4 oz fresh or frozen (defrosted) cranberries

3 Tbsp sugar

175 g/6 oz raspberry jam

1 Tbsp lemon juice

Icing sugar to dust

FILLING

Sift together the flour, baking powder, cinnamon and salt into a medium bowl; set aside.

In a large bowl with an electric mixer, beat the butter until creamy, 30 seconds. Add sugars and beat until light and fluffy, 2 minutes. Beat in egg, vanilla essence and lemon rind. Stir in flour mixture until a soft dough forms.

Scrape the dough on to a piece of clingfilm or greaseproof paper. Using the clingfilm or paper as a guide, shape the dough into a flat disk, and refrigerate until firm enough to roll, 1 to 2 hours.

Lightly grease 2 large non-stick baking sheets. On a lightly floured surface, using a floured rolling pin, roll out one-third of the dough 3 mm/⅛ in thick. (Keep the remaining dough refrigerated.) Using a 7-cm/3½-in star-shaped cutter, cut out an even number of biscuits. Using a 2.5-cm/1-in or 4-cm/1½-in star-shaped cutter, cut out the centre of half the biscuits. Arrange the biscuits on baking sheets 1 cm/½ in apart. Refrigerate 15 minutes. Pre-heat the oven to 350°F/175°C/Gas 4.

Bake until just set and the edges are golden, 8 to 10 minutes. Transfer the baking sheets to wire racks to cool slightly. Then transfer the biscuits to the wire racks to cool completely.

In a food processor fitted with a metal blade, process the cranberries, sugar, jam and lemon juice. Scrape into a medium saucepan, and, over medium heat, cook until mixture is reduced to about 250 ml/8 fl oz, 8 to 10 minutes, stirring often. Leave to cool, stirring occasionally.

Spread about 1 teaspoon of the cranberry mixture on to each star to within 1 cm/½ in of the edge. Arrange the cut-out cookie stars on a wire rack. Dust liberally with icing sugar; then carefully place over whole stars, gently pressing together. Allow the biscuits to set for 1 hour at room temperature.

TIP

To dust again with icing sugar before serving, cover the filled centres with small rounds of greaseproof paper first.

Christmas Cut-out Biscuits

These biscuits can be cut out in any shapes you can find: trees, angels, reindeer, bells or stars.

MAKES ABOUT 72
(DEPENDING ON SIZE OF CUTTERS)

250 g/8 oz plain flour	1 Tbsp vanilla essence
2 tsp baking powder	½ tsp lemon essence
½ tsp salt	
120 g/4 oz unsalted butter, softened	**ICING**
250 g/8 oz caster sugar	375 g/12 oz icing sugar
1 large egg	2–3 Tbsp milk
Grated rind of 1 lemon	1 Tbsp lemon juice
1 Tbsp lemon juice	Red and green food colouring (optional)

Sift the flour, baking powder and salt into a medium bowl. In a large bowl with an electric mixer, beat the butter until creamy, 30 seconds. Add the sugar and continue beating until light and fluffy, 1 to 2 minutes. Beat in the egg, lemon rind and juice and the vanilla and lemon essences until well-blended. Stir in the flour mixture until blended.

Form the dough into a ball and divide into 3 pieces. Flatten each piece to a circle, and wrap each tightly in clingfilm. Refrigerate for several hours or overnight until dough is firm enough to handle.

Pre-heat oven to 350°F/175°C/Gas 4. On a lightly floured surface, using a floured rolling pin, roll out one dough circle 3-mm/⅛-in thick. Keep the remaining dough circles refrigerated. Using floured biscuit cutters, cut out as many shapes as possible, and transfer the shapes to 2 large ungreased baking sheets 2.5 cm/1 in apart.

Bake until just coloured around the edges, 8 to 10 minutes. Transfer baking sheets to the wire racks to cool slightly. Then transfer the biscuits to the wire racks to cool completely. Repeat with the remaining dough.

Into a medium bowl, sift the icing sugar. Stir in 2 tablespoons milk and lemon juice, adding a little more milk if the icing is too thick. Spoon about one-third of the icing into a small bowl and another one-third into another small bowl. Add a few drops of red coloring to one bowl and green to the other, mixing until you have the desired shades.

Spoon the three colours into three separate paper cones. Pipe designs and decorations on to each biscuit. Leave to set for about 2 hours, then store in airtight containers with greaseproof paper between the layers.

Three Kings Bread

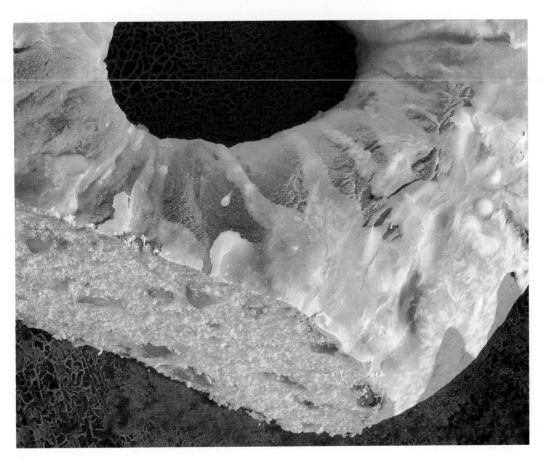

Three Kings Bread, or *Rosca de los Reyes*, is eaten in Mexico and Puerto Rico on Twelfth Night, January 6, the day the three kings brought Jesus gifts. A tiny ceramic doll, coin or bean may be hidden in the bread. The person who finds it throws a party on Candlemass, February 2.

BREAD MACHINE RECIPE—MAKES 1 500-G/1-LB LOAF

1 egg	2 tsp yeast
120 ml/4 fl oz water	3 Tbsp chopped walnuts
2 Tbsp powdered milk	2 Tbsp raisins
60 g/2 oz butter	3 Tbsp glacé cherries
3 Tbsp sugar	
2 tsp grated orange rind	**ICING**
1 tsp salt	90 g/3 oz icing sugar
250 g/8 oz strong white flour	1 Tbsp milk or cream
	¼ tsp vanilla essence

Put all dough ingredients except the fruit and nuts in the bread tin in the order suggested in the instructions. Set for white or sweet bread, dough stage. Press start. Add the fruit and nuts at beeper or after the first kneading.

When the dough is ready, remove from the tin and punch down. Leave to rest for 5 minutes. Preheat the oven to 400°F/200°C/Gas 6. Butter a 45-cm/18-in baking sheet. Roll the bread into a rope. Bring ends of the rope together to form a ring, and place the bread on baking sheet. Insert a ceramic doll, dried bean, or foil-wrapped coin into the dough from the underside. Cover the dough and put in a warm place to prove until doubled, 45 minutes to 1 hour.

Bake until golden, about 25 minutes.

Make the icing by combining the sugar, milk and vanilla essence. It should be thin enough to drizzle, but not runny. Adjust the milk if necessary. When the bread has cooled slightly but is still warm, drizzle the icing over it.

Panettone

This is an Italian Christmas bread distinguished by its tall, domed shape.

BREAD MACHINE RECIPE—MAKES 1 500-G/1-LB LOAF

60 ml/2 fl oz milk	½ tsp ground star anise
2 eggs	250 g/8 oz strong white flour
40 g/1½ oz butter	2 tsp yeast
3 Tbsp sugar	3 Tbsp pine nuts
½ tsp salt	2 Tbsp sultanas
1 tsp grated lemon peel	60 g/2 oz chopped candied fruit
1 tsp vanilla essence	1 Tbsp flour

Put all the ingredients except the pine nuts, raisins, fruit and the last tablespoonful of flour in the bread tin in the order suggested in the instructions. Set for white bread, dough stage. Press start.

The high sugar content interferes with the rising action of the yeast, so it is kneaded after the first rising. Remove the dough and punch down. Toss the candied peel with 1 tablespoonful flour, then gently knead the fruit, sultanas and pine nuts into the dough. Put the dough in a buttered tin and turn so all the sides are greased. Panettone is traditionally baked in a tall, cylindrical tin. Use a 500-g/1-lb coffee tin. Set it in a warm place, cover loosely and leave to prove until doubled in volume.

Bake in pre-heated 350°F/175°C/Gas 4 oven until golden and a skewer inserted comes out clean, 30 minutes.

Lamańce

This is a traditional Polish sweet dish for serving at the Christmas eve feast. Lamańce means broken, reflecting the fact that some of the biscuits are broken in the dip or that they should not be quite so perfect in shape.

MAKES 64

175 g/6 oz plain flour	**DIP**
25 g/1 oz butter	60 g/2 oz poppy seeds, ground
120 g/4 oz icing sugar	60 g/2 oz ground almonds
1 egg yolk	2 Tbsp honey
3 Tbsp soured cream	300 ml/10 fl oz soured cream

Grease several baking sheets. Sift the flour into a bowl and blend in the butter. Stir in the sugar, egg yolk and soured cream to make a soft dough. Cut the dough in half and wrap in clingfilm. Chill for about 15 minutes, or until firm enough to roll out.

Pre-heat the oven to 350°F/175°C/Gas 4. Roll out half the dough to an oblong measuring 20 x 40 cm/ 8 x 16 in, then cut this into four 10-cm/4-in squares. Cut the squares in half diagonally to make triangles. Repeat with the second piece of dough. Place the biscuits on the baking sheets. Bake for about 8 to 12 minutes, until golden. Cool on wire racks.

For the dip, mix the ingredients together, then lightly crush about four of the biscuits into it. Mix well, then serve the biscuits with the creamy dip.

◄ *Panettone*

GLOSSARY

Bake blind To bake an unfilled pastry case. To prevent the sides falling in and the base bubbling, non-stick paper and beans are used in order to weigh down the pastry during cooking.

Beat To mix food together with a wooden spoon or electric mixer in order to incorporate air into the resulting mixture.

Binding Adding eggs, cream or melted fat into dry ingredients to hold ingredients together.

Beating

Blanch Par-boiling usually refers to vegetables which are cooked for a short time in boiling water.

Boiling Cooking in liquid at 212°F/100°C.

Caramelise To cook sugar until melted and brown either by dissolving and boiling or by grilling.

Crimping Making decorative edging for pastry.

Curdle When fresh milk separates into solids and liquids caused by overheating or adding acid. Also *Dredging* when beaten mixtures separate when adding eggs too quickly or too cold.

Dariole Small straight-sided round mould used for small cakes and desserts.

Dice Cut into small cubes.

Dredge Sprinkle food with sugar or flour.

Dropping consistency The consistency of a mixture, neither stiff nor runny, when it will slowly fall from a spoon when shaken.

Dust see Dredge.

Fold To mix ingredients using a gentle figure-of-eight motion and a metal spoon. *Folding* Usually applies to mixtures which have previously been beaten to incorporate air.

Gluten Proteins found in wheat which form part of the chemical process when making risen breads.

Ice To coat with icing.

Infuse To steep or heat gently in order to extract flavour usually from a spice such as a vanilla pod or a blade of mace.

Knead To stretch and fold mixtures to ensure even mixing of ingredients. Refers to yeast-based mixtures in particular.

Leaven see Prove.

Meringue Whisked egg whites and sugar beaten until stiff. Used to top pies or cooked in small mounds in a low oven until crisp.

Kneading

Pass To press through a sieve.

Praline Almonds and sugar cooked together until caramelised. Sometimes crushed to garnish cakes or powdered and used as a flavouring.

Prove To set aside mixture to allow rising agents to expand the dough to twice its original size.

Punch down To punch risen dough to expel air.

Purée To pass ingredients such as fruit through a sieve, blender or food processor to form a liquid or paste.

Relax or rest To set aside pastry which needs to allow the gluten, which has been stretched during the rolling process, to contract. This reduces the risk of shrinking during cooking. Some batters need to relax to allow starch cells to expand in the liquid, thus producing a lighter effect when cooked.

Ribbon To whisk ingredients until the mixture thickens sufficiently in order to leave a ribbon-like trail when the whisk is dragged through the mixture.

Rind The coloured part of citrus fruit skin. Used grated or thinly pared for flavouring.

Rising agents The active ingredient used to make mixtures rise either during the cooking process or before cooking. These include yeast, whisked egg white and baking powder.

Roulade Thick, flat cake spread with cream or icing and rolled.

Scald To heat milk until just boiling.

Scalding point The moment just before boiling when the liquid is bubbling around the edges of the pan but not bubbling in the middle.

Sift To pass flour or icing' sugar through a sieve to remove lumps.

Spring-release tin Baking tin with hinged sides to facilitate the easy removal of cakes.

Stirring Mixing with circular movements.

Ring tin Ring-shaped baking tin used for cakes.

Whipping Beating eggs or cream until frothy or stiff using a whisk.

Sifting

Whipping

Pared citrus rind

INDEX

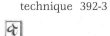